Civil War Memories

CIVIL WAR MEMORIES

Contesting the Past in the United States since 1865

ROBERT J. COOK
University of Sussex

Johns Hopkins University Press
Baltimore

Printed in the United States of America on acid-free paper
2 4 6 8 9 7 5 3 1

Johns Hopkins University Press
2715 North Charles Street
Baltimore, Maryland 21218-4363
www.press.jhu.edu

Library of Congress Cataloging-in-Publication Data

Names: Cook, Robert J., 1958– author.
Title: Civil War memories : contesting the past in the United States since 1865 / Robert J. Cook.
Description: Baltimore : Johns Hopkins University Press, 2017. | Includes bibliographical references and index.
Identifiers: LCCN 2017004274 | ISBN 9781421423494 (hardcover : alk. paper) | ISBN 9781421423500 (electronic) | ISBN 1421423499 (hardcover : alk. paper) | ISBN 1421423502 (electronic)
Subjects: LCSH: United States—History—Civil War, 1861–1865—Influence. | United States—History—Civil War, 1861–1865—Social aspects. | Collective memory—United States.
Classification: LCC E468.9 .C559 2017 | DDC 973.7/1—dc23
LC record available at https://lccn.loc.gov/2017004274

A catalog record for this book is available from the British Library.

Johns Hopkins University Press uses environmentally friendly book materials, including recycled text paper that is composed of at least 30 percent post-consumer waste, whenever possible.

To the memory of Derek Bevan

CONTENTS

ACKNOWLEDGMENTS

Anyone foolhardy enough to write a book of this scope must owe a fistful of debts, not only to giants in the field of Civil War memory like David Blight and Caroline Janney but also to those strangers, friends, and family members who have contributed in myriad ways to a research project of long duration. All scholars require money and time to undertake their work successfully. On this score I gratefully acknowledge the assistance provided by a British Academy / Leverhulme Senior Research Fellowship and a term of institutional leave from the University of Sussex that, together, gave me a valuable year and a half away from teaching to write the book. I thank especially David Brown, Adam Gilbert, Patrick Kelly, and two anonymous readers for Johns Hopkins University Press for their probing comments on an initial draft of the manuscript. It goes without saying (but I am constitutionally bound to say it) that, in spite of their heroic efforts, any mistakes in the text are all my own.

Generous friends across the United States provided me with accommodation and psychological support on research trips across the Atlantic, especially (in strictly alphabetical order) Roy Adolphson, Claire Awtrey, Jennifer Awtrey, Julianne Borton, Joy Harvey, Barbara Holmlund, and John Zeller. I thank John Neff and Jarod Roll for inviting me to test out some ideas on Jefferson Davis's death at a public lecture at the University of Mississippi in November 2014. I am grateful as well to Bob Jones of Louisville for sharing his experiences as a Civil War reenactor and to Jennifer Ford, head of the Department of Archives and Special Collections at Ole Miss, who not only provided me with help on my memorably cold visit to Oxford but also enabled me to identify Dudley McEwan Featherston as the likely author of an anonymous Lost Cause oration in the university archives. Thanks also to the Chautauqua County Historical Society for permission to publish from the Albion W. Tourgée Papers; to my efficient editors at Johns Hopkins University Press, Elizabeth Demers and Meagan Szekely; to my expert copy editor, Beth Gianfagna; to all my supportive colleagues in History and American Studies at the University of Sussex; and especially to my parents, Margaret and John.

My wife, Andrea Greengrass, has had to live with this project on a daily basis. I thank her for her skilled work on the index but most particularly for her love and support over the years. This book is dedicated to the memory of her late father, who is greatly missed by me, Andrea, Martha, Daniel, and all our family.

Civil War Memories

Introduction

On the evening of June 17, 2015, Emanuel AME Church in Charleston, South Carolina, was hosting one of its regular Bible study classes. Widely known as the oldest African American congregation south of Baltimore, "Mother Emanuel" was steeped in history. In 1822, one of its cofounders, Denmark Vesey, had organized an abortive slave revolt that was brutally suppressed by the city's white authorities. Today's parishioners were far too welcoming to question why a young white man, slight of build with blond hair, had chosen to join them that night. But after an hour of rich discussion and biblical exegesis, they were shocked when the stranger pulled out a gun. Somehow, twenty-six-year-old Tywanza Sanders summoned the courage to try to persuade him to lower his weapon. "You don't have to do this," said the young African American. The man had no intention of aborting his mission. "Yes," he replied. "You are taking our women and taking over the country."[1] Then he began firing with lethal purpose. Within seconds, six women and three men, including Sanders and the church's respected pastor, Clementa C. Pinckney, were dead or dying. The cold-blooded killer strolled out into the warm night air, got into his car, and made good his escape.

Coming as it did at a time of heightened racial tension in the United States, generated by several high-profile incidents in which black men had been killed while being apprehended by police, the massacre triggered bitter responses from some African Americans. "We're not worth the air they don't want us to breathe," commented Charleston resident Jareem Brady the day after the murders."[2] The nation's first black president, Barack Obama, was more circumspect, but he implored his fellow Americans to consider the broader context in which the killing of black people occurred. Quoting Martin Luther King Jr.'s words after the slaying of four black girls at a Baptist Church in Birmingham in 1963, he remarked of the victims: "They say to us that we must be concerned not merely with who murdered them but about the system, the way of life, the philosophy which produced the murderers. Their death says to us that we must work passionately and unrelentingly for the realization of the American Dream."[3]

The sickening events at Mother Emanuel constituted one of the deadliest race hate crimes in modern American history. The suspect, Dylann Storm Roof, was soon arrested in North Carolina and returned to Charleston.[4] Internet photographs of Roof showed the young man waving a Confederate battle flag and posing beside a car bearing a Confederate license plate. Most observers regarded these images as proof that the killer was a white supremacist sympathetic to the right-wing, neo-Confederate movement that linked its opposition to a range of alleged scourges in contemporary America to the failed southern bid for independence in the early 1860s. Stunned into action by the atrocity, many southern Republicans, including Governor Nikki Haley of South Carolina, concluded that it was time for responsible politicians to end their tolerance of, or even support for, controversial Confederate symbols. With Haley's backing, the South Carolina legislature voted in July 2015 to remove the familiar red, white, and blue St. Andrew's cross from the grounds of the statehouse in Columbia. "It is a new day in South Carolina, a day we can all be proud of," announced the governor optimistically, "a day that truly brings us all together as we continue to heal, as one people and one state."[5]

The Charleston murders initiated a wider debate in the United States about displays of the Rebel battle flag. The fierce public response to the massacre impelled major corporations such as Amazon, eBay, Sears, and Walmart to announce that they would no longer sell Confederate-flag merchandise. The battle flag, said one corporate representative, had "become a contemporary symbol of divisiveness and racism."[6] "We never want to offend anyone with the products that we offer," stated another.[7]

The public conversation quickly extended to other reminders of the proslavery Confederacy. Southern communities in particular were divided by debates over whether Rebel street names should be altered and whether Confederate statues erected in the late nineteenth and early twentieth centuries should be removed—all in the pursuit of better race relations in the present. In August 2015, the University of Texas at Austin responded to pressure from students and took down a statue of southern president Jefferson Davis that had been installed on the college's South Mall in the 1930s. Cities including Baltimore and New Orleans also initiated moves to eradicate statues of Confederate generals and politicians. Rev. Shawn Anglim, a black Methodist minister in downtown New Orleans, claimed that he had been unaware of a monument to Jefferson Davis near his church until it was defaced after the vigilante killing of an unarmed African American youth, Trayvon Martin, in Florida in 2012. Now he belonged to a ministerial group that demanded the removal of offensive Rebel statuary. Anglim described such symbols as "hurtful." "They continue to divide people as they were intended to do, and they will keep doing it in subtle and profound ways," he said.[8]

White conservatives were divided in their response to these developments. Gerald Warner, a commentator on the right-wing Breitbart website, accused opportunistic leftists of using the Charleston massacre to further their "agenda of cultural genocide against conservatism, tradition, and the South. . . . Now, they feel, is the time to airbrush out of history every tradition that is an obstacle to their new, rootless, alien society based on intolerant political correctness." Warner exhorted those who opposed "the culture warriors of the left" to flaunt the battle flag: "Hoist it high and fly it with pride, it proclaims a glorious heritage."[9] But amid the criticism there were signs that a significant number of southern conservatives were unwilling to sustain the status quo. In June 2016, the Southern Baptist Convention passed a resolution urging "our brothers and sisters in Christ to discontinue the display of the Confederate battle flag as a sign of solidarity of the whole Body of Christ, including our African American brothers and sisters."[10]

The charged public response to the Charleston slayings highlighted the continuing impact of the Civil War on American life. This book explains why this brutal industrial war has been long remembered in the United States.[11] It does so by examining it through the lens of "historical memory," a term that scholars have used (cavalierly at times) to explain how groups of all kinds construct accounts of the past by a process of selective remembering and forgetting.[12] Writing in the 1920s, the pioneering French sociologist Maurice Halbwachs contended that personal memories are inherently unstable and unreliable, that they are determined by the present rather than the past, and that they are generated within a social framework.[13] This study confirms the wisdom of Halbwachs' insights into what he called "collective memory" by demonstrating how socially constructed autobiographical memories helped to feed powerful group memories of the Civil War. It also shows how these group memories combined with other factors such as interparty competition and racial strife to forge consolidated, ideologically driven grand narratives that survived the passing of the wartime generation.

This book invites tough questions about the functions of collective memory. The story of Civil War remembrance since 1865 corroborates sociologist Barry Schwartz's view that it is both a model of and for society.[14] It not only reflects social relations in a given polity but also helps to shape those relations. Of course, collective memories alone do not make societies. Societies are made and remade by the constant interaction—sometimes peaceful, often violent—of people and institutions with varying degrees of influence. The ability to construct a plausible and broadly hegemonic narrative of a group's past, however, must be seen as an important component of social power. The Jim Crow South provides a classic exemplar. In the late nineteenth century, dominant whites in the region developed a coherent narrative—part fact, part fiction—of the southern past that made white dominion in the form of racial segregation appear natural, and therefore hard to contest, to many blacks as well as most whites. Martin Luther King's deputy Ralph Abernathy grew up in rural Alabama in the 1930s. He recalled that while African Americans knew segregation was wrong, they "felt too intimidated by the pervasiveness of it and by the fact that it seemed so old and so ingrained, a part of the landscape, like the slant of a hillside or the hang of a massive oak tree."[15]

As one would expect of such a divisive event, no single "memory" of the Civil War has ever existed. During the last three and a half decades of the nineteenth century, Americans forged four principal strands of Civil War memory: Unionist, emancipationist, southern, and reconciliatory.[16] These grand narratives, charted in part 1, were fashioned largely by those who lived through the sectional conflict. They continue to influence the way it is "remembered" today, even by Americans who have no direct connection with those who fought and suffered in it.

Unionist memory of what northerners once routinely called "the War of the Rebellion" was the Yankee victors' memory. Nationally dominant during the Reconstruction period, a divisive postbellum era that generated powerful historical memories of its own, this recounting focused public attention on the Civil War as a glorious people's war to safeguard the most important republic on earth. As well as being written into contemporary histories and participants' memoirs, it was evident in Republican Party campaigns and the commemorative activities of the main Federal veterans' organizations, including the Grand Army of the Republic. Massive tributes to the northern cause such as the triumphal memorial arch to Union troops in Brooklyn, the Michigan Soldiers' and Sailors' Monument in Detroit, and bronze equestrian statues to Federal generals in Washington, DC (those featured prominently in the opening sequence of the Emmy Award–winning TV series *House of Cards*) lost their power to move Americans long ago. However, their dedication ceremonies were attended by tens of thousands of people who, even half a century after the war's end, possessed a direct or secondhand memory of a conflict they judged to be noble and patriotic. While Unionist memory sometimes assisted the pursuit of racial justice by incorporating the destruction of slavery as a secondary and often self-congratulatory theme, its primary focus was on the Civil War as a contest that had saved the United States as a nation with a unique democratic mission in the world.

By 1900, the American republic was an assertive imperialist power in which the mass of its nonwhite population was disenfranchised, legally segregated, and liable to be lynched with impunity. Some black leaders, including the former abolitionist Frederick Douglass and a dwindling number of white allies, tried to sustain a second strand of Civil War memory—one that emphasized the central role played by the abolition of slavery and loyal US Colored Troops in saving the Union—in order to bolster their calls for equality under the law. Initially, this emancipationist memory of the Civil War overlapped significantly with its predominantly white Unionist counterpart. But as the latter waned as a result of consensual pressures, the emancipationist narrative developed into a marginalized "counter-memory" nurtured largely by African Americans.[17] In the first half of the twentieth century, most whites and many blacks had little or no idea of its existence because blacks simply lacked the power to keep their distinctive account of the Civil War before the public.

The defeated Confederates, abetted by some disillusioned southern white Unionists, fostered their own counter-memory of the "War between the States" or the "War of Northern Aggression." After 1865, the South's "Lost Cause" was crafted initially by embittered former Confederate officers and elite white women who assumed responsibility for interring the Rebel dead. In the late 1880s, as grieving white southerners recovered from war, defeat, and what they regarded as the horrors of black and Yankee rule during Reconstruction, they fashioned what historian Gaines M. Foster has called the "Confederate celebration"—a new, self-confident phase of the Lost Cause that was more conducive to regional economic growth and to reconciliation with the North.[18] Aging Rebel veterans, insistent that they had fought as patriots for quintessential American principles of states' rights and self-government, collaborated in this vast commemorative project with younger middle-class white women who joined chapters of a new organization, the United Daughters of the Confederacy (UDC). The Daughters played a critical role in sustaining a potent remembrance of southern suffering and heroism that helped not only to bolster their own social status but also to sustain racial segregation into the second half of the twentieth century. White southerners who resisted the civil rights movement of the mid-twentieth century were children of the Confederate celebration. The Lost Cause's reach was long as well as deep.

The classic image of the antebellum South as a mythic realm of handsome cavaliers, white mansions, benevolent masters, and happy slaves proved an enticing one for many northern as well as southern whites, particularly members of the postwar generation trying to make their way in a ruthlessly competitive capitalist society. Its allure helps to explain the emergence of a particularly durable fourth strand of Civil War remembrance. This reconciliatory strand conditioned and was conditioned by the surging American nationalism of the late Gilded Age. It played a major role in cementing better feeling between North and South after the ferocious bloodletting of the 1860s. Its instrumental, consensus-building function appealed especially to governing, business-minded elites in both sections and drew considerable emotional power from Americans' yearning to put the divisive past behind them and renew the nation-building project begun by their Revolutionary sires. Its most obvious manifestations included Blue-Gray reunion meetings between Union and Confederate veterans ready to pay tribute to the courage of their opponents, romantic novels and plays that often featured northern men marrying southern women, and celebration of selected heroes of the war—US President Abraham Lincoln and Rebel commander Robert E. Lee in particular—on both sides of the old divide.

This sentimentalized, intrafamilial narrative of the war, never wholly triumphant because of the conflict's lingering hatreds, represented an accommodation between northern and southern viewpoints—one that acknowledged the fortitude with which the defeated Confederates had fought for their perceived rights under the original Constitution as well as the necessity of a Union victory for the greatness of the modern American republic. Crucially, it became the national government's preferred mode of publicly representing the war—indeed, Washington's support helps to explain its predominance over the other modes of remembrance outside the South after 1900. While the government's drive for sectional reconciliation at this time was predictable, its ritual acts of remembering required a significant amount of forgetting to bring northern and southern whites together. As historian David W. Blight has made clear, it was African Americans who paid the highest price for national amnesia.[19]

Part 2 of this study assesses the history of Civil War memory since the Progressive era. It covers a period in which the original participants and their immediate kin surrendered custody of war remembrance to broader mnemonic communities—ones in which "memories" of the Civil War were transmitted primarily, though by no means exclusively, via the realm of mass culture. Remembrance in the modern period was partly the work of organizations like the

UDC whose members treasured personal memories of the veterans and their families as well as the commemorative rituals in which their forebears had participated. But it was promoted mainly by the construction of artificial memories by creative artists and the relentless advance of consumer capitalism. The Civil War's appeal to individuals with no personal experience of the conflict was apparent everywhere in the modern era. Author Margaret Mitchell possessed family ties to the Confederate wartime generation, but the same could not be said for the millions of non-southern fans who read her popular novel, *Gone with the Wind* (published in 1936), or who later watched the Selznick studio's lavish film version of the book. Similarly, the Civil War centennial of the early 1960s, deeply flawed though it was in execution, and Ken Burns's *The Civil War*, a runaway success when it was first screened on national television in 1990, introduced the war to new generations of Americans far removed from its intercommunal violence.

Reformers and mainstream politicians in the twentieth century used Civil War memory to stir civic activism and American patriotism. Progressive campaigners, for example, used the protean memory of Abraham Lincoln as a weapon in their battle against the trusts, while President Franklin D. Roosevelt and other New Dealers (some of them creative artists like Carl Sandburg) deployed it to promote social change and orient Americans in the fight against fascism.

Memories of the war and its aftermath also influenced racial politics during the modern era because the conflict remained unfinished business for African Americans nurturing their emancipationist strain of historical memory. The latter was increasingly at odds with the dominant reconciliatory and southern (Lost Cause) narratives that depicted the war primarily as a white men's fight. While southern Democrats consistently relied on Lost Cause myths and symbols to combat growing pressure on racial segregation, assertive blacks began to contest displays of Confederate heritage that smacked to them of white supremacy. The modern battle over Civil War memory began when segregationists took up the Rebel battle flag as a symbol of resistance to racial integration in the late 1940s. Indeed, much of the support for the flag and other manifestations of the South's revolt against the United States can be traced to remembrance not of the Civil War but of the nonviolent civil rights movement.

At the start of the sesquicentennial commemoration in 2011, the British weekly journal *The Economist* contended that the Civil War's ability to move Americans was "finally passing."[20] Now that segregation was gone and the South was no longer impoverished, claimed the magazine, the old sectional fissure had ceased to be a divisive factor in the United States. The claim was not entirely invalid. Civil War memories were no longer genuinely "felt" memories in the way that southern author Robert Penn Warren had described them in 1961, when many Americans could still remember veterans of the internecine conflict.[21] The murdering hand of Dylann Roof and subsequent debates over the destruction of Confederate symbols, however, left little doubt that constructed memories of a bitter civil war fought long ago retained the power to mobilize Americans in the politically and racially polarized present.

PART ONE

THE POSTWAR PERIOD

CHAPTER ONE

A Fractured Country and Its Fractured Memories

Secession and Civil War

Slavery, nativism, and competing nationalisms ignited the United States's gathering crisis in the nineteenth century. In the mid-1850s, the country's interregional party system collapsed under a welter of pressures that included not only northerners' hostility toward the expansion of racial bondage but also popular concerns that mainstream party politicians were no longer responsive to their fears about mass immigration from Europe. The resulting realignment spawned a new political organization, the Republican Party, which represented the interests of northerners and demonized wealthy southern slaveholders. While the party's radical wing included many people who opposed the existence of slavery on moral grounds, a majority of Republicans were more concerned about the impact of the aristocratic "Slave Power" on whites, especially on the economic opportunities of settlers in the country's western territories. Reluctant to attack slavery in the states where it was entrenched, Republicans found common ground in their core policy of congressional prohibition of slavery extension.

The Republicans embraced nonextension to curtail what they regarded as slavery's detrimental influence on a vigorous republic whose citizens were convinced they lived in the freest polity on earth. Many white southerners, however, saw it as an attack on their honor and self-respect and a gross violation of their property rights under the 1787 Constitution. They also regarded it correctly as an assault on their political power, for a prohibition against the admission of more slave states into the Union would mean a rise of northern influence and a lessening of their own. Therefore, when the Republicans elected Abraham Lincoln president in November 1860 with a plurality of the popular vote garnered almost entirely in the North, southern separatists began maneuvering to take their states out of the Union.

They faced a difficult task. Roughly three-quarters of white southerners did not own slaves.[1] However, even non-slaveholding whites understood that their liberties were defined mainly by the fact that they were not black chattel. Fears of what the enslaved might do if they were ever freed from the disciplining and supposedly civilizing ties of bondage permeated the predominantly rural South, especially the fertile plantation districts where slaves often outnumbered whites. Secessionists therefore played heavily on the racial fears of ordinary folk, especially the widespread anxiety that once in power the antislavery Republicans would foment unrest among the blacks. These fears were rooted in historical memories of the bloody Haitian slave rebellion of the late eighteenth century and of Nat Turner's unsuccessful slave revolt in Virginia in 1831 as well as in direct experience of everyday black resistance to the slave regime. One southern radical proclaimed that the Republicans' election victory constituted "an open declaration of war" against the South, presaging "all the horrors of a San Domingo servile insurrection, consigning her citizens to assassinations and her wives and daughters to pollution and violation to gratify the lust of half-civilized Africans."[2]

In most states, secessionists also had to dispel opposition from opponents who regarded secession, even in the face of Lincoln's election, as a gamble that was not worth taking. Fierce debates in hastily convened conventions prompted memory wars across the Deep South.

Before 1861, myths surrounding the War of Independence and revered Founders such as George Washington and Benjamin Franklin had contributed significantly to the development of early American nationalism. Southern Unionists, desperate to hold together the sentimental bonds of Union, turned to a rich store of historical memory to make their case. In Georgia, Benjamin H. Hill tried to stem the radical tide by lauding "[o]ur glorious revolution," and urging his fellow citizens to avoid rash decisions in the same manner as General Washington, the father of the country.[3] A leading Virginia Unionist told the state's secession convention in Richmond that "his old, patriotic father, born amid the thunders of the Revolution," had implored him to "save this Union, or never let my eyes rest upon you again."[4]

Appeals to romantic nationalism anchored in a heavily mythologized past posed an obvious threat to the secessionists, inducing some of them to disparage the country's Revolutionary heritage. "I bade selfishness avaunt, when my heart turned toward the Government of my fathers," intoned the slaveholding Georgian Thomas R. R. Cobb, "I saw the glories of Bunker Hill and Monmouth, and Saratoga, and Yorktown, clustering around it.—I recalled the story of her struggles as an aged ancestor who bled in her cause recounted it to infant ears around the winter's fire." But, continued Cobb, "the cruel hand of Northern aggression" had snapped his attachment to the Union, and he now saw before him only an "idol . . . whose deformity and ugliness disgusted while they pained me!"[5]

Most states' rights politicians at the height of the secession crisis, however, understood the power of sentimental historical memories of the Revolution to affect their constituents and sought to channel rather than dismiss them. Jefferson Davis, a Mississippi planter-politician elected president of the new Confederate States of America in February 1861, insisted that secession was entirely consistent with the actions of the Founders, who had been forced by oppression to secede from the British Empire. Republicans like President-elect Abraham Lincoln countered by arguing that the Union was the precious fruit of the Founders' work and that therefore it must remain unbroken.

Lincoln was not averse to employing mnemonic appeals of his own in order to prevent civil war. His first inaugural address on March 4, 1861, included a lyrical appeal to breakaway Confederates, the gist of which had been suggested by his new secretary of state, William H. Seward. "I am loth to close," concluded Lincoln. "We are not enemies, but friends. We must not be enemies. Though passion may have strained, it must not break our bonds of affection. The mystic chords of memory, streching [*sic*] from every battle-field, and patriot grave, to every living heart and hearthstone, all over this broad land, will yet swell the chorus of the Union, when again touched, as surely they will be, by the better angels of our nature."[6] No American leader has tried to marshal the past so powerfully in the service of the present. Tragically, many among those whom Lincoln described in his speech as "my dissatisfied fellow countrymen" no longer recognized themselves as his compatriots.[7]

The conflict unleashed by the South's bombardment of Fort Sumter early in the morning of April 12, 1861, and President Lincoln's subsequent call for volunteers to suppress what he and a majority of his fellow northerners regarded as a rebellion against the legal government of the United States was long and sanguinary. It was made so by several factors: the ferocity of Confederate resistance to the North's invasion of the homeland; a murderous combination of modern warfare and premodern medicine that resulted in at least 750,000 combatant deaths; and the tardiness with which the more industrialized and urbanized North brought its superior resources to bear on the predominantly agricultural South.[8]

Those resources included manpower and industries based in the slave South. While Lost Cause advocates later worked to create an impression that southerners had been united behind the Confederate war effort, the reality was different. Non-slaveholding white Unionists hostile to the region's plantocracy supplied 300,000 troops to the Union Army.[9] About two-thirds of them came from border states like Kentucky, Maryland, and Missouri that did not join the Confederacy. Each of these slave states contained important cities that the Confederacy could ill afford to do without. Union control of Louisville, Baltimore, and St. Louis provided the Federals with vital supply centers as well as sources of additional manpower. Beyond these areas, mountainous districts of Virginia, Tennessee, and North Carolina furnished significant numbers of Union soldiers.

The war was fought principally in two main theaters on either side of the Appalachian Mountains. For the first two years of the conflict, the Confederates outperformed their opponents in the east, partly because of the relative superiority of their generals, including Thomas J. ("Stonewall") Jackson, a puritanical college professor who ran the Federals ragged in the fertile Shenandoah Valley, and Robert E. Lee, a wealthy slaveholding Virginian who rejected command of the Union Army after the attack on Fort Sumter. Jackson and Lee were aggressive soldiers who believed the South could not afford to fight a purely defensive war against an enemy that could put more and better equipped troops into the field. In June 1862, Lee assumed command of the Army of Northern Virginia at a critical moment in the war when the Confederate capital of Richmond was imperiled by the advance of Union general George B. McClellan's Army of the Potomac, organized after the debilitating rout of Federal forces at the First Battle of Bull Run the previous summer. In a series of fluid engagements known as the Seven Days' battles, Lee, assisted by Jackson and his other leading corps commander, James Longstreet, drove his cautious opponent away from the capital. He then raided boldly into northern Virginia and Maryland, inflicting another smashing defeat on the Federals at Second Bull Run, and resisting uncoordinated assaults by McClellan's army at the bloody Battle of Antietam, in which nearly 3,600 Americans were slaughtered on a single day.

The Army of Northern Virginia's accomplishments bolstered southern morale and brought the Confederacy to the verge of international recognition. Lee's men inflicted brutal punishment on the Army of the Potomac at Fredericksburg in December 1862 and Chancellorsville in May 1863, before striking north again in the summer of 1863, this time as far as the free state of Pennsylvania. On July 1, the eastern theater's two great armies crashed into one another outside Gettysburg. In vicious fighting south of the small college town, Federal forces ranged along Culp's Hill and Cemetery Ridge repulsed heavy attacks along the Union line, most famously on the third and final day when, in an advance known later as "Pickett's Charge," Lee launched a disastrous assault on the enemy center. Total casualties over the three days' butchering numbered more than 51,000.

Five months after this carnage, Abraham Lincoln delivered a pithy funeral oration at a dedication ceremony for the new "Soldiers' National Cemetery" on Cemetery Hill. His "Gettysburg Address," subsequently revered as a canonical document of America's civil creed, was suffused with the president's typically purposeful use of historical memory. The United States, he reminded an appreciative audience, was "conceived in Liberty" and committed to the startling proposition "that all men are created equal." Surveying the newly dug graves of the Union dead, he urged northerners to renew their commitment to military victory on the basis that the sacrifices of these men in behalf of a nation "so conceived, and so dedicated" should not be "in vain." Henceforth, those who died for the republic would play a key role in driving remembrance and commemoration of a transformational conflict that Lincoln concluded would steel Americans' resolve "that this nation shall have a new birth of freedom; and that this government of the people, by the people, for the people, shall not perish from the earth."[10]

In hindsight, the Confederate defeat at Gettysburg signaled the beginning of the end for the would-be southern nation. The decisive breakthrough came in the western theater, where the Federal armies had won strategic victories at Shiloh, Perryville, and Stones River. By the close of 1862, Union forces had secured a firm grip not only on the loyal border slave states but also portions of Arkansas, Tennessee, and Louisiana, including the port of New Orleans. Violence afflicted many citizens living in border areas, its spread accelerated not only by the murderous activity of irregular forces on both sides but also by mounting attacks on African Americans by angry local whites and by Federal hard-war policies such as the suspension of habeas corpus and wholesale arrests of suspected Confederate sympathizers. In the spring of 1863, Union general Ulysses S. Grant began his final campaign against Vicksburg, the last remaining Rebel stronghold on the Mississippi River. The town's defenders surrendered on July 4, leaving the strategic waterway in Union hands and the Confederacy divided. Although Federal forces under William S. Rosecrans flirted with disaster at Chickamauga the following September, Grant and his chief lieutenant, William Tecumseh Sherman, quickly salvaged the situation by beating Braxton Bragg's Confederate Army of Tennessee on the heights of Lookout Mountain and Missionary Ridge. These actions secured Chattanooga for the Union, resulted in Bragg's replacement by Joseph E. Johnston, and set the stage for Sherman's relentless drive south toward the vital railroad hub of Atlanta, which fell after a short siege at the beginning of September.

This crucial victory revealed the close connection that existed between home front and battlefield by virtually guaranteeing Lincoln's reelection in the

November US presidential election. Sherman, meanwhile, abandoned his supply base and cut a morale-sapping swath of destruction, first through the heartland of Confederate Georgia to the Atlantic coast at Savannah, and then north through the Carolinas. His subordinate, George H. Thomas, remained behind to destroy what was left of the Army of Tennessee at the one-sided Battles of Franklin and Nashville.

By this time, Grant, now the Union's general-in-chief, had moved east at President Lincoln's request to oversee the struggle against Lee's depleted but battle-hardened Army of Northern Virginia. Both Lincoln and Grant understood that the only way for the North to win was to subdue Confederate resistance by applying constant military pressure on the enemy across every front. "Concentration in time" would prevent southerners from using reinforcements to relieve individual pressure points.[11] Both men knew this attritional strategy would result in heavy losses, but, aware that northern manpower must tell eventually, they did not flinch from it. In exceptionally bloody fighting in the Wilderness, at Spotsylvania, and Cold Harbor—major engagements in the Overland Campaign of 1864—Grant repeatedly turned Lee's flank in Virginia, forcing him to retreat until his dwindling forces were bottled up in trenches around the town of Petersburg, twenty-five miles below Richmond.

Among the troops besieging Petersburg in late 1864 and early 1865 were African American regiments commanded by white officers. By early 1862, many northerners acknowledged that they would never subdue the Rebels without striking at slavery and making use of black manpower. Slaves cultivated crops that helped supply the Confederate armies. They also dug trenches, built fortifications, and worked in essential industries. Seizing control of this labor in pursuit of Union war aims, however, was no easy matter. Lincoln knew that racial prejudice was endemic in the North and that pro-Union slaveholders in border states like Maryland and Kentucky would oppose any attempt by the government to interfere with their property rights. Four days after Lee retreated from Antietam in September 1862, the president issued his preliminary Emancipation Proclamation stating that he would declare free all slaves in Confederate-held territory on January 1, 1863

Branded a military measure rather than an act of justice toward the enslaved, the edict divided the North and enraged white Unionists in the loyal border states. Democrats inside and outside the army were particularly vociferous in their opposition to it. Party leaders exploited that opposition and enjoyed significant successes in the midterm elections by contending that Lincoln's administration was trying to "abolitionize" the conflict. However, a majority of Republicans and Union troops welcomed the proclamation as evidence that the administration was finally getting tough on the Rebels. Lincoln did more than simply ride out the storm; he now sanctioned the enlistment of black troops as well as emancipation. By the end of 1863, regiments of US Colored Infantry were filling up quickly. Although they were composed mainly of former slaves, significant numbers of northern free blacks also joined the ranks of volunteers. Their stalwart performance at several engagements that year, including an unsuccessful assault on Battery Wagner outside Charleston in July, convinced growing numbers of prejudiced whites that black men could fight effectively. The sight of former slaves wearing Union blue and carrying guns enraged many Confederates. When presented with the opportunity, as at the Battle of the Crater outside Petersburg on July 30, 1864, they gave them little quarter.

Lincoln's Emancipation Proclamation freed relatively few slaves. Its chief impact was to transform the army into an agent of liberation. As the Federals pressed deeper into the Confederacy, more and more slaves abandoned their masters and made the difficult journey into Union lines. They were not always well received, and the death rates in some government camps were high. But constant Union military pressure and slave flight combined with rising internal dissent to bring the Confederacy to the verge of destruction. So desperate was the situation that some Rebel leaders, including Jefferson Davis and Robert E. Lee, contemplated offering freedom to slaves mustered into the South's armed forces, now heavily depleted because of rampant desertion. The Union breakthrough at Petersburg in early April meant that only a handful of black companies were organized before the South capitulated.[12]

Hotly pursued by Grant's Federals, Lee's Army of Northern Virginia surrendered at Appomattox Court House, west of Richmond, on April 9. Receiving Lee at the home of Wilbur McLean, the Union commander offered his rival generous terms in line with President Lincoln's desire, expressed in his recent second inaugural address, that the country should approach the peace "with malice toward none; with charity for all."[13] Grant permitted the Confederates to return to their homes after signing paroles and giving up most of their weapons. He also allowed officers to retain their sidearms and horses and subsequently extended permission for anyone, regardless of rank, "who claimed to own a horse or mule [to] take the animal to his home."[14] When faced with the prospect of a triumphant salute by his own army, he ordered the guns to remain silent. The war was over, he declared, and "[t]he rebels are our countrymen again."[15]

Although Grant's terms reflected the yearning for peace of most northerners, their impact was lessened six days later by the shocking murder in Washington of President Lincoln at the hands of an embittered Rebel sympathizer, the actor John Wilkes Booth. Confederate diarist Kate Stone hailed Booth for ridding "the world of a tyrant" and making "himself famous for generations."[16]

The grinding-mill claimed its most famous victim two weeks before Sherman accepted the surrender of Confederate troops under Joseph Johnston in North Carolina. America's civil war was virtually over.

Aftermath

The war left a bitter legacy on both sides because the damage it inflicted was so extensive. Those areas of the South worst affected by the fighting—rural places like the Shenandoah Valley, northern Virginia, and whole swaths of the Mississippi Valley—were devastated, as were many cities that had felt the full force of northern military might, notably Atlanta, Richmond, and Columbia, the capital of South Carolina, which burned in February 1865. Vast numbers of draft animals and livestock were gone as were the valuable investments locked up in nearly four million slaves. All told, the region's bid for independence cost it two-thirds of its assessed wealth. More costly still was the loss of human lives. By war's end, at least one in three Confederate soldiers, compared with one in six Federals, were dead.[17] Roughly 50,000 civilians had also perished.[18] Many were killed in deadly guerrilla fighting between Unionists and Confederates in mountainous eastern Tennessee and the bitterly divided loyal slave states of Missouri and Kentucky.

Legions of Union and Confederate corpses rotted in unmarked graves. Many bodies lay barely hidden in churned-up fields and shattered pine woods, the bleached bones ripe for picking by foraging hogs and rude disinterment by industrious farmers. Huge numbers of disabled and disfigured men returned to their communities with only their families to care for them. Many would die of their wounds and war-related ailments in the months, years, and decades to come. Others would struggle to rebuild their lives in postwar society, their sense of selfhood as shattered as their broken bodies.

The war's impact was also felt acutely by female noncombatants on both sides. While the fighting raged, women of all classes had been drawn inexorably into the conflict. In the North, farm wives sewed flags and made uniforms and spent long days in the fields tending to crops and livestock. Urban working women in industrial cities like Philadelphia, Pittsburgh, and New York, many of them European immigrants, labored for wages in armaments factories where fatal explosions were not unknown. Patriotic elite and middle-class women, often devout Protestants, served as nurses, joined voluntary organizations like the US Christian Commission and the US Sanitary Commission, and raised money for soldiers' relief by holding fairs in the larger cities. In the Confederacy, women who lived on farms and plantations worked mainly by slaves confronted the alarming prospect of having to supervise their human property with limited male assistance. Most supported the war effort with varying, sometimes extreme, degrees of enthusiasm, as did their urban peers, who clubbed together to form local soldiers' aid societies. One group of Richmond ladies raised enough money to fund construction of a gunboat to defend the Confederate capital.[19]

The disproportionately high loss of life among Confederate men placed a heavy emotional and physical burden on their female kin. Southern women regarded care and remembrance of the dead as the special responsibility of their sex. They adopted familiar mourning rituals, such as the wearing of black and the preservation of sacred keepsakes. If they had a body to bury, they prepared the corpse for burial and tried to secure the services of a Christian minister to conduct the funeral ceremony. Southern white women's leading participation in wartime burial and grieving activities was captured in William De Hartburn Washington's popular painting *The Burial of Latané* (1864). Widely disseminated as an engraving, the image purported to depict a real event in which the Federals had prevented an Episcopalian clergyman from presiding over the burial of Captain William Latané after his death on the Yorktown Peninsula in June 1862. In the center of the painting a woman in mourning dress delivers the burial rites in what Virginian John R. Thompson's poem—Washington's inspiration—described as "accents soft and low." The only male character in the scene is "the faithful slave" resting on the shovel with which he has dug the "the sod" where the hero lies "with his fame, his country, and his God."[20]

Modern scholars posit the existence of a close connection between individuals' experiences of traumatic events and the formation of powerful historical memories capable of being transmitted across generations.[21] Southern whites may not have been so traumatized that they were unable to defend white supremacy after 1865, but undeniably the majority of Confederates were stunned by the sickening realization that so much suffering had come to nothing. The pain of grief at the loss of so many family members and neighbors was thus exacerbated by the shock of military defeat. These powerful sensations were particularly raw after Lee's surrender at Appomattox. "We have been robbed of every-thing except our memories—God has kept them green," asserted Jefferson Davis's strong-willed wife, Varina, in a revealing statement that mixed defiance, regret, and piety in equal measure.[22] In the months and years that followed, those memories would feed white southerners' interpretations of their struggle for independence and steel their refusal to bow down before their conquerors.

Some northern travelers in the region in the spring and summer of 1865 remarked on the Rebels' willingness to abide by the result of the war, including their grudging acquiescence to the demise of slavery as well as the Confederacy. While war weariness, pragmatism, and the desire for social order prompted such responses, many southerners harbored a deep, visceral hatred of the

Yankee invaders. This was particularly true of the Confederate officer class, composed disproportionately of wealthy men from slaveholding families, and white women from the same high-status group. All had possessed a major stake in the patriarchal slave system, the security of which would have been guaranteed by the attainment of Confederate military victory. These angry southerners vented their fury against the Yankees who had destroyed the hierarchical world on which their power had been based. Tellingly, although most recognized that the dream of Confederate independence was over, they did not admit that secession had been a grievous mistake, let alone indicate a readiness to prostrate themselves at the feet of their haughty oppressors. "We feel deep, unutterable regret at our failure," wrote Alabamian Robert Park, "but no humiliation. We have done nothing wrong."[23] The Confederates viewed themselves as a suffering Christian people. They did not regard military defeat as God's final judgment on them.

Elite southerners often considered themselves paternalists in matters of race. Indeed, many members of the old planter class regarded blacks, notably certain house slaves, as members of their extended family. However, they shared with most non-slaveholding whites in the region an unshakable conviction that people of color were racially inferior, incapable of working without coercion, liable to lapse into a state of barbarism if left to their own devices, and undeserving even of the basic civil rights that a majority of northern Republicans now wished to bestow on them. When US Supreme Court Justice Salmon P. Chase visited the South in May 1865, he found local leaders willing to cooperate with federal authorities but adamantly opposed to the enfranchisement of the former slaves. "It is curious to observe," he remarked, "how little they seem to realize that any change in personal or political relations has been wrought by the war."[24]

The conflict had been especially hard on the impoverished freedpeople. Thousands of them had died in unsanitary "contraband" camps established by Federal authorities, and many had had their lives uprooted when their masters "refugeed" them to areas of Secessia far from the main centers of fighting. Others had been impressed by the Confederate military to labor on fortifications. Yet the fact was, as prominent free black leaders quickly observed after Lincoln issued his preliminary Emancipation Proclamation, conflict between northern and southern whites presented oppressed people of color with a historic opportunity to improve their situation. This was why Frederick Douglass and Martin Delany supported the enlistment of black men into the Union armed forces. During the bleak antebellum years, abolitionists had used highly selective memories of black support for the American cause during the Revolution and the War of 1812 to demonstrate that the race was manly, brave, and patriotic and therefore deserving of equal treatment by whites.[25] Military service during the Civil War enabled blacks to build on this narrative framework. Those US Colored Troops who fought at places like Port Hudson, Battery Wagner, Millikens Bend, Olustee, and Petersburg believed their service to the nation should not only promote the liberation of their race but also guarantee black men equality under the law as American citizens.

In spite of widespread illiteracy among the enslaved, few former bondsmen and women did not know the significance of Confederate defeat or remember the day they secured their freedom. Some retained a clear understanding that they played an active role in their own liberation. William Sherman Jr., a former slave interviewed in the 1930s, recalled that he and a cousin working on a Georgia plantation, had "slipped off" and precipitated the flight of several hundred slaves to Union lines during the Federals' march through the state.[26] He also explained that his father had adopted General Sherman's name and passed it on to his son. Renaming oneself after Union commanders like Sherman and Grant was not an uncommon practice among the freedpeople. William Sherman Jr. and many other black men carried the memory of Union victory and emancipation as a badge of pride as well as identity.

Actions like this bore witness to a rising tide of black assertiveness. Justice Chase found Florida blacks forming Union Leagues to defend themselves and promote their citizenship rights within weeks of Abraham Lincoln's murder in April 1865. As the institutional restraints of slavery broke down, blacks began to leave their farms and plantations, searching for loved ones from whom they had been separated in bondage and seeking alternative employers who would pay them wages under the Yankees' new free-labor regime. Many black folk simply took a temporary holiday from work, confirming whites' worst fears that former slaves would not labor without discipline. Others moved from the countryside into the region's towns—partly for security, partly for work, and partly to take advantage of separate black social institutions, including churches and fraternal organizations. Here they competed for public spaces with whites, often displaying a pronounced unwillingness to grant their former masters the deference they expected.

For resentful whites, stunned but not cowed by defeat, this social upheaval constituted a world turned upside down. They moved quickly to reassert their dominance over the emancipated slaves. During the fall of 1865, southern state legislatures, working under provisional governors appointed by Lincoln's successor, Andrew Johnson, passed new laws to restrict the mobility of blacks and restore them to a state of virtual slavery. These "black codes" were enacted in a climate of rabid anti-black violence in Alabama and several other states, including notionally loyal Kentucky, where slavery remained legal until ratification of the Thirteenth Amendment in December. Attacks on African Americans, especially US Colored Troops, who were the most hated component of the

Yankees' military occupation force, mounted in all the former border slave states as well as the vanquished Confederacy. They testified to the strength of local whites' detestation of emancipation and the prospect of black civic equality. Coupled with the election of many prominent former Confederates to Congress, the codes and the violence accompanying them represented a direct challenge to the victorious North. The Yankees' response would determine the framework for postwar Reconstruction—part constitutional crisis, part labor revolution, and part battle over the memory and meaning of the Civil War.

Northerners had never been united during the war. Pro-peace Democrats, derided as "Copperheads" by their Republican opponents, had grown increasingly critical of the bloodletting as it continued unabated—their opposition to Lincoln's alleged tyranny peaking in 1864, when their efforts helped General George McClellan to capture 45 percent of the popular vote in that year's presidential election. Grassroots opposition to the war had also been manifested in opposition to the Emancipation Proclamation and to the imposition of the draft. Ferocious rioting in Manhattan in July 1863 was directed against powerful Republicans seeking to embroil white working-class people in a war not of their making and, most lethally, against impoverished free blacks, whom the mobs perceived to be the favored beneficiaries of the Republicans' bloody abolition war.

The Republican Party itself was by no means united on strategy. Lincoln's slowness in finding generals to match the caliber of Lee and Jackson frustrated many of his co-partisans, as did his efforts to control the process by which Confederate states were reintegrated into the Union, his charitable attitude toward the Rebels, and his moderate position on equal rights for blacks. Wartime divisions in the North guaranteed that the victorious northerners would not act with one voice in the interrelated struggles over Reconstruction, sectional reconciliation, and the memory of the Civil War.

Some of those cleavages were evident in northerners' response to the assassination of President Lincoln on Good Friday 1865. Some Radical Republicans who considered him excessively conservative on matters of race and too generous in his attitude toward southern traitors responded to his death with equanimity. They believed that Andrew Johnson, a Tennessee Unionist, would be tougher on these matters because of his well-known hostility to the planter class. A number of Protestant ministers, more sure of God's intentions than the president had ever claimed to be, contended that the killing marked a new phase in the divine master plan for remaking the benighted South. Copperheads too, like Confederates, had little cause to mourn Lincoln, a man they loathed as a ruthless dictator. The predominant northern reaction to the slaying, however, was one of shock. This shuddering emotion initially overcame many people's desire for reconciliation and fed angry cries for revenge against the Rebels. The president had been popular with many ordinary folk in the victorious section, especially with the soldiers themselves, who had valued his support for their sacrifices in behalf of the nation.

As well as turning out in huge numbers to view his remains en route from Washington to his tomb in Springfield, Illinois, northerners often coupled their grief with demands that Confederate leaders should be punished for their crimes against the republic. The widespread conviction that secession had resulted from an orchestrated plot by planter-politicians to destroy the Union led many northerners to assume that Jefferson Davis and other Rebel leaders were behind the events at Ford's Theatre. The assassin, John Wilkes Booth, was cornered and killed in late April at the end of a frenetic manhunt through northern Virginia; his fellow conspirators were tried by a military tribunal and executed in July. After Davis was captured in Georgia while fleeing to join the one remaining Confederate army in the field in Texas, he was incarcerated and briefly manacled in Fortress Monroe. Federal authorities quickly launched efforts to tie him to Lincoln's murder. That fall another tribunal tried Henry Wirz, the officer in charge at the notorious Andersonville stockade in Georgia, for the mass murder of Federal prisoners of war. With memories of the president's death still raw and the sufferings of Union soldiers highlighted by the trial, the tribunal sought to implicate Davis in the proceedings. Wirz, however, refused to cooperate with those efforts, and he went to the scaffold alone in November 1865.

The Swiss émigré proved to be a partial lightning rod for northerners' hatred of the Rebels. Remarkably, given the scale of retribution after other internecine conflicts, he was one of the very few Confederates executed by the US government after Appomattox.[27] Jefferson Davis languished in prison, but his confinement would prove to be temporary. The desire for vengeance against the Rebels took different forms in the years ahead: notably the insistence of Radical Republicans like Congressman Thaddeus Stevens of Pennsylvania that Washington should disempower the planter aristocracy entirely and remake the criminal South in the image of the free-labor North.

The Purposes of Civil War Memory after 1865

Five major factors impelled remembrance of the Civil War in the years immediately following its termination: the existence of a limited yet viable domestic market for war narratives; the combatants' desire for public validation and vindication; individual and collective commemoration of the soldier dead; the prospect of gaining federal largesse through proof of wartime loyalty to the US government; and fierce interparty combat fueled by war-born enmities. Each proved strong enough to give the Civil War deep resonance into the late nineteenth century.

A flurry of histories, biographies, and memoirs appeared in the early years of Reconstruction. One reason for this initial burst of publications was the desire of some individuals to make money out of a searing event that had affected so many people. Politicians, soldiers, and journalists rightly sensed the existence of a market for books about the war and sought to cash in on the demand. Because America's urban middle-class was still growing at the time, this market was relatively limited in size compared with its successor in the 1880s and 1890s. It was large enough, however, to bear the release of hefty pro-Union accounts of the Civil War bearing sonorous titles that boasted their authors' commitment to what one modern scholar has termed ironically the "Cause Victorious."[28] Although these "national" histories were published in the rapidly urbanizing northeast, the same metropolitan presses joined smaller local ones in issuing many early war books aimed at niche markets. In the thinly populated western state of Iowa, for example, the Burlington-based journalist Lurton Dunham Ingersoll, known to all his readers as "Linkensale," rushed out an account of Hawkeye troops that was published in Philadelphia and Dubuque and touted in newspapers across the state.[29] Such books, together with the first regimental histories like A. F. Sperry's account of the Thirty-Third Iowa Volunteer Infantry, printed in Des Moines in 1866, testified to the central role played by local communities in the Civil War. Sperry, a schoolteacher from the small town of Pella, concluded his book by suggesting that while his comrades would lose their wartime organization they "would mostly be neighbors still."[30] Communities like his provided an important early market for war books, because northern readers, including the veterans themselves, thirsted to learn more about the conflict and the role they had played in it.

The marketing possibilities for books about the leading commanders on both sides were greater still. Northerners and southerners were especially keen to read about Stonewall Jackson, the famed Rebel commander who had led the Federals a merry dance in the Shenandoah Valley. John Esten Cooke, an impoverished Confederate cavalry officer who had no fondness for Yankees, was the first author to profit from the widespread demand for knowledge about Jackson. In 1866, he crafted a commercially successful biography that emphasized the general's peculiarities and heroism. Sagely, he excised anti-Union passages that had appeared in the 1863 edition of the book, a version aimed solely at Confederates, in order to render Jackson a bold and somewhat eccentric figure more attuned to northern tastes. Cooke was also the first writer to make a lot of money out of romanticizing the recent bloodletting. He wrote *Surry of Eagle's-Nest*, a novel about Jackson's "cavalier" soldiers on campaign, for the widest popular readership. Its success indicated the marketability of Civil War fiction only months after the killing had ended. Public enthusiasm for his work soon waned but not before he had made enough money to restore his plantation home in the Shenandoah Valley.

The desire of many individuals to vindicate their actions in the court of public opinion constituted a second major impulse behind early acts of Civil War remembrance. Confederate military commanders felt a pressing urgency to explain their part in the war because they confronted a battery of slurs leveled by what one North Carolinian described as the "lying tongues of Yankee Scribblers."[31] Robert E. Lee was already planning to write a history of his Virginia campaigns by the summer of 1865. His problem was a dearth of written evidence to prove that he and his men had fought as well as they could have done against a numerically superior foe. In November, he appealed to one of his former corps commanders, Jubal A. Early, for help. All his records, he said, had been destroyed in "the conflagration and retreat from Richmond." He asked General Early to "repeat" his reports of operations in 1864 "and send me copies of such letters, orders &c of mine . . . and particularly give me your recollection of our effective strength at the principal battles." His only concern, he iterated, was "to transmit, if possible, the truth and do justice to our brave soldiers."[32]

Despite assistance from Early and other officers (not to mention financial inducements from excited publishers), Lee's efforts to compile an accurate account of his campaigns foundered on the conflicting and partial nature of the evidence provided by his lieutenants as well as on his own decision to accept the post of president of Washington College in Lexington, Virginia. But by turning to his fellow Confederates for help at this time he exemplified the social nature of early Civil War remembrance. Nobody, not even General Lee, could recall with any degree of precision the historic events in which they had participated. Everyone required the assistance of comrades to help him piece together his reminiscences of the recent conflict.

General Early, a Confederate exile in Canada in 1865–66, had better luck than Lee in committing his story to paper. His attempts to justify his wartime conduct were motivated initially by the fact that Lee had relieved him of command after he had failed to defeat Philip H. Sheridan's rampaging Federal army in the Shenandoah Valley in the final stages of the Civil War. Although Early prided himself on his good memory (he would soon gain a reputation as a leading historian of the Lost Cause), the irascible Rebel needed all the help he could get to reconstruct the past. Planning to write a history of his campaigns in the Shenandoah Valley, he asked one of his engineers to send him copies of reports as well as maps of his major battles.[33] These materials enabled Early to write an account of his operations that was published initially in Canada in 1866. He dedicated the book "to the Memory of the Heroic Dead, who fell fighting for Liberty, Right, and Justice" and sent a copy to his revered commander.[34] Lee thanked him guardedly. The account, he told Early, "corresponds generally with my recollection, though I cannot pretend to the accuracy of your statements, without giving the subject more investigation than I now have time to devote."[35] Less than a year after the Civil War, its very "facts" seemed elusive, even to warriors who had fought for the same cause. It was little wonder, then, that such a complex and fiercely contested event would generate divergent historical memories and overarching interpretations.

Refighting the Civil War in print was a relatively elite pastime in the Reconstruction era, restricted primarily to officers on both sides. Grief for the soldier dead, however, the third main cause of Civil War remembrance after 1865, was a feeling shared by large numbers of ordinary people, North and South. Its most tangible manifestations lay in a variety of linked commemorative projects, the most important of which were the building of cemeteries, the construction of monuments, and the staging of elaborate public ceremonies to mourn those who had sacrificed their lives for their respective countries. In the immediate aftermath of so much killing, none of these sensitive activities were ideologically neutral.

After the war, the US government intensified its efforts to ensure that as many of its dead soldiers as possible were interred in graves of its own making. This necessitated a formidable program of cemetery construction that highlighted the centralizing impact of the Civil War on the American state as well as the conflict's spur to American patriotism. No national cemeteries had been built to honor the republic's military heroes after the War of Independence, the War of 1812, or the US-Mexican War. The enormous casualties of the Civil War, however, wrought a sea change in the public's attitude toward death in the nation's service. Northerners demanded that the sacrifice of the 360,000 mostly volunteer soldiers who had laid down their lives for the republic should be properly recognized. Their government responded impressively.

A report commissioned by US Quartermaster General Montgomery Meigs in October 1865 revealed the scale of the problem: tens of thousands of Union corpses scattered across the South and vulnerable to desecration by disgruntled Confederates. The previous year, Meigs had instigated the building of a national military cemetery on the Arlington estate owned by Robert E. Lee's wife, Mary Custis, across the Potomac River from Washington, DC. Now he instructed military officers and reburial teams to scour the South for loyal bodies. These teams collected up the Federal dead (their efforts to locate corpses often aided by former slaves) and then reinterred them in government cemeteries built on or near the great battlefields of the war or adjacent to hospitals and prisons. Pittsburg Landing National Cemetery (now Shiloh National Cemetery), for example, contained bodies disinterred from 178 locations on the 1862 Shiloh battlefield and 565 separate spots in the Tennessee Valley.[36]

The remains hauled to the graveyard at Marietta, Georgia, came from 1,970 different places.[37] By March 1870, a total of 309,225 Federal bodies, many of them unidentified, had been gathered up under the government's care at a cost of more than $3 million.[38] The Republican-dominated Congress passed legislation to mark, beautify, and protect these places, thereby guaranteeing their function as prime physical sites of Civil War remembrance for generations to come.

Not all Federal soldiers were interred in these new, well-ordered US cemeteries. Removing soldiers' corpses from the theater of war was an expensive business, but some individuals and families, usually officers' relatives, were able to bring home the remains of their loved ones. Buried in local cemeteries across the North and the upper South, these bodies were joined over time by rising numbers of Union veterans who died after Appomattox. Civil War monuments, funded by regimental comrades and the wider community, were often built in these places.[39] Peaceful village and town cemeteries therefore functioned alongside national cemeteries as sites of mourning for the Union dead, their headstones and funerary monuments tangible focal points for collective northern tributes even before the institutionalization of Union Decoration (Memorial) Day in 1868. White southerners were no less afflicted with sorrow at the human cost of war. Their commemorative gaze, however, was directed toward their own sacrificial dead.

Enduring hatreds incurred by the wartime killing made the burial of fallen combatants a controversial process. Few northerners in the conflict's immediate aftermath suggested that slain Confederates—men who had taken up arms against the authority of the United States government—should be buried at the taxpayer's expense alongside the white and black bodies of the hallowed Union dead. (While African Americans were often buried in separate sections of US cemeteries like Arlington, they were always included in the government's reinterment program.) The latter's exclusion of Rebels, however, was often resented by southern whites. One Richmond newspaper observed that while "their Government" was extending lavish care to Federal corpses, "[t]he nation contemns our dead. They are left in deserted places to rot into oblivion."[40]

Determined that southern heroes should not be allowed to molder without due care and honor, local women who had experienced what historian Paul H. Buck referred to as "the triple agony" of physical suffering, loss, and defeat stepped into the breach.[41] They did so by forming Ladies' Memorial Associations across the South. These groups, often extensions of wartime soldiers' relief societies, were composed largely of white women from the urban upper class. Numbering about seventy by the spring of 1866, they depended on close cooperation with men who helped with fundraising, disinterred Confederate corpses, hauled bodies into existing cemeteries, buried them in special plots, and delivered speeches at funerals and other commemorative events. The women, however, took the lead in organizing and funding a range of substantial reburial projects, contracted directly with the menfolk to undertake essential labor, planned the construction of monuments, and were the prime movers behind the initiation of Confederate Memorial Day. Within a year of the war's end, then, southern women who could be seen walking the streets of the defeated South in mourning garb had embarked on a collective public effort to gather up and remember the region's fallen heroes—an effort that was remarkable not only because it was led by a sex that had been heavily constrained by antebellum patriarchy, but also because of its scale and efficiency. As early as May 1866, for example, 16,000 Confederates had been buried in Richmond's Oakwood Cemetery.[42]

The activities of the Ladies' Memorial Associations quickly assumed the guise of what historian William A. Blair calls "a form of guerrilla warfare through mourning."[43] These elite women mourned not only the soldiers who had laid down their lives for their country but also the loss of that country. "We are a distinct and separate nation," wrote the Virginian Isabel Maury in January 1866, "and I wish our customs to be as distinct as we are."[44] Political intent was most apparent at events to commemorate Confederate Memorial Day. While no single date for this public acknowledgment of the southern nation's sacrifices existed at this time, the spring of 1866 witnessed a plethora of commemorative activities across the region. Buildings and private homes were draped in black crepe, businesses were closed, and images of Confederate heroes were flaunted openly on the streets. In Richmond, uniformed Confederate veterans assembled in regimental groups and marched in military formation to Hollywood Cemetery. There a crowd of about twenty thousand people watched or participated in the decoration of graves, including that of the revered cavalry commander, J.E.B. Stuart, who had perished in the Overland campaign of 1864.

Speeches delivered at memorial ceremonies attested to the strength of southern feeling. "We retract nothing, recant none of our principles," intoned one minister at White Sulphur Springs, West Virginia.[45] Henry A. Wise, the Commonwealth's former governor who had been an outspoken secessionist, told a funereal gathering in Winchester in October 1866 that southerners should look to their dead for the confidence to resist submission to the Yankees. General Jackson, he averred, would have "demanded" the withdrawal of all occupying forces . . . as well as the restoration to southern whites of their civil rights under the law. "A lost cause!" he intoned, "If lost it was false; if true, it is not lost!"[46]

Large demonstrations of unrepentant Rebels troubled northerners, particularly when coupled with evidence that many southern whites had no intention of allowing loyal (pro-Union) blacks to occupy public spaces for their own purposes. In April 1866, shortly before African Americans celebrated the first anniversary of the liberation of Richmond by Union troops, the Baptist church at the center of event planning was burned down. Although the procession passed off peacefully—as many as two thousand people marched in a parade watched by at least fifteen thousand spectators—subsequent public displays by black Republicans in cities like Norfolk and New Orleans were contested violently.

Fears that rebellion was rearing its ugly head again induced many federal officials to crack down on Confederate memorialization efforts. In January 1867, huge crowds turned out in New Orleans to honor the body of Albert Sidney Johnston as it passed through the city on its way to its final resting place in Galveston, Texas. Johnston, one of the South's leading commanders at Shiloh, had been killed on the first day of the battle. His posthumous progress through the South enabled prominent Rebel generals like Braxton Bragg, James Longstreet, and Richard Taylor, as well as thousands of ordinary Confederates to pay their respects to the deceased and his cause. Anticipating another flagrant demonstration of enthusiasm for the rebellion, the federal officer in charge in Texas refused to allow a similar procession. His immediate superior, Union cavalry hero Major General Philip Sheridan, upheld the decision. "I have too much regard for the memory of the brave men who died to preserve our Government," he said, "to authorize Confederate demonstrations over the remains of any one who attempted to destroy it."[47]

The US authorities' efforts to suppress public displays of affection for the Confederacy proved more successful than their attempts to curtail white supremacist violence directed against blacks. This was largely because most Confederate veterans were pragmatic enough to know when to tone down their displays of affection for their old cause. Robert E. Lee cautioned publicly against commemorative activities that would sustain festering wounds, on the grounds that such behavior would prevent the reintegration of the southern states into the Union on the best possible terms for the former Rebels. As southern men scaled back their involvement in Confederate memorialization exercises under the watchful gaze of the federal authorities, the Ladies' Memorial Associations grew in influence. Their labors in behalf of the Confederate dead would help to sustain the Lost Cause during the turbulent years of military Reconstruction.

The distinction between loyalty and treason, central to disputes over how the fallen on both sides should be remembered, also played a key role in the fourth driver of Civil War memory after 1865: the concerted attempt by many individuals to secure government compensation for services undertaken, and damages suffered, during the Civil War. Remembrance of one's loyalty to the

United States could unlock a vital source of income during the late nineteenth century. While the financial importance of loyal memories was most evident in the sphere of pension provision—by the 1890s, Washington was paying relatively generous pensions to Union veterans—their significance during the Reconstruction years lay primarily in the actions of the Southern Claims Commission. Congress created this three-man federal panel in 1871 to hear claims for damages caused to loyalists' property by the US military during the Civil War. In the course of its ten-year career, the panel received 22,298 claims totaling more than $45 million. It paid out $5 million.[48] The Commission's desire to defend the public purse and its determination to equate loyalty with active support for the Union in the difficult conditions of the wartime South thus placed a premium on the construction of personal narratives of the past that fit closely with the Republican commissioners' own sense of what constituted patriotic citizenship.

White southerners, especially female claimants with relatives in the Confederate Army, found it almost impossible to secure damages. However, the panel looked kindly on petitions from a small number of single or separated white women who remembered that they had provided positive assistance to the Union cause. For example, an Alabamian named Rachel Cole was able to show that she and a neighbor had helped fugitive Union prisoners and Confederate deserters reach Federal lines. The commissioners also rewarded white men who could recall convincingly that they had voted against secession and fought for the Union. Individuals sometimes found that forgetting the past could be as useful as remembering it. A Virginian, Joseph Segar, won damages with a strong claim to be a Union man, but he wisely neglected to mention his antebellum backing for slavery and states' rights.

Initially, the commissioners assumed that only whites had owned property in the slave South. They were therefore surprised to be confronted with many claims from African Americans. Although some blacks were able to recall serving in the US military or aiding Union prisoners, the freedpeople's lack of corroborating evidence and constrained ability to act under slavery induced the commissioners to relax their equation of wartime loyalty with active citizenship. Instead, they were persuaded by the assertion that "all the colored people were for the Union" and allowed the majority of claims submitted by blacks who had been free or enslaved during the Civil War.[49]

Civil War Memory and Reconstruction Politics

The distinction between remembered loyalty and treason galvanized party competition in the Reconstruction era. Even though the military outcome of the Civil War had been decisive, the conflict generated a string of issues that politicians could use to mobilize voters.

As well as engendering lasting hatreds, the war had sapped confidence in existing institutions. Many Americans feared that the war had fatally undermined the country's political system. They talked a good deal about the "Mexicanization" of the American republic, by which they meant either the end of political stability or the encroachment of military despotism.[50] Some people genuinely feared that another civil war was just around the corner. Supporters of President Andrew Johnson's lenient policies for the post-emancipation South were convinced that Radical Republicans wanted to plunge the country into greater chaos in order to punish southerners for secession. Some ardent Republicans believed that Johnson was preparing to follow the example of Napoleon III in France and stage a coup d'état. Senator Oliver Morton of Indiana stated that if war resulted, he would "rush it with the same spirit, and the same men who had crushed the rebellion."[51] A few irreconcilable Confederates, Jubal Early among them, hoped that northerners would fall out over Reconstruction and allow former Rebels like himself to regain the initiative. "My hope is in a collision over the spoils of office between the parties in the North," wrote the general in August 1866, resulting in an opportunity "for the southern states to recover their independence."[52]

The specter of a second civil war was not exorcised completely until the disputed presidential election of 1876 was resolved peacefully the following year. Political violence in the South repeatedly undermined the Republicans' efforts to remake Dixie in the North's image and ultimately ensured that local whites would retain their dominance over blacks even while they abandoned their dreams of separate nationality from the Yankees. Memory played a critical role in the battles over Reconstruction policy, fueling southern Democrats' campaigns to "redeem" their section from the humiliation of "carpetbag" rule as well as Republican efforts to ensure that dangerous former Confederates did not make a swift return to power.

The war had made a disastrous impact on the Democratic Party, once a highly effective national coalition embracing politicians and voters on both sides of the Mason-Dixon Line. As well as dividing the party along sectional lines because most proslavery southern Democrats supported secession, the conflagration had pitted war supporters against antiwar Democrats in the North. Although some War Democrats cooperated with Republicans in new Union Party coalitions in the early 1860s, a majority of northern Democrats emerged from the conflict determined to return their battered party to national power. Northern Democratic strategists had a vested interest in either suppressing or downplaying wartime memories because their rebuilding project was a two-stage enterprise. It required them, first, to sideline the Peace Democrats, who had been discredited in the public's eyes by Union victory. If they embraced these former "Copperheads" too openly, they risked alienating conservative northerners who regarded outspoken peace men like Clement L. Vallandigham of Ohio and Fernando Wood of New York as allies of the breakaway Confederacy. Reviving bitter memories could only remind northern voters that the party was tainted with treason. It made more sense to focus voters' attention on the present and future: to stress that sectional reconciliation was essential for the nation's welfare, to call for the speediest possible readmission of southern states to Congress, and to oppose the Republicans' divisive support for black male suffrage. During the early years of congressional Reconstruction, when tens of thousands of southern white men were prohibited from voting, national Democratic strategists knew they would have to focus primarily on courting northern support. But as the power of the former Rebels returned, their advocacy of sectional reconciliation and white rule would assist the second stage of their political strategy: the rebuilding of political links with southern Democrats.

Former Confederates who supported the Democrats before the war had good reasons to return to their old partisan allegiance because most northern Democrats favored amnesty for former Rebels, states' rights, and white supremacy. When they spoke nationally—in Congress, for example—many southern Democrats, even before the final restoration of home rule in 1877, saw the advantage of mouthing sectional reconciliation to consolidate their renewed connections with their northern allies and to isolate vindictive Republicans. At home, however, they frequently styled themselves as guardians of Confederate memory in order to unite local voters behind their leadership. It was in this guise that they led the assault on carpetbag rule.

Like the former Rebels, northern Republicans also had much to gain by sustaining sectional memories of the Civil War after 1865. Their grand narrative of the conflict lauded the party's vanguard role in mobilizing northerners to defeat the evil designs of southern traitors. In late 1865 and early 1866, this arresting narrative framed the response of centrist and Radical Republicans to what they saw as alarming signs of a Confederate resurgence in the South. Insisting that wartime loyalty to the US government must be the basis of Reconstruction, they passed the Civil Rights and Freedmen's Bureau bills largely to benefit the hard-pressed freedpeople. Any expectations they had of formulating policy in collaboration with President Andrew Johnson, however, were quickly dashed. Johnson vetoed both bills and in doing so initiated a vicious political struggle that opened up new fissures in an already deeply divided country. In the early phase of this battle, the Republicans seized on Unionist memories of the late conflict to win support from anxious white voters in the North.

The mnemonic dimension of the battle over Reconstruction was greatly complicated by Johnson's actions. The Tennessee Unionist, a onetime Jacksonian, had received the vice presidential nomination of the Republican-headed National Union Party in 1864 because of his likely appeal to War Democrats. An insecure man with no love for secessionists, white abolitionists, or African Americans, his aim was to transform the victorious wartime coalition into a permanent organization of northern and southern conservatives under his leadership. This made the president's chief policy goals—reunion, reconciliation, and white supremacy—similar to those of the northern Democrats. Neither he nor they had reason to sustain inconvenient war memories that would inhibit the forging of cross-sectional alliances. Johnson's support for political realignment and his desire for a speedy Reconstruction also appealed to some conservative Republicans who chafed at the influence of antislavery Radicals in their party. However, there were two fatal flaws in the president's plans. First, he failed to recognize northern Democrats' determination to retain their party identity. Second, he underestimated the importance of war-generated issues and memories to northern voters.

Congressional Republicans responded to Johnson's challenge by passing the Civil Rights and Freedmen's Bureau bills over the president's vetoes and by creating a special committee to consider additional action. The Joint Committee on Reconstruction took testimony from a range of individuals, including Union military officers, southern white Unionists, and even a few leading former Confederates such as Robert E. Lee and Alexander H. Stephens. Although its members were interested in learning about current conditions in the South, several individuals called to testify reached back in time to bolster their arguments. One Virginia legislator remembered that conservative men in his state had only backed secession reluctantly after Fort Sumter and contended that no one he knew still entertained "the project of finally seceding from the Union, and setting up southern independence."[53] Union general Rufus Saxton, on the other hand, recalled that during the war African Americans had made "excellent soldiers." Insisting that the former slaves shared "all the vices and all the virtues of our common humanity," he drew on his experience as a commander in South Carolina to assert that they had demonstrated their capacity to work for wages without coercion.[54]

The Joint Committee heard that most former Confederates resented the US government and were making life dangerous for Unionists of both races. Its July 1866 report was attached to a draft constitutional amendment making the freedpeople US citizens and guaranteeing them "the equal protection of the laws."[55] Written by Senator William Pitt Fessenden, whose youngest son had perished in the Union debacle at Second Bull Run, it justified the measure as necessary to ensure that northerners did not squander the fruits of their hard-won victory. Fessenden reminded readers that the unrepentant Rebels had waged war against the government for four years "with the most determined and malignant spirit, killing in battle, and otherwise, large numbers of loyal people."[56] Republican leaders, rashly denounced by Andrew Johnson as insurrectionists, had no intention of allowing the intemperate president to wrest the mnemonic initiative from them.

Johnson hoped that the National Union convention in Philadelphia in August would kick-start his attempts to forge a viable coalition of patriotic Democrats and conservative Republicans. The gathering was noteworthy for its early attention to reconciliatory symbolism. A band played Union and Confederate war songs, and delegates applauded and wept as Darius Crouch, a relatively minor Federal commander, entered the hall arm-in-arm with Governor James Orr of South Carolina. Occurring just days after a well-publicized massacre of blacks in New Orleans, this kind of political theater disgusted many northerners who considered it too soon after Appomattox for such fraternal demonstrations. Pro-Johnson candidates were trounced in the midterm elections, proving northern voters' disdain for politicians who wanted them to forget the consequences of southern treason. Emboldened by victory, congressional Republicans in February 1867 turned most of the former Confederacy over to military rule and empowered federal commanders to oversee elections in which black men could vote.

The new southern Republican regimes sired by Congress were fragile entities—heavily dependent for survival on US military protection as well as the votes of newly enfranchised blacks and some white Unionists. Most former Rebels regarded these interracial carpetbag regimes as illegitimate, imposed on them by Yankees in a further attempt to "mongrelize" and degrade the South. More vicious attacks on southern Unionists ensued, some of them the work of a shadowy new terrorist group, the Ku Klux Klan. Founded in Pulaski, Tennessee, the Klan claimed to represent the spirit of deceased Confederates. Clad in white costumes, its members, many of them Rebel veterans, roamed the countryside at night attacking Republicans in their homes. The Klan and similar terrorist groups were supported by powerful southern Democrats—leading former Rebels like Major General John B. Gordon of Georgia who knew that their return to local power and the restoration of white supremacy were heavily dependent on sustaining memories of the Confederates' war.

Northern Democrats were divided over how their party should approach the 1868 presidential election. The nomination of a notorious Peace Democrat such as Indiana's George Pendleton would mean, as one midwesterner asserted, that "every man who took part in the war will be unable to support him without stultifying himself and acknowledging he did wrong."[57] The anticipated need to parry Republican assaults on their allegedly treasonous past even induced some leading Democrats to consider nominating Chief Justice

Salmon P. Chase as their presidential candidate. Chase had an impressive record as a supporter of the Union and of equal rights for blacks. His racial egalitarianism, however, was too much for most Democrats to stomach, and in the end the party passed over Chase, Pendleton, and Andrew Johnson. In July 1868, it nominated for president the former New York governor, Horatio Seymour, on a platform opposed to congressional Reconstruction. Seymour's running mate was a prominent Union general and conservative, Frank P. Blair Jr. An outspoken opponent of black equality, Blair had recently issued a public letter announcing that a Democratic president would oust the Republican regimes in the South with military force. It was no surprise that Blair's nomination received strong backing from delegates representing states of the old Confederacy.

The Democrats' hopes of a swift revival after Appomattox were dashed by their opponents' adept use of historical memory. At their Chicago convention in May, the Republicans nominated for president Ulysses S. Grant, the leading Union commander of the war. Grant had played his cards wisely over the past two years, refusing to support Andrew Johnson in his losing battle against congressional Republicans. His victory helped to unify the party after some of its senators had voted controversially against the impeachment of Andrew Johnson, by this time a very lame duck. It also signaled the Republicans' determination to hold on to the votes of Union veterans. The soldiers had recently formed a new patriotic organization, the Grand Army of the Republic (GAR). Although notionally a fraternal rather than a political group, a majority of the GAR's members were Republicans. The organization would function as a prime institutional carrier of Civil War memory for the remainder of the century. It would also operate as an unofficial arm of the Republican Party. Although the Democrats had their own short-lived soldiers' organization, the White Boys in Blue, they found it difficult to shed the taint of treason so quickly after the war.

One reason for this was white southerners' escalating campaign of violence against black and white Unionists, which enabled northern Republicans to wave the so-called bloody shirt as a perennial reminder of the threat posed to the country by Democrats. The political cartoonist, Thomas Nast, was an expert manipulator of northern voters' Civil War memories and the contemporary fears to which they were connected. Nast, a German-born immigrant, worked for the Republican newspaper, *Harper's Weekly*. During the 1868 election campaign, he bombarded readers with a barrage of sulfurous imagery that played on northerners' anxieties about a Confederate revival. "The Democratic Hell-Broth," printed at the end of October, featured Frank Blair, Horatio Seymour, and Confederate cavalry commander Wade Hampton. Nast depicted the three men as witches from Shakespeare's *Macbeth* stirring a boiling cauldron marked

"C.S.A." and "K.K.K." An accompanying text, the witches' curse, raised up vivid recollections of Democratic crimes:

> Hand of Treason, reeking red,
> Poison-fang of Copperhead . . .
> Skull of prisoner at Fort Pillow,
> Blood of freedman at Camilla,
> Hampton's torch, Fred Douglass's fetter,
> Booth's revolver, Blair's letter . . . [58]

Powerful images like this, combined with persistent Republican reminders that Seymour had sympathized with New York draft rioters in 1863, helped General Grant secure a clear majority of the white vote in New England and the Midwest. Abetted too by the votes of southern blacks and the fact that Virginia, Mississippi, and Texas remained unreconstructed and therefore unable to participate in the canvass, the Union hero triumphed with 214 electoral college votes over Seymour's 80.

Northern joy at Grant's triumph soon soured. The president's failure to eliminate corruption induced reform-minded Liberal Republicans to oppose his reelection in 1872. Convinced that existing prohibitions against many former Confederates were contributing to graft and to the persistence of Reconstruction-era violence, and that bloody-shirt rhetoric was merely a tool of venal spoilsmen in their party, leading Liberals demanded not only a general amnesty act but also an end to anti-southern abuse. Savvy Democratic leaders, recognizing the weakness of their political position, urged their co-partisans to embrace a "new departure," by which they meant public acceptance of the Thirteenth, Fourteenth, and Fifteenth Amendments that had enhanced the rights of the freedpeople. This pragmatic maneuver set the stage for their embrace of Horace Greeley, the breakaway Liberals' presidential candidate.

The maverick editor of the antislavery *New York Tribune* was a public supporter of sectional reconciliation, having played a formative role in securing the release of Jefferson Davis from prison in May 1867. In the midst of his 1872 presidential campaign, Greeley told an audience in Pittsburgh, "The war is ended, let us again be fellow countrymen, and forget that we have been enemies."[59] Mainstream Republicans, however, had no intention of letting their opponents dominate the debate over Civil War memory. Despite the removal of voting and officeholding prohibitions from the vast majority of former Confederates in May 1872, they disparaged calls for historical amnesia. "If we remember, with any gratitude the 500,000 soldiers who perished in the [wartime] struggle," asserted the *Nation*, "we can never consent that the party which was sneering, dabbling, and hindering while they were fighting shall in its old form and character again come to the front."[60] Thomas Nast rallied patriotic citizens to the Republican standard with scathing visual attacks on the Democratic candidate. Several cartoons trashed Greeley's reconciliatory appeals. One depicted the apostate New Yorker grasping the hand of the ghost of John Wilkes Booth. Another showed him shaking hands with an armed southerner trampling the American flag and murdered blacks.[61] Still fearful that wartime issues had not yet been settled, the majority of voters reelected Grant in a landslide. The result also owed something to Greeley's unpopularity among Democrats. Many had long memories of Greeley's commitment to antislavery before the war and simply stayed at home on election day.

During the next four years, Democrats used a combination of fraud, intimidation, and violence to redeem southern states like Mississippi from military rule. Sensing that northerners were growing tired of Reconstruction, President Grant proved increasingly reluctant to protect embattled southern Republicans with federal troops. Evidence of corruption within the administration and the reconstructed southern states convinced some Republicans, keen to secure the return of breakaway Liberals to the fold, to oppose further federal intervention in the South. In Massachusetts, for example, they formally declared their determination to commit the party's proud past "to history."[62] However, the rising tide of southern violence and the unpalatable prospect of the Democrats returning to national power sharpened political minds. In January 1876, James G. Blaine, a Republican presidential aspirant, launched a vitriolic attack on Jefferson Davis in the US House of Representatives during a debate over whether Congress should remove the remaining officeholding disqualifications from a handful of high-ranking Confederates. Moving to exempt Davis from any amnesty legislation, Blaine denounced the Rebel president as the witting "author . . . of the gigantic murders and crimes at Andersonville."[63] Five months later, one of Blaine's staunchest backers, Robert G. Ingersoll of Illinois, delivered a powerful speech at the Republican national convention in Cincinnati. Ingersoll, a Union veteran celebrated and reviled as a formidable purveyor of sectional spleen, lauded "the plumed knight" from Maine for preserving in Congress what northern "soldiers won on the field" and for snatching "the mask of Democracy from the hideous face of rebellion."[64] While Blaine lacked sufficient support to secure the nomination on this occasion, the Republicans' decision to nominate another Union veteran for president spoke volumes for the rebellion's continuing influence on contemporary American politics.

Rutherford B. Hayes, the Republican candidate in 1876, was widely respected as a brave Union officer who had been wounded several times in the Civil War. Although his fellow partisans regarded him as a reform-minded Republican who could appeal to Liberals hostile to corruption and sectionalism, Hayes quickly realized that northern voters' fears of a Confederate resurgence might tip the balance in a close contest in which the Democrats had nominated for president Samuel J. Tilden, a wealthy New York lawyer who had publicly supported a compromise deal with the South during the secession crisis. "[T]he true issue in the minds of the Masses," Hayes told Republican leaders, "is simply, shall the late rebels have the government?"[65] Incidents such as the Democrats' massacre of blacks in Hamburg, South Carolina, in July imparted considerable force to this overtly sectional strategy. In one livid campaign speech, Senator Oliver Morton of Indiana denounced the Democrats as "gangrened instigators of rebellion" and "slave drivers who have lost their occupation."[66] Bitter memories of the Civil War bound Union and Confederate veterans to opposing sides in the presidential election contest and played a major role in an unprecedented turnout of more than 81 percent. They did not, however, decide the result of a tight race whose outcome, it rapidly became clear, would depend largely on the decision in South Carolina, Louisiana, and Florida—the only southern states where the Republicans retained power.

Democrats claimed the electoral college votes of each of these states, expecting thereby to win the presidency for the first time in two decades. Republicans, however, immediately announced their determination to contest the votes of all three states in order to secure Hayes's victory. This decision threatened to confirm persistent fears that the Civil War had permanently destabilized the American polity. Hotheads on both sides, including some of Jubal Early's diehard allies in the South, seemed ready to plunge the country into another war. Most leading former Confederates, however, had no wish to risk another conflict, even if they received the green light for military action from belligerent northern Democrats like conservative Union general George McClellan. Bradley T. Johnson, a former Rebel commander, drew a shrewd lesson from the recent past to alert his fellow Confederates to the need to stay their hand. "I believe experience has shown," he wrote, "that the party in America which makes use of armed force in resisting officers acting under the forces of the law is always unsuccessful & is overthrown." Witness, he recalled, what he referred to as US Secretary of State William Seward's "trick of making us fire on Sumpter [*sic*]" in order "to unite the North." "In this struggle," he insisted, "the party that begins violence will have the sentiment of the country rise against it & crush it."[67]

Although Samuel Tilden was not supine during the crisis, his co-partisans in Congress, desperate for political legitimacy after years of being taunted as traitors by the Republicans, agreed to create a bipartisan electoral commission to determine the status of the contested votes and to abide by its decision. The concession disappointed irreconcilables from Lee's old Army of Northern Virginia. "I had fixed my heart upon the fact that the democracy would hold what they had now—with arms if necessary," wrote one of their number despairingly.[68] But even when the commission declared Hayes the winner by one vote, pragmatic southerners—not least those involved in secretive negotiations to settle the crisis peacefully—understood that the Republicans' victory would finally bring Reconstruction to an end. And so it proved. After his inauguration President Hayes, strongly supported by reformist elements within his party, withdrew all federal military support for the South's remaining Republican governments.

Hayes's narrow political triumph did not terminate the influence of Civil War memories in mainstream politics. Even as the Ohio veteran was preparing to enter the White House, the former Confederates were in the process of fashioning their distinctive Lost Cause interpretation of the Civil War into a powerful strain of historical memory—one that would help to solidify their still unsecured dominion over blacks at home and ultimately defy Yankee efforts to cast the Confederates' independence struggle as sedition and rebellion.

CHAPTER TWO

The Resurgent South and Its Lost Cause

Origins of the Lost Cause

A strange thing happened after the Civil War. In 1865, victorious northerners expected to transmit their version of events to future generations of Americans. By 1900, however, those Yankee expectations had been dashed, partly by the emergence of a powerful losers' memory of "the War between the States." While northerners did not fully embrace the Lost Cause, a majority of them reached an accommodation with it by embracing an even more potent reconciliatory strain of historical memory that consigned the struggle to save the Union and destroy slavery to the margins of the nation's memory bank. Popular culture in the twentieth century would pay relatively little attention to the North's triumphant narrative of "the War of the Rebellion." Instead of drooling over actors portraying Federal heroes like Grant and Sherman, American moviegoers would thrill to the exploits of the Ku Klux Klan, admire the decency of doomed cavaliers like Ashley Wilkes, and swoon over the dark good looks of the ultimate Confederate antihero, Rhett Butler.

The roots of the Lost Cause lay in the determination of many southern whites, including those from pro-Union slave states like Missouri and Kentucky, to commemorate the South's abortive bid for independence. Its rise was interwoven with the crusade against Reconstruction, the consolidation of white supremacy under Democratic rule in the 1890s, and the emergence of a "New South" committed to industrial and commercial progress. Constructed, like all historical memories, by different groups possessing their own agendas, it was a plastic strain of memory that smoothed the process of change in a conservative region that remained impoverished and underdeveloped long after military defeat. During its first inward-looking phase, in which embittered Confederate leaders played a formative role, the Lost Cause was cloaked in the culture of loss and mourning by communities across the South. But by the time Confederate President Jefferson Davis died in December 1889, it had begun to break free of its funerary grip and develop into a public celebration of the southern cause as a patriotic American fight. This transformation, which opened up pathways to reconciliation with the North, was the work of key remembering agents such as rank-and-file Confederates and younger southern white women whose members were heavily influenced by the turmoil of Reconstruction. The United Confederate Veterans (UCV) and United Daughters of the Confederacy (UDC), two of the most energetic carriers of Civil War memory in the United States, would transmit what its members regarded as the timeless values of the plantation South into the modern yet racially segregated world of the twentieth century. Jim Crow was sustained by the regionally dominant memory they constructed.

Shortly after learning of Lee's surrender at Appomattox, Father Abram J. Ryan, an anti-abolitionist Roman Catholic priest who had served unofficially as a chaplain in the Confederate Army, penned a heart-felt tribute titled "The Conquered Banner" to his doomed nation's starry battle flag. Accepting the reality of defeat, Ryan urged his Rebel compatriots to "[f]url that banner, for 'tis weary; Round its staff 'tis drooping dreary." Acknowledging also that there was no longer "a sword to save" his country and that "its people's hopes are dead," he glimpsed the power of southern myth in the uncertain future. Consumed with grief (his own brother had perished in the conflict), he wrote passionately of "the blood which heroes" had invested in the flag:

> Furl that Banner! True, 'tis gory,
> Yet 'tis wreathed around with glory,
> And 'twill live in song and story,
>   Though its folds are in the dust:
> For its fame on brightest pages,
> Penned by poets and by sages,
>   Shall go sounding down the ages—
> Furl its folds though now we must.[1]

Ryan's morbid stanzas were terrible poetry. However, they touched raw emotions in the wounded Southland and would remain popular among whites in the region for many decades. The priest's insistence on the nobility of the Confederates' struggle spoke to their yearning for vindication in the eyes of the world. Even though their cause had drowned in a sea of blood, they refused to accept that their proslavery republic had been, in the words of one crowing Yankee broadside, "conceived in sin, born in iniquity, [and] nurtured by tyranny."[2]

The work of vindication was well under way by the late 1860s. What historian David Blight has called the initial "diehard era" of the Lost Cause was fashioned as a coherent discourse by unrepentant former Confederates writing in a highly charged political climate.[3] They included not only Richmond editor, Edward Pollard, whose book, *The Lost Cause,* appeared in 1866, but also West Pointer Albert Taylor Bledsoe and former Confederate Vice President Alexander H. Stephens. Justifying a beaten cause, denigrated as evil by large numbers of northerners, was not an easy venture, but these writers warmed to the task. Collectively, they developed a two-pronged defense of the South that would grow in potency over time.

The first prong was developed by Bledsoe and Stephens. Their objective was a critical one: to demonstrate that secession, the immediate trigger for civil war, had been legal under the federal Constitution of 1787. By proving this they could show that the North's invasion of the South had been unlawful. Failure to make this claim stick would, they believed, doom the Confederates at the bar of history. As Bledsoe, an old classmate of President Jefferson Davis, put it succinctly in his 1866 tome, *Is Davis a Traitor; or Was Secession a Constitutional Right Previous to the War of 1861?*, "[I]t is precisely as this question is decided, that the Jacksons, the Johnsons, the Lees, and the Davises of the South, will be pronounced rebels and traitors, or heroes and martyrs; that the South itself will be disgraced, or honored, in the estimation of mankind."[4]

The defenders of secession argued their case on the basis of the compact theory of the Constitution—the doctrine that the Union founded at Philadelphia had been a voluntary one with many powers reserved to the individual states. They contended, as Jefferson Davis had asserted in his inaugural address of February 1861, that the Confederates were patriots attempting to preserve fundamental American principles of state sovereignty and self-government. In his two-volume *Constitutional View of the Late War between the States* (1867–70), Alexander Stephens vigorously denied that "[t]he matter of Slavery, so-called," had played a significant part in the decision to secede. The millions of dollars invested in slaves, he reckoned, were "but as the dust in the balance, compared with the vital attributes of the rights of Independence and Sovereignty on the part of the several States."[5] Southerners, he insisted, had fought to preserve "the Federative Principle," the fount of human liberty. "The Cause which was lost by the surrender of the Confederates," he avowed, "was only the maintenance of this Principle by arms. It was not the Principle itself that they abandoned."[6] Convinced that the liberty-loving South had been crushed by centralism and tyranny, both Stephens and Bledsoe damned Abraham Lincoln for his refusal to allow peaceable secession.

The defense's second point was that the North had prevailed only because of its overwhelming numbers. Rebel troop strength, or lack of it, had been a particular concern of Robert E. Lee and other Confederate generals at the end of the war. Pollard gave credence to this view in *The Lost Cause.* He claimed, for example, that Lee had held Richmond and Petersburg at the beginning of 1865 "with not more than thirty-three thousand men," compared with the enemy's legions of more than 160,000.[7] The Richmond editor did not attribute Yankee victory solely to numbers. Among other things he was highly critical of Jefferson Davis's executive leadership. However, warped statistics like these enabled him to elevate Lee's superior talents as a commander over those of Grant and to deflate the arrogant Yankees' claims about their military prowess.

The broad purpose of these two lines of argument was to establish that the Confederates had fought heroically against insuperable odds to defend not slavery but their rights under the old Constitution. Their proponents developed them for internal and external consumption. Domestically, the claims appealed to white southerners' sense of victimhood and bolstered their self-perception as valiant crusaders for American liberty. Externally, they had the advantage of attracting northern conservatives during the ongoing fight against congressional Reconstruction. While these early Lost Cause authors acknowledged that the independence struggle was over and that slavery was dead, they condemned ongoing northern efforts to "subjugate" white southerners. Bledsoe blasted the North's "great war of coercion" and slammed Radical Republicans' "schemes of vengeance" against their conquered foe.[8] Stephens called the 1867 Military Reconstruction Act "one of the most palpable usurpations of Power to be found in the history of the world" and urged northerners to fight for national liberty by driving "the usurpers from their places" at the ballot box.[9] Chillingly, in view of the violence being inflicted on the freedpeople, Pollard openly declared his reasons for resisting congressional policy. "[T]he war," he asserted, "did not decide negro equality; it did not decide negro suffrage; it did not decide State Rights, although it might have exploded their abuse; . . . it did not decide the right of a people to show dignity in misfortune, and to maintain self-respect in the face of adversity. And these things which the war did not decide, the Southern people will still cling to, still claim, and still assert in them their rights and views."[10] In later years, supporters of the Confederacy would downplay the linkage between the white South's liberation war and subjugating African Americans. During Reconstruction, few people were ignorant of that connection.

Aside from their own racial prejudices, one reason why so many northerners eventually became blind to that linkage was the romanticization of the Confederate cause by southern novelists. Although John Esten Cooke began the task of crafting a sentimental memory of the plantation South that would appeal to northern readers, most southern writers during Reconstruction had no wish to accommodate Yankee tastes. However, even while they breathed defiance toward the conquerors, they joined Cooke in mythologizing the Old South. Angry women writers like Sallie F. Chapin, Sarah J. C. Whittlesey, and Sarah Dorsey, proud former Confederates all, depicted the antebellum South as a harmonious society peopled by paternal planters and pampered slaves. Their goal was not reconciliation between the sections; rather, like Pollard and other male political writers, they sought to affirm the vanquished Confederacy at a moment when its people were being forced to suffer the humiliations of carpetbag misrule.

Over time, the fictional realm of the plantation South would help to reduce northern hostility toward Dixie by providing an alluring backdrop for intersectional romances between northern men and southern women. Sallie Chapin's representative novel, *Fitz-Hugh St. Clair* (1872) did no such thing. The book idealized the eponymous hero's plantation home, but it subverted northern dreams of mastery over the South. Chapin narrates how St. Clair, a Confederate officer, convinces his father's New York friend, Mr. Winthrop, of the evils of Reconstruction, marries his daughter Lucie, and returns with her to South Carolina to combat the "reprobates" who have enslaved the state's "noble" whites.[11] Yet even while Chapin gave voice to her people's racial fears by having St. Clair predict the horrors of black rule, the book's accompanying illustrations furnished readers with a formula for calming those anxieties.[12] Depictions of contented slaves undertaking worthwhile manual labor and basking in the leisure time provided by their kindly masters signaled that African Americans posed no threat to whites as long as they were subordinated.

Lost Cause arguments were disseminated not only in books but also in regional magazines with telling titles such as *The Land We Love* and *Our Living and Our Dead.* These journals had limited circulation and were read mainly by white southerners. They printed a range of articles and poems designed to vindicate the Confederacy and console readers over the sacrifices of its menfolk. *The Land We Love* was edited by Daniel Harvey Hill, a former Rebel general and devout Christian. While his magazine urged southern whites to come to terms with defeat, it also helped to sustain the idea that they were, as Methodist minister R. H. Rivers of Tennessee put it in one article, "the greatest sufferers in the struggle." "[A] nation," stated Rivers, "derives no honor from blood-thirsty Attilas that sweep like a desolating storm over homes of innocence and Edens of peace and loveliness." Rivers, like Hill, was prepared to consider reconciliation but only if northerners would accept that southern heroes like Lee and Jackson were true American patriots who "fought for principle, and struggled with manly courage for what they believed to be right."[13]

In October 1870, the Lost Cause received a major boost with the sudden death of the Confederacy's most revered commander, Robert E. Lee. The general had spent his final years as president of Washington College in Lexington, Virginia. The position suited him. It reflected his resolve to be useful to the postwar South in a civic capacity while remaining out of the limelight. Publicly, he encouraged southern whites to accept the reality of their situation, cooperate with US authorities, and work to restore the devastated region for which they had fought so tenaciously. This outwardly responsible stance would later assist Lee's incorporation into the pantheon of America's Civil War heroes. Yet it masked his profound hostility toward Republican efforts to make the freedpeople equal under the law. Notwithstanding his reluctance to attract publicity, the former slaveholder cooperated with northern Democratic attempts to win votes on the back of sectional reconciliation and white supremacy during the 1868 presidential election campaign. Lee's August public letter, signed by more than thirty leading Confederates, acknowledged the demise of slavery, advocated reconciliation between the sections, and urged northerners to let the South alone and thereby allow relations between the races to "soon adjust themselves on a basis of mutual kindness and advantage."[14]

The news of Lee's death stunned his many southern admirers. "I am just beginning to realize the General's death," wrote one former Rebel officer, "and it weighs as a crushing loss on us all. One of the saddest thoughts is that so great a link to the noble & glorious past is gone, and I fear now that the restraining influence of his example is not with us. Our people may degenerate more quickly."[15] Fears that Lee's demise would sever southern whites' connection to the liberation struggle of the 1860s were understandable. Their illustrious commander, however, proved more useful to the Lost Cause dead than alive.

In the fall of 1870, most former Confederates lived in states governed by biracial Republican coalitions that were backed by small numbers of US troops garrisoned in the main towns. This did not stop them from publicly mourning the death of their military chieftain, nor did it prevent their leaders from using Lee's demise for political advantage. New Orleans was a case in point.

The Crescent City was home to thousands of former Confederates after the war. Its imposing cemeteries contained the bodies of many fallen Rebels, and the place was a thriving center of Confederate memorial activity. In 1869, a group of leading citizens, including former general Braxton Bragg, formed the Southern Historical Society (SHS) to promote the collection, preservation, and dissemination of materials "illustrating the nature of the struggle from which the country has just emerged, defining and vindicating the principles which lay beneath it, and marking the stages through which it was conducted to its issue."[16] Most of the city's Confederate veterans and elite women who belonged to the local Ladies' Memorial Associations hated Louisiana's Radical Republican regime. Headed by carpetbag governor Henry Clay Warmoth and bolstered by a black militia as well as federal troops, the state government was reviled widely as a Yankee imposition. Matters were not helped by the fact that James Longstreet, Lee's favorite corps commander in the Army of Northern Virginia, led the militia. In 1867, Longstreet joined the Republican Party on the pragmatic grounds that it was better for whites than blacks to control the ruling party. The general was immediately denounced by most leading former Confederates as a treasonous southern "scalawag," thus setting the stage for his demonization in the lore of the Lost Cause.

The announcement of Robert E. Lee's death provided embittered New Orleans Confederates with a chance not only to mourn the South's peerless soldier but also to isolate their political enemies. Initially, Democrats who opposed Warmoth's regime took care not to antagonize the Republicans. Instead of lauding Lee for his genius at defeating Yankees on the battlefield, they hailed his restrained conduct after Appomattox. Many Unionists in the city, including businessmen who were anxious for peace and social stability, responded by acknowledging Lee's patriotic course after 1865. Even the state's black lieutenant governor, Oscar J. Dunn, decorated his home in mourning cloth. Not all Republicans, however, were willing to pay homage to the deceased, for Lee was still widely regarded as a traitor to his country. Mayor Benjamin Flanders pointedly refused to lower the flag on city hall to half-mast as a mark of respect.

It was not long before Lee's admirers openly displayed their contempt for the general's detractors. On October 18, 1870, they held a grand memorial service in the city's St. Charles Theatre. White southerners packed the ornate building to honor their aborted nation's greatest son. Prominent Rebel commanders, including Braxton Bragg, Pierre G. T. Beauregard, and John Bell Hood, listened from the stage as successive speakers expounded floridly on Lost Cause themes. One declaimed the constitutionality of secession, while another praised Lee's "masterly and heroic energy" in the service of a magnificent Christian civilization.[17] The proslavery minister Rev. Benjamin M. Palmer, unbowed by military defeat, made race the centerpiece of his keynote address. God and history would vindicate the Confederacy, he insisted, because race (by which he meant possession of a white skin) was the key to greatness. In a city where black equality was fiercely contested, the contemporary resonance of Palmer's address was clear to all. By acclaiming Robert E. Lee as a Confederate hero, the opponents of Republican rule in Louisiana left their enemies in no doubt that the interconnected struggle for home rule and white supremacy would continue.

The South Redeemed

In addition to sparking heavily politicized memorial activities in New Orleans and other southern towns, General Lee's death spurred Lost Cause advocates to redouble their efforts to exonerate the Confederacy and jettison Radical Republican rule. Lee had frowned on commemorative exercises because he feared they would provoke a damaging response from the federal authorities. Now that he was gone, his many admirers among the Confederate officer class felt free to organize more effectively. Within weeks of his demise, former Rebel leaders in Virginia had founded the Association of the Army of Northern Virginia as the first significant Confederate veterans' organization. Rival Lee monument associations had also been set up in Lexington and Richmond.

None of these groups played as important a role in the development of the Lost Cause in the 1870s as the Southern Historical Society. The SHS made little headway in its early years, but it was energized after passing into the control of Jubal Early and his Virginia-based officer clique. More than fifty delegates convened at White Sulphur Springs in West Virginia in August 1873, where they heard an unrepentant Jefferson Davis insist that southerners were "cheated rather than conquered" and Early pronounce on the goals of the Society.[18] Clad in Rebel gray, the uncompromising general insisted that former Confederates would attend the "bar" of history "as patriots demanding our rights and vindicating the true principles of the government founded by our fathers."[19]

Three years later, the organization began publishing the *Southern Historical Society Papers* (*SHSP*). From its inception this journal strengthened and expanded the Lost Cause narrative of "the War between the States" by publishing battle and campaign reminiscences, sketches of leading commanders, and Confederate documents. Throughout its long existence (the last volume was published in 1959) the *SHSP* built on the original foundations of the Lost Cause while simultaneously providing a forum for the settling of various scores among the former Rebels' military hierarchy. Many of those involved in the project were venomous Yankee haters determined to counter what they regarded as the lies propagated by northern writers like William T. Sherman. Dabney H. Maury, a Confederate general who was one of the Society's leading organizers, dismissed Sherman's 1875 memoirs in the first volume of its *Papers* as "unsavory" and "yielding no fruit to the toiler after historical truth."[20] Instructively, while he was more positive about Virginia's Union general George H. Thomas in the same essay, he had privately welcomed the death of "the Rock of Chickamauga" in 1870. "Life was probably a curse to him," he wrote, "But I hope he will not feel the Change agreeable."[21]

The elite diehard phase of the Lost Cause lasted into the mid-1880s. It differed from its later celebratory manifestation in acknowledging that southern whites had not been a unified force in defending the homeland against the Yankee hordes. Because defeat resulted in part from internal divisions widened by Union military pressure, many pioneer exponents of the Lost Cause had blamed selected Rebel leaders for failure. In his 1866 account of the Confederates' war, Edward Pollard criticized Jefferson Davis's administration and contended that leadership flaws were at least as responsible for military collapse as inferior numbers. He also assailed several of the Rebels' highest commanders, Jubal Early included, for their poor military performance. Such attacks contributed to an escalating debate between high-ranking Confederates over key tactical and strategic decisions during the war. The most vitriolic of these debates—that concerning the performance of James Longstreet—illustrated the close connection between Civil War memory and contemporary politics.

In the immediate postwar years, most former Confederates rightly regarded Longstreet as one of the most effective corps commanders of the Civil War. His reputation, however, plummeted when he joined the carpetbag regime in New Orleans. It was no accident that Longstreet's loudest traducers were the Virginians who dominated the SHS. Determined to exalt Robert E. Lee after his death in 1870, they found the scalawag Longstreet a useful foil to deflect rumbling criticism of Lee's battlefield tactics. Pollard, for example, had criticized "[t]he failure of Gen. Lee" to stop the Federals occupying the high ground at the end of the first day of the Battle of Gettysburg in July 1863.[22] Jubal Early sought to rebut such charges by initiating what one scholar has described as "one of the cleverest orchestrations of innuendo and unsubstantiated accusations in American historiography."[23] Addressing an audience in Lexington in January 1872, he charged that Longstreet had single-handedly lost the climactic battle in Pennsylvania by refusing to execute what he claimed to have been Lee's wish to attack the Union left at sunrise on the second day. The assertion was false because Lee had signaled no such daybreak assault, but Early had personal reasons for making it. His own conduct at Gettysburg had been less than exemplary. Lacking explicit orders from his superiors, he had failed to occupy Cemetery and Culp's hills at the end of the first day's fighting and knew that Longstreet's embrace of the Republicans made the Georgian an ideal scapegoat for what many former Confederates regarded as the decisive defeat of the war.

Early gained support for his calumny of "Old Pete" from Lee's staff officers who seized the chance to bolster their general's reputation. One of the most important of these military aides, Lexington minister William Nelson Pendleton, backed up Early's claims in January 1873. Longstreet, he contended, had been guilty of "culpable disobedience" and "treachery."[24] The anti-Longstreet brigade was then joined by many high-profile former Confederates who also welcomed the chance to elevate Lee at the expense of his junior commander. Braxton Bragg, Wade Hampton III of South Carolina, and Lee's nephew Fitzhugh all commended Early for disseminating what they saw as the truth about the Battle of Gettysburg.

James Longstreet was no shrinking violet. He vigorously defended himself against the mounting charges and was generally corroborated by loyal staff officers. However, he made the mistake of trying to boost his reputation at Lee's expense, for example, by alluding to his superior's overconfidence at Gettysburg. This strategy alienated the majority of white southerners, who were in no mood to read criticism of their lamented hero from a political apostate. Longstreet provided enough evidence to prove that claims about a sunrise attack order were false. But by the end of the century, his high military reputation had been shredded by his opponents' operations.

The close relationship between politics and historical memory was conspicuous in southern whites' continuing efforts to throw off the Radical Republican yoke in the 1870s. Their struggle met with increasing success as Republican regimes across the region collapsed under pressure from insurgent Democrats. The enemies of Republican rule in the postwar South enjoyed several advantages in the fight for political power after 1868. First, they could count on most ordinary whites' hostility to racial equality. Second, many of them were willing to use murderous violence to achieve their ends. Third, the South's vulnerable Republican coalitions were increasingly split along racial lines, a fracture that made it difficult for Radicals to secure cooperation between lower-class whites and newly enfranchised African Americans. Fourth, they could rely on northerners' own divisions over Reconstruction to increase opposition to congressional policy above the Mason-Dixon Line. And fifth, they could readily connect their contemporary political campaigns to vivid memories of the Confederate struggle.

Elite white opponents of Republicanism in the South agreed on the need to restore home rule and white domination, but they were not united on the means to achieve this end, nor on their vision of the region's future. The main tension lay between violent white-line Democrats such as Martin W. Gary and Matthew C. Butler in the South Carolina upcountry and more paternalistic conservatives like James Kemper and Fitzhugh Lee in Virginia and Wade Hampton in the South Carolina lowcountry. While all these men had been Confederate officers, the former were willing to stir up grassroots hatred of blacks to mobilize white voters behind their leadership. The latter, by contrast, were less eager to invoke hostility toward African Americans. This was partly because the paternalists feared that the excesses of hardliners might incur the wrath of the federal authorities and partly because they hoped to attract electoral support from blacks who knew their place.

White leaders across the South also disagreed about the merits of the "New South" project which called for the economic development of the region with the assistance of outside capital. Social conservatives like Jubal Early were deeply suspicious of New South proponents like Governor Kemper and his fellow Confederate general John B. Gordon of Georgia. They not only feared that the modernizers would further corrupt their beloved Southland by promoting its shift from a stable agrarian society to a more fluid industrial one, but also sensed correctly that their pro-business opponents had a clear incentive to advocate North-South reconciliation because they wanted to attract Yankee investment.

Tensions between diehard former Confederates and pragmatic supporters of economic growth surfaced over the modernizers' willingness to suppress war memories at the behest of northern Democrats. When Jubal Early told Robert E. Withers, a Virginia politician and fellow Confederate officer, that southern leaders were too keen to keep war issues out of the 1872 presidential election campaign, Withers retorted that harping on about northern mistreatment of Confederate POWs and other highly charged subjects could only play into the hands of prominent Republicans like Oliver Morton of Indiana. "[E]very Northern democrat in Congress, without exception," he added, "deprecates the revival and discussion of these matters."[25] Early was similarly rebuffed in October 1875 when he and other irreconcilables, Lee's son Rooney among them, tried to make the unveiling of a statue to Stonewall Jackson in Richmond an occasion for Confederate defiance. "Our Democratic friends North," wrote Governor Kemper, a member of Virginia's short-lived Conservative Party, "express great anxiety that nothing shall happen on the 26th to hurt the party. They say Morton & Co. would pay a half million to get some of our boys to tear down and trample on the U.S. Flag on that day."[26]

Although modernizers and diehards were committed to overturning Republican rule, their differences over how to do this were connected to their treatment of African Americans in the altered political climate of Reconstruction. Ratification of the Fifteenth Amendment in 1870 had enfranchised black men across the country, and some Virginia Conservatives, including paternalists like Governor Kemper, saw the wisdom of appealing to elements of this new constituency. When organizing the parade to Stonewall Jackson's statue in 1875, Kemper sanctioned requests to participate from black ministers and militiamen appreciative of the general's sponsorship of a Sunday School for enslaved children. Early was furious. Richmond blacks, he complained, would seize the chance to vaunt their support for equal rights. Kemper stood his ground, basing his argument on a sentimental strain of the Lost Cause that emphasized black loyalty to the white race under slavery. If local blacks "humbly and decorously" wished to pay tribute to Jackson, he asked, who was Early to complain? "If your Father's negroes followed his body to the grave, and if many hundreds of freed negroes followed Jackson's body to his grave, I don't see anything in the present arrangement so new, so strange or so monstrous as to astonish you or to fire your rage."[27]

Such friction, however, could not conceal the fact that most white southerners shared the overriding commitment of leading Democrats and Virginia Conservatives to the restoration of white supremacy. This commitment helped to drive the popularity of the Lost Cause in the 1870s, even in states that had never been part of the Confederacy and subjected to military rule. In Kentucky, as in Missouri, white Unionists often shared their onetime opponents' horror of emancipation and aversion to equal citizenship for blacks. Former Confederates in Kentucky easily seized the initiative from disaffected Unionists, building monuments to Rebel heroes like General John C. Breckinridge, whose Lexington statue was funded partly by a generous donation from the Democratic-controlled state legislature. Like their peers in other parts of the South, they also sought to control the historical record by writing accounts of the liberation struggle and collecting documents and relics. A branch of the SHS was founded in Lexington in 1878. One of the Lost Cause's most prominent supporters in Kentucky was Henry Watterson. Born in Washington, DC, he had a checkered career as an antebellum southern Unionist who fought briefly for the Confederacy, edited a Rebel paper in Chattanooga, and then fled to Cincinnati, where he issued a Republican newssheet. He finally settled in Louisville, becoming editor of Kentucky's leading paper, the *Courier-Journal*, and shifting his political allegiance from the Liberal Republicans to the Democratic Party. Like many other pragmatic conservatives from the divided border regions, he was an enthusiastic New South booster who coupled his admiration for the values and sacrifice of the Old South with public backing for racial paternalism and sectional reconciliation. By the late 1880s, the efforts of Lost Cause proponents in Kentucky had proved so successful that many people were unaware that the state had supplied more Union than Confederate volunteers. One resident confessed at the time of Jefferson Davis's death that although the state had sent more than 70,000 men into the Union Army "you never hear a Kentuckian refer to it, with pride." He conceded too that he had only discovered the truth by reading his wife's Sunday School paper.[28]

The political power of Lost Cause imagery and ritual was evident throughout Reconstruction but nowhere more so than in South Carolina during the fiercely contested election contest of 1876. By this time the Palmetto State was one of only three southern states in which the Republicans still retained political power. Governor Daniel Chamberlain's administration was especially vulnerable to attacks from former Confederates. The state had become a byword for corruption after publication of James S. Pike's *The Prostrate State* (1874), a one-sided exposé of Radical misrule authored by a northern Liberal Republican committed to Confederate amnesty and speedy sectional reconciliation. Chamberlain's embattled regime was excessively dependent on black votes as well as federal military support. Although Grant's administration had suppressed Klan activity in the state in the early years of the decade, high levels of violence and intimidation against black Republicans continued to sap the local government's political strength.

In 1876, white supremacist Democrats led by former Confederate generals Martin Gary and Matthew Butler determined to put an end to their humiliation at the hands of Yankees and African Americans. Their campaign strategy called for strong displays of Lost Cause allegiance across the state. The public face of the Democrats' "redemption" crusade was Wade Hampton, an aristocratic cavalry commander who had lost a brother and a son in the Civil War. Convinced of the rectitude of the Rebel cause, Hampton played a vanguard role in Confederate memorial activities in the 1870s, serving as president of the state's Confederate Survivors' Association and the SHS's most prominent supporter in South Carolina. A paternalist who valued the loyalty of his black "body servant," Kit Goodwyn, he provided the ideal front man for violent white-line Democrats in a gubernatorial contest they hoped would seal the fate of their Republican enemies—a representative of the old chivalry who would unify white South Carolinians without unduly antagonizing Washington in the midst of a crucial presidential election.

South Carolina Democrats aimed to forge a white supremacist consensus in the state with a redemption campaign that combined force with pageantry. The shock troops of the contest were red-shirted members of local rifle clubs made up largely of former Confederate soldiers energized by Hampton's candidacy. They not only provided physical support for the party's gubernatorial candidate but also reminded South Carolinians that the Confederate past had meaning in the troubled present. The Lost Cause's capacity to excite whites across the state was evidenced by the large crowds turning out to welcome General Hampton at carefully orchestrated political rallies during the fall of 1876. Progressing eastward from the upcountry to Columbia, Hampton was escorted by enthusiastic files of Confederate veterans. The cavalcade welcoming him into the town of Ninety Six was reputedly two miles long. At the rallies Hampton expressed his reverence for the continuing sufferings of the southern people, the crowds sang stirring hymns reflective of the Confederacy's Christian roots, and young women dressed in white invoked the spotless nature of the Lost Cause.

Although black men were not demonized at these rallies, the Red Shirts assaulted them when necessary. At the town of Hamburg on the Columbia River in July, white-line paramilitaries that included a young planter named Benjamin R. Tillman shot several captured black militiamen in cold blood. Other acts of violence accompanied the gubernatorial campaign, which culminated in November with Hampton's crushing victory and the state's subsequent redemption from Republican rule. Once installed in office, the new governor conveniently forgot the violence that had helped secure his victory and even promised education and a degree of political influence to South Carolina blacks. Future political power in the state, however, would lie not with old-style paternalists like Hampton but with uncompromising white supremacists like Ben Tillman. Tillman had not fought for the Confederacy because of an eye tumor in 1864. However, his proud memories of the Red Shirt campaign would help make this consummate demagogue one of the South's most powerful political leaders by the close of the century.

Jefferson Davis, the New South, and the Transformation of the Lost Cause

The Lost Cause began to mutate into a more open second phase in the second half of the 1880s. Three main shifts in its development were apparent. First, it grew more inclusive. Second, as the remarkable public response to Jefferson Davis's death in 1889 revealed, it became less a manifestation of collective grief and more of what historian Gaines Foster describes as a "celebration" of the Confederate struggle.[29] Third, its exponents acquiesced to reconciliation with the North on condition that the Yankees conceded that white southerners had fought as brave American patriots to defend the original Constitution. As the transformation occurred, intransigent conservatives surrendered the initiative to angry white populists or New South adherents keen to move forward on the basis of a mythic southern past of their own making.

While the overthrow of carpetbag rule instilled southern leaders with greater self-confidence, it proved no more successful than capitalist boosterism as a solution to their region's many social problems. Urban growth, industrialization, and widespread poverty in the towns and countryside intensified class tensions, racial conflict, and political strife. As a result, many Democratic politicians relied heavily on the Lost Cause to augment their own power by rallying local whites behind their leadership. They sought a stratified society in which blacks were subordinated permanently and in which whites, whatever their status, acknowledged a common allegiance to the timeless values of the Confederacy.

The South's political volatility after Redemption complicated their task. In Virginia, former Confederate general William Mahone led the revolt of a biracial "Readjuster" coalition against the rule of fiscally conservative "Bourbon" Democrats. Although the state's ruling elite tried to discredit Mahone as another scalawag like Longstreet, their invocations of Confederate memory had limited effect—not only because of their foe's Rebel credentials but also because he articulated profound grievances held by the state's hard-pressed white farmers, many of whom were themselves Confederate veterans. Initially, Mahone found it difficult to reach out to black voters because his men had participated in a massacre of US Colored Troops at the Battle of the Crater in July 1864. In the end, his ability to secure federal jobs for Virginia blacks trumped African American concerns about his past. At the height of Readjuster power in the state, black Republicans secured 27 percent of Virginia's places in the US Treasury Department and 38 percent of those in the Post Office.[30]

While William Mahone's proud record as an effective Confederate commander helped to insulate him from Bourbon attacks, veterans' support for his political insurgency against Virginia's Democratic leadership revealed the extent of grassroots antagonism toward ruling elites in the post-Reconstruction South. This antagonism, which had its origin in antebellum and wartime class fissures, could be glimpsed in the growing memory work of rank-and-file Confederates. Wartime reminiscences written by ordinary Rebels, though fewer in number compared with their Union peers, constituted one manifestation of this development.

These writings included a remarkable series of newspaper articles written in 1881–82 by Sam R. Watkins, a noncommissioned officer in the First Tennessee Infantry, a hard-fighting regiment in Braxton Bragg's ill-starred Army of Tennessee. Watkins, a typically unrepentant Confederate, was motivated to record his memories by his conviction that "[t]he histories of the Lost Cause are all written out by 'big bugs,' generals and renowned historians," and that he had as much right to tell his story as anyone else.[31] He also wrote because southern commanders like Jubal Early and Joseph E. Johnston paid little heed to the experiences of the rank-and-file, preferring to lard their texts with self-justifying accounts of battlefield tactics and campaign strategy. Watkins was determined that his comrades, many of whom had perished in the war, would not be forgotten by history. Thus he recalled how, while defending a Confederate salient at the Battle of Kennesaw Mountain in July 1864, he was saved by his regimental colleague, William A. Hughes. Nearly twenty years after the event, Watkins could still remember hearing "the roar," feeling "the flash of fire," and seeing his friend "grab the muzzle of the gun, receiving the whole contents in his hand and arm, and mortally wounding him." "Reader," wrote Watkins, "he died for me."[32]

As well as ensuring that unsung heroes like William Hughes were remembered for giving "their lives to their country's cause," Watkins openly criticized commanders who, he believed, had let down the Confederacy.[33] Braxton Bragg, he maintained, was a poor leader of the Army of Tennessee. "None of General Bragg's soldiers ever loved him," he claimed. "They had no faith in his ability as a general. He was looked upon as a merciless tyrant."[34] Watkins was scathing about the tendency of Confederate officers to look down on their men. "[A] private had no right to know anything . . . and that is today why generals and colonels and captains are great men," he asserted ironically.[35]

Sam Watkins wrote against the grain in the 1880s. Most of the Civil War reminiscences composed in the late nineteenth century, a period of intense public interest in the conflict, shunned irony as well as Watkins's willingness to record the horrors of battle. However, his insistence that southern soldiers had a right to tell their story was emblematic of ordinary Rebels' growing involvement in Civil War memorialization, a trend that resulted in the creation of the United Confederate Veterans, a powerful new soldiers' organization comparable to the Federals' GAR, in July 1889. His willingness to criticize southern elites, moreover, was representative of the seething class tensions within southern society after the war. Insurgent politicians who tried to capitalize on these social divisions were understandably wary of the socially conservative function of much Lost Cause rhetoric. The violent South Carolina Democrat, Ben Tillman, generally avoided talk of Confederate glories despite his youthful support for the southern war effort. Instead he mobilized the state's distressed white farmers by fueling their racial anxieties, by denouncing local pro-business elites, and by reminding his constituents how supposedly ordinary Red Shirts like himself had thrown off Radical rule during Reconstruction.

The mutating Lost Cause, however, proved to be an effective weapon in the political armory of wealthy New South boosters. In the spring of 1886, modernizing Georgia Democrats seized on public appearances by the elderly Jefferson Davis to unite local whites behind their rule. By the end of the decade, they had installed the former president into a pantheon of Confederate heroes whom they deemed essential role models for the region's next generation.

Jefferson Davis survived the Civil War for nearly a quarter of a century. After his release from Fortress Monroe, the Mississippi planter tried his hand at business without conspicuous success. Struggling with money problems in the 1870s, he was rescued by the diehard Confederate author Sarah Dorsey, who owned an estate named Beauvoir on Mississippi's Gulf Coast. She heard that Davis was in financial trouble and invited him to live in a cottage at Beauvoir. Before her death in 1879, Dorsey deeded the property to the former president. It was here that Davis, still uniquely stateless after the war, wrote his two-volume *Rise and Fall of the Confederate Government* (1881). Less a history of his controversial administration than an intellectual defense of the Confederacy, the work was a major contribution to the Lost Cause canon. In it Davis expounded at length on the constitutionality of secession, downplayed the role of slavery in Civil War causation, attacked power-hungry Republicans for instigating the conflict, depicted the Confederates' liberation struggle as a noble crusade against consolidated government, and insisted that while the struggle had been shown to be "impracticable . . . this did not prove it to be wrong."[36]

Jefferson Davis's public conviction that southerners were a proud, patriotic American people who had nothing to be sorry for made him a useful figure for forward-looking New South boosters like former Confederate general John B. Gordon and the innovative young journalist, Henry W. Grady, who edited the *Atlanta Constitution*. In the spring of 1886, Grady invited Davis to attend the unveiling of a monument to Redeemer statesman Benjamin H. Hill in Atlanta in order to promote Gordon's candidacy for Georgia governor. The *Constitution* urged its readers to greet Davis as an authentic southern hero. They needed little persuading. Huge crowds of white men, women, and children turned out to welcome the old president and his youngest daughter, Winnie, on their progress through the Deep South. Bands played Rebel war songs like "The Bonnie Blue Flag," flowers were strewn everywhere, and a cannon (installed on Davis's train by the *Constitution*) heralded the president's arrival in towns and villages along the route.

In Atlanta, Davis shared the stand with General Gordon who was branded "the hero of Appomattox" for his prominent role in Lee's final campaign. Grady introduced the president to the crowd as "the uncrowned king of our people," adding, "The resurrection of these memories that for twenty years have been buried in our hearts, have given us the best Easter we have seen since Christ was risen from the dead."[37] Davis made only cursory remarks on this occasion, but his special popularity with Confederate veterans was evident for all to see. In Savannah, where he again appeared on a stage with Gordon, he was mobbed by hundreds of old soldiers moved by his unguarded assertion that a cause as noble as the Confederacy could "never die."[38] Many of these same veterans, excited by the renaissance of Rebel leaders they could respect and enchanted by Winnie Davis, newly dubbed the "daughter of the Confederacy," turned out in large numbers to vote Gordon into office later in the year.

The warmth and affection with which so many white southerners of every age greeted Jefferson Davis on his southern tour of 1886 and his visit to the Georgia state fair in Macon the following year demonstrated that time and events had restored his reputation in the Southland. While many northern Republicans continued to regard him as the arch criminal, a majority of former Confederates and their lineal descendants enthusiastically embraced him as the living embodiment of their heroism and suffering since 1861.

It was for this reason that the sudden death of the South's "best beloved" in New Orleans in December 1889 initiated a remarkable collective response across the region.[39] Long lines of people gathered at city hall to view his body, which lay in state in a partially open coffin for four days. Confederate veterans, many of them bearing the scars of war, were prominent visitors, their memories "busy with the long ago—with things that were past, but not forgotten."[40] Some former Rebel officers harbored bitter recollections as they entered the flower-strewn death chamber. Davis's unreconstructed friend, Jubal Early, was among the mourners. So was St. George T. C. Bryan, a Confederate officer from Virginia who told his brother how "the Cripples and inferm [*sic*] of the Nation were passing in review, for every sick room and infirmary and home of the aged had sent out their tenants to look upon a face which had seen and felt the flush of victory . . . and crushing out of a Nation[']s Liberty."[41] Not all the visitors, however, were old soldiers. According to one press report, the vast throng also included "tattered old darkies, in turbans and guinea callicos," large numbers of white schoolchildren from the city's denominational schools, Roman Catholic priests, and white women, some of whom were mothers of Rebel soldiers killed in the war.[42]

Shortly before noon on December 11, a glorious springlike day, the casket lid was closed for the final time, and the coffin was removed to an improvised catafalque outside city hall. A silk Confederate battle flag was thrown over the casket along with Davis's Mexican War sword. The military funeral, carefully orchestrated to demonstrate the Mississippi statesman's service to the United States as well as the Confederacy, was watched by a vast throng who had gathered in Lafayette Square. One reporter observed that the prevailing mood was "almost festive." New Orleans, he wrote, "looked more as though arranged for some great celebration, some public holiday."[43] Yet the spectators fell silent when the service began. John Galleher, Louisiana's Episcopalian bishop who had served as a Rebel chaplain in the war, delivered a short address in which he depicted the deceased as the Confederacy's own Christ who had suffered for his people. After the funeral, the onlookers watched respectfully as a detachment of soldiers transferred the casket onto "a handsomely decorated caisson" that bore a black-clad catafalque consisting of six upturned cannons functioning as columns and a canopied dome ornamented in bronze with a furled American flag draped on either side.[44]

The several "divisions" involved in the funeral procession then moved into line behind the caisson. They included not only hundreds of Confederate veterans carrying tattered battle flags but also numerous civic organizations and a dozen young white women who had persuaded the marshal that the route was not too long for them to traverse. While a division of African Americans scheduled to participate at the back of the march did not materialize, more than twenty Union veterans based in the South paraded without formal permission from the national GAR. One newspaper report described how, as the procession moved slowly through the streets, "[t]he clank of sabers and tramp of iron-shod feet re-echoed along the interminable lines, while the soul subduing dirges blended with the solemn booming of the minute gun."[45]

More than three hours later, the long cortege drew to a halt in Metairie Cemetery, which housed vast mausoleums for the armies of Tennessee and Northern Virginia. Again, huge numbers of people attended. They watched as an honor guard bore the coffin up a mound to the foot of a towering monument to Stonewall Jackson. Accompanying the casket, still draped in the flag of the Confederacy, were Davis's grieving widow, Varina, and the late president's "faithful negro body servant," Robert Brown.[46] After a short burial service, everyone sang "Rock of Ages." Soldiers then carried the coffin around the mound to the open doorway of the burial vault. Women representing various Ladies' Memorial Associations and a number of southern governors, including Governor Gordon of Georgia, the new UCV's commander, fell into line behind the family. Finally, the casket was placed in the vault, the Rebel flag was removed, and guns from Captain Beanham's battery fired three rounds as the family descended.

Jefferson Davis's funeral witnessed an open demonstration of postbellum Confederate veneration by ordinary white southerners of every age. To the consternation of northern Republicans, local people turned out en masse to mark the president's passing—not just in New Orleans but at memorial services in towns across the region. These parallel gatherings had been instigated by John B. Gordon, who urged his fellow southern governors to organize memorial events timed to coincide with the main event in New Orleans.[47]

On the day of the funeral, businesses across the South were closed as a mark of respect to the deceased, public buildings and private homes were draped in black, and stores prepared memorial displays in their windows. Confederate veterans, white women, and schoolchildren participated in these services, which featured addresses by local dignitaries. Three thousand people, one-third of them women, convened at the Texas state capitol in Austin to hear music and speeches, while a large crowd packed Metropolitan Hall in Raleigh, North Carolina, where another of Davis's loyal wartime "body servants," James Jones, was present. The citizens of Charleston, South Carolina, poured onto the streets. As many as thirty thousand people watched Confederate orphans, veterans, and cadets from the city's Military Academy march in separate groups to the Grand Opera House, which had been copiously decorated by local women. There they joined Confederate veterans and mothers to hear a bevy of old Rebels address the mourners. The stage itself was crowded with images and objects redolent of the doomed Confederacy including a portrait of Jefferson Davis, the flag of the CSS *Shenandoah*, one of the South's most feared raiders, and the banners of various infantry regiments. Reflecting on these impressive demonstrations of affection for the dear departed southern nation and its president, a local newspaper asserted that they were evidence that Charleston "does not forget—never can forget—her sons whose lives were offered a willing sacrifice for the principle of self-government . . . [and] the man who, in his own person, embodied this principle, and who expatriated himself in defence [*sic*] of the doctrine of State rights."[48]

Jefferson Davis's funeral obsequies demonstrated that by 1889 the Lost Cause had become "a Southern civil religion."[49] Its distinguishing rituals and symbols were all in place: The public display of Confederate emblems like the Rebel saltire and faded regimental flags; the ubiquitous presence of Confederate soldiers, many of them disabled and disfigured; prevalent images of southern military heroes of the Civil War; even the prominence of a few faithful blacks. All these things testified to the potency of a historical memory infused and invigorated with Christian notions of fidelity, suffering, and blood sacrifice. By acknowledging Davis as their dear "chieftain" who, as "the manacled prisoner of Fortress Monroe," had suffered on their behalf, white southerners rejected northern claims that the Confederate president was an exceptional figure—a treasonous has-been, "chained to a dead past" as one Republican newspaper put it, who had long ago been consigned to the dustbin of American history.[50] Instead, they asserted, his cause, the Founders' cause of liberty and self-government, was their cause too.

The emotional services in New Orleans and other southern towns and cities had a strikingly cathartic effect on the region. Reports of people weeping and of faltering eulogies indicated that Jefferson Davis's death released a welter of pent-up grief by providing members of the wartime generation with a chance to grieve publicly and communally for the deaths of at least a quarter of a million other southern men in the service of the Confederacy. The crowds in New Orleans and elsewhere, however, were not made up entirely of older men and women who had lived through the war. Their almost festive nature indicated that the Lost Cause was in transition. The orchestrated rituals associated with Jefferson Davis's death helped white southerners of all ages to move on without relinquishing the past.

The close involvement of New South boosters in the funeral arrangements confirmed that the second phase of the Lost Cause would be broadly compatible with southern progress under the leadership of modernizing white elites committed to sectional reconciliation, capitalist enterprise, and the consolidation of white supremacy as a means of suppressing class conflict between members of the avowedly superior race.

Henry Grady joined Governor Gordon in using Jefferson Davis's death to promote policies of economic development and local white control of African Americans. Grady was the son of a Confederate officer who had been killed in fierce fighting around Petersburg, Virginia. As his formative role in Davis's southern tour of 1886 had shown, he understood the emotional power of the Lost Cause—not just personally but also for the majority of southern whites. Instead of rejecting the Confederate past, he harnessed it in pursuit of a prosperous southern future built on northern-backed economic growth. After receiving the doleful news from New Orleans, his *Atlanta Constitution* proclaimed Jefferson Davis "the last of the mighty leaders of the lost cause!"[51] Grady's interest in the intergenerational transmission of Confederate memories induced him to dispatch a sculptor to New Orleans to mold Davis's death mask, this in preparation for the construction of a statue in honor of the deceased statesman. On the day after Davis's death, the editor told Atlantans that it was essential to raise money for a lasting physical monument to the president. The monument's purpose, he said, was to "educate" southerners who had no personal memories of their liberation war. Poignantly, for he too would be dead by the end of the year, Grady told the crowd: "I have a boy who is the hope of my life, and there is no man living or dead to the base of whose statue I would send him sooner to learn the duties of a citizen and a patriot, than the statue of the golden hearted gentleman whose death we mourn today."[52]

Henry Grady thus conceived and branded the industrializing, socially conservative, and racially repressive New South not as a rejection of the Old South but as a filial extension of it. His go-ahead newspaper went out of its way in the days after Davis's death to scotch the idea that antebellum politicians had been opponents of progress. They were, contended the paper, intensely practical men: "This practical spirit of the old south enabled her people to wage a four years' war against tremendous odds, and that same spirit, surviving today in her young men, has brought the new south to the front."[53]

In the hands of boosters, the celebratory phase of the Lost Cause proved to be as compatible with sectional reconciliation as it was with southern modernization. Governor Fitzhugh Lee urged Virginians to mourn Davis's passing and in doing so iterated that US citizenship "does not require us to treat as unknown the records of the past." However, he also made it clear that the United States was "our common country."[54] The day after Davis had been laid to rest, Henry Grady assured an elite audience in Boston that southern whites were patriotic Americans loyal to the reunited republic. Only ill-conceived Republican attempts to enforce black rights generated tensions between the sections. These tensions would be erased, he said, if northerners left the South's best men alone to settle this question in their own time. They could be confident, he insisted, that southern whites loved African Americans. And to prove it he marshaled sentimental memories of his "old black mammy" cradling him in her arms when he was a young child and of another slave tending his dying master on a battlefield of the late Civil War. "[M]ay God forget my people—," he cried theatrically, "when they forget these!"[55]

The modernizers' instrumental use of Confederate memory and commemoration rendered Jefferson Davis's last years a watershed in the progress of the Lost Cause. After his death, white southerners' insistence that they, like their chieftain, had always acted as American patriots grew increasingly shrill. "All that the Southern people demand," asserted one South Carolina editor on the day before the funeral, "is recognition of their patriotic purpose in the act of Secession, that the Confederate war was a war of independence and not a conspiracy, and that having done their best endeavor in what they believed to be right and having failed, they are worthy to stand side by side as American citizens with those of other sections of the Union who fought for what they believed to be right and succeeded."[56] Despite the region's tribulations, Democratic leaders' confidence in their ability to shape the region's destiny had risen enormously after Redemption. The stage was now set for an open celebration of the Old South and the vanished Confederacy.

The Confederate Celebration

Evidence that the Lost Cause was shedding its mourning clothes in favor of triumphal garb followed hard on the funeral obsequies for Jefferson Davis. On May 6, 1890, an excited crowd numbering at least one hundred thousand gathered in Richmond, Virginia, to witness the unveiling of an enormous equestrian statue to Robert E. Lee. Twenty years in the making, the monument was the occasion for a joyous collective tribute to the Confederacy's most respected soldier. The dwindling minority of white southerners who remained unreconciled to military defeat mingled with the majority who regarded Lee as a great American as well as southern patriot. Speakers at the event downplayed the general's ability to thrash the Yankees, preferring instead to laud his commitment to duty and honor. Although Confederate flags flew everywhere, so too did the Stars and Stripes.

William H. Payne, a former Rebel officer, was present among the multitude. He hated northerners, despised New South advocates like Grady and Gordon who preached reconciliation, took a dim view of "the mockery of the U.S. flag" flying over the monument, and complained bitterly about the presence in Richmond of the southern renegade, James Longstreet.[57] However, Payne was so elated by what he called "the glory of the hour" that he declared himself "too full of reverence, love and passionate exultation of *the Confederate* spirit which was everywhere manifested, to worry over Longstreet."[58] The great commander's statue, he considered, was one of the best he had ever seen.

The Confederate celebration or "spirit" as Payne called it, took root in the last decade of the nineteenth century. It did so at the same moment that white southerners hammered the final nail in the coffin of black equality by creating a racially segregated society in which African Americans were reduced to second-class citizens by a dense patchwork of degrading state and municipal laws. The freedpeople, whose political influence had been steadily eroded by the marginalization of the region's Republicans after Reconstruction, were finally disempowered by new state constitutions that contained all manner of creative ways of circumventing the Fifteenth Amendment. Worse still, they were subjected to a wave of ferocious white violence manifested in the heinous phenomenon of lynching.

Although the reasons behind the rise of a Jim Crow society in the American South were complex, its formation was connected closely to the political and economic instability that wracked the region in the 1890s. The Lost Cause triumphed at this historical juncture because it offered something to whites of all classes. Democratic politicians and well-to-do white southerners embraced it as a cultural tool to foster an intraracial consensus that would sanction their claims to oversee the postwar social order. The agrarian insurgency launched by the Farmers' Alliance and its successor, the Populist Party, posed a major challenge to their influence, not only because of its class-war dimension but also because it threatened in some places to unite angry farmers across racial lines. Constructing an invented and idealized past in which all southern whites had supported the liberation struggle of 1861–77 made perfect sense to many Democratic leaders and to the planter-merchant-industrialist elite that, internal tensions notwithstanding, broadly supported the maintenance of Democratic rule.

A majority of southern whites embraced the Confederate celebration because it offered them identity and vindication, because it helped to confine and emasculate avowedly dangerous African American men, and because it acted as a cultural salve at a time of acute social stress. Two new popular organizations ensured that memories of the Confederates' war would persist into the twentieth-century South. In the vanguard of the celebration were, first, aging rank-and-file soldiers belonging to the United Confederate Veterans, and, second, younger white women who joined the United Daughters of the Confederacy. Assisted by an influential new magazine, the *Confederate Veteran,* and popular southern novelists like Thomas Nelson Page and Thomas Dixon Jr., these allied groups generated considerable support for a wide range of commemorative activities at both the local and state levels. Together they added important layers to the original Lost Cause narrative of the late 1860s that would help make certain elements of southern myth attractive to many northerners.

The UCV won a mass following in the 1890s by cultivating the support of ordinary Confederate soldiers, men like Sam Watkins who had been marginalized during the diehard period of Lost Cause activity dominated by Jubal Early's clique of Army of Northern Virginia officers. By 1896, there were already 850 UCV camps in existence, a number that had nearly doubled eight years later.[59] Approximately eighty thousand former Rebels belonged to the organization in the early years of the twentieth century, somewhere between one out of every three or four Confederate veterans left alive.[60] These men joined partly for the camaraderie. The UCV excelled at staging reunions. Most of these were relatively modest local affairs, but large regional and state gatherings were held throughout this period. The organization's annual meetings in Richmond in 1896 and Atlanta in 1898 attracted about one hundred thousand and sixty thousand former Confederates, respectively.[61]

Many of those who attended reunions subscribed to the *Confederate Veteran* magazine which was founded in 1893, the same year that Jefferson Davis's remains were transported, amid more Rebel pageantry, to their final resting place in Richmond's Hollywood Cemetery. The monthly journal's editor, Sumner A. Cunningham, had been a low-ranking Tennessee officer during the Civil War. His stated purpose in inaugurating the venture was to assist "communication between Confederate soldiers and those who are interested in them and their affairs" and "to furnish a volume of information which will be acceptable to the public, even to those who fought on the other side."[62] Although the first volume featured a poem in memory of General Albert Sidney Johnston and a call to support construction of a monument to Jefferson Davis, the *Veteran* flourished because it appealed directly to ordinary Rebels who rated their contribution to the Lost Cause at least as highly as that of most high-ranking officers and civilian leaders. Because veterans were the main contributors and subscribers, the journal's life span was roughly equivalent to that of their cohort. Its last issue appeared in 1932.

The self-confidence injected by the UCV and the *Confederate Veteran* into the celebratory phase of the Lost Cause was exhibited in several ways, not only the annual marking of Confederate Memorial Day, but also support for monument building and the veterans' keen interest in Civil War history. Initially, southern whites erected relatively few common-soldier monuments to commemorate the sacrifice and heroism of all those who had served in the armed forces of the Confederacy. Such memorials proliferated, however, during the early years of the twentieth century. Virginians, for example, unveiled at least eighty-three statues honoring the service of rank-and-file soldiers between 1900 and 1919, compared with just thirty-four between 1880 and 1899.[63] Although many Rebel veterans lived in poverty, those who could afford to do so contributed precious funds to the raising of these inert tributes to patriots who had fought, in the words of the most common inscriptions, for the defense of "states rights," "local self-government," or "constitutional liberty."[64]

The *Confederate Veteran* also played its part, spearheading a successful campaign to build a monument to Sam Davis, the "boy hero of the Confederacy," in Nashville. Davis, a young volunteer who served with Sam Watkins in the First Tennessee Infantry, had been hanged by Union troops as a spy in 1863. For Sumner Cunningham and many other southern veterans, Davis was the archetypical Confederate: obscure, courageous, suffering, and as much a hero as any famous general.

UCV members' determination to mark their past in bronze and stone was motivated by a strong urge to cement their place in history and to teach lessons of duty, honor, principle, courage, and civic sacrifice to future generations of southerners. Their commitment to the intergenerational transmission of Civil War memory led them to support the formation of the United Sons of Confederate Veterans in 1896.[65] The Sons assisted the UCV in its task of remembering the Confederacy, principally by helping to raise funds to build monuments and perpetuating Memorial Day rituals, and by participating in collective projects to document the liberation struggle.

The veterans and their male offspring were joined in their efforts to remember the South's war for independence by the new UDC. Although some Ladies' Memorial Associations remained active into the late nineteenth century, their upper-middle-class and aging membership hindered expansion. In September 1894, delegates, responding to a call emanating from Caroline Meriwether Goodlett of Nashville and Anna Davenport Raines of Savannah for the creation of a federation of Confederate women's groups, met in Nashville to form what was originally called the National Association of the Daughters of the Confederacy. In spite of the fact that membership was restricted to female descendants of Confederate veterans, the organization took off quickly. It boasted thirty thousand members within ten years and nearly one hundred thousand by 1918.[66] Most of these new recruits belonged to the South's growing urban middle-class and had been born after 1850. Although their most vivid recollections were normally of Reconstruction rather than the Civil War itself, younger Daughters had heard lurid tales of Yankee vandals from their elders and experienced the poverty and loss occasioned by defeat. Both the Confederate struggle for independence and its humiliating aftermath loomed large in their autobiographical memories.

The UDC's rapid expansion testified not only to the widespread popularity of the Confederate celebration but also to bourgeois white women's desire to participate fully in society. Joining the UDC imparted status to members and enabled them to engage in a range of activities—lobbying state legislators for funding, for example—formerly belonging to the male sphere. Although a minority of Daughters such as Rebecca Latimer Felton of Georgia fought for women's suffrage, most were conservative in their social attitudes. However, while they tended as a result to be enthusiastic supporters of monuments for Confederate generals and statesmen, their class background and gender also made them determined to mark the active role of women in the South's liberation war. Like the Confederate veterans, most Daughters were strong advocates of racial segregation and black disfranchisement. But their relative youth and social position caused them to be more receptive to change and to sectional reconciliation (as long as reconciliation took place on southern terms) than male diehards or Ladies' Memorial Association members.

Together the UDC and UCV constituted a powerful cultural front for the transmission of a highly politicized Confederate memory in the modern age. Tensions did exist between the two groups. The male veterans viewed the past and the present in resolutely patriarchal terms. Although they acknowledged the support that women, especially mothers, had given to the Confederacy, they regarded themselves as the principal guardians of the Rebel past. At their reunions, veterans liked nothing better than to be acclaimed by young women dressed in white. Such attention confirmed their conviction that they represented the epitome of southern courage, manhood, and chivalry. On the whole, however, the aging soldiers and the youthful Daughters cooperated effectively with one another. The women respected the veterans' accomplishments in behalf of the South and concurred with their view that the world should know that the Confederates had fought for rights and principles that contemporaries must respect. For their part, the often impoverished veterans generally appreciated the UDC's impressive efforts to mark the past, especially in (what was for them) the difficult arena of fundraising for monuments. The South's stone tribute to Jefferson Davis and the Confederate cause in Richmond, for example (dedicated in 1907), would never have been completed had not the UDC taken over fundraising at a critical moment when UCV efforts had fallen far short of the required target. Their most important collaboration, however, was the consolidation of the Lost Cause narrative through their close attention to, and censorship of, Confederate history.

The veterans were determined to make the Lost Cause reverberate across the ages by writing about their wartime experiences. In an era when professional history was still in its infancy, contributors to the *Confederate Veteran* labored to establish what they regarded as the truth of the Civil War. This truth, they believed, had been warped by Yankee writers eager to stigmatize Confederates as traitors and proslavery fanatics. They would bear it no longer. As one defiant Virginian told northerners in July 1894, "[H]enceforth if you slander us, we will retaliate; henceforth we will play the part of the lion instead of the cur; henceforth we will assert our manhood at least; and if this be treason, you must make the most of it you can."[67]

Both the UCV and UDC created historical committees to encourage members to engage in the work of disseminating the facts of what they usually called "the War between the States" in opposition to the North's vindictive "War of the Rebellion" or the term "Civil War," which denied southern nationhood. While Rebel soldiers filled the pages of the *Confederate Veteran* and other journals with personal accounts of wartime experiences, the Daughters wrote hundreds of papers for discussion at local meetings. Mildred Lewis Rutherford of Athens, Georgia, the UDC's most influential historian, directed that the organization's local chapters should prepare accounts of plantation life (including faithful slaves), the real reasons for secession, women's role in the war, and Confederate history in general. In undertaking the work of generating what they regarded as a true narrative of the war, both groups rejected the view that only professional scholars, trained in the science of writing "objective" history at American universities, could tell the epic story of the South's heroic struggle for independence. As the UDC's historian-general Adelia Dunovant asserted at the national convention in 1898, "How . . . can [science] be applied to the attributes of the soul?"[68]

In this spirit, southern women in the late nineteenth and early twentieth centuries devoted themselves to the preservation of important Confederate sites such as Jefferson Davis's former residence in Richmond and Mississippi's Old Capitol in Jackson. They also collected tangible objects from the war, including evidence of women's material contributions to the war effort, and placed them in public spaces such as the Confederate Relic Room in the South Carolina State House in Columbia. The same women joined male veterans in supporting the use of public funds for the creation of state archives that would house precious documents from the 1860s. While their campaigns were often hindered by government parsimony, by 1920 every southern state had created its own repository for documents generated by the storied past.

The result of this fevered historical activity was a collective updating of the Lost Cause narrative. It contained many elements of the original tale, especially the latter's insistence that secession had been a constitutional act unconnected to slavery, but it placed greater emphasis on the social harmony that supposedly had prevailed in the antebellum and Confederate South as well as the heroic contribution of rank-and-file Rebels and southern women to a politically legitimate war effort—all within (certainly as far as the UDC was concerned) a framework of virtuous patrician leadership. The updated narrative also placed great stress on the slaves' putative fidelity to their masters. This was a vital element of the story at a time when southern white men and women believed that African Americans had lapsed into barbarism after emancipation. Fondly remembering individual blacks, often house slaves or wartime "body servants" like those on show at the time of Jefferson Davis's death, provided some whites with a source of comfort in an age of vicious racism and a model of behavior for contemporary African Americans. It also sapped the strength of northerners' crowing claims that emancipation imbued the Union cause with the glow of morality.

In order to embed this particular truth in the physical as well as the literary landscape, some southerners began calling for monuments to be built to the faithful slave. One of the first such memorials, the project of Samuel E. White, a former Confederate officer and cotton textile mill owner, was dedicated in Fort Mill, South Carolina, in 1895. The monument featured images of a mammy cradling a child on the porch of a plantation house and a field slave resting on a log. It was dedicated to "The faithful slaves / who, loyal to a sacred trust, / toiled for the support / of the army with matchless / devotion, and with sterling / fidelity guarded our defenceless [*sic*] / homes, women and children, during / the struggle for the principles / of our 'Confederate States of / America.' "[69]

Another major new component of the Lost Cause narrative was a carefully crafted memory of Reconstruction that highlighted the humiliations inflicted on defeated southerners by their Yankee conquerors. Most appalling of those humiliations was so-called Negro rule. In her 1887 memoir, Susan Dabney Smedes, the daughter of an impoverished Mississippi planter, described the postwar era as "terrible years" when "[t]here was not much law in the land."[70] As well as documenting the financial travails of her beloved father, Thomas, she recalled how local people had been forced to crush striking black farm laborers and how the Republican governor, Adelbert Ames, a "narrow and puritanical" New Englander, had seemed "to have hated the Aryan race of the South."[71] In similar fashion, the UDC historian Mildred Rutherford insisted that the imposition of black suffrage "was a crime against the white people of the South."[72] To Laura Martin Rose, a Mississippi Daughter who wrote a laudatory essay on the postwar Klan, Reconstruction was "the dark cloud that enveloped the Southland."[73]

Historical truth, of course, was elusive. A few southern writers recognized this. One former Rebel observed that the confused first day's fighting at the Battle of Chickamauga in 1863 had "about as many errors to its credit as any battle ever fought."[74] For most UDC and UCV members, however, the truth was simple enough. It was their narrative of the Lost Cause. Insidiously, this dogmatic conviction impelled both organizations to censor history texts that did not disseminate the truth as they saw it. Southern states took their recommendations seriously, ensuring that generations of local schoolchildren were reared on books that ignored slavery as a factor in Civil War causation and depicted blacks as dupes in the South's struggle to save America from its Radical Republican foes. Teachers who failed to toe the line faced serious repercussions. Enoch M. Banks, a Georgia native, resigned his position as a professor at the University of Florida after the state's UDC president and other guardians of Lost Cause orthodoxy demanded his dismissal. Banks had had the temerity to mark the fiftieth anniversary of the Civil War by telling readers of the *New York Independent* that in 1861, the "North was relatively in the right, and the South was relatively in the wrong."[75]

The white South's selective account of its Civil War–era past was a formidable weapon in the hands of politicians during the 1890s. Even US Senator Ben Tillman of South Carolina, no friend of pro-business Democrats, cherry-picked elements of it to promote his efforts to disfranchise the state's black population. Convinced that African Americans had been ruined by emancipation, Tillman joined his ally Governor John Gary Evans in asserting that disfranchisement would save hardworking white farmers from a repeat of Reconstruction. When the topic of voting rights came up in the Palmetto State's 1895 constitutional convention, a body dominated by white Democrats, he regaled his fellow delegates with recollections of the horrors stanched by Red Shirts like himself. Only two whites joined the six black delegates in the convention in voting against the new constitution. Tillman's brother George, a Confederate veteran and postwar terrorist, remarked at the close of proceedings that South Carolinians were not a "free people," because if they were free they would have "negro slavery" and "the Confederate States government" instead of debating black suffrage and owing fealty to Washington. Nevertheless, even this diehard could look to the future with some optimism. He called the new constitution a "rainbow of hope" and a demonstration of his "faith in the Anglo Saxon race." Here lay the paramount significance of fostering southern historical memory. Nothing could go wrong, George Tillman insisted, "unless we forget that we are white men, Carolinians, and Democrats."[76]

By 1900, the Lost Cause had a tight grip on the southern states, including some like Kentucky and Missouri that had never joined the Confederacy. Its triumph was the work of countless white remembering agents—principally Confederate officers and rank-and-file soldiers, middle- and upper-class women, and Democratic politicians of all stripes—who made it one of the most durable of America's historical memories. Its regional triumph, however, was less surprising than its wider national influence. How the once mighty Union cause lost its sting is the subject of the next two chapters.

Remembering the Victors' War in the Gilded Age

The Victors' Narrative

The United States' military victory over the proslavery Confederacy generated a powerful collective memory shot through with millennial triumphalism. Julia Ward Howe's famous "Battle Hymn of the Republic," published in February 1862, espied an immanent God "in the watch-fires" of the northern armies and "the fateful lightning of His terrible swift sword" wreaking his judgment on wicked Rebels and their iniquitous peculiar institution.[1] But as unrepentant white southerners rallied behind the Lost Cause, the disseminators of this potent strain of memory grew anxious. In the fall of 1875, one of the North's most eminent generals, William T. Sherman, urged his former army comrades to write about their wartime experiences, "for the time is coming and is near at hand when the truth connected with our war must be told and the truth will vindicate itself."[2] Twelve years later, Sherman had begun to doubt that the truth as he saw it would be vindicated. "[T]he Rebels," he wrote, "succeed in their claim to have been the simon pure patriots and 'Union men' of our day and generation. They have partially succeeded and may completely succeed."[3]

The victors' memory was originally a robust construction. The most influential Unionist remembering agents were Federal soldiers whose efforts to cement remembrance of their sufferings and sacrifice in behalf of the nation took several forms—not only their own commemorative activities (often assisted by male and female kin) but also their influence within the postwar Republican Party. Even after Washington had acquiesced to home rule for the South, many Republican leaders were determined to ensure that treason-tainted Democrats did not foist forgetfulness on the American people in their nefarious attempts to regain power.

In certain respects, the results of this enormous communal effort to remember the Union cause were impressive. Surely, all those passionate speeches, reams of strident text, and thousands of stone monuments would enable the Unionist narrative of national salvation and the abolition of slavery to endure for all time? It was not to be. The pressures for national unity were too strong, and the North's commitment to justice for African Americans proved too weak for the Unionist strain of memory to predominate over its reconciliatory and Lost Cause competitors. In the end, the purposeful cause of General Sherman and his comrades was undermined by most northerners' desire for consensus and white southerners' willingness to embrace the Stars and Stripes on their own terms. As the anxious general feared, the bluecoats' deeds would not be privileged over those of their Confederate foes in the annals of the restored republic.

The contours of the Unionist grand narrative were established in the 1860s and early 1870s. Amateur historians were the first to stitch together this stirring story of how northerners had saved the nation. Joel T. Headley, a New York journalist who had been ordained a Presbyterian minister, released the first edition of his two-volume history, *The Great Rebellion*, before the conflict had ended. He had no doubt that blame for the war should be fastened on "the southern conspirators" who sought "[t]he perpetuity of slavery . . . because the power they sought to obtain was founded on it."[4] Henry Wilson, author of the even longer *History of the Rise and Fall of the Slave Power in America*, concurred. "[I]t is now more clearly seen," wrote the wartime Republican senator, "that the dark spirit of slavery was the inspiration of these crimes against the peace, the unity, and the life of the nation."[5] Secession leaders, he contended, "had been for so many years preaching disunion and plotting treason" that they hailed Lincoln's election "as the opportunity long sought for, to break up the Union and found a confederacy based upon slavery."[6] Even Horace Greeley, the maverick Republican editor who helped secure Jefferson Davis's release from prison, insisted in his *American Conflict* that the main danger to the antebellum republic had been posed by "*general* saturation by and subjugation to the despotic ideas and aims of the Slaveholding Oligarchy."[7]

John W. Draper, an English-born scientist who was president of the New York Medical School, was the first genuine scholar to produce an account of the recent bloodletting. His three-volume *History of the American Civil War* was published between 1867 and 1870. In keeping with other Unionist tomes, his text depicted secession as the result of a slaveholders' conspiracy and the military outcome of the resulting conflict as just retribution for southern sins. The early Lost Cause proponent, Albert Taylor Bledsoe, pronounced Draper's history execrable—"literally stuffed with the lying traditions, the cunningly devised fables, and the vile calumnies, with which a partizan press and a Puritanical pulpit have flooded the North."[8]

In addition to holding the "Slave Power" responsible for the deaths of hundreds of thousands of Americans, these early Unionist historians praised the way the majority of northerners had responded to the imminent danger posed to the republic. Greeley paid tribute to "the valor of our soldiers, the constancy of our ruling statesmen," and, more prosaically, to the ordinary citizens who purchased war bonds.[9] Headley marveled not only at the great *rage militaire* that greeted the Confederate attack on Fort Sumter but also the rapid and peaceful demobilization of the Union Army four years later. The war, he concluded, "had been the people's war—the people had carried it on, and having finished their own work, quietly laid aside the instruments with which they had accomplished it, and again took up those of peaceful industry."[10]

In the eyes of these authorities (whose analyses soon found their way into northern school textbooks), the Union war effort represented the most noteworthy instance in human history not only of grassroots republican patriotism but also of collective moral virtue. The abolition of slavery was central to their claims that the North had waged a just war. Henry Wilson hailed the Emancipation Proclamation as "the great historic event of the war," more memorable even than the battles themselves, while Headley called Lincoln's famous edict "the greatest event of the Nineteenth Century—the one that will forever be the distinguishing feature of this memorable war."[11] Wilson went a step further, linking the crusade for the Union to wartime efforts in Congress to end racial discrimination as well as slavery. Although large numbers of northern whites in the late nineteenth century bolstered their self-esteem by hailing the emancipation of the slaves as well as the preservation of the Union, relatively few of them insisted that equality under the law must be a precondition for sectional reconciliation. The connection between Union victory and racial equality, however, informed the waning struggle over Reconstruction along with Republican efforts to enforce black voting rights after 1877. It was not lost entirely, moreover, on a discernible minority of Union veterans who sensed, more than most northerners, that the new oppression of African Americans represented a major setback for their cause.

The soldiers who had won the war spearheaded early remembrance and commemoration of their sacrifices in behalf of the nation. In doing so, they burnished the central features of the Union narrative laid down by the conflict's first chroniclers. Although the carnage bred a degree of cynicism in the United States, the dominant note among the North's demobilized troops was not a negative one. Even men who been disabled as a result of the fighting insisted that they had performed a necessary civic duty. Entrants to a left-handed penmanship contest for amputee soldiers in 1865 and 1866 reflected movingly on their bodily sacrifice on the altar of the republic. As well as remembering some of the horrors of battle—the "shrieks of the wounded and groans of the dying"—they articulated pride in their achievements and reflected openly on the ideological dimensions of the war.[12] One writer observed that he was "but one among many who have played an active part in rescuing our country from the hands of traitors."[13] Another contended that he and his comrades had "fought with too herculean strength and vigor for light, liberty, truth, justice, integrity, fidelity and Christianity . . . than to permit slavery, oppression, monarchy, and everything that was base, vile, and degrading to rule our glorious 'land of the free' and 'home of the brave.'"[14]

Some of the entrants rejoiced openly not only in having helped to save the country but also, like Headley, Wilson, and other northern historians of the day, in the war's destruction of slavery: John H. Raymond, a New Englander, copied the text of the Emancipation Proclamation with his one remaining arm. Although the cash prizes on offer may have induced some entrants to put a positive slant on their literally shattering experiences, most of the essays reflected many Union soldiers' firm, patriotic resolve in war and peace.

The Soldiers Who Saved the Republic

Life after Appomattox was often very hard for Union veterans, as it was for the vast majority of former Confederate soldiers. America's postbellum era, one of capitalist excess and fierce competition for material improvement, witnessed many casualties, including traumatized, depressed, diseased, and impoverished soldiers.[15] Large numbers of former Federals were expected to reintegrate quickly into society without the assistance of a modern diagnosis of post-traumatic stress disorder or, at first, significant financial help from government. Finding it hard to readjust to civilian life, many became addicted to alcohol and were prone to violent mood swings. Some committed suicide. Despite their hardships, however, large numbers managed to retain their self-respect, even in the face of the wider population's growing lack of interest in their achievements. They did so through a combination of self-help and local (often family) support. By recalling and commemorating their wartime service, many former soldiers nurtured a strong sense of identity. Their acts of remembrance also contributed significantly to the early consolidation of the victors' narrative.

Veterans' groups were the most important conduits of Unionist memory. Northern soldiers began forming their own fraternal organizations soon after Appomattox. They included not only elite groups such as the Society of the Army of the Tennessee in which membership was open only to officers, but also mass membership organizations like the Military Order of the Loyal Legion of the United States and the Grand Army of the Republic that were open to all ranks. Smaller organizations, including the Crippled Soldiers Association and various POW groups, helped to sustain bitter collective memories that the wider society preferred to bury.

Founded in the spring of 1866 by a coterie of middle-ranking Union officers, the Grand Army proved to be the most influential of the new veterans' groups. As the Civil War drew to a close, Major Benjamin F. Stephenson of the Fourteenth Illinois Infantry talked to his regimental colleague Chaplain William J. Rutledge about the future of Union soldiers after their demobilization from the army. Rutledge apparently insisted that Union veterans would "naturally desire some form of association by which they could perpetuate their experiences as soldiers of the Union, and at the same time cultivate such a spirit of loyalty that a rebellion would be impossible in this country in the future."[16]

The GAR held its first "grand convention" in July 1866 and its inaugural national encampment four months later in Indianapolis. Section 6 of its founding Declaration of Principles highlighted the war-born nationalism and moral purpose at the heart of the Unionist narrative. This passage pledged members to maintain "true allegiance to the United States of America based upon paramount respect for and fidelity to the national Constitution and laws manifested by the discountenancing of whatever may tend to weaken loyalty, incite to insurrection, treason, or rebellion, or in any manner impair the efficiency and permanency of our free institutions, together with a defence [*sic*] of universal liberty, equal right, and justice to all men."[17]

The organization grew quickly after a slow beginning. Membership stalled in the early 1870s. The leadership erred in instituting a complex set of Masonic-style grades, and many cash-strapped veterans could not afford their annual dues in the midst of a deep economic depression. By the end of the decade, however, the Grand Army was beginning to attract large numbers of Union veterans, and posts were being formed across the Midwest, the Northeast, and in parts of the South. In 1890, more than 350,000 former soldiers and sailors, most of them in middle age, belonged to the GAR, about one-third of all Federal servicemen still alive at that date.[18]

Remarkably, given the segregated nature of the Union Army during the Civil War and the pervasive racism of the Jim Crow era, the organization maintained a relatively strong commitment to interracialism, based on its recognition that African American men had proved their fealty to the Union by fighting to quell the rebellion. Not all GAR posts were integrated. The national organization condoned segregated departments in Louisiana and Mississippi; a system of blackballing gave prejudiced white members the means to exclude black applicants; and in some towns, former US Colored Troops preferred to create their own posts. Across the old free states in particular, however, many GAR posts were integrated by the presence of small numbers of blacks. Their existence testified to the war's liberalizing impact on the racial attitudes of many white Union veterans.

The Grand Army served several purposes. First, it provided practical assistance to veterans in the form of limited financial aid. Second, it acted as a powerful mouthpiece for veterans' interests, especially when it came to lobbying for federal pensions. Third, the organization actively sought to propagate Civil War memories—specifically to diffuse the Unionist narrative of the late conflict. This was deemed essential not only to recognize the sacrifice of the North's two million citizen-soldiers but also, as the GAR's "Declaration of Principles" made plain, to guarantee the future safety of the United States. How, reasoned Federal veterans, could the republic possibly survive if its people forgot why and with what consequences northerners had gone to war in 1861?

GAR members recalled their military service in different ways. At post meetings, held in local rooms or purpose-built halls, they conjured the fraternal atmosphere of the campfire by regaling one another with stories of the war. Such tales nurtured a range of feelings: sadness and melancholy as well as triumph and a sense of vindication. Some veterans wrote up these personal accounts of Civil War experience for publication in veterans' newspapers such as the *Soldiers' Tribune* and the *National Tribune*. A small minority published them as book-length memoirs. Posts also collected and lobbied for funds to build monuments intended, like those of the Lost Cause, to commemorate their own and their fallen comrades' sacrifices in behalf of the nation and to stand as markers of personal courage and civic duty to future generations. In addition, GAR members participated in reunions that were staged regularly, often on a regimental basis, from the early 1880s onward. They attended the organization's annual departmental and national encampments, which attracted vast gatherings of Union veterans before World War I. Former US Colored Troops participated regularly and enthusiastically in commemorative exercises, often in close cooperation with white GAR members. Aware of the importance of transmitting remembrance of their patriotic service to future generations, the Grand Army officially recognized male and female youth auxiliaries with the creation of the Sons of Union Veterans of the Civil War in 1881 and the Auxiliary to Sons of Union Veterans six years later.

The GAR's most important contribution to the construction of Union memory was its institutionalization of Union Decoration Day or, as it was more commonly called by the end of the century, Memorial Day. One of the prime movers behind this innovation was the GAR's third commander-in-chief, Major General John A. Logan, a raven-haired War Democrat and postwar Republican who had been one of Sherman's leading corps commanders. Aware that many communities were already marking the graves of fallen Union soldiers with spring flowers, Logan issued an official order in 1868 designating May 30 as Decoration Day. Several northern states declared the date a legal holiday and, after the GAR became a real force in the land in the early 1880s, the veterans spearheaded efforts to make it a regular event on the calendar of villages, towns, and cities across the country. On the Sunday before Decoration Day, veterans often attended a special religious service held to mark the occasion. There they heard a local minister applaud their marvelous service to the republic and expound on its meaning for Americans in the present. On the day itself, businesses closed as a mark of respect, and long parades of veterans and civic groups marched from a downtown location to the local cemetery to hear patriotic speeches and see schoolchildren place flowers on the graves of Union soldiers.

The growing popularity of Decoration Day rituals in the North highlighted the importance of female assistance to the veterans. In relative terms, Unionist women exercised less mnemonic influence than their Confederate peers. Federal veterans were jealous of their own achievements, and, unlike former Rebel soldiers, they experienced no political barriers to their early attempts to commemorate them. Northern women, certainly members of America's rapidly growing white middle class, also possessed more avenues for self-fulfillment and civic engagement than female southerners. However, members of the GAR-affiliated Woman's Relief Corps (WRC), of whom there were more than one hundred thousand in the late nineteenth century, played a vital role in transforming Decoration Day "from a holiday into a holy day" dedicated to community-wide reverence for the citizen-soldiers who had saved the republic.[19] As well as persuading local politicians and businessmen to support the annual patriotic display, they also mobilized large numbers of schoolchildren to participate in the day's carefully orchestrated events. They appeared regularly at GAR social events, joining in the singing of wartime favorites like "Marching through Georgia" and in the process affirming the veterans' sense of manhood. They also inveighed frequently against the Lost Cause and raised precious funds to aid distressed former servicemen and build monuments to the great Union cause.

Government assistance for the veterans was not entirely absent in the first decades after Appomattox. As discussed in chapter 1, the US War Department acknowledged the service of the country's fallen defenders by gathering their corpses into new national cemeteries. The central state, its power enhanced by the mobilization of wartime resources, helped its surviving soldiers in at least two ways. As well as providing limited pensions for badly disabled soldiers, Washington bolstered self-esteem by welcoming back the veterans as heroes of the republic. Whereas, in the late twentieth century, no federal demonstration of support for Vietnam veterans was held until seven years after the last American troops left Saigon, the US government in 1865 staged a grand review for its eastern and western armies just six weeks after Appomattox. President Andrew Johnson and General-in-Chief Ulysses S. Grant watched from the reviewing stand as tens of thousands of uniformed Federals marched down Pennsylvania Avenue over two days. Huge crowds lined the route and applauded joyously as the weary troops paraded before them.

Northern municipal and state governments also financed victory parades. The Iowa state legislature waited until the late summer of 1870 to sponsor a reunion for former Union troops living inside its borders, but the "boys in blue" reveled in the chance to meet their old comrades again. As many as thirty thousand Union veterans descended on Des Moines for what one leading newspaper called "the most magnificent pageant the State has ever witnessed."[20] Seemingly endless columns of Federal volunteers paraded through the city center in their civilian clothes. This event was noteworthy not only for quadrupling the capital's population (the veterans brought with them about twenty thousand women and children), but also for seeing General Sherman nearly crushed to death by an excited crowd outside the statehouse. Disabled soldiers, embodied symbols of the Civil War, were the objects of particular veneration, for their personal sacrifice in behalf of the republic was painfully visible. The impressive parade through town included at least a dozen carriages containing maimed soldiers. "These wounded heroes were the objects of the deepest admiration by all," noted one reporter, "and the showing of an arm shortened by half by rebel shot or shell, was an eloquence that carried its own glory and story with it."[21]

Government help for the veterans increased over time, largely through the soldiers' own lobbying efforts. Washington and many northern states funded the creation of a number of soldiers' homes that housed impoverished veterans. The federal government also moved, more slowly than most veterans would have wished, to create a relatively generous system of pensions for Union veterans. The Dependent and Disability Pension Act of June 1890 virtually guaranteed a government pension to all surviving northern troops, regardless of whether they had been injured in the Civil War; three years later Union veterans' pensions made up 43 percent of all US government expenses.[22] More so than in the South, where the tax base was smaller, northern public officials dug deep into the public purse in order to memorialize the Union cause. In the 1890s, for example, the Iowa legislature spent about $400,000 to construct a soaring Soldiers' and Sailors' Monument in Des Moines and vast stone monuments to Iowa's fallen sons on southern battlefields like Shiloh and Vicksburg.[23] While expenditures on this scale were not uncontroversial, they demonstrated substantial northern public support for remembrance and commemoration of the Union war effort. They also revealed the symbiotic relationship between the veterans, the construction of Union memory, and the Republican Party. The progress of this relationship would help determine the fate of African Americans into the twentieth century.

Emancipation Remembered

No one knew better than Frederick Douglass the importance to African Americans of keeping memories of the Union cause fresh in the minds of the northern public. The nation's leading black spokesman understood that restoring amity between northern and southern whites required a large measure of historical amnesia and that such amnesia could only damage the former slaves. As he asked pertinently in July 1875, "If war among the whites brought peace and liberty to the blacks, *what will peace among the whites bring*?"[24] Only one strain of Civil War memory offered hope to the freedpeople: an emancipatory reading of the conflict that highlighted the destruction of slavery *and* racial prejudice as its most important outcomes. If white Americans could be held to this radical understanding of the Civil War, they would surely find it difficult to reoppress people of color in their midst. Although the former Confederates were quick to demonstrate their hostilty to such an interpretation, three overlapping groups of remembering agents in the United States evinced varying degrees of commitment to it: African Americans, Union veterans, and Republican politicians. A consensus among them on the emancipationist meaning of the Civil War could render Unionist memory a powerful weapon in the ongoing struggle for black rights.

African Americans possessed a strong historical consciousness informed by their searing experience of bondage and war and their attachment to millennial forms of Protestantism that saw the hand of a just God in worldly events. While they lacked the financial resources to build expensive monuments, black communities across the United States nourished a rich commemorative culture. Before the war, northern free blacks had celebrated British West India emancipation with a day of speeches, song, and food. After Appomattox, African Americans on both sides of the Mason-Dixon Line remembered the Civil War at several points in the year, including Emancipation Day, Decoration Day, and Lincoln's birthday. In Texas, much of which had remained in Rebel hands until the end of the war, blacks commemorated their liberation on June 19 ("Juneteenth"), the day in 1865 when Federal authorities had notified them of their freedom.

Although participants in these events welcomed the fact that northern victory had saved the United States, their overriding interest in this achievement lay in its biblically informed consequences: their release from the dark night of captivity and the glorious prospect of equal rights. Emancipation Day was a joyous, often boisterous, occasion in the black community. African Americans of all classes typically congregated in a local church or park to hear an oration and a public reading of Lincoln's famous proclamation. This gathering was often preceded by a procession of black Union veterans or militiamen followed by musicians and fraternal organizations. Some parades were more lavish than others. The Juneteenth celebration in San Antonio in 1883 included baseball players, ministers, firemen, teachers, schoolchildren, and a float containing "young girls costumed as 'Columbia and the States of the Union.' "[25] Women participated actively in these occasions, decorating carts and preparing food, but men usually delivered the speeches and read out the Emancipation Proclamation.

African Americans numbered among the most prominent supporters of Decoration Day in the southern states after 1865. David Blight credits Charleston blacks with inaugurating the tradition on May 1, 1865, when hundreds of liberated slaves and a number of white Unionists gathered at a burial ground for Federal troops sited on the city's racecourse, until recently a pleasure ground for wealthy planters. After marching around the track, they strewed flowers on the graves of the fallen, heard addresses from local ministers, and sang spirituals and patriotic songs such as "America."[26] Then everyone gathered before the grandstand where Union officers, ministers, and white abolitionists delivered speeches. Although white Unionist involvement in Decoration Day declined in the South as opposition to black equality intensified, African Americans continued to mark the event collectively. By the end of the century, they were virtually the only people who continued to observe it at Federal cemeteries like Andersonville in Georgia.

Speeches on these commemorative occasions covered a range of topics. During the early years of Reconstruction, orators often made the connection between black loyalty to the Union and the ongoing struggle for equality. As the prospects for equal justice dimmed, they dwelt increasingly on the progress made by blacks since their liberation. Celebrations of Emancipation Day became increasingly restricted as southern whites limited blacks' access to public space and as middle-class African Americans, preoccupied with what they saw as the urgent need to appear respectable in the eyes of contemptuous whites, tried to crack down on disorderly conduct on communal occasions. Yet many ordinary blacks continued to claim a stake in the Civil War—a conflict from which growing numbers of whites seemed keen to exclude them.

Black Federals spearheaded this effort, frequently articulating in public, often in their capacity as Union League or GAR members, how their efforts had helped to save the country, liberate the race, and bolster demands for equal rights under the law. One of the most active of these former soldiers was George Washington Williams, a free black Pennsylvanian who enlisted in the Union Army as a youth in 1864. After the war, Williams, a Baptist minister and loyal Republican, was strongly involved in Reconstruction-era politics in Ohio. On July 4, 1876, he delivered a passionate address in which he insisted that black folk must be regarded as central, not marginal, actors in American history. As evidence he proffered the slave who "threw down his hoe, took up his musket, and saved the country."[27] Williams's efforts to memorialize the black contribution to northern victory were nothing short of heroic. In the following decade he penned an extended account of the US Colored Troops and campaigned vigorously, though ultimately unsuccessfully, for a national monument to honor their sacrifices in behalf of the nation.

The race's most strident advocate of an emancipationist reading of the Civil War, however, was Frederick Douglass. The former Union Army recruiter made one of the most important speeches of his life on April 14, 1876, at a ceremony held in Washington, DC, to dedicate a monument to Abraham Lincoln. Designed and sculpted by Thomas Ball, the bronze statue in Lincoln Park depicted the martyred president holding a copy of the Emancipation Proclamation in one hand and raising up a bondsman with the other. It was funded largely by African Americans, most of them US Colored Troops. Although historian Kirk Savage has criticized the paternalistic imagery as fundamentally racist, the dedication ceremony itself demonstrated the racially liberal promise of Union victory.[28] Not only was the nation's foremost black leader the keynote speaker, but powerful whites, including President Grant, were in the audience. Douglass used the occasion not to lavish hollow praise on Lincoln—a man who had told him that blacks should emigrate from the United States—but instead to deliver a nuanced tribute to a president who had recognized that the only way to save the Union was to free the slave.

While the leonine Radical Republican's claims that Lincoln "was preeminently the white man's President" and that blacks were "at best only his step-children" can easily be interpreted as criticism of his subject, he publicly acknowledged the president as "our friend and liberator."[29] The accolade was heartfelt. Ball's statue was physical evidence of the esteem in which ordinary blacks held Lincoln, and Douglass genuinely appreciated the late president's capacity for growth on matters of race. But the acknowledgment also made sense politically. Lincoln was the martyr-hero of the Union cause. By committing himself and his race to an antislavery interpretation of that cause, Douglass hoped to prevent northern whites from backsliding on equal rights.

As well as embracing Lincoln as the liberator of his people, Douglass was often at pains to remind northern audiences of why they had fought the Civil War. He told a Decoration Day gathering in his former hometown of Rochester, New York, in 1882, that brave "loyal men, true to the Republic in the hour of supreme peril, [had] dashed themselves against a wanton, wicked and gigantic rebellion, and suppressed it beyond the power to rise again."[30] Sectional rhetoric like this appeared to place Douglass on the same side of the memory wars as another major cohort in Gilded Age society: white Union veterans. But to what extent did the bluecoats, just starting to organize with real intent, share his emancipationist narrative of the Union cause?

The answer to this question is complex. Abolishing slavery had been a means to an end for most northerners. The vast majority of white soldiers who enlisted in the Union Army during the war held negative views of blacks—sometimes extremely negative ones. However, daily encounters with slaves and the stubborn resistance of southern whites combined to soften some of those prejudices. By war's end, most Union troops regarded themselves at the very least as practical abolitionists who had come, like President Lincoln, to realize that the only way to save the best government on earth was to strike decisively against the institution that had spawned secession.

In some of the earliest personal accounts of the Civil War, Federal soldiers explicitly acknowledged the assistance they had received from southern slaves. In November 1863, Major Samuel F. M. Byers was captured in fierce fighting at Missionary Ridge in Tennessee and taken to an enemy prison camp at Columbia, South Carolina. He dedicated his first book, *What I Saw in Dixie* (1868), to Edward Edwards, a slave who helped him escape. "Our chains fell off together," recorded Byers, "and I would not now ask a privilege or right from my Country that I would not willingly accord to him."[31] Although abolitionists were present in the ranks from the start, most northern volunteers had not enlisted to liberate black men. However, by 1865, their wartime experience gave significant numbers of them empathy for the southern population most visibly loyal to the Union. And many of the rest could see that memorializing emancipation as a major achievement of the war added luster to their own sacrifice.[32]

Most Union soldiers who wrote or spoke publicly in the late nineteenth century about their wartime experiences couched their narratives in republican and Christian terms, prioritizing the contribution that their comrades, living as well as dead, had made to American and even world history. As one contributor to the *National Tribune* put it boldly in May 1883, men of the Army of the Potomac must "rank with the soldiers of Thermopylae, Marston Moor and Bunker Hill" after crushing "the most powerful rebellion in the history of nations." Like Unionist historians, the veterans extolled the *rage militaire* of 1861 as wondrous evidence of grassroots vigilance, the only safeguard of a healthy democracy. The same writer explained how northerners had arisen "majestically to meet the emergency presented" and "vindicate their right to control the destinies of the Republic." He added that while the public had not been ready to free the slaves in the late spring of 1862, Army of the Potomac veterans had played a critical role in the destruction of slavery, washing away that foul "stain upon the national escutcheon with their blood."[33]

Many veterans attending dedication ceremonies during the 1880s dwelt on emancipation as a major achievement of the war that had been essential to the preservation of national unity. In July 1886, the twenty-third anniversary of their bloody work on the left of the Federal line at Gettysburg, surviving members of the Ninety-Ninth Pennsylvania Infantry gathered on the old battlefield to mark the erection of a monument to the regiment's valor close to the site of Devil's Den. They heard E. K. Martin describe how, at Gettysburg, "liberty was engaged in the most desperate struggle she ever entered upon in all the travail of the ages." A Confederate victory, he pronounced, would have ensured that American freedom "remained a paradox": "This lovely section of our commonwealth [would have become] the edge of a slave mart, re-enacting perhaps the scenes of Senegambia and the Soudan. It is yonder marble shaft, rising from the crowning point of this immortal field, its base sentinelled by the dead heroes who repose where they fell that in a more imposing sense represents 'Liberty Enlightening the World.'"[34] Two years later, Brigadier General Nirom M. Crane told a group of New York veterans on the same field that by "your deeds and suffering this grand and glorious Nation was preserved, and the curse of slavery was forever wiped out from this continent, and millions of human beings forever made free."[35]

Norwood Penrose ("Pen") Hallowell, a Massachusetts Quaker with strong antislavery sympathies who had enlisted in the Federal Army as a youth, had not watered down his views by the time he delivered an address in Harvard's Memorial Hall in 1896. He warned his audience to abhor "the sentimental sophistry that since there were heroism and fidelity to conviction on both sides, we may commemorate those virtues of both armies as American, and thereby try to forget there were ever two armies or two causes." Loyalty to "conviction" might be laudable, he conceded, but not all convictions were equally worthy of praise. "Slavery and polygamy were convictions," he said: "Such monuments as Memorial Hall commemorate the valor and heroism that maintained certain principles,—justice, order, and liberty. To ignore the irreconcilable distinction between the cause of the North and that of the South is to degrade the war to the level of a mere fratricidal strife for the display of military prowess and strength."[36]

Black emancipation was inscribed on a number of northern war memorials around the turn of the century. In May 1902, General Lew Wallace, a Shiloh veteran who had found fame and fortune as the author of the historical romance *Ben Hur: A Tale of the Christ*, presided at the unveiling ceremony of a handsome Soldiers' and Sailors' monument in Indianapolis. The giant limestone column, funded by the state of Indiana and dedicated to the common soldiers of the North, featured statues of Columbia trampling the Rebel flag and a freed slave holding his broken chains aloft.

While very few of these tributes to emancipation depicted African Americans as agents in their own liberation, Augustus Saint-Gaudens's dramatic representation of the black Fifty-Fourth Massachusetts Infantry's assault on Battery Wagner in 1863 was a striking exception. Dedicated in May 1897 on Boston Common in the presence of African American veterans, the bronze memorial frieze depicted armed black Union troops marching beside their patrician white commander, Robert Gould Shaw, who was shown on horseback. In a moving speech, the renowned Harvard thinker William James (who had not fought in the 1860s and publicly opposed militarism and imperialism) urged listeners to draw essential republican lessons from "[t]he great war for the Union," for it would soon be "like the siege of Troy, it will have taken its place amongst all other 'old, unhappy, far-off things and battles long ago.'" Among those lessons, he said, was the fact that the United States was "founded in what we may call our American religion . . . that a man requires no master to take care of him." And that when the spread of slavery endangered the republic, Shaw and his men had proved "that in such an emergency Americans of all complexions and conditions can go forth like brothers, and meet death cheerfully if need be, in order that this religion of our native land shall not become a failure on earth."[37]

In lauding the destruction of slavery, some white Federal veterans commented positively on the contribution made by blacks to Union victory. They did not usually write at length about them in the manner of African American authors like George Washington Williams, but many did so anecdotally and with some feeling. Like Samuel Byers, they often incorporated recollections of assistance received from southern slaves, or they noted, sometimes with condescension and ingrained prejudice, the bravery of black troops under fire. Captain Henry Romeyn told readers of the *National Tribune* in 1887 that US Colored Troops had performed with "courage and conspicuous gallantry" at the Battle of Nashville in December 1864.[38] H. B. Turrill, an Ohio veteran, recalled that black soldiers involved in an engagment in Mississippi had fought with a "valor . . . equal to the white troops" and that they had retreated with better discipline. Taken prisoner by the Rebels, he also remembered seeing the corpses of murdered Colored Troops. The Confederates, he wrote, boasted of taking "no 'nigger' prisoners."[39]

Although the bluecoats frequently alluded to the wickedness of the slaveholders' rebellion, the achievement of emancipation, the courage of black Federals, and the loyalty of most slaves, they did not generally depict African Americans as equal participants in the war to save the Union. Only a minority of them, moreover, concurred with Frederick Douglass and other black spokesmen that ending prejudice against color, as distinct from emancipation, was a cause that was at least as important as saving the nation. Yet some white veterans did make the connection delineated by Lincoln in his Gettysburg Address between the war for the Union and the ongoing struggle for equality in the United States.

The most visible supporter of African American rights among white Union veterans was Albion Winegar Tourgée. Tourgée enlisted in a New York regiment at the beginning of the Civil War and injured his spine at First Bull Run after being struck by a gun carriage in the Federals' pell-mell retreat to Washington. He reenlisted in the 105th Ohio early the following year and fought in the narrow Union victory at Perryville in Kentucky. Like many other soldiers, Tourgée was radicalized by his encounters with slavery. His regiment refused to return fugitives to their masters, and he personally witnessed disturbing scenes on a plantation. By late 1862, he was calling for "a thorough and complete revolution and renovation," a conviction he took with him to the occupied South during Reconstruction.[40]

In North Carolina's reforming constitutional convention of 1868, derided by white conservatives as a "Gorilla Convention" because it contained fifteen black delegates, Tourgée invented a false memory of the Rebels' massacre of Colored Troops at Fort Pillow to assist his efforts to empower the state's large population of freedpeople.[41] "If I ever forget that day and its lesson in noble manhood," he said (disregarding the fact that he had been nowhere near the fort in April 1864), "and ever fail to give my voice and strength for the equal, political, and civil rights to that race which gave one hundred and eighty thousand such hero[e]s in the darkest hour of the conflict . . . may God forget me and mine forever."[42] Tourgée did what he could as a teacher and Republican judge to improve conditions for local blacks, but white-line Democratic violence proved increasingly demoralizing and threatened his marriage. In 1879, he published a novel based on his experiences as a carpetbagger titled *A Fool's Errand*. As well as detailing North Carolina whites' aggressive efforts to resist black equality, the book poured withering criticism on Republican reformers who had withdrawn support for military Reconstruction in the early 1870s. It sold well. Many northerners were already disillusioned with President Hayes's policy of southern home rule and open to new ideas about how to constrain the burgeoning power of the former Confederates.

During the 1880s, Tourgée joined Frederick Douglass in trying to mobilize popular support for black rights. This cause was endangered nationally in 1883 by the US Supreme Court's decision in the *Civil Rights Cases* that Fourteenth Amendment prohibitions against racial discrimination applied only to states and not to private individuals. Douglass blamed the ruling on a failure of memory, and Tourgée concurred. Now domiciled in upstate New York, he redoubled his efforts to remind northerners of what they had fought and died for. In 1884, he published *An Appeal to Caesar*, an attempt to demolish widely accepted ideas about black inferiority that was grounded partly in remembrance of Colored Troops' courage during the Civil War. "We speak of the past as dead," he wrote, but the truth was, for better or worse, that "it cannot die. . . . To-day is as Yesterday made it, and To-morrow will be shaped by To-day."[43]

Two years later, he published *The Veteran and His Pipe*, a collection of essays in which a Union amputee conveys his thoughts on the war's larger meaning to his pipe, "Blower." Tourgée appealed to the bluecoats' self-respect in order to persuade them to hold open the door of memory. "COMRADE:" he wrote, "If you have succeeded in forgetting the impulse that made you, for a time at least, a hero, and regarding your wounds as "poor dumb mouths" that testify of personal peril, rather than the immortal cause in which they were won, you can hardly feel surprise that the veteran is remembered chiefly as a pensioner . . . and 'the soldier vote' considered a political commodity, to be purchased by the promise of public plunder."[44] The old soldier proceeds to recall how, in 1865, dying for the nation was seen as "more of a privilege than a hardship." Union volunteers, he ponders, "died for the rights of man, for the perpetuity of a government founded on liberty, in deadly conflict with a republic based on the principle of slavery."[45] Although the general thrust of this text was pessimistic—the veteran observes that his views are becoming increasingly unfashionable—Tourgée was not the only Federal veteran dissatisfied with, as one writer to the *National Tribune* put it, "the present deplorable [treatment] of the colored people in the South."[46]

When, in the fall of 1884, in a desperate effort to save his family's finances, former Union commander and ex-president Ulysses S. Grant embarked on his own Civil War memoirs, he fashioned a characteristically lucid narrative that depicted the Union cause as just and patriotic. Unlike some other Union veterans, Grant had little to say about the military performance of US Colored Troops. However, notwithstanding his wish for sectional reconciliation, he insisted, like most ordinary northern veterans, that the Confederate cause was "one of the worst for which a people ever fought, and one for which there was the least excuse."[47] He also reiterated his support for black suffrage during Reconstruction and his conviction that African Americans, having been "brought to our shores by compulsion . . . should now be considered as having as good a right to remain here as any other class of our citizens."[48]

William T. Sherman was another prominent Union veteran calling for the enforcement of black rights in the 1880s. An opponent of black equality during the Civil War, the Union general described African Americans in his 1875 memoir as "simple in character" and suggested he had not favored using them as soldiers because he did not want the Confederates to claim that northerners could not win without the help of slaves. However, he resented suggestions that he had been indifferent to African Americans' fate during his famous march through Georgia and the Carolinas. "[A]s regards kindness to the race," he wrote, "encouraging them to patience and forbearance, procuring them food and clothing, and providing them with land whereon to labor, I assert that no army ever did more for that race than the one I commanded in Savannah."[49] After the war, Sherman had little time for Radical Reconstruction and supported reconciliation with the South on northern terms. But as the political and cultural influence of the former Confederates mounted, the general began to reconsider his position on black equality before the law.

In 1888, Sherman used the august forum of the *North American Review* to speak out. To make his point, he enlisted his memories of a newly liberated slave named "Bob" who was serving Union officers after the fall of Fort McAllister outside Savannah in 1864. Although his prose betrayed his prejudices, he recalled with a degree of empathy the black man's yearning for freedom, expressed most courageously when Bob told his former owner, a captured Confederate officer, that he was now working for the Federals. "Slavery," Sherman confirmed to Bob's humbled master, "is gone, and the Southern Confederacy a thing of the past."[50] Blacks, wrote the general, should be allowed to vote on the basis of their loyalty to the Union and their coerced fidelity to the Confederacy. Failure to give them equal rights, he added (raising fears of an impending race war in the South that Grant also noted in his memoirs), would result in "another war, more cruel than the last, when the torch and dagger will take the place of the muskets of well-ordered battalions."[51]

Union veterans' insistence that they had waged a great patriotic war to save the republic and in the process destroyed a wicked institution that had been the source of incalculable human misery made most of them, at best, hesitant supporters of reconciliation with their Confederate foes in the 1880s. Their participation in that decade's small number of Blue-Gray reunions on some of the old battlefields of the Civil War—at Wilson's Creek in August 1881, for example, and Gettysburg in July 1887—give a false impression of the extent to which they were uninterested in the future of African Americans or invested emotionally in reconciliation. The former Federal soldiers who journeyed to Wilson's Creek fraternized willingly with their old foes, but they also sought reassurance that the Confederates accepted the outcome of the Civil War and spoke to local blacks about their current situation.[52] Some Union veterans vigorously opposed inviting former Confederates to attend commemorations marking the twenty-fifth anniversary of the Battle of Gettysburg in July 1888.[53] By this time, many Federal volunteers were becoming receptive to the idea of reconciliation, but they would not embrace it fully until they were convinced that the cause for which they had fought had been entirely vindicated.

They certainly made no secret of what they thought about the Confederacy. When, in June 1887, Grover Cleveland, the first Democratic president to be elected after the war, proposed returning captured Rebel flags in the government's possession to their states, GAR members across the country responded angrily, and Cleveland was forced to shelve the idea. When Jefferson Davis died in December 1889, few bluecoats mourned his passing. The *National Tribune* denounced the president's "unutterable wickedness" in bringing about the Civil War and blamed him for continuing the fight long after it had been lost. "He caused the sacrifice of a million lives," asserted the veterans' paper, "in order to keep 4,000,000 negro[e]s in slavery."[54]

Memory of the Union cause was cresting at this moment. Why then, given the veterans' widespread interest in voting rights enforcement and frequent insistence that nation-saving and emancipation were closely related achievements, was the cause of equal rights for loyal African Americans as lost as the defeated Confederacy by the early 1890s?

The Republican Party, Unionist Memory, and the Fading Struggle for Racial Justice

In July 1886, an excited throng of Union veterans gathered in Ottawa, Kansas, to welcome one of their most popular leaders to town for a soldiers' and sailors' reunion. The state's governor, John A. Martin, a former Union officer who had fought in the Atlanta campaign, prefaced the eagerly anticipated appearance of General John A. Logan by describing the Civil War as seeming "like a dream, so long ago did it happen." His memory was sharp enough, however, to recall how quickly the people's armies had dispersed. Their struggle, he told the crowd, "was not a struggle in this country for Union, but it was a struggle for popular government on the field of the world." When "Black Jack" was introduced, the bluecoats went wild. The general repaid them with a stirring speech in which he commended Kansans for the progress their state had made since the war. Like Governor Martin, he invoked the way that veterans "sometimes, in our dreams, think we are in battle again." But these were dreams, not nightmares, he said, because they culminated in victory. "The war for freedom, and the destruction of slavery," he pronounced, "is ended."[55]

Logan made several political points in his speech. Predictably, he backed government pensions for Federal soldiers on the basis of their patriotic sacrifice. "In a few more years," he said, "we will have to go to the cemeteries, the hill-sides, the brooks, the marshes, and rivers to ascertain the history or wants of the soldier. The evidence of decay is on us to-day." But he also demanded the equal protection of the laws for all American citizens. Union veterans, he claimed, "thought slavery the curse of the soil, and civilization . . . and desired that liberty might grow up on its grave." They should now act "on the line of giving justice to all. . . . The trouble has been, they do not act harmoniously, because they are told that these things must be forgotten and laid to rest in the grave of oblivion forever."[56]

General Logan was one of the most prominent Republicans of the day. His calls for the federal government to assure equal treatment for African Americans were far from exceptional. During a period when elections were studded with military rhetoric and imagery, he and other Republican leaders campaigned vigorously on this issue, often combining their statements with appeals to northern voters' memories of the Civil War. This appeared to place them on the same side as Frederick Douglass and Albion Tourgée in the ongoing contest to enforce black rights, partly on the basis of African Americans' wartime loyalty to the United States. This is unsurprising. Both Douglass and Tourgée regarded themselves as supporters of the Republican Party, alongside the GAR one of the two most powerful institutional carriers of Unionist memory during the Gilded Age. Drawing their support mainly from the North, the Republicans had led the fight against the Slave Power. The two Radicals were wary of the party's ability to equivocate on controversial issues, but they believed that the Republicans' antislavery past rendered them a progressive force preferable to white supremacist Democrats. Many ordinary blacks invested millennial hopes in Republicanism too, hoping that its fiery destruction of the proslavery rebellion and contribution to their own liberation would translate into postbellum support for equal rights.

Their hopes were not unjustified. The Radical wing of the Republican Party had included many staunch antislavery supporters who possessed a strong moral attachment to the notion of a color-blind society, at least insofar as this notion meant that blacks should be treated as citizens of the United States and enjoy equal treatment under the law. Convinced that the empowerment of southern blacks was the only way of countering the former Confederates' treasonous impulses, the Republicans had delivered on a portion of the equal rights agenda by passing the Fourteenth and Fifteenth Amendments to the Constitution.

Civil War memories remained central to Republican symbolism and rhetoric in the 1880s. Douglass's and Tourgée's warnings about the dangers of amnesia were echoed by many mainstream Republicans as Reconstruction drew to a close. In 1878, for example, Iowa Governor Samuel J. Kirkwood moaned that "some of our people seem to desire to ignore the fact that we have ever had a civil war, or to insist that if it shall be remembered at all it shall be only as an unfortunate and foolish quarrel in which both sides were about equally wrong and neither side especially to blame—that at least each side believed itself to be right and was fighting according to its convictions, and that no blame should attach to him who has convictions and has the courage to fight for them."[57]

While the two Radicals' longer-term diagnosis was correct—amnesia could only hurt the cause of equal rights—their main problem was not that northern whites were in danger of forgetting why they had fought the Civil War. It lay rather in the prosaic reality that Republican leaders wanted to sustain emancipationist memories of the Union cause not so much because they cared about blacks per se, but because they feared the corrosive impact that southern whites' increasing control over the freedpeople would have on their own political power. Their anxieties increased when Democratic successes in the 1878 midterm elections, assisted by widespread violence and intimidation in the South, revealed the dangers inherent in President Rutherford B. Hayes's restoration of home rule. In fact, the pursuit of equality under the law and the maintenance of Republican power in Washington were seemingly compatible goals, for federal enforcement of the Reconstruction amendments could ensure that southern black men remained a counterweight to the mounting influence of the former Confederates. The majority of African Americans and white Union veterans who participated in Gilded Age politics were Republicans, and both these constituencies remembered emancipation as a major achievement of the Civil War.

Union veterans tended to vote Republican in the Gilded Age because the party of Lincoln offered the best defense of their wartime achievements. Although Democrats did make periodic efforts to contest the bluecoat vote (for example, by running one of the heroes of Gettysburg, General Winfield Scott Hancock, for president in 1880) and made inroads into it with their appeals to working-class men and immigrants, they never managed to wrest it fully from their political foes. Republican politicians across the Northeast and Midwest were the staunchest supporters of federal pensions and offices for the former servicemen, as well as the veterans' many commemorative efforts. Six Republican presidents occupied the White House between 1869 and 1901. All six were former Federal officers who had served the Union cause in one capacity or another.

Republicans, however, did not agree on policy issues in the 1880s. The party's relationship with African Americans was a particular source of contention.

Liberal reformers associated with the GOP had opposed close ties with blacks since the early 1870s. They blamed the connection for political corruption and violence and regarded it as an obstacle to necessary cooperation with southern white elites. Mainstream Republicans also disagreed about how to break up the so-called Solid South after Reconstruction—whether they should continue to support party regulars (who were predominantly black) or make overtures to disaffected whites hostile to the old Confederacy's conservative regimes. Frustrated by the inability of the US Justice Department to convict whites who infringed black voting rights, President Chester A. Arthur threw his support behind white independents like William Mahone's Readjusters in Virginia.

The Readjusters' loss of power in 1883 led most Republican leaders to fall back on their traditional connection to African Americans. This reversion did nothing to impress the liberal "Mugwumps" who deserted the party after it nominated James G. Blaine for president in Chicago in 1884. The "plumed knight" had a deserved reputation as a spoilsman and was a staunch supporter of protection for American manufacturing, a policy opposed by the free-trade reformers. As well as being hit by the Mugwumps' defection, Blaine and his running mate, John A. Logan, were hampered by continuing violence, economic coercion, and vote-rigging in the South.

To offset their problems in 1884, Republican campaign managers stoked remembrance of the Civil War by using familiar battle songs to mobilize bluecoat voters. Political campaign songs of the day included "John A.'s Body" sung to the stirring tune shared by "John Brown's Body" and "The Battle Hymn of the Republic." It included the chorus:

> Tramp, tramp, tramp, the boys are marching,
> Marching with spirits just the same
> As when 'neath the starry flag, we cut down red treason's rag,
> At the magic sound of John A. Logan's name.[58]

Another, titled "Marching for Logan" and sung to the tune of the soldiers' favorite, "Marching through Georgia," conjured memories of an emancipation war:

> Hurrah! Hurrah! we bring the Jubilee!
> Hurrah! Hurrah! the sword that sets us free!
> So we sing the chorus from Chicago to the sea
> As we go marching for LOGAN![59]

In this acrimonious contest, the Republicans touted themselves, as they had done in every general election since 1864, as saviors of the Union. They also repeatedly attacked the Democratic candidate, Grover Cleveland of New York, for securing a substitute to fight on his behalf during the Civil War and denigrated his running mate, Thomas A. Hendricks of Indiana, as a contemptible Copperhead. But for the first time since Appomattox, Republican efforts to use Civil War memory in the pursuit of national power culminated in failure.

The result was close and initially in doubt. "If the 'C.S.A. on horseback' undertake to give us trouble," one agitated Nevadan told Logan, "allow me to tender you my support and friendship with my purse and if necessary my *sword*."[60] Once it became clear that Cleveland had carried the electoral college with the help of the Democratic South, many Republicans were distraught at the prospect of surrendering power to men whom they regarded as enemies of the country. "[W]hen I sit down & think," one New York GAR leader wailed to Logan, "that you & I who gave four years services in the field to maintain the supremacy of our national Gov[ernment] have lived to witness the humiliating spectacle of seeing the Party who endeavoured to destroy it again in control[,] it makes my heart sink."[61]

Although Blaine lost the election in part by surrendering key northern battlegrounds like New York and New Jersey, his failure to secure a single electoral college vote in the South led Republicans to cry foul. The *New York Tribune* denounced what it called "the new rebellion against the establishment of manhood suffrage," and the paper's influential editor, Whitelaw Reid, urged General Logan to write his memoirs of the Civil War in anticipation of a presidential run in 1888.[62] Assured that he would be paid "handsomely for the time employed," Sherman's popular corps commander responded enthusiastically.[63]

The result was a modern political tract, steeped in the Unionist narrative and dedicated to "the young men of our Country," titled *The Great Conspiracy*. In it Logan charted what he called "the mad effort" of a small coterie of slaveholding politicians "to destroy the best government yet devised by man upon this planet."[64] The book also recounted the story of Copperhead treason, blacks' enlistment into the armed forces of the United States, and the destruction of slavery. He concluded by speculating that if Abraham Lincoln could return to the United States he would find "that many legitimate fruits of our Union victories had been filched from us." Instead of encountering the republic he expected, one "where all men are equal before the law, and protected in their rights," he would be confronted not by slavery but its successor: "the heartless and galling system of African Peonage." Logan made no secret of his conviction that the former Confederates had regained power by using widespread fraud and violence. "Already," he warned, "we see the signs of great preparations throughout the Solid South. Already we hear the shout of partisan hosts marshalled behind the leaders of the disarmed Rebellion, in order that the same old political organization which brought distress upon this Land shall again control the Government. The old chieftains intend to take no more chances. They feel that their Great Conspiracy is now assured of success, inside the Union."[65]

Logan's insistence that Union veterans should resist contemporary pressures to forget the sectional conflicts of the past had everything to do with Republican leaders' realization after the shock of defeat in 1884 that they needed to shore up their African American and bluecoat constituencies. His death two years later did nothing to alter their strategic thinking. At the Republican national convention in Chicago in June 1888, delegates (many of them former Union soldiers) nominated Senator Benjamin Harrison of Indiana, a survivor of Shiloh, for president. They also pledged support for veterans' pensions and "effective [federal] legislation to secure the integrity and purity of elections." The platform was permeated with reminders of the Union cause. As well as honoring Lincoln, "the immortal champion of liberty and the rights of the people," it also prayed for the recovery to health of General Philip Sheridan, one of the few top Union commanders still alive. And, "[in] the spirit of those great leaders" and the party's "own devotion to human liberty," the convention congratulated the people of Brazil for emancipating that country's slaves.[66]

General Lew Wallace, a friend of Harrison, accepted a commission to write the nominee's campaign biography. He worked quickly and produced a sixty-five thousand–word text on schedule. With an eye on two of the party's main voting blocs, he praised the Union Army as "the noblest army the world ever saw, in arms the most capable, to principle the most devoted" and lauded US Colored Troops' "skill and courage" in the final stages of the Civil War.[67] Wallace also described Harrison's "compassion and sympathy" for fugitive slaves and condemned President Cleveland's attempt to return captured Rebel flags to the treasonable South.[68]

Harrison lost the popular vote to Cleveland, but he triumphed narrowly in the electoral college by winning key northern states. Crucially, the Republicans also won back control of both houses of Congress for the first time since 1875. Although the tariff was the main issue in the campaign, the Republicans' use of Unionist memory helped to keep the majority of veterans on their side. One midwestern editor granted that the result was first and foremost a protest against free trade. But, he added, "It is second, a rebuke to the unpatriotic course of the Administration toward Union soldiers and their dependent wives and children. No man who insults the defenders of the Union as Mr. Cleveland has wantonly and repeatedly done, can ever be President a second time."[69]

Restored to national power, the Republicans launched a belated effort to break the Democrats' stranglehold over the South by enforcing the right of blacks to vote under the Fifteenth Amendment. Early in 1890, Congressman Henry Cabot Lodge of Massachusetts, a non-veteran (born in 1850) who had a strong sense of the moral worth of the Union war effort, cosponsored a mild bill providing for federal supervision of elections in districts where at least one hundred petitioners requested it. What Democrats called the "force bill" received guarded support from Albion Tourgée. The old Radical Republican not only testified in its favor in Washington but also endorsed it in the pages of the monthly magazine *Forum*. "It should not be forgotten," he reminded readers, "that there are 50,000 [black men] still living who wore the federal blue and fought for the freedom of their race."[70]

Republican congressmen summoned memories of black military service to make their case for the elections bill in the House. Union veteran Marriott Brosius of Pennsylvania asked legislators if they could "forget" that "in the darkest hour of the night of our trial . . . we made a covenant with him [the black man] sealed with his blood and ours and witnessed by heaven, that when the war was over and the nation saved he should enter into the enjoyment of the blessings and glories of citizenship?"[71] Jonathan Rowell of Illinois, another former Federal, reminded his colleagues that, unlike treacherous Democrats, African Americans had fought for the Union "upon a hundred fields of battle . . . with a loyalty that never was excelled."[72]

The Republicans also heaped scorn on their opponents' efforts to conjure nostalgic memories of slavery to defeat the bill. Nils P. Haugen of Wisconsin had been too young to fight in the Civil War, but he knew the Lost Cause's power to erode equal rights in the present. When a Virginian waxed lyrically about his friendship for blacks on the basis of his sustenance by an enslaved wet-nurse, Haugen retorted witheringly: "It is not the first time that the 'dear old black mammy' has been called into requisition on that side of the chamber. God only knows how many Democratic statesmen the dear old lady is reponsible for. [Laughter on the Republican side.] We simply ask you, gentlemen, that you extend that same consideration to her brothers, her sons, and her uncles that you professedly and confessedly have for the 'old mammy,' her sisters, her daughters, and her aunts."[73]

The bill passed the Republican-controlled House of Representatives in June 1890. Thereafter it foundered on the shoals of contemporary politics and hard economic reality. Far West Republicans like William Stewart of Nevada were keen not to alienate southern politicians whose support they required for a silver purchase act intended to ease currency flows. There were also widespread fears that the legislation would damage trade with the South. Several New South advocates, including John B. Gordon of Georgia, denounced the bill as outrageous and threatened to boycott northern goods if Congress passed the act. Other southern politicians conjured memories of Reconstruction by raising fears that the Republicans were trying once again to impose a disastrous black supremacy on the region. After the party suffered losses in the midterm elections later in the year, a handful of Republican senators played their part in defeating the legislation, which was finally shelved early in 1891. While many Republicans, black and white, despaired, Senator Stewart rejoiced. The bill's demise, he said, "has terminated the unnatural strife between the North and the South."[74]

The defeat of Lodge's elections bill helped to render generations of African Americans politically powerless. Southern states' efforts to disfranchise black men proceeded apace in the aftermath, and not until the late 1950s did Congress begin to undermine their handiwork. The bill's demise also severed the once progressive connection that had existed between politicized memories of the War of the Rebellion and black rights.

Union veterans, the majority of whom remained Republicans, did not simply abandon their conviction that liberating the slaves had been a great achievement. The theme continued to resonate in Memorial Day and monument dedication speeches. A minority of white veterans, moreover, did not join President Harrison in giving up on practical efforts to halt the steady erosion of black rights and security. In late 1891, Albion Tourgée founded the biracial National Citizens' Rights Association (NCRA) to publicize outrages against African Americans and pressure the Republican Party into renewing its commitment to equal rights. His mailbag was full of letters from whites, many of them Union veterans who were avid readers of his "Bystander" column in the Chicago *Inter-Ocean* which regularly flailed northerners and southerners for their mistreatment of African Americans. They approved his initiative and linked their support for it to their Civil War experiences. Alexander Martin, a sixty-year-old former serviceman from Kansas, explained his interest in the NCRA by recalling that "when a Soldier was in Need he allys found a frand in the collered man."[75] Some of these veterans expressed deep frustration with the Republicans for failing to pass the Lodge bill. "I get angry," wrote one of Tourgée's correspondents, "when I think of the opportunity the Republican Party has had to fulfill *all* the pledges given during the Rebellion to the white and *Black* and have failed to make them good. I gave three years and more of the best part of my life for a Government of *all* the People and it was expressly understood and declared from 1861 to 1865 that all the Pledges given by the Republican Party should be redeemed. [N]ow I *demand* the same treatment for my dusky Brother that I ask for myself."[76]

Determined to transmit an emancipationist memory of the war across the ages, J. H. Wimpey, a Missouri resident who had fought with the Sixth Kansas Cavalry, requested an NCRA enrollment certification "to pass with my discharge down to my grand children to show them that, in the conflict for Nationality and freedom, I stood on the right side and to show them that my gratitude or manhood was not so shriveled up and small as to oppose extending equal rights and protection to my colored comrades in arms that stood beside me when rebel cannon was hurling missiles of death into our ranks."[77]

The NCRA never got off the ground, partly because Albion Tourgée's limitations as an organizer prevented him from making it a working coalition of blacks and whites. Neither he nor his Republican allies were able to prevent Cleveland's election to a nonconsecutive second term in 1892, the Democrats' subsequent repeal of Reconstruction-era enforcement legislation, or the US Supreme Court's landmark ruling in the case of *Plessy v. Ferguson* (1896) that racially separate facilities were legal under the US Constitution as long as they were notionally equal.[78] Vivid recollections of the great patriotic war to save the Union had provided Republicans and progressive northerners (often one and the same) with a usable past for three decades. But as Sherman and many other former Federals had feared, the tide of Unionist memory was now fast receding. The cause of black equality with which the War of the Rebellion had been imperfectly aligned would be swept away with it.

The Rocky Road to Sectional Reconciliation

Consensual Pressures

The pressures for reconciliation between the warring sections intensified as the years passed. Support for renewed North-South amity was always apparent above the Mason-Dixon Line, even during the war itself, when Peace Democrats sought in vain to bring the conflict to a swift end. The ferocity and extent of the killing between 1861 and 1865, however, made reconciliation a difficult task for anyone attempting it in the decade and a half after Appomattox. Horace Greeley got little thanks from his fellow northerners for helping to release Jefferson Davis from prison in 1867 or when he ran for president with Democratic backing five years later. James Longstreet's collaboration with the Republicans rendered him infamous to many southern whites. Despite passage of an amnesty act for former Confederates and sporadic calls for sectional harmony, the protracted political struggles of Reconstruction kept war-related issues at the fore. While even Davis acknowledged northerners' charitable aid to the white South during a deadly yellow fever epidemic in the summer of 1878, such generosity across regional borders did not put an end to Civil War hatreds.

Yet by this date, powerful groups in American society were clamoring for sectional peace. Not just northern Democrats and their New South allies but also urban businessmen keen to increase their profits in the country's rapidly expanding national market and social reformers determined to improve Americans on both sides of the wartime divide. Frances Willard headed the Woman's

Christian Temperance Union (WCTU), one of the era's most successful reform groups. She was a staunch supporter of the antislavery Republican Party before the Civil War. However, in the late 1870s and early 1880s when her crusading organization began operations in the South, she took care not to antagonize local whites by trumpeting the Unionist narrative. During a successful tour of the region in 1881, Willard dwelt sentimentally on the limited evidence of Blue-Gray fraternization on the battlefield. Addressing a large gathering of Union and Confederate veterans later in the decade, she soothed southern feeling by quoting Father Abram Ryan's poem "The Sword of Lee" and proclaiming unity among northern and southern whites on the basis that they were "one Anglo-Saxon race."[1] White southern women, appreciative of Willard's reconciliatory approach and her organization's willingness to accept racial segregation, responded warmly and joined the WCTU in large numbers. The first major southern delegation attended a national convention in 1881. "There has been music in your coming," gushed one northerner, "We listened once for your footsteps as those of an advancing enemy, but to-night we clasp hands lovingly—our cause, our country is one."[2]

During the 1880s, influential northern and pro-business southern Democrats spearheaded the process of reconciliation. When Ulysses S. Grant succumbed to throat cancer at his home in New Jersey after completing his memoir of the Civil War, they seized the chance to make his funeral a mighty statement of intersectional friendship. President Grover Cleveland placed Union hero and fellow Democrat, Winfield Scott Hancock, in charge of proceedings. Grant lay in state at city hall in New York for two days in August 1885. An estimated quarter of a million people filed past the coffin to pay their respects.[3] When Grant's son Fred requested the presence of two Rebel generals as pallbearers, Cleveland readily complied. He appointed Joseph E. Johnston and Simon Bolivar Buckner to partner Union heavyweights Sherman and Sheridan. Hancock also made Robert E. Lee's nephew, Fitzhugh, an official aide. Lee, an active supporter of the New South project, shared the view of some leading southerners, Jefferson Davis among them, that Grant was one of the more palatable Yankee commanders because of his honorable treatment of Confederates at Appomattox.

The funeral was a grand affair. Although Federal units predominated, Hancock ensured that Confederate veterans marched in the long procession from city hall to the newly prepared gravesite in Riverside Park. More than 1.5 million spectators watched from the sidewalks, while at the same time some southern whites, leading Confederates among them, participated in parallel memorial services.[4]

Not everyone was impressed with this carefully crafted display of sectional reconciliation. Some Confederate veterans belonging to Jubal Early's network of diehard officers welcomed Grant's demise: "Never was a Cancer a bonanza before," rejoiced Dabney H. Maury.[5] Grant's lieutenant William T. Sherman also took a dim view of the proceedings. "The line of Union and Rebel, of loyalty and treason, should be kept always distinct," he told his former corps commander Grenville M. Dodge, a wealthy businessman and influential Republican.[6] Dodge concurred, but he could see which way the wind was blowing. "As long as our veterans live it will be," he replied presciently, "but the tendency all the time is, to wipe out history, to forget it, forgive, excuse and soften, and when all the soldiers pass from this age it will be easy to skip into the idea, that one side was as good as the other."[7]

Modern scholars suggest that sectional reconciliation required northerners to forget why the Civil War had been fought and that the tragic cost of abandoning an emancipationist narrative of the conflict was the forfeiture of justice for the liberated slaves.[8] In pursuing this argument, they take issue with older nationalist scholars such as Paul Buck who celebrated North-South reconciliation as one of America's "noblest achievements."[9] There is something to be said for the arguments of both parties. Another bloody civil war between American whites would certainly have been an appalling event. On the other hand, there can be no doubt that good feelings were restored, as Frederick Douglass and Albion Tourgée knew they would be, at the expense of politically and culturally disempowered African Americans. Yet two vital questions remain: How and when was the once vigorous Unionist memory of the War of the Rebellion finally trumped by the fraternal, lily-white narrative of sectional reconciliation?

The Civil War's chief remembering agents in the Gilded Age—Confederate and Union veterans—played an active role in the reconciliation process, but not through any desire to forget on their part. Their contribution came primarily in two forms: first, their often grudging willingness to concede that their enemies had fought courageously for a principled and authentically American cause; second, Union veterans' mounting conviction that their erstwhile foes could be trusted as loyal compatriots. It was not primarily the veterans, however, who chose to forget, or at least suppress, the reasons for, and the issues generated by, the violence of the Civil War. It was, rather, their children and grandchildren, as well as Americans with no personal connection whatsoever to the war who opted to put the past behind them and focus on a national future that they hoped would be largely untainted by the damaging fissures of the mid-nineteenth century.

The tectonic shift in Civil War memory that resulted was partly the work of publishers and writers who sought to promote national unity by remembering the war as a collective *American* experience involving the soldiers of both sides. This project, which began in the late 1870s, came to fruition in the second half of the 1890s—the decisive phase in the uneven and incomplete process of sectional reconciliation—when a majority of surviving veterans finally embraced the spirit of fraternalism without denying the rectitude of the cause for which they had fought.

Cultural Foundations of Sectional Amity

During the mid-1870s, supporters of closer ties between the warring sections seized on the centenary of the American Revolution as a way to advance their nationalist aims. The Philadelphia International Exposition, staged during the summer and fall of 1876, was intended to showcase American material culture to the world. Its promoters hesitated to foreground productions that looked back to the divisive Civil War. The star of the exhibition would not be Lincoln or Grant but the father of the nation, George Washington, a Virginia slaveholder whom New England poet James Russell Lowell acclaimed in a timely ode reminding northerners and southerners of their shared past. However, the organizers could not ignore completely the fact that the exposition was being held in one of the North's leading cities barely more than a decade after Appomattox. The hanging of a gigantic history painting of the Battle of Gettysburg in the American art exhibition revealed the inherent difficulty of prioritizing national unity so soon after four years of fratricidal carnage.

The state of Pennsylvania originally commissioned Peter F. Rothermel's painting to mark the contribution of its soldiers at the only Civil War battle fought on local soil. The huge canvas depicted the moment when Federal troops, gathered behind a stone wall at the center of the Union line on Cemetery Ridge, repulsed Pickett's Charge on the climactic third day of the engagement. Rothermel had walked the field and spoken to surviving participants in an effort to produce an accurate visual record of the decisive moment in the fighting. In the end he struggled, like all chroniclers of past events, to find a single truth and resorted to a good deal of artistic license. As well as incorporating Pennsylvanian George Meade, commander of the Army of the Potomac, into the work, he placed an invented Union private at the center of the composition. The soldier straddles the wall wielding a rifled musket as a club, ready to dash out the brains of any one of the brutish-looking Confederates shown advancing from the right-hand side of the picture.

Rothermel's history painting had been acclaimed when first exhibited at the Philadelphia Academy of Music in 1870. Meade, Sherman, and other luminaries delivered speeches testifying to its worth as a tribute to the heroism of the citizen-soldiers who had saved the Union. Its showing at the centennial exhibition, however, proved more controversial. Several critics thought it injected an unnecessarily sour note into an event intended to celebrate American unity and innovation. Clarence Cook, a reviewer for the *New York Tribune*, claimed the painting would "sow ill-will and discord, and re-open wounds once closed."[10] The critics focused particularly on Rothermel's depiction of the battle as a maelstrom of intercommunal violence. In Cook's words, it was "a picture of blood and fury, of men—of brother-men, of fellow citizens—murdering one another in the lust of hate; of soldiers, brave men of the South and North, in the spasms of mortal agony; of dead men with blue faces and swollen hands—horrors piled on horrors."[11]

The controversy sparked by the exhibition of Rothermel's *Battle of Gettysburg* at an event intended to show the world that America was back on track demonstrated that sectional reconciliation was a slow-growing phenomenon—its development hindered not only by the hatreds generated by the war itself but also by the political controversies of Reconstruction. Although several metropolitan critics disliked Rothermel's work, many people viewing it in the American art building in Philadelphia probably regarded it as a valid tribute to the Union volunteers' heroic service. One irate southerner reported that when the painting was given a preliminary showing on the centennial grounds, it received "the attraction of every northern man. They gather in crowds around it, and laugh and jeer over the 'rebels,' whom 'they beat so badly,' to use their terms. 'They deserved all they got,' and similar expressions of hate, were heard on every side, and rebel and rebellion in their Yankee mouths."[12]

The debate over how artists of all kinds should depict the Civil War continued apace in the late 1870s and 1880s. As popular interest in the war grew, cultural entrepreneurs based predominantly in the urban and industrial Northeast responded to demand by delivering literary and artistic products that would attract white American consumers on both sides of the Mason-Dixon Line. By the mid-1880s, literature couched in the kind of reconciliatory terms preferred by Rothermel's hostile critics sold better than books and poetry likely to stir up old animosities. To many Americans, reconciliation made perfect financial as well as political sense.

Union and Confederate veterans, significant numbers of them now members of the country's burgeoning middle class, were important consumers of Civil War–related literature in the nineteenth century. One of the leading entrepreneurs to tap into their growing desire to publicize, commemorate, and make sense of the most important event in their lives was Alexander K. McClure, a Liberal Republican who edited the Philadelphia *Weekly Times*. In the spring of 1877, McClure inaugurated a series of articles in which veterans from both sides gave their accounts of various military topics relating to the recent conflict. Many of these essays were collected in *Annals of the War*, a substantial tome published two years later. McClure's objective was partly reconciliatory. He believed his project would correct "the grave errors of the . . . strongly partisan histories" in vogue since 1865.[13] The continued vitality of sectionalized memories meant that his aim was only partially realized. Many writers, among them Confederate General Joseph Johnston, who took Sherman to task for criticizing his conduct of the Atlanta campaign, were bent on burnishing their reputations and settling old grievances. A few even lingered on the horrors of war. Some, however, including the novelist John Esten Cooke, depicted the conflict as a realm of adventure or looked forward to closer ties between the sections.

Among the latter was General Richard Taylor, a Rebel commander in the Trans-Mississippi theater. Taylor's own memoir, *Destruction and Reconstruction* (1879), was one of the best of the genre. It shone a harsh light on the fighting and made no attempt to hide the author's dislike of Yankee "brigands" like Sheridan who had "ravaged" the Shenandoah Valley "with a cruelty surpassing that inflicted on the Palatinate two hundred years ago."[14] Yet in his piece for McClure, Taylor remembered the generous way his men had been treated when they surrendered in May 1865. He pondered "what years of discord, bitterness, injustice and loss would not our country have been spared had the wounds of war [been] healed by . . . the hands that fought the battles."[15] As well as being a barbed criticism of congressional Reconstruction, which had already fallen into disrepute with many northerners, the comment anticipated a reconciliation grounded partly in the veterans' recognition of their shared experience of warfare and mutual courage on the battlefield.

This motif featured prominently in an even more successful series of Civil War articles that was printed in *Century* magazine between November 1884 and November 1887. *Century* was one of several new journals in this era looking to find subscribers among the country's expanding population of middle-class readers. Its richly illustrated series on the war was phenomenally popular. In the first six months, circulation nearly doubled to 225,000, and by its close the exercise had generated a profit of $1 million.[16] *Battles and Leaders of the Civil War*, a handsome four-volume edition that included many new articles, was released in 1888. It sold some seventy-five thousand copies.[17]

Century editor Richard Watson Gilder, a Pennsylvania veteran, and his deputies Robert Underwood Johnson and Clarence C. Buel shared Alexander McClure's desire to promote reconciliation between former enemies and at the same time turn a profit. In pursuit of these mutually reinforcing goals, they deliberately sought to downplay controversies by enjoining contributors to eschew politics—the reasons for secession or Lincoln's decision to issue the Emancipation Proclamation, for example—in favor of narrating their place in an epic American war, a compelling national experience shared by brave men on both sides. According to Johnson, an Indianan with family ties to a Confederate general, the series originated in a debate with Buel about which battle of the conflict had been the bloodiest. Believing that northerners and southerners would respond positively to a series of war essays that dealt with events "in an unsectional way," the two men persuaded Gilder to back their project.[18] Chosen to lead the operation, Johnson offered celebrity soldiers like Grant, Sherman, and Longstreet substantial sums of money to contribute their insiders' reflections to the series. Grant initially refused, but his family's desperate need for money caused him to relent. The magazine eventually paid him $4,000 for four pieces.[19] His account of the Battle of Shiloh was a huge success after Johnson persuaded the general to offer more than just dry facts. Indeed, it led *Century* to close a contract for Grant's memoirs.

When Grant penned the passage in his reminiscences describing Lee's surrender at Appomattox in April 1865, he used the description to advance good feeling between the sections. In greeting Lee, "a man of much dignity," Grant claimed he felt "sad and depressed . . . at the downfall of a foe who had fought so long and valiantly." He remembered how, after the official surrender terms had been signed, several of his officers asked to visit acquaintances in the Army of Northern Virginia: "They went over, had a very pleasant time with their old friends, and brought some of them back with them when they returned."[20] Most of the articles in *Century*, *Scribner's*, and other popular journals of the period intentionally promoted the impression that the Civil War, while undeniably fierce and tragic, had ended long ago with brothers shaking hands with brothers, each party cognizant of the bravery and gallantry of the other.

Much of the Civil War literature of the 1880s and 1890s marginalized women and African Americans as active participants in the conflict. The Union and Confederate commanders who benefited financially from their writings focused tightly as requested on military campaigns and battles. While they sometimes incorporated women in support roles and blacks as local color, their emphasis on manly courage fed a contemporary preoccupation with the vigor of white American manhood occasioned by the rise of a salaried middle class and mass immigration from Europe.

Century did accept a limited number of pieces by women, including a handful of southern writers. These women often couched their reminiscences in sentimental terms and assisted the editors' reconciliatory objectives. Constance Cary Harrison, who married Jefferson Davis's private secretary after the Civil War, prefaced her essay "Richmond Scenes in '62" with the statement that her aim was not to narrate "the history of those awful Seven Days." Instead, she claimed, her intention was "only to speak of the other side of that canvas in which heroes of two armies were passing and repassing, as on some huge Homeric frieze."[21]

The tendency of this vast body of literature to suppress the horrors of war left a handful of writers dissatisfied. They included Ambrose Bierce, a Union veteran from Ohio. Unlike most authors who made the Civil War their central theme, Bierce wrote in a sardonic, at times gothic, style that mocked deluded ideas about the glories of death in war. His short story, "What I Saw of Shiloh," published in 1881, has none of the romance that permeated many war stories of this period. In the gathering gloom, the narrator encounters corpses strewn over a blood-soaked field. He finds only one man still barely alive, "a Federal sergeant, variously hurt" who lies "face upward, taking in his breath in convulsive, rattling snorts, and blowing it out in sputters of froth which crawled creamily down his cheeks, piling itself alongside his neck and ears. A bullet had clipped a groove in his skull, above the temple; from this the brain protruded in bosses, dropping off in flakes and strings."[22] For Ambrose Bierce the Civil War, as it proved for many disturbed veterans, was one terrifying memory after another.

Bierce's conviction that the war had been an unmitigated disaster for ordinary Americans on both sides prevented him from embracing the North's triumphant victory narrative. Although he retained a bluecoat's belief that he had fought in a better cause than his Confederate foes, he was repelled by the efforts of those he called "loyalty's hot-gospellers" to tout the moral superiority of the Union cause.[23] His wartime experiences alone led him to reflect with a jaundiced eye on his youthful decision to enlist in the Federal Army. Once, he confessed to readers of the *San Francisco Examiner*, he had been "sufficiently zealous for universal and unqualified Freedom. . . . There were other issues involved, but they did not count for much with me. I am now glad that they were involved, for their presence as threads to the Fate-woven fabric of events spares me the disquieting consciousness of misguided zeal."[24] Bierce's cynicism helped to make him a public advocate of reconciliation. He supported the return of the government's Rebel flags, and he refused to join other northerners in condemning Jefferson Davis after his death in 1889.

The depoliticization of Civil War memory, consciously abetted by the editors of *Century* and other prominent journals, hastened the process of reconciliation. In 1894, a young northern writer, Stephen Crane, authored *The Red Badge of Courage*, perhaps the best novel ever written about the Civil War. Born in Newark, New Jersey, in November 1871, Crane had no autobiographical memory of the late conflict, but he was one of many young Americans in the late nineteenth century who possessed personal connections to it. He cherished the sword that he inherited from his Uncle Wilbur, a Union veteran traumatized by his experiences at the Battle of Chancellorsville in May 1863, and was probably acquainted with veterans of the 124th New York Infantry, who saw action at the same crashing engagement that had taken a toll of more than 30,000 casualties on both sides.

Already acclaimed by nationally prominent figures like William Dean Howells and Hamlin Garland as one of the most promising exponents of literary realism in America, Crane had planned to write "a pot-boiler" about the Civil

War to supplement his income.[25] One day in 1893, he was flicking through old copies of *Century* in a friend's New York studio. Reading accounts of tactics and strategy that eschewed references to the feelings of individuals, he exclaimed, "I wonder that some of those fellows don't tell how they *felt* in those scraps. They spout enough of what they *did*, but they're as emotionless as rocks."[26] Instead of contributing to the growing pile of Civil War dime novels like *Fighting for the Right* (1892) and *A Victorious Union* (1893) by Oliver Optic (William Taylor Adams)—popular adventure books written for young boys in the new spirit of North-South brotherhood—he started work on a more substantial book that he hoped would make the war a genuinely felt experience for his readers.

Crane placed a young Union soldier, Henry Fleming, at the center of his tale of a raw recruit's first taste of battle. The battle is not named, but internal evidence reveals it to be Chancellorsville. There is no reference to the war as an ideological conflict. Henry has enlisted in the romantic pursuit of glory, not to save the Union or free the slaves. The impressionistic narrative focuses solely on his experience of war and his rapid transition to manhood. On the first day of the engagement, Henry behaves like a coward. He runs away after his first confused encounter with the Rebels and receives his "red badge of courage" when a fleeing Federal soldier strikes him in the face with a rifle butt. When he returns to the regiment, his comrades, seeing his wound, treat him as a hero. Only on the second day of the fighting does he act with genuine courage, retaining the regiment's colors while under fire. His motive for doing so, however, is not ideological zeal but the realization of his own inadequacy. Crane did not stint on exposing the horror of combat. At one point in his retreat, Henry encounters a ghastly corpselike figure, a "spectral soldier" who "seemed always looking for a place, like one who goes to choose a grave."[27] Nature is all about, an inert, uncaring witness to the human brutality and suffering in its midst. Despite its ironic treatment of soldierly behavior in combat, Crane's psychological investigation ends on a positive note. Henry has been tested successfully by war. Entering it a boy, he emerges from it a man.

The Red Badge of Courage made Stephen Crane nationally and internationally famous. It also contributed unwittingly to sectional reconciliation by denuding the conflict of its politics. The book's main focus on the relationship between war and manhood was representative of a broader trend in late-nineteenth-century American society to remember the Civil War as a shared national event that had important lessons for contemporaries, especially modern young men who seemed preoccupied with the idea of making money. Judge Oliver Wendell Holmes Jr., a prominent Massachusetts veteran who had been wounded several times in the war, told graduating students at Harvard University on Memorial Day 1895 that they should shun the easy life. War, he said, though "out of fashion," taught the value of pain and suffering such as that he had witnessed at Spotsylvania's "dead angle" where, after a day's fighting in May 1864, "the dead and dying lay piled in a row six deep." Pray "not for comfort," he urged, "but for combat; to keep the soldier's faith against the doubts of civil life, more besetting and harder to overcome than all the misgivings of the battle-field."[28]

By the early 1890s, ardent exponents of the Union cause, certainly those people who proclaimed its moral superiority over the proslavery Confederacy, were on the defensive. Three important events of that tumultuous decade—the creation of the country's first National Military Park at Chickamauga and Chattanooga in 1895, the hard-fought presidential election contest of 1896, and the Spanish-American War of 1898—helped to ensure that Civil War memory entered the twentieth century as a support for, not a sapper of, domestic unity.

Good Feeling (and Bad) at Chickamauga

Despite a trickle of early Blue-Gray reunions and the high visibility of some Confederate generals at Grant's funeral service, concrete manifestations of sectional reconciliation had been in limited supply during the 1880s. When southerners tried to build a monument to mark the high tide of the Confederacy at Gettysburg, they were rebuffed by outraged Union veterans, including Lucius Fairchild, commander-in-chief of the Grand Army. Several Confederate groups in Virginia subsequently refused to attend a Blue-Gray parade to dedicate a monument to Pickett's Charge in Richmond, Virginia, because of the participation of a GAR post from Philadelphia. The Gettysburg battlefield became an emphatically Unionist shrine, so cluttered with regimental monuments that one unsympathetic newspaper called it "our national museum of monstrosities or chamber of horrors."[29]

Not all Federal veterans were happy with this state of affairs. Among them was journalist Henry Van Ness Boynton, an anti-Grant Republican who had fought at the Battle of Chickamauga and been wounded at Missionary Ridge. Boynton's personal commitment to reconciliation was evident as early as the winter of 1876–77 when he participated in the covert negotiations culminating in the election of fellow Ohioan Rutherford B. Hayes and the termination of federal military occupation of the South. This commitment may have been increased by his involvement in some of the testiest battles over Civil War memory to take place within the ranks of the North's veteran community.

One of Boynton's leading antagonists was William T. Sherman. Boynton had been enraged by the general's self-serving memoir of 1875 that burnished the Union commander's own reputation at the expense of other leading figures on both sides of the late war. The work, claimed Boynton, was "the gigantic wrong of the false historian."[30] Sherman, he insisted, had been "largely responsible" not only for the "disgraceful surprise" attack by Rebels on the first day at Shiloh but also a "bloody failure" at Chickasaw Bayou during the Vicksburg campaign.[31] As well as ignoring these stains on his record, the general had failed to credit George Thomas for protecting the Federal retreat at Chickamauga and minimized the accomplishments of Thomas's "magnificent" Army of the Cumberland in which he (Boynton) had fought.[32] Sherman responded by attacking Boynton in print and dismissing him as "a notorious slanderer" who was easily corrupted—a slur that prompted the angry journalist to call for a retraction and, when he failed to receive it, to demand that his illustrious opponent should be court-martialed for conduct unbecoming an officer.[33] In the late 1880s, Boynton's two chief aims—greater recognition for the Army of the Cumberland and the restoration of good feeling between North and South—came together in his efforts to turn the old Chickamauga battlefield into a tangible symbol of renewed good feeling between the sections.

Chickamauga was an ideal site for bringing Union and Confederate veterans together in a common cause. Because the battle in northern Georgia had been a tactical Rebel victory, it offered white southerners a better site for reconciliatory ventures than Gettysburg, a place of Union triumph that remained jealously guarded by the GAR. The fact that it lay wholly within the borders of a former Confederate state also meant that the material benefits accruing from its preservation—battlefield tourism, for example—would contribute mainly to local prosperity. On the other hand, Thomas's stubborn rearguard action in the final stages of the battle meant that northern veterans could regard the bloody engagement as a strategic victory, one that had guaranteed the Union possession of nearby Chattanooga and thereby paved the way for the Federal successes at Missionary Ridge and Lookout Mountain, sites that Boynton sought to preserve in connection with Chickamauga.

Henry Boynton floated his idea of a battlefield park after visiting Georgia in 1888. "There is," he told readers of the *Cincinnati Gazette*, "no other great battlefield of the war where Northern and Southern veterans could meet harmoniously and with equal satisfaction to preserve the field of their magnificent fighting."[34] The reception was overwhelmingly positive. In February 1889, a group of former Confederate and Federal officers met in Washington to form the Chickamauga Memorial Association, dedicated to making Boynton's vision a reality. The Association held its first official meeting the following September at the annual reunion of the Society of the Army of the Cumberland, a prominent veterans' organization whose members had a keen sense of their accomplishments relative to their peers who had fought in the Federal Army of the Tennessee. Governor John B. Gordon of Georgia, a prominent advocate of southern industrialization and sectional reconciliation, told the assembled veterans that they should "bury the foul spirit of discord so deep that no blast of partisan political trumpet . . . can ever wake it to service again."[35]

The former soldiers' efforts to gain federal funding in the name of sectional peace attracted bipartisan support in the US House of Representatives Committee on Military Affairs. Insisting that "[t]he political questions which were involved in the contest do not enter into this view of the subject," the committee designated the proposed park "in all its aspects a purely military project."[36] In the summer of 1890, Congress appropriated $125,000 to create the Chickamauga and Chattanooga National Military Park and provided for the organization of a three-man commission (which would include former Confederate General Alexander P. Stewart) to oversee its development. Boynton, the park's first historian, took the lead in marking the key sites, including regimental positions in battle. Although he was aided by reports from the government's *Official Records of the War of the Rebellion*, his task was a difficult one. Accurate labeling of events that had taken place in the early 1860s could be a frustrating exercise. At one point, Federal brigade commander John B. Turchin accused Boynton of self-promotion after the two men fell out over the placement of markers showing where Turchin's unit had fought.

In September 1895, more than fifty thousand people, many of them veterans from both sides of the late conflict, attended dedication ceremonies held over three days in Chattanooga and on the battlefield at Chickamauga. The limits of sectional reconciliation were uncovered when Governor William C. Oates of Alabama, a Confederate amputee, blamed the Civil War on Puritan fanaticism and derided the idea that Union troops had fought to free the slaves. After northern veterans made their views known by calling on Oates to desist, their political representatives weighed in with remarks of their own. Governor Urban A. Woodbury, a Vermont Republican who had lost an arm at First Bull Run, gave no quarter when he insisted that "we cannot teach our children but that they [the Rebels] were wrong."[37] For the most part, however, good feelings prevailed. US Vice President Adlai E. Stevenson, an Illinois Democrat who had not served in the war, commended the bravery of soldiers on both sides and hailed the fact that they were now meeting "as brothers—under one flag, fellow-citizens of a common country."[38] This view, bolstered by Ohio Governor William McKinley's statement that national unity was the Civil War's "glorious reward," explains why so many Union veterans, Boynton among them, were willing to fraternize with their Rebel foes.[39] The country was reunited. The Union was safe. They had won the war. The former Confederates, on the other hand, were pleased that old enemies like Boynton did not try to thrust black emancipation down their throats and that leading northerners publicly acknowledged their courage as American soldiers. The shoots of reconciliation were bursting out everywhere—nowhere more importantly than in the contested arena of party politics.

The Election of 1896

The presidential election of 1896 was a watershed event in the history of Civil War memory because it demonstrated a newfound willingness on the part of national Republican leaders to temper their once instinctive sectionalism. Grover Cleveland's election for a second term in November 1892 had seemed to confirm the impotence of the Republicans' sectional rhetoric. Cleveland's administration, however, soon ran into serious trouble. In 1893, the country was hit by a deep depression that halted economic activity and imposed enormous hardships on farmers and industrial workers. The result was widespread poverty and social unrest, culminating in May 1894 in a bitter strike of railroad workers at the Pullman Palace Car Manufacturing Company outside Chicago that ended only when President Cleveland dispatched federal troops to break the dispute.

Many farmers across the United States mobilized behind the leadership of the agrarian Populist Party that threatened to destroy the major parties' stranglehold over the American political system. Like the WCTU and other reform groups seeking to organize nationally, the Populists had a clear stake in fostering sectional reconciliation. In the 1892 election, they had placed a Union and a Confederate general on their presidential ticket in a bid to attract northern and southern voters. The party's appeal was to class, not section. Four years later, against a background of continued social unrest (15 percent of American workers remained unemployed), progressive Democrats hostile to the pro-business eastern wing of the party seized control of the national convention in Chicago and successfully promoted an uneasy fusion with the Populists on the basis of support for currency inflation.

One of the shrillest speeches at the convention was delivered by Senator Ben Tillman of South Carolina. Harboring his own presidential ambitions and hoping to unite southern and western farmers behind the free coinage of silver, the tub-thumping Tillman introduced himself as hailing from the South, "the home of secession." The announcement went down badly in the Chicago Coliseum, but the senator pressed on, insisting that bimetallism was "a sectional issue." Southerners, he said, now looked to the West, "asking our brethren of those States to unite with us in restoring the government, the liberty of fathers, which our fathers left us."[40] Tillman's open embrace of secession was a tactical mistake. William Jennings Bryan of Nebraska, the dark-horse candidate at the convention, understood the danger of parading treason before a national audience. His electrifying "Cross of Gold" address left "no taste of sectionalism in the mouth" and secured the nomination for himself.[41]

The "Popocrat" threat to the established order induced Republican leaders, still heavily reliant on the financial backing of northeastern manufacturers and the votes of Union veterans, to adapt their use of Civil War memory to the altered times. Their presidential candidate, William McKinley, was a highly respected Union officer who had fought against Lee at Antietam and Early at Kernstown and Cedar Creek. However, while he was a proud defender of the Union cause, a supporter of the Lodge elections bill, and a renowned advocate of high tariffs to bolster American manufactures, Major McKinley was also receptive to the idea of sectional reconciliation. This made him an ideal candidate in an election contest in which Republican strategists like his close ally, the Cleveland businessman Mark Hanna, hoped to appeal to conservatives everywhere by highlighting the irresponsible fusionists' reliance on class warfare and easy money.

Some Republican newspapers were quick to cite Ben Tillman's Chicago gaffe as proof of southern treason in 1860–61 and link it to the Popocrats' alleged attempts to destabilize the country in the present. But for the most part, Republican leaders, backed by a corporate-funded war chest of nearly $4 million, deployed Civil War memory in a more nuanced fashion in 1896 than they had done previously. Rather than instinctively waving the bloody shirt and connecting their opponents to the Rebellion, they tried to fashion a more usable past, one that would unite conservative, patriotic Americans on both sides of the old sectional divide behind McKinley, protective tariffs, and the gold standard.

Instead of reminding voters that former Confederates and Democrats could not be trusted to run the government, the Republicans ran an aggressively nationalist campaign designed to focus public attention on the perils of internal disunity. Bryan and his cohorts, they claimed, were modern-day secessionists, trumpeting class warfare at a time when the country needed social cohesion. One of the Republicans' main targets was a northern Democratic governor, John P. Altgeld of Illinois, who had used his authority to try to block the use of troops to defeat the Pullman strike. Such action, claimed the Republican press, was precisely the kind that had endangered the republic after Lincoln's election. "In 1861," commented *Harper's Weekly*, "some of the States undertook to enforce the doctrine that the Federal government had not the power to prevent them from leaving the Union. Their attempt was defeated after a terrible war."[42]

Conjuring memories of the secession crisis enabled Republican campaign managers to avoid inconvenient references to wartime emancipation that could only alienate southern conservatives. The failure of the Lodge bill and the consolidation of Jim Crow meant the party could no longer be regarded as a credible vehicle for racial equality. Its 1896 platform condemned lynching but barely touched on the desperate need for federal enforcement of black voting rights in the South. Instead, the Republicans' mnemonic appeals that year played on grassroots fears of social unrest and labor conflict. Thus, when the fusionists tried to unite hard-pressed westerners and southerners against the capital-rich Northeast, General Daniel Sickles, one of McKinley's leading backers, denounced the strategy as "sectionalism—of which the rebellion was the offspring."[43]

As Sickles's comment revealed, enduring Unionist memories of the Civil War were not entirely absent from the campaign. The prospect of a tight election made the Midwest, home to roughly four hundred thousand surviving Federals, the major political background. In an effort to secure it for McKinley, party strategists advertised the candidate's exemplary war record and proclaimed that Bryan's inflationary policies would damage the value of the soldiers' pensions. That fall they also financed a tour of the region by a group of high-profile Union generals, including Sickles. The Patriotic Heroes' Battalion crisscrossed the region by rail and was greeted by enthusiastic congregations of veterans at every stop. The train was decked out in red, white, and blue and streamed with banners proclaiming the danger that Bryan posed to the nation.

Although the Republican efforts to energize Union veterans involved rhetorical denigration of secession, party leaders blamed the rebellion on a small group of elite southern traitors. More significantly, they acknowledged the bravery and, without irony, the civic responsibility of ordinary Confederate veterans. During his "front porch campaign," McKinley hosted groups of voters at his home in Canton while his energetic opponent toured the country delivering hundreds of political speeches. These stage-managed meetings included a reception for veterans of both sides in October. The mingling of the Blue and the Gray proved to be uncontroversial. One midwestern Republican editor accustomed to lambasting Democrats and Rebels commented that

> the breaking down of party lines in this year's campaign will more thoroughly unify the American people than any other event since the British troops laid down their arms at Yorktown. We have faced Confederate soldiers in battle array, have met and talked with numbers of them since the war, and we are free to say that we would rather trust that portion of them, in control of the government, who are now standing firmly for the preservation of the National honor and the business safety of all the people, than to trust northern or any other men in control who advocate National dishonor to serve the interests of millionaire silver kings. Confederate soldiers were disloyal to the Nation but they were not dishonest.[44]

Republican efforts to paint the election as a contest between social order and secessionist-style anarchy in which American patriots on both sides of the Mason-Dixon Line had only one choice took many forms. One hard-hitting cartoon cleverly played on wartime memories in order to demonstrate the gulf in experience between the two candidates. It contrasted McKinley as a sturdy Union soldier "upholding his country's honor" with Bryan (born 1860) as a baby shaking his rattle.[45] After an election that elicited turnouts as high as 95 percent in several states, McKinley won a crushing victory in the electoral college by carrying the Midwest. Although virtually all southern and far western states went for Bryan, the Republican Party's readiness to regard rank-and-file Rebels in a positive light confirmed the growing support for sectional reconciliation in the country at large. As president, William McKinley would continue to fashion war remembrance into a weapon of consensus.

Major McKinley Goes to War Again

The Spanish-American War of 1898 proved to be the tipping point in the history of Civil War memory in the United States, not only because it finally convinced Union veterans that their erstwhile foes could be trusted as compatriots but also because it sealed the federal government's commitment to reconciliatory forms of Civil War commemoration.

Initially, President McKinley was cautious about fighting Spain. For a few weeks, anxious Republican leaders were forced to remind the public about his military record as evidence that he possessed the manly backbone to stand up to a monarchical European foe. McKinley's reservations quickly wilted in the face of rising jingoism whipped up by the popular press, including the papers of William Randolph Hearst, who signed up the celebrated young novelist Stephen Crane to report on conditions in Cuba for the *New York Journal*. Although some southerners found the idea of volunteering unattractive, support for the war—which began in April—was not hard to find in Dixie. A handful of leading former Confederates, keen to demonstrate their courage and patriotism, immediately offered their services to the government. McKinley, who had publicly endorsed sectional reconciliation in his inaugural address, jumped at the opportunity. He appointed Rebel cavalry officers Fitzhugh Lee and Joseph Wheeler to command US volunteer units.

The new battlefield park at Chickamauga in Georgia was turned into a training ground, Camp George H. Thomas, for volunteers from all parts of the United States. Many of these young recruits spent their spare time scouring the site for Civil War relics like bullets and cannon balls. Some talked with the small number of Union and Confederate veterans in the ranks. One New Englander observed that he and his comrades "knew little of the history and conditions" surrounding the Civil War and that the questions they addressed to a former Rebel "were almost as ludicrous as his answer."[46] But white northern and southern recruits in the camp generally mixed well with one another. After the US victory at San Juan Hill in early July 1898, the military bands of northern regiments played southern tunes, and those from southern units reciprocated.

The patriotic spirit engendered by the war was a revelation to many Americans. En route to Cuba with his regiment of "Rough Riders," Colonel Theodore Roosevelt marveled at the sight of so many American flags flying in New Orleans. As a young boy, Roosevelt had watched from a high window as Abraham Lincoln's coffin passed by the family home in Manhattan. As an adult, he was a keen enthusiast of the Civil War in particular and war in general as testing grounds for American manhood. He could not have dreamed in the "bygone days of bitterness," he wrote, that former Confederates would turn out in such large numbers to celebrate Old Glory and contribute so many sons "to fight and die under it."[47]

Southern support for the war against Spain, certainly the support indicated by the involvement of high-profile Confederate officers, was welcomed by most Union veterans because it seemed proof that the old Rebels could again be trusted as loyal citizens of the United States. Their chief organ, the *National Tribune*, drew readers' attention to the fact that many of the country's military commanders were Union veterans, but it also featured engravings of "battle-tried leaders" like southern heroes Fitzhugh Lee and Joseph Wheeler.[48] Sumner Cunningham's *Confederate Veteran* magazine welcomed what it saw as the region's broadly positive response to the conflict on the grounds, established by Jefferson Davis and other Lost Cause proponents, that "it verifies the truth, oft declared, that motives of Southern men in the 'civil' war were for the good of the government established by the founders of this republic."[49]

American naval supremacy in the Caribbean and the Pacific helped to secure victory by August 1898. McKinley, warming to the task of empire building, used Civil War memory to solicit public and congressional support for his expansionist foreign policy. During the fall, while diplomats negotiated a peace treaty with Spain in Paris, the president told midwestern audiences that military action in the 1860s and the 1890s had expanded liberty and civilization. He went out of his way to praise the unity with which the country had fought the Spaniards and informed an audience in Omaha, Nebraska, that the victors of Manila Bay and Santiago were worthy successors to the heroes of the Revolution, to Grant and Sherman, and, he added (apparently to ringing applause), "of Lee, Jackson, and Longstreet."[50] McKinley, who now had his eyes on annexing the Philippines, also told audiences that they should not squander the fruits of victory.

The president's need to secure Senate approval for the Treaty of Paris (signed with Spain in October) induced him to travel south in December 1898. In Atlanta for a celebratory peace jubilee, he told an audience at the Georgia statehouse that it was time the federal government accepted responsibility for the care of Confederate graves. "[S]ectional lines," he said, "no longer mar the map of the United States. Sectional feeling no longer holds back the love we bear each other."[51] McKinley's overtures seeemed to pay dividends when the Senate narrowly ratified the peace treaty. Northern Republicans cast most of the yea votes, but the treaty only scraped through with backing from a handful of southern Democrats, including Alexander S. Clay of Georgia, William V. Sullivan of Mississippi, John L. McLaurin of South Carolina, and Confederate veteran Samuel D. McEnery of Louisiana.[52]

Two days before the crucial vote in Washington, Filipino insurgents led by Eduardo Aguinaldo had begun a bloody revolt against US occupation of the Philippine Islands. The three-year insurrection intensified domestic debates over the country's new global role. Undaunted, President McKinley mixed Unionist and reconciliatory strains of Civil War memory to boost popular support for his counterinsurgency efforts in the Pacific. As historian Mike Sewell has observed, many members of his own party "remembered the Civil War as a conflict justified by God's Providence" and responded positively to suggestions that the kind of hard-war policies endorsed by Abraham Lincoln could secure humanitarian ends once again.[53] At Sioux Falls, South Dakota, on October 14, 1899, McKinley stated that the United States intended to suppress the Philippine insurrection "just as we put down any rebellion against the sovereignty of the United States," yet he also lauded "the gallant and intrepid Joe Wheeler" whom he described as "a great cavalry leader of the Confederate army."[54] Six months later, speaking at Antietam (one of five Civil War battlefields designated a National Military Park in the 1890s), the president insisted that the courage displayed by the American soldiers on both sides of the late conflict was "the common heritage of us all." The patriotic northerners and southerners now "fighting and dying" in the Pacific, he asserted, were fighting for "the flag that represents more than any other banner in the world the best hopes and aspirations of mankind."[55] In this rhetorical formulation, millennial hopes that northerners had once invested in the War of the Rebellion were now shared by Americans on both sides of the Mason-Dixon Line in their common undertaking of imperial mission. Not all Americans, however, were convinced by the president's creative use of historical memory. In one startling broadside, McKinley's anti-imperialist critics in the North equated him with Jefferson Davis because of what its authors saw as his betrayal of cardinal American principles.[56] History does not record his response, but it seems unlikely that the patriotic major would have been amused.

Accommodations

President McKinley was assassinated in Buffalo, New York, in September 1901 and therefore did not live to see his country defeat the outgunned Filipinos.

But he did live to witness a signal advance in the progress of sectional reconciliation. In June 1900, just eighteen months after the president had announced his backing for federal care of the Rebel dead, Congress sanctioned the reburial of Confederate soldiers in Arlington National Cemetery. By 1902, 267 former Rebels were interred there in a separate plot.[57] These were men who had died in Union prisons and hospitals during the war and whose bodies had not been returned to the South under the auspices of the Ladies' Memorial Associations.

Other symbolic measures followed. In 1905, Congress finally authorized the return of captured Confederate battle flags to the southern states. When President Cleveland had proposed this initiative in 1887, he had been forced to back down by opposition from the GAR and other loyal organizations. Eighteen years later, the move no longer seemed controversial. In 1906, US Secretary of War William Howard Taft granted a United Daughters of the Confederacy (UDC) request for the construction of a large Confederate memorial in Section 16 of Arlington cemetery, where the Rebel dead had been reinterred. In July 1913, Woodrow Wilson, the first southern-born president since Andrew Johnson, addressed a large gathering of Union and Confederate veterans at Gettysburg on the fiftieth anniversary of the great battle. Wilson, renowned as a historian of the Civil War era, was a committed American nationalist who once asserted that "*because* I love the South, I rejoice in the failure of the Confederacy."[58] At Gettysburg he celebrated the Civil War as a shared experience between brave American men on both sides. "We have found one another again as brothers and comrades in arms," he proclaimed, "enemies no longer, generous friends rather, our battles long past, the quarrel forgotten—except that we shall not forget the splendid valour, the manly devotion of the men then arrayed against one another, now grasping hands and smiling into each other's eyes."[59]

President Wilson's florid paean concealed almost as much as it revealed. Significant southern backing for the Spanish-American War shifted the balance between sectional and reconciliatory strains of Civil War remembrance decisively in favor of the latter; it did not mean that those older, angrier strains had been obliterated completely. Sectional reconciliation took place in the United States not, as Wilson indicated, primarily because the veterans were willing to forget the issues and passions of the Civil War, but for two different reasons. First, the majority of Union and Confederate soldiers reached an accommodation with one another without surrendering their conviction that their own cause had been right. Second, Americans who had no ties to the Civil War—recent European immigrants, for example—as well as many younger native-born people like Stephen Crane who did have family connections to the veterans were far too preoccupied with the present and future to spend their lives refighting old battles from the past. To varying degrees, all of these groups were enveloped by the era's nationalist surge. Some more than others were seduced by the romantic, lily-white culture of reconciliation that bolstered the growing consensus.

A minority of people on both sides resisted the juggernaut of sectional reconciliation until the day they died. Former Confederate guerrillas began holding reunions in the late nineteenth century. Although they sought to explain wartime excesses such as William Quantrill's deadly August 1863 raid on Lawrence, Kansas, by pointing out the brutality of Unionist "bushwhackers," few demonstrated signs of repentance. Instead they reveled in their murderous effectiveness. "We had nothing to regret in that we had dun only wishied we had dun more," stated one Missourian.[60] Regarded as common criminals by most northerners and with a good deal of distaste by Lost Cause advocates eager to celebrate the chivalry of Confederate statesmen, soldiers, and women, the guerrillas' unsentimental recollections of the war rendered them out of step with the era of better feeling between North and South.

Because they were more numerous, better organized, and more respectable than the aging Rebel guerrillas, former prisoners of war on both sides posed more of a problem for sectional reconciliation. Understandably, many of these men found it impossible to forget the suffering of their youth or to forgive those whom they held responsible for that torment. Of the roughly 410,000 soldiers imprisoned during the Civil War, an estimated 56,000 died in captivity.[61] Those who survived hell-holes like Andersonville, Georgia, and Elmira, New York (camps where the death rate was 29 and 24 percent, respectively) were determined to keep their own pain and that of their comrades before the public.[62]

Attempts by northern and southern POWs either to blame the enemy or to excuse the sins of their own side obstructed the pace of reconciliation in the 1870s and 1880s. Realizing the damage wrought by bitter prison memories, the editors of *Century* magazine purposely excluded contributions from POWs from their original War Series. However, POW organizations like the Society of the Immortal 600, a group of Confederate officers used as human shields by the Federals during the siege of Charleston in 1865, continued to publicize the issue into the twentieth century. Soldiers' newspapers such as the *Confederate Veteran* and the *National Tribune* as well as published papers disseminated by the Military Order of the Loyal Legion of the United States also kept sectional feeling alive, as did one-sided prison memoirs written by embittered POWs. These texts made it difficult for many former servicemen to abandon their conviction that they had fought against a barbarous enemy.

Some of the rancor over prison conditions dissipated as time passed. In 1889, Herbert Collingwood wrote a reconciliation-themed novel titled *Andersonville Violets* in which a Confederate guard refuses to shoot a Union prisoner who escapes from Andersonville. Collingwood offered the novel as a contribution to better feeling between the sections. The book, he wrote, "would present food for sound and healthful thought, unblinded by partisan feeling or sectional hatred. The war is over forever. It can never be fought again. We have but one flag."[63] During the late nineteenth and early twentieth centuries, northern states dedicated monuments to their prison dead in the national cemetery at Andersonville. Despite the occasional barbed remark from a northern speaker, most of the ceremonies took place without significant controversy.

Women allied to the veterans on both sides, however, rarely hesitated to sustain the festering issue of prison conditions. In 1893, the GAR-affiliated Woman's Relief Corps purchased the old prison site at Andersonville to ensure that the terrible suffering of northern POWs would never be forgotten. More controversially still, in May 1909, the UDC dedicated a monument in the village of Andersonville to Henry Wirz, the camp's infamous commander who had been executed after the Civil War. Union veterans, used to demonizing Wirz as the supreme embodiment of Rebel barbarism, were outraged. James Tanner, a severely disabled former Federal who spearheaded the fight for Union veterans' pensions, numbered among those appalled by the announcement of the UDC's project. Normally a strong advocate of reconciliation, Tanner publicly assailed the Daughters for planning this shocking act. "It is time to speak out man-fashion in a dignified way," he told the GAR's National Encampment in 1906, "and let the country know that the Grand Army of the Republic makes its dignified protest against the exaltation of the man who sent to horrible death so many of our comrades and who caused such inexpressible anguish in the hearts of the people of the North."[64] UDC members, angered by what they saw as northerners' failure to remove the beam from their own eye and convinced that Wirz should go down in history as a martyr to the Confederacy, were unmoved by such protests.

Despite the difficulties posed by the contested memory of guerrilla warfare and squalid prisons, sectional reconciliation was a reality by the early twentieth century in part because the veterans and their allies reached an accommodation with each other over time. Essentially, they agreed to differ over key issues on which compromise was difficult—issues such as who was to blame for the war and the mistreatment of prisoners and civilians—and maintained the right to insist on the superior virtue of their respective cause. On the other hand, they found a modicum of common ground in a recognition of mutual valor and civic commitment.

After the Spanish-American War, signs of support for sectional reconciliation began to swamp evidence of lingering difference. Blue-Gray reunions, for example, became more prominent features of the commemorative landscape. At these events, praise for the courage of old enemies was always forthcoming as the veterans of both sides came to understand that public recognition of their own bravery would be enhanced by such generous acknowledgment.

Many elite figures, moreover, worked to fashion a consensual memory of the conflict that would bolster a social and political order in which they had an important stake. Heroic role models from America's brothers' war served their purpose well. In 1902, Charles Francis Adams Jr., a leading northern businessman who had served in the Union Army, celebrated Robert E. Lee as a spotless leader whose virtues of "courage, devotion, patriotism" and "high sense of duty and personal honor" should be revered nationally in a churning society beset by the problems of modernity.[65] Woodrow Wilson, whose own father briefly served as chaplain in a Confederate infantry unit, praised Abraham Lincoln for his charitable attitude toward defeated white southerners as well as his commitment to national unity.

Unlike Jubal Early and his clique of Confederate diehards, most proponents of the celebratory Lost Cause publicly acknowledged that they were loyal citizens of the United States. In 1904, Dudley McEwan Featherston, the son of a Confederate brigadier general from Mississippi, extolled the Rebel dead in words that looked clearly to the future as much as to the past. "Never in the world's history," he boasted, "did any people adjust themselves to circumstances or accept a situation with a nobler devotion . . . than the Confederate soldier, and this in itself should demonstrate to the world, their loyalty to-day to the flag of our government."[66]

Although UDC members, just like the old Rebels who belonged to the United Confederate Veterans (UCV), were jealous guardians of southern history and swift to resent any Yankee slight, they did not regard their activities as seditious. Most Daughters were visible members of the South's new urban bourgeoisie. Their remembering activities, ranging from historical preservation to textbook censorship, entrenched the cultural power of their class, which had been built on the violence and political success of white supremacist Democrats in the region. Broadly supportive of economic progress within a socially and politically conservative framework, such well-to-do women had no interest in being seen as traitors. Their aim, rather, was to continue the efforts of Jefferson Davis and other Lost Cause ideologues to prove that the Confederates had been the true American patriots of the 1860s. Unsurprisingly, given that the War of Independence offered white southerners a readily available memory site at which they could demonstrate their allegiance to the United States, many UDC members also belonged to the Daughters of the American Revolution, a national civic group that not only marginalized the role of blacks in the nation's founding but also segregated its chapters along the color line. These southern women generally were responsive to reconciliatory overtures from the North. As long as Yankees were willing to recognize the courage and high-mindedness of the Confederates and to avoid criticism of southern race relations, the Daughters proved ready to act as contemporary patriots.

Union veterans numbered among the least conciliatory groups in the United States. However, their heavy investment in turn-of-the-century American nationalism gave them a considerable stake in the reconciliation process. This was because they viewed America's rise to great power status as a vindication of their own sacrifices in behalf of the Union and regarded evidence of renewed southern allegiance to the republic as confirmation of their victory. Predictably, GAR members were ardent supporters of the era's flag cult. One of the Grand Army's leading initiatives in the early 1900s was to place the Stars and Stripes in the country's common schools. GAR posts raised funds for this purpose and sent former soldiers into classrooms to teach American children about the meaning of duty and sacrifice for the nation. While the Grand Army had the trappings of a militaristic organization, its patriotic members saw their conduct as a natural extension of their wartime republican service—and a necessary one too, given the imperative need for social cohesion in an age of mass immigration and rapid urban and industrial growth.[67]

Tellingly, while many white former Federals continued to acknowledge their shared links to black Civil War veterans, younger servicemen who had fought against Spain exhibited no desire to acknowledge their fellow black soldiers as equals. Having mixed with one another in their training camps, white northern and southern Spanish War veterans clearly found it easier to embrace the spirit of sectional reconciliation than older GAR members, who jealously guarded sectionalized memories of "their" war and refused to allow Spanish War veterans to join the Grand Army. Unlike the GAR, the much smaller United Spanish War Veterans organization segregated its posts on both sides of the Mason-Dixon Line. Union veterans, argues historian Barbara Gannon, "remembered a war against slavery in which its members fought with former slaves and rejected racial segregation. In contrast, the USWV created all-black state-level organizations because black military service was less central to their wartime memory."[68]

The national growth of reconciliatory sentiment and the contemporaneous rise of Jim Crow induced many African Americans to make accommodations with the past. Some of those people who attended the inaugural park ceremonies at Chickamauga and Chattanooga in 1895 journeyed on to Atlanta to visit that ambitious city's Cotton States and International Exposition. It is likely therefore that many Civil War veterans were among the racially segregated audience that heard one of the most famous speeches ever delivered by a race leader in the United States.

Booker T. Washington, the principal of Tuskegee Institute in Alabama, had been born a slave in 1856 and later attended a black teacher training school in Virginia run by a paternalistic Union officer named Samuel C. Armstrong.

He intended his "Atlanta Compromise" address of September 18 to reassure southern whites, in the midst of intensifiying violence against African Americans in the region, that the liberated slaves were not a threat to the master race. Instead, he urged, blacks should be treated as a valuable economic resource within a framework of physical separation.

Washington relied on several rhetorical strategies to make his argument. They included a carefully crafted use of historical memory to engage the interest and sympathy of white listeners. In words laced with the kind of nostalgia deployed by Henry Grady in Boston six years earlier, he asked whites to see black folk not as beasts and criminals but as "the most patient, faithful, law-abiding, and unresentful people that the world has seen"—a people who had proved their "loyalty to you in the past, in nursing your children, watching by the sick-bed of your mothers and fathers, and often following them with tear-dimmed eyes to their graves."[69] Hoping as well for "a blotting out of sectional differences" and "a willing obedience among all classes to the mandates of the law," Washington signaled his support for the modernizing agenda of the New South: social order, material progress, and sectional amity forged on the back of the Confederate celebration that incorporated blacks mnemonically only as faithful slaves.[70]

Booker T. Washington's controversial accommodation with segregation thus involved an accommodation with the historical memory of the former Rebels. At a time when some southern blacks, those attending Memorial Day ceremonies at Andersonville, for example, continued to cherish the example of armed black men, the South's leading black spokesman eschewed an emancipationist narrative of the Civil War and chose to parrot the Lost Cause verities of Henry Grady and other oppressors of his race. His choice was determined largely by the vicious white supremacism of the 1890s. However, the cost—blacks' acknowledgment of their second-class status—was high. In November 1902, Washington invited the UCV's commander, General John B. Gordon, to speak at Tuskegee. Gordon told the black students of his admiration for "the Negro race who with so much faithfulness befriended and cared for the wives and sisters of the Confederate soldiers" in a war to maintain slavery. "[T]he Southern white man," said the former Klansman, "is the best friend the Negro in the South has."[71]

In truth, African Americans had few friends anywhere during this era. While many Union veterans, their immediate families, and even some blacks reached an accommodation with the Confederate celebration, white Americans more generally were seduced completely by what Nina Silber has termed "the romance of reunion."[72] Embracing key elements of the reconciliatory and Lost Cause narratives, this flowering culture was highly sentimental—and profoundly racist.

The Culture of Reconciliation

The culture of sectional reconciliation, nationally dominant by the early 1900s, was manifested most powerfully in popular literature. Its highly selective remembrance of the Civil War and Reconstruction mirrored a deeply prejudiced society in which African Americans were increasingly oppressed. It also contributed to the ideological scaffolding on which white supremacy was constructed, North as well as South, in the late nineteenth and early twentieth centuries.

Fictional accounts of the recent past by southern authors like Joel Chandler Harris, Thomas Nelson Page, and Thomas Dixon Jr., contributed immensely to the cementing of reconciliation between old enemies. Harris, a Georgian best known for his Uncle Remus tales, tended to favor white yeomen over aristocratic cavaliers as his central characters. This did not prevent him from fashioning idealized southern communities populated by warmhearted whites and blacks bound closely to one another by ties of mutual affection. Bondage had been no barrier to such relations, he averred, because it was "to the glory of the American character and name, that never before in the history of the world was human slavery marked by such mildness, such humanity, as that which characterized it in the United States."[73]

Page was a well-connected Virginian whose stories were taken up enthusiastically by northeastern magazines. He specialized in plantation narratives that depicted the antebellum period as a golden era in which southern women fell in love with northern men against a background of sectional conflict. Like Harris, he profited greatly from American readers' growing receptivity to sectional reconciliation in the 1880s and 1890s. Although he publicly defended lynching, Page often mediated the consummation of an intersectional love affair in his tales through the narrative voice of a faithful slave. One of his best-loved stories was "Meh Lady" (1887), an account of a plantation woman who falls in love with a Union officer, Captain Wilton, to whom she is distantly related. After Wilton is wounded in battle, Meh Lady's loyal slave, the narrator Unc' Billy, conveys him to the plantation, where romance eventually blossoms. The original idea for the story came not from Page but from Robert Underwood Johnson, who had masterminded *Century*'s reconciliatory War Series. After reading a love story by the German writer Gotthold Ephraim Lessing, which highlighted the virtues of the warring Prussians and Saxons, the editor suggested that Page try something similar.[74] Having found the formula for success, Page was happy to share it with others. "Get a pretty girl and name her Jeanne . . . ," he advised an aspiring female novelist from Louisiana, "Make her fall in love with a Federal officer and your story will be printed at once!"[75] The formula permeated all forms of popular American literature in the late nineteenth century. Bronson Howard's play *Shenandoah* (1889) brought together no fewer than five pairs of lovers separated by the Civil War.

Northerners, women especially, were avid readers of plantation romances for three main reasons. First, such books offered a compelling imaginative realm to which Yankees, troubled by the many strains of industrial society, could retreat. In this respect they were the fictional equivalents of the South's new tourist resorts that were promoted by developers as warm, exotic havens for upper-class city dwellers. Second, by imagining reconciliation in terms of marriage between a northern man and a southern woman, the tales confirmed northerners' understanding of the power relations underpinning the restoration of sectional amity. Third, the fact that the stories were populated by faithful blacks struggling to cope with the demands of freedom corroborated many northern readers' view of how race relations should operate in the new era of high imperialism and Jim Crow. They therefore stiffened the powerful strain of Anglo-Saxon racism that had been challenged by the sectional conflict but that now seemed to have most white Americans in its grip.

In this respect, Reconstruction proved to be a critical site of mnemonic consensus for northern and southern whites. While they often agreed to disagree about controversial war issues, most Americans at the start of the twentieth century concurred that it had been a mistake to impose black and carpetbag rule on the former Confederates. This conviction, encouraged initially by Democrats and Liberal Republicans, was strengthened by the defeat of the Lodge elections bill and a growing sense among many northerners that African Americans had regressed since emancipation. It took root also with the help of nationalist historians—not only gentleman amateurs like James Ford Rhodes who bemoaned passage of the Fifteenth Amendment but also a new generation of professional scholars centered at Johns Hopkins University in Baltimore and Columbia University in New York. William A. Dunning and his mentor, former Tennessee Unionist John W. Burgess, were the architects of what later became known as "the Dunning school." While both men saw much to admire in congressional Reconstruction, they argued that government efforts to impose black suffrage on the Rebels had been a grievous political mistake, partly because blacks had not been ready for the vote and partly because the move had fanned the flames of white supremacism.[76] Their critical interpretation of federal policy after the war, rendered even more negative by other racially prejudiced white scholars, would serve as the standard scholarly account of this decisive period of American history for at least half a century.

Academic interpretations of Reconstruction, heavily influenced by the social and intellectual milieu in which they were constructed, corresponded closely with accounts of the same period written by the untrained female historians of the UDC and novelists like Thomas Nelson Page and Joel Chandler

Harris. Page's *Red Rock: A Chronicle of Reconstruction* (1898) sold one hundred thousand copies within two years of publication.[77] Set "somewhere in that vague region partly in one of the old Southern States and partly in the yet vaguer land of Memory," it depicted Reconstruction as a period when whites, once the inhabitants of "a goodly land" ruled by the most just of oligarchies, were "subjected to the greatest humiliation of modern times" but "reconquered their section and preserved the civilization of the Anglo-Saxon."[78] In *Gabriel Tolliver* (1902), Harris developed a tale of southern lovers set in the normally close-knit Georgia community of Shady Dale. The village's attempts to recover from the shock of war are upset by the arrival of a Yankee carpetbagger, Gilbert Hotchkiss, an "ill-informed emissary of race hatred and sectional prejudice" whose plans to destroy the community's social fabric are thwarted by local whites and loyal blacks, including Uncle Plato, a right-thinking freedman who avers spiritedly that "[w]hen my marster tu'ns his back on me I"ll tu'n my back on him."[79]

African Americans were relatively marginal characters in these books—either useful allies of the white central characters or dupes of power-hungry carpetbaggers like Gilbert Hotchkiss. They were invested with real threat in the insidious fiction of Thomas Dixon Jr. Dixon was a Baptist minister and friend of Ben Tillman from North Carolina. His uncle Leroy McAfee had fought for the Confederacy. Fearful, like many of his white contemporaries that miscegenation and mass immigration from southern and eastern Europe were polluting America's racial stock, he penned his third novel, *The Clansman* (1905), as a tribute to the postwar Klan of which both his uncle and his father had been members. Dixon's virulently racist text featured a romantic plotline that inverted standard northern narratives of Yankee men marrying southern women. *The Clansman*'s pro-southern yet broadly reconciliatory central narrative paired Rebel soldier Ben Cameron with Elsie Stoneman, the daughter of a Radical Republican congressman modeled on Thaddeus Stevens. Unlike Page and Harris, Dixon portrayed some of his African American characters as dangerous—none more so than Silas Lynch, a mixed-race protégé of Austin Stoneman, who seeks to humiliate Cameron and his fellow southerners. When a group of blacks rape Cameron's childhood sweetheart, Marion Lenoir, he joins the Klan, which proceeds to serve summary justice on the rapists and redeem the country for Anglo-Saxon civilization. The book tapped into the prevailing zeitgeist. One Union veteran told Dixon that he disagreed with his views about blacks but added that "time may prove . . . my wife's hearty endorsement of the work to be the more correct view."[80] He was right. *The Clansman* soon sold more than a million copies. Eager to capitalize on his achievement, Dixon turned the book into a play that was received enthusiastically by audiences on both sides of the Mason-Dixon Line.

The national appeal of Dixon's racist views was apparent in August 1908, when a white mob rampaged through the black neighborhood of Springfield, Illinois, destroying property and assaulting African Americans. Such events were depressingly commonplace in the early twentieth century, but for some white liberals this riot was particularly shocking because it occurred in the hometown of Abraham Lincoln, the Great Emancipator. Moved to action, a group of them initiated steps to create an interracial organization dedicated to promoting black civil rights through the federal courts.

The National Association for the Advancement of Colored People (NAACP) was the product not only of moral outrage at the violence in Springfield but also of an awareness on the part of some reformers that Americans had lost touch with their civil war. Several of the organization's founding members, including Mary White Ovington, Henry Garrison Villard, and Charles Edward Russell were progeny of antebellum abolitionists. Acting as direct heirs of the old antislavery movement, they invited delegates to attend an inaugural conference in New York City in late May 1909.

A number of speakers at this event made it clear that the creation of the new organization was a conscious act of historical remembrance. "As the years have passed," said William Hayes Ward, editor of the *New York Independent*, "and a new generation has come which has no memory of the Civil War or the Proclamation of Emancipation, and no knowledge of the efforts made during the period of reconstruction and the adoption of the Fourteenth and Fifteenth Amendments to reduce the Negro back to a condition of serfdom, we need not wonder that the old fervor of sympathy has much subsided, while at the same time there has been a readiness to apologize for old wrongs; and we have even seen the effort, too often successful, to pervert the history of the old struggle."[81] Another speaker, Burt G. Wilder, a scientist at Cornell University who had served on the medical staff of the 55th US Colored Infantry, testified that African Americans had fought hard for the Union. The black man's claim to equal rights, he avowed, "was earned during the Civil War by the general conduct of soldiers of African descent, by their valor, by their initiative under trying conditions, and by their deliberate self-sacrifice for the sake of a principle."[82]

The founding of the NAACP was a rare moment of brightness for African Americans in the era of Jim Crow. The runaway national success of Thomas Dixon's work confirmed that selective white memories of the past were freighted with vicious racism. Sectional reconciliation was a positive development in many respects, but, as Frederick Douglass had predicted all along, it was accomplished at the expense of African Americans. As the veterans of both sides passed from the earth, Civil War memories as usable as those peddled by Dixon, Page, McKinley, and others would continue to influence the ways Americans reflected on their receding past, their troubled present, and their uncertain future.

PART TWO

THE MODERN ERA

Distant Drums in an Age of Global Warfare

All Dust and Ashes

By 1920, fewer than 15 percent of all the soldiers who had lived through the Civil War were still alive.[1] Stewardship of Civil War memory was passing rapidly from the wartime generation to its direct descendants. The veterans' daughters and granddaughters, sons and grandsons possessed vivid personal memories of their war-scarred relatives and the commemorative activities of the late nineteenth century in which they themselves had often played an active role. Inez Smith of Detroit, Michigan, and Grace Hosmer of Farmington, Minnesota, were daughters of deceased Union soldiers. In 1939, they looked back with feeling to a time when the heroes of the republic were in their pomp.

Smith recalled that Memorial Day "or Decoration Day as we called it then" had always been "a memorable day in my life." She used to walk down Main Street, holding her father's hand, "his blue chest all decked with medals—the bright blue ribbon with white stars around his neck with his proudest possession, the Congressional Medal of Honor hanging from it (he won it for saving the colors at Chancellorsville), his cane beating a sharp, military, rat-tat-tat on the sidewalk." Now, Smith reflected sadly, "[t]he fine stalwart men" of the Grand Army were "[a]ll dust and ashes . . . and only memories in the heart of a little girl grown up."[2]

Hosmer remembered that her midwestern village possessed a strong GAR post: "They were all men in the prime of life, vigorous, jolly, and how they did enjoy their comradeship together." She had always looked forward eagerly to the post's annual campfire on New Year's Day at which the former soldiers' wives served dinner to local residents. After the meal, she and other children participated in a program that included recitations and army songs. On Memorial Day, she joined her fellow citizens on the customary pilgrimage to the cemetery, where there used to be just a few graves. Now, mused Hosmer poignantly, there were more than forty graves. "All through the years I have laid flowers on the graves of those men that I saw passing one by one, until now none is left."[3]

The familial determination of women like Inez Smith and Grace Hosmer to honor the veterans helps to explain the persistence of Civil War memories after the passing of the wartime generation. It does not, however, account for the widespread appeal of the interconnected reconciliatory and Lost Cause narratives or the sanctification of Abraham Lincoln in the first half of the twentieth century. There was strong demand for the Civil War in American popular culture between 1914 and 1945. Audiences flocked to watch movies such as *The Birth of a Nation* and *Gone with the Wind*, while authors like Stephen Vincent Benét, Douglas Southall Freeman, Margaret Mitchell, and Carl Sandburg found their lives transformed by formidable sales of their literary works. These artistic productions stimulated the interest of many white Americans who had scant connection to the Confederate or Union war efforts. Taking on artificial memories of redoubtable southerners like Ben Cameron and Scarlett O'Hara or national role models like Abraham Lincoln, consumers across the United States developed an attachment to a conflict they had never known.

Civil War memory's primary influence in the cultural realm after 1914 did not signify its wholesale disappearance from domestic politics. Once the Republicans had abandoned their support for black rights and Federal veterans were no longer a significant voting bloc in the United States, it ceased to influence competition between the major political parties. However, politicians would continue to draw on dominant Civil War narratives and symbols to attract and orientate voters in a confusing world. During the Great Depression, pro-business Republicans competed with New Deal–era liberals and radicals to make Lincoln a usable hero for hard-pressed working people. Southern Democrats were more likely to turn to Robert E. Lee as the man for the crisis. Their reliance on bitter memories of Reconstruction to fight the statist New Deal provided a particularly striking reminder of the Civil War's capacity to affect contemporary racial politics. The strength of Jim Crow made it difficult for black folk to gain a hearing in white America during these years. But Africans Americans were far from supine. They rightly sensed that the growing power of the federal government after 1933 and the United States's entry into World War II rendered their emancipationist counter-memory an increasingly formidable weapon in the race's ongoing struggle for equal treatment under the law.

Sanctifying Lincoln in the Progressive Era

The popularity of Abraham Lincoln in the early decades of the twentieth century furnished clear evidence of the Civil War's temporal reach. Lincoln, a sectional hero at best for the first thirty years after his death, now emerged as a genuinely national icon. This transformation demonstrated how remembrance of the Civil War in the United States changed over time in response to fundamental social shifts occasioned by the rapid advance of industrial capitalism. While not everyone loved the sixteenth president, his "memory" was firmly enshrined in the hearts of a majority of his people by the time his imposing marble monument was dedicated in Washington, DC, in 1922.

Abraham Lincoln's rise as the patron saint of American civil religion was partly a function of Progressive-era reformers' preoccupation with order and consensus. Although some northerners had indulged in hagiography after the president's assassination in April 1865, Lincoln remained a controversial and elusive figure during the political battles of the late nineteenth century. Many white southerners loathed him for launching a brutal war of conquest. Blacks like Frederick Douglass applauded his support for emancipation but understood his mixed motives. Although northerners, especially Republicans, were broadly admiring, they disagreed on the reasons for his alleged greatness and the personality traits responsible for his rise to fame. It was left to Progressive reformers and politicians to fashion a narrative that made Lincoln a president who could command the respect of a majority of ordinary Americans.

These Progressives included the muckraking journalist, Ida B. Tarbell. Her writings and public talks painted Lincoln as the quintessential democratic hero, a supremely human figure whose training on the American frontier had equipped him with character traits that enabled him to rise above the ordinary without abandoning his empathy for common folk. As well as self-reliance, industriousness, and self-improvement—essential virtues for anyone trying to thrive in the Social Darwinian flux of fin-de-siècle America—those traits also included the ability to tell right from wrong. Tarbell recounted a tale of Lincoln witnessing the "shocking cruelty" of the slave mart in antebellum New Orleans. "The whole thing was so revolting," she wrote, "that Lincoln moved away from the scene with a deep feeling of 'unconquerable hate.' " " 'Boys,' he told his companions, 'let's get away from this. If ever I get a chance to hit that thing, I'll hit it hard.' "[4]

For crusaders like Tarbell, an adeptly packaged memory of Lincoln, grounded in a plausible amount of fact, constituted a powerful weapon in the contemporary battle against corruption and concentrated corporate wealth. Jane Addams, a pioneer in Chicago's settlement house movement, also played an important role in connecting Lincoln to contemporary reform. She associated the late president closely with her beloved father. Just four years old when Lincoln died, Addams distinctly remembered "the day [in April 1865] when I found on our two white gate posts American flags companioned with black. I tumbled down on the harsh gravel walk in my eager rush into the house to inquire what they were 'there for.' To my amazement I found my father in tears, something that I had never seen before."[5]

One day her father drove her into Madison to visit Old Abe, a bald eagle that had served as mascot for the Eighth Wisconsin Infantry. The bird was guarded by a uniformed veteran who told children about the many battles it had survived. Addams recalled that while standing beneath the capitol dome she was transfixed by "the image of the eagle in the corridor below and Lincoln himself as an epitome of all that was great and good. I dimly caught the notion of the martyred President as the standard bearer to the conscience of his countrymen, as the eagle had been the ensign of courage to the soldiers of the Wisconsin regiment."[6] "Is it not Abraham Lincoln who has cleared the title to our democracy?" she closed the second chapter of her autobiography: "He made plain, once for all, that democratic government, associated as it is with all the mistakes and shortcomings of the common people, still remains the most valuable contribution America has made to the moral life of the world."[7]

Although the sectional heat had gone from northern politics by the early twentieth century, leading politicians grasped the utility of the burgeoning Lincoln myth. Nobody used it more effectively than Theodore Roosevelt—like Addams and Tarbell, another child of the Union cause. McKinley's successor as president of the United States waged a fierce battle to curb the power of the trusts. In doing so, the charismatic New Yorker presented himself in the Lincolnian garb of a pragmatic moderate with a strong moral core. The war against the corporations, he maintained, was akin to the late war against slavery. Observers were attracted by the historical connections. One 1904 cartoon depicted Lincoln holding the president by the hand and pointing him toward the public good.

When Roosevelt and his supporters abandoned the Republicans to found their own political organization, the Progressive Party, the Civil War analogies became even more frequent. Roosevelt compared his mainstream opponents to James Buchanan, the nation's ineffective executive during the secession crisis. Delegates attending the new third party's national convention in Chicago in August 1912 gustily sang the stirring Union anthem, the "Battle Hymn of the Republic," at every opportunity, thus injecting their reformist cause with millennial zeal as well as historical legitimacy. Roosevelt cherished the "Battle Hymn." But in keeping with the times, he sought southern approval for it by inducing the Georgia novelist Joel Chandler Harris to call publicly for its embrace below the Mason-Dixon Line.

Also consistent with contemporary practice was the Progressives' decision to hold a racially segregated convention. This surrender to Jim Crow did not prevent them from citing Lincoln's paean to democracy in his November 1863 Gettysburg Address. Reformers of all stripes valued the Address during this period. Tellingly, they directed their attention almost exclusively toward the late president's concluding utterance that "government of the people, by the people, for the people shall not perish from the earth." Lincoln's opening contention that the republic had been founded on the basis that all men were created equal—an insistence that had obvious implications for the treatment of African Americans—was conveniently sidelined.

Popular admiration for Abraham Lincoln increased apace during the second decade of the twentieth century. This was partly owing to the amount of attention lavished on the centenary of his birth in 1909. Urban reformers and public officials, particularly in the North, regarded the commemorative events of that year as an ideal way to inculcate European immigrants with core American values. Lincoln's early poverty, his tender-heartedness, and his now legendary capacity for self-improvement and hard work made him an immensely attractive figure to many of the country's new arrivals, who were taught in synagogues, churches, and public schools to love the sixteenth president. His unique service to the republic enabled northern municipal authorities to use him as a conduit for modern-day American nationalism. Among immigrant and native-born children alike reverence for Lincoln went hand in hand with the Pledge of Allegiance, the singing of the national anthem, and salutes to Old Glory. In Chicago, an elite-dominated planning committee prepared for the Lincoln centenary in close cooperation with ethnic community leaders. Commemorative events were staged in schools, halls, and places of worship across the teeming metropolis. Speakers routinely eulogized Lincoln for his humanity, resourcefulness, and patriotism, while young children recited famous speeches like the Gettysburg Address and the reconciliatory Second Inaugural.

Abraham Lincoln's importance as a symbol of consensus and nationhood was underlined by growing emphasis on his insistence that the defeated southerners should be treated charitably. In 1906, *Scribner's Magazine* published a short story titled "The Perfect Tribute" by Mary Raymond Shipman Andrews, a southern writer born in 1860 who had moved to upstate New York after marrying a Republican lawyer. The tale was awash with the kind of Blue-Gray sentimentalism that propelled popular enthusiasm for sectional reconciliation during this period. It recounts how a downcast President Lincoln left Gettysburg believing that his short address had failed to stir the passions because it elicited no applause from the audience. The next day, walking on the outskirts of Washington, he is nearly knocked down by a young lad from a good southern family who wants a lawyer to write a will for his brother, a Confederate officer grievously wounded at the Battle of Gettysburg. Unaware of Lincoln's identity, the boy escorts the president to a nearby prison hospital. The stricken Rebel takes an immediate shine to the stranger, and the two men shake hands warmly. Captain Blair tells the lawyer that he has been reading President Lincoln's recent address in the papers and that he has heard from a reliable source "that when it was ended it was as if the whole audience held its breath. . . . One might as well applaud the Lord's Prayer—it would have been sacrilege." Although the wounded Confederate admits the speech is "all wrong from my point of view," he rhapsodizes over its excellence. "The bitterness of the fight has faded for me," he says: "I only feel the love of country, the satisfaction of giving my life for it. The speech—that speech—has made it look higher and simpler—your side as well as ours. I would like to put my hand in Abraham Lincoln's—[.]"[8] Of course, the officer then dies, his hand gripping that of the kindly man by his bedside. Andrews's saccharine fiction was extremely popular. *Scribner's* published a school edition for the centenary. It sold more than half a million copies by the early 1940s.[9]

Lincoln's image as a conciliator was powerful and ubiquitous in the early twentieth century. Many stories and visual texts placed his clemency at their heart, including Jean L. G. Ferris's popular painting *Lincoln's Last Official Act*, which showed the president pardoning a Confederate prisoner after an appeal from the condemned soldier's wife. The country's new movie industry also caught hold of the symbolism. No early film director did more to popularize and humanize Abraham Lincoln than David Wark Griffith, whose pioneering epic, *The Birth of a Nation*, took America by storm in 1915.

Griffith was the son of a slaveholding Confederate officer. Born in 1875, he moved to California after making his reputation as an accomplished director of one-reel films for the Biograph Company in New York. Inspired by watching European-made historical epics like *Quo Vadis*, Griffith determined to make an American blockbuster. An admirer of Thomas Dixon's fiction, he purchased the rights to *The Clansman* and another novel, *The Leopard's Spots*, for $2,000 and 25 percent of the profits.[10] He then collaborated on the screenplay for a silent movie originally titled *The Clansman* and based predominantly on the novel and play of the same name. Shooting for the film began in the summer of 1914. The main characters, including the evil mulatto Silas Lynch and the would-be rapist Gus, were all played by white actors. African Americans were only employed on the set as extras.

Griffith's purpose in making *Birth of a Nation* (the film was retitled on Dixon's advice) was didactic as well as profit-oriented. He wanted to tell what he regarded as the true story of the Civil War and Reconstruction. Convinced that Americans in a new age of mass culture would learn about the past through visual media rather than reading history books, he set about creating a convincing narrative that would educate as well as thrill audiences willing to pay $2 each for the privilege. As well as citing "experts" on the period such as Albion Tourgée, James S. Pike, and Woodrow Wilson (carefully reworked quotations from authorities like these appeared as intertitles to guide viewers through the action), he tried to ensure that scenes, props, and costumes were as historically accurate as possible. To achieve this, Griffith used original images by Mathew Brady, one of the Civil War's leading photographers, to fashion a number of sets, and designers pored over *Century*'s *Battles and Leaders* volumes to ensure maximum authenticity for military props used in the war scenes.

Beginning on the eve of the Civil War with the visit of the northern Stonemans to their southern Cameron cousins, the film depicts the nation's bloody fissure as a family quarrel. The first part of the movie then proceeds with an account of the breakup of the Union before enacting battle scenes, all filmed in the Hollywood hills, from the war. Part two focuses on Reconstruction, charting the malign impact of black rule on the defeated former Confederates. The film climaxes with the dramatic ride of mounted white-robed Klansmen into the town of Piedmont and the reunion of North and South represented principally by the marriage of Confederate veteran Ben Cameron to the Radical Republican's daughter, Elsie Stoneman, played by fragile beauty Lillian Gish.

After its release in early 1915, the film was a major success with audiences nationally. The *Brooklyn Eagle* "guessed" that as many as ten million Americans saw it in just over two years.[11] There were several reasons for its enormous popularity, not least the technical proficiency of the action scenes and the virulence of racial prejudice in the United States at the time of its release. However, Griffith also won over audiences by successfully mingling Lost Cause themes and images with reconciliatory motifs. Like President Wilson, whose historical work he admired, the director was a proud southerner *and* American. His "true" history of the Civil War era favors his native region in most respects. *Birth of a Nation* depicts happy, contented slaves on the Camerons' antebellum plantation and faithful freedpeople who help rescue their former master from the Radicals' clutches. It also attributes secession to the South's justifiable determination to protect states' rights, elides the attack on Fort Sumter from the narrative of war causation, shows the courage of outnumbered Confederate troops in the siege of Petersburg, and vindicates fully the South's campaign against Reconstruction.

Northern moviegoers had been reared to interpret Reconstruction as a colossal mistake, and doubtless many had found the mythically cohesive Old

South of Thomas Nelson Page and other romantic novelists a compelling alternative to their own unforgiving and ethnically diverse industrial society. As southern blacks moved into their cities in growing numbers to find work, many northern whites probably identified closely with Griffith's obsession with racial purity and sectional reconciliation on a white-line basis. However, it is unlikely that so many northerners would have responded positively to Griffith's epic if it had been a purely Confederate film. As it was, they could applaud at the point when Grant accepts Lee's surrender at Appomattox, acknowledge the director's respect for white Union soldiers (two of whom defend Ben Cameron's father when he takes refuge from marauding blacks in their besieged cabin), and, crucially, appreciate his admiration for Abraham Lincoln.

Lincoln appears in *Birth of a Nation* as "the Great Heart." He not only pardons Ben Cameron after hearing an impassioned appeal from the Rebel officer's mother but also rejects the Radical Republicans' efforts to impose a harsh peace on the white South. His assassination, therefore, is a tragedy for the whole country—an event that obstructs the rapid coming together of the white American family after four years of sad bloodletting. Griffith's Lincoln is not the Great Emancipator. Censors actually prevented the director from incorporating evidence of the president's support for black colonization. Instead, he is Lincoln the merciful, the Great Heart who would have saved white southerners from so much pain had he lived.

Griffith's stirring melodrama was as controversial as it was popular. Audiences and critics loved it. African Americans and their white allies found its racism repellent. The NAACP, still in its infancy, launched a concerted campaign against the film, as did William Monroe Trotter, a crusading Boston newspaper editor who was the son of a black Civil War soldier. Several northern cities banned it on the grounds that it was racially inflammatory. Hostility emanated from some surviving white Union veterans who, made aware of the movie's pro-southern bias by the early publicity, regarded *Birth of a Nation* as a threat to their dual wartime achievement of nation-saving and the destruction of slavery. A number of Grand Army posts denounced the movie. "While it pretends to teach history," contended a group of angry veterans in Lawrence, Kansas, "it teaches a lie. It begets racial prejudice."[12] One Iowa post condemned its "exaltation and vindication of secession" and denigration of the North "for waging war for the suppression of the rebellion of 1861." It also laid into the movie on the grounds that it "insults and dishonors the colored race . . . a race who are just emerging by their own efforts from the slough of ignorant bondage unto the light of education and intelligence and manhood."[13]

Outraged comments like this from the dwindling band of Federal volunteers did not reflect the prevailing view among white Americans. The phenomenal popularity of *Birth of a Nation* consolidated reconciliatory and Lost Cause strains of remembrance in the United States. The terrific visual power of Griffith's sweeping epic not only confirmed white southerners' understanding of their recent past but also enabled large numbers of non-southern viewers to identify with the South's suffering and courage in the Civil War era. The broadly positive response to the film demonstrated the capacity of modern cinema to generate viewers' empathy with societies different from their own, different both in terms of time and geographical space. Cultural historian Alison Landsberg has described the process by which new technologies such as film, and later television, embed constructed memories into popular culture as "prosthetic." Memories of this kind, she contends, exist at the junction of personal and collective experience: "They are privately felt public memories that develop after an encounter with a mass cultural representation of the past, when new images and ideas come into contact with a person's own archive of experience."[14] As the twentieth century wore on, most Americans would "remember" the Civil War either as direct descendants of the wartime generation or, more often, as modern consumers moved to take on artificial memories by a range of devices, including romance, narrative, and visual spectacle.

Birth of a Nation was filmed against the backdrop of a global conflict from which the United States remained aloof until April 1917. Griffith made clear his reservations about the utility of war by revealing its damaging human consequences in the panoramic battle scenes and in intertitles such as "War claims its *bitter, useless sacrifice.*"[15] Yet he was no pacifist. When Germany's renewal of unrestricted submarine warfare finally induced President Wilson to intervene on the side of Great Britain and France, the celebrated director supported the decision along with a majority of Progressive reformers convinced that Prussian militarism represented a genuine threat to the more perfect world they hoped to build.

This dramatic turn of events ensured that another layer of wartime memories would be piled on those generated by earlier conflicts. Notwithstanding significant grassroots resistance to the draft that may have been influenced, in the South, by transmitted memories of opposition to Confederate conscription, more than four million Americans served in the country's armed forces during the struggle against the Central Powers. About one million of them saw active service, of whom just over fifty thousand died in combat on the Western Front.[16] White northerners and southerners fought alongside each other in the trenches, further cementing the process of sectional reconciliation. African Americans were organized into racially separate units, as they had been during the Civil War. But in this conflict, few all-black regiments were entrusted with combat operations.

Abraham Lincoln constituted an important reference point and mobilizing tool for Americans fighting the kaiser. As one might have expected of a Democrat whose father had been a slaveholding Confederate, Woodrow Wilson's admiration for his predecessor had its limits. He and Secretary of War Newton D. Baker were convinced that Lincoln had meddled excessively in military affairs, and they gave General John J. Pershing, the son of a Union sutler who commanded the American Expeditionary Force, "a free hand" in France despite his Republican proclivities.[17] Wilson's stalwart nationalism and liberal instincts, however, made him appreciative of Lincoln's usefulness as a rallying point for the war effort. In seeking to mobilize support for the war, his administration invoked the Gettysburg Address to buttress claims, previously made by interventionists like Theodore Roosevelt, that the Allies were fighting to promote democracy.

Allusions to Lincoln also helped ordinary Americans accept President Wilson's assumption of war powers and in some cases to make sense of the substantial US death toll in the Meuse-Argonne sector of the Western Front. Many commentators noted the parallels between the two presidents. Abraham Lincoln, pronounced Rabbi Stephen S. Wise, a prominent American Zionist, had fought to ensure that the Union would never again be endangered and that "the negro" could not be reenslaved. In the same way, Woodrow Wilson was "seeking to bring about a reordered world in which there shall be no tolerance of Kaiserism nor possibility of militarism."[18] At first, many African Americans embraced the idealism of the fight. "Free the World as Lincoln Freed Us!" intoned black religious leaders at a mass meeting in Chicago in February 1918.[19]

The sixteenth president's considerable symbolic power rested in the fact that the majority of Americans admired him as both a representative man and a national statesman. This duality was represented awkwardly in 1916 when a monument was raised at the site of his birthplace in central Kentucky. An association whose members included Ida Tarbell and the satirist Mark Twain purchased the Lincoln family farm near Hodgenville. It then became the site of a birthplace memorial composed of a reconstituted log cabin enclosed by a Doric temple. By this time, however, the government had initiated plans to build a more impressive tribute to Lincoln, one that emphasized his heroic persona. Some politicians supported the idea of building a "Lincoln Road" between Washington, DC, and Gettysburg. This American version of the Appian Way would include a highway for automobiles and horse-drawn vehicles, bordered by trees and decorated by flowers along the median strip. The plan appealed not only to the country's expanding automobile lobby and to developers but also to reformers keen on reverencing Lincoln while simultaneously harnessing the democratic potential of the internal combustion engine to a characteristically Progressive vision of utility and progress. In the end, this project lost out to a more orthodox form of commemoration: the construction of a new memorial on the National Mall in Washington.

The genesis of the Lincoln Memorial, the most imposing of all America's Civil War monuments, occurred in Congress at the beginning of the twentieth century. Republicans, restored to national power by the election of 1896, established an architectural commission to design a new ceremonial landscape at the heart of the federal capital. This body's 1902 report called for the building of a templelike structure at the west end of the Mall on an axis connecting it with equestrian monuments of leading Union generals at the base of Capitol Hill. In a nod to sectional reconciliation, the commission envisaged a memorial bridge across the Potomac that would link the temple to Arlington National Cemetery, the former Custis-Lee estate in Virginia that was now a repository of Confederate as well as Union dead. Progressives behind the "City Beautiful" movement who wanted to civilize a chaotic urban environment endorsed the project as a way of improving the nation's capital. Northern Republicans and statist reformers backed it because they wanted to dramatize the enhanced power of the federal government. By the end of the decade, Lincoln's memory had been embraced by a broader coalition that included social Progressives and liberal Democrats such as Woodrow Wilson. In 1911, Congress finally created a bipartisan commission charged with overseeing the construction of a lasting tribute to the sixteenth president.

Designed by Henry Bacon Jr. and incorporating Daniel Chester French's gigantic marble statue, the Lincoln Memorial was finally completed at a cost of nearly $3 million in 1922.[20] Some midwestern Progressives opposed the idea of a Greek temple being raised to the Man of the People, but the classical design served the purposes of governing elites wanting to place Abraham Lincoln at the center of a national memory of the Civil War embedded in the culture of sectional reconciliation. Those elites anticipated southern opposition to the monument by making its overriding focus the president's role in unifying the modern republic to which they paid allegiance and not his role as the Great Emancipator. Visitors stepping inside the building are immediately met with the words:

> IN THIS TEMPLE
> AS IN THE HEARTS OF THE PEOPLE
> FOR WHOM HE SAVED THE UNION
> THE MEMORY OF ABRAHAM LINCOLN
> IS ENSHRINED FOREVER

The inscription demonstrates the extent to which the emancipationist component of Unionist memory had been swept away by the tide of reconciliation. Written by the art critic Royal Cortissoz, it makes no reference to the abolition of slavery. This omission was deliberate, for Cortissoz had no intention of undermining the memorial's central message of restored American brotherhood.

"The memorial must make a common ground for the meeting of the north and the south," he told Henry Bacon. "By emphasizing his saving the union you appeal to both sections. By saying nothing about slavery you avoid the rubbing of old sores."[21]

President Warren G. Harding, a pragmatic Republican striving to maintain a balance between the conservative and reformist wings of his party, led the dedication ceremony on May 30, 1922. Harding accepted the monument on behalf of the nation before a crowd of about thirty-five thousand that included elderly Confederate and Union veterans as well as a number of African Americans who were directed to a segregated section of the audience. Virtually all the speakers, among them Chief Justice William H. Taft, stressed Lincoln's paramount contribution to national salvation.

Robert Russa Moton, Booker T. Washington's successor as head of Tuskegee Institute, was the day's only orator who threatened to sound a discordant note. In his original text, he insisted that the new memorial would be "but a hollow mockery, a symbol of hypocrisy" as long as "any group within the nation is denied an equal opportunity for life, liberty and the pursuit of happiness."[22] He also criticized the federal government for failing to end the violence against blacks, which had reached a new pitch after World War I. After scrutinizing his draft, the organizing committee deemed these sentiments unfit for an intersectional love feast and reined him in. The unfortunate Moton made no reference to the errors of the government in the speech that he actually delivered and must have nearly choked on his claim that the country, the South especially, had been making steady "progress" in race relations "in the spirit of the great Emancipator."[23]

The Propaganda of History

The two decades after 1918 witnessed publication of some of the most popular Civil War books ever written as well as the emergence of important new schools of academic thought on the conflict's origins. Most of these works were produced in a spirit of national unity or, in the South, leaned in the direction of the celebratory Lost Cause tradition as it was perpetuated by patriotic southern organizations like the United Daughters of the Confederacy (UDC). While a small number of African American historians fought valiantly against a tide of Civil War remembrance that relegated blacks to the margins of the country's past, the few passionate defenders of the once potent Union cause seemed like dinosaurs upon the landscape.

The best-selling Civil War–related books of the 1920s were unashamedly middlebrow works. Written for a wide readership, they depicted the war as an epic American conflict that had resolved the dilemmas posed by slavery and finally secured national unity. Carl Sandburg's two-volume *Abraham Lincoln:*

The Prairie Years (1926) drew mostly rave reviews for its exhaustive and sympathetic portrait of Lincoln's early life. Sandburg, a left-wing midwestern poet whose father had migrated to the United States from Sweden, gained fame by tapping into the enduring popular image of the martyred president as a plain man who had transcended his constricted background through the application of homespun American virtues. In Sandburg's telling, Lincoln's now-famous character traits—his industry, humanity, wit, humor, and melancholy—grew organically out of the testing prairie environment. "In the short and simple annals of the poor," reflected the poet, "it seems there are people who breathe with the earth and take into their lungs and blood some of the hard and dark strength of its mystery."[24] Lincoln, thought Sandburg, was certainly one of those people. Yet he was much more than that. He was also a skillful politician whose considerable ambition drove his career forward. Sandburg's Lincoln, like Ida Tarbell's, was a man with a deep moral core. But he was also a remarkably adept professional politician. "Without the cunning of a fox," wrote Sandburg, "without a wilderness sagacity, without natural instincts such as those guiding wild geese on thousand-mile flights, he would have gone down and under in stalking a presidential nomination."[25]

Stephen Vincent Benét's sprawling prose poem, *John Brown's Body* (1928), sold 130,000 copies in 1928–29 and was awarded a Pulitzer Prize for literature.[26] It attracted readers because it too infused its subject with epic grandeur. Benét, a Pennsylvanian whose grandfathers had fought on opposite sides of the Civil War, conceived his tribute to hard-won national progress as an American Illiad. The war he depicts is a national tragedy shared primarily by whites on both sides. The poet pays respect to both the Union and Rebel causes without mourning the death of the slaveholding Confederacy at the hands of the industrializing North. "John Brown is dead, he will not come again," rejoices Benét. "Out of [his] strong sinews the tall skyscrapers grow, / Out of his heart the chanting buildings rise, / Rivet and girder, motor and dynamo[.]"[27]

Benét's controlled descriptions of battlefields like Fredericksburg, where Union troops shelter behind a breastwork of two dead comrades ("One had lost his back, / Scooped out from waist to neck with a solid shot, / The other's legs were gone") drew power from readers' memories of more recent killing on the Western Front.[28] Some professional scholars, convinced that World War I had been caused by a series of fatal mistakes by European leaders, began to suggest that the origins of America's own season of bloodletting lay not in reasoned arguments about states' rights or the dangers of slavery expansion but in a combination of irrational fanaticism and political misjudgment.

Avery O. Craven and James G. Randall pioneered the "revisionist" school that reinterpreted the Civil War as "a needless war" brought about by radicals and incompetent leaders on both sides.[29] Craven, who lectured at the University of Chicago and was the son of antislavery Quakers, regarded war as an evil that must be avoided at all costs. Randall taught American history at the Urbana-Champaign campus of the University of Illinois. His influential 1940 essay, "The Blundering Generation," was charged with his memories of World War I in which so many "young men" had been "used as cannon fodder."[30] In contrast to the writers of the late nineteenth century, who had tended either to romanticize the intercommunal violence of the 1860s or suppress its horrors, Randall insisted that his readers must see the Civil War for what it really was: a "ghastly scourge . . . in which prison misery and preventable disease took heavier toll than bullets and in which desertion, corruption, and greed were as widespread as romantic gallantry."[31]

The revisionists' conviction that the Civil War had not been inevitable placed them in a very different interpretive camp from Charles Beard, one of the country's leading historians, who cowrote *The Rise of American Civilization* with his wife, Mary, in 1927. Both authors were middle-class Progressives with a long-standing interest in the operations of modern society. In their important two-volume study, the Beards described the Civil War as the result of an irrepressible class conflict between "the capitalists, laborers, and farmers of the North and West" and "the planting aristocracy of the South."[32] The result of Union victory, they contended, was the triumph of northern industrial capitalism, its forced imposition on the agrarian South, and an array of modern problems that the Beards deplored, just like the good reformers they were.

Tellingly, despite their differences over whether the Civil War could have been prevented, the revisionists and the Beards wrote histories that comported well with the existing racial order in the United States. Neither interpretive school showed much interest in African Americans: the revisionists criticized supposedly fanatical abolitionists, while the Beards insisted that material factors had played a more significant role in bringing about the Civil War than moral opposition toward slavery. Neither camp, moreover, posed any challenge to the prevailing hostile memory of Reconstruction that remained a major obstacle to social change in the South.

In fact, one of the best-selling history books of the 1920s was Claude G. Bowers's *The Tragic Era*, an overblown and entirely conventional account of the horrors of Reconstruction. Bowers, an Indiana Democrat, wrote the book to revive popular support for his party after its disappointing defeat in the 1928 presidential election. It was, he claimed immodestly, "the true story" of a period in which "the Republican Party solidified its power by bayonets and corruption" and "the most tremendous indictment of that party ever penned in history."[33] Although academic historians doubtless envied Bowers's sales, they failed to critique his racially biased interpretation of Reconstruction because most of them agreed with it. By this time, even white Republicans adhered to the received wisdom on postbellum military occupation, carpetbag government, and the empowerment of ignorant blacks.

During the interwar period, African American scholars posed the main challenge to these dominant paradigms. The educator Carter G. Woodson spearheaded efforts to sustain an emancipationist counter-memory of the Civil War and Reconstruction in the era of Jim Crow. Woodson had been born in Virginia after the war. His parents were former slaves. Working on farms and in coal mines, he saved enough money to enroll at Berea College, a former abolitionist oasis in eastern Kentucky. He excelled there and went on to undertake postgraduate work at the University of Chicago and Harvard, where he gained his doctorate in 1912. Three years later, he attended an exhibition in Chicago to mark fifty years of black progress since emancipation. Aware that such events masked the continuing subjugation of the race, fellow boarders at the city's segregated YMCA urged him to create an organization to promote African American history. He cofounded the Association for the Study of Negro Life and History (ASNLH) in 1915.

Although black families during this period regularly transmitted stories of slavery, the Civil War, and white violence during Reconstruction, powerful constraints on black schooling, especially in rural areas of the South, helped to ensure that most African American children had only the most rudimentary understanding of the race's past. While the outspoken black nationalist Marcus Garvey urged his followers to remember that they had a glorious history, the past he conjured was largely an Afrocentric one. Booker T. Washington, on the other hand, had counseled blacks to focus on the present and future; the past he acknowledged was heavily inflected with Lost Cause myths about black fidelity under slavery.

Aided by financial support from philanthropic whites, Carter Woodson's ASNLH soon emerged as a credible vehicle for the promotion of serious scholarship on black history in North America. Woodson patronized a group of talented young African American historians, including Lawrence D. Reddick, Alrutheus A. Taylor, and Charles H. Wesley, who published their work in the ASNLH's *Journal of Negro History*. During the 1920s, the periodical showcased academic essays challenging orthodox accounts of African Americans' allegedly passive and marginal role in the country's past. The ASNLH expanded its reach by inaugurating Negro History Week in 1926 and by introducing the *Negro History Bulletin* to assist hard-pressed black schoolteachers, excessively dependent on secondhand school textbooks that, in the impassioned opinion of the veteran reformer Charles Edward Russell, gave no hint that slavery was "a great and terrible moral evil" and often peddled Lost Cause accounts of the rise and fall of the Confederacy.[34]

One of the ASNLH's major goals was to develop a robust counternarrative to the prevailing Dunningite interpretation of Reconstruction. Alrutheus Taylor made a particularly important contribution with two articles on Reconstruction in South Carolina. While acknowledging that the state's postwar Republican regime had engaged in its fair share of corrupt activities, Taylor convincingly detailed the discredited state government's accomplishments in policy areas such as education and land reform. Unsurprisingly, Claude Bowers overlooked these findings when he wrote *The Tragic Era*, a book denounced by blacks as a "lynching in prose."[35] However, they provided a useful resource for the formidable black intellectual W.E.B. Du Bois when he embarked on his own pathbreaking history of Reconstruction as a response to Bowers's disturbingly popular work.

The first African American to receive a doctorate from Harvard University and a founding member of the NAACP, Du Bois possessed a pellucid understanding of the connection between an emancipationist memory of the Civil War and the ongoing fight for civil rights. In 1909, he had written a biography of John Brown, lauding the fiery abolitionist's willingness to use force to end slavery. The book was a commercial failure in part because one of the NAACP's white founders, Henry Villard, slammed it in two anonymous reviews. (The paternalistic businessman was so worried about Du Bois's interpretation that he wrote his own study of Brown, praising the antislavery radical for his moral commitment but criticizing him for resorting to violence.) Four years later, Du Bois, now editor of the NAACP's monthly magazine, the *Crisis*, devised a historical pageant that was performed at the federally funded National Emancipation Exposition held in New York City in October 1913. Called *The Star of Ethiopia*, Du Bois's spectacular production was staged by more than 350 black schoolchildren, teachers, actors, and dancers, and watched by more than 14,000 people during its short run.[36] Its aim was to strengthen black identity by dramatizing the race's active role in history. Among the cast was a black Civil War veteran who proclaimed, "I represented Ethiopia in the Civil War. I am a Union soldier. I fought for Old Glory. Who says that Ethiopia has done nothing for civilization? When civilization was about to fail in America, Ethiopia saved it."[37]

The migration of more than one and a half million southern blacks to the increasingly urban, industrial North between 1910 and 1930 brought about limited improvements in the living conditions experienced by African Americans. The move northward generally translated into better though still inferior schooling, greater opportunities for collective activism, and a measure of political influence. Unlike their southern peers, northern blacks were not prevented from voting. Their concerted opposition played a key role in Congress's decision in 1923 to shelve a controversial UDC proposal to build a national monument to the black mammy in Washington. However, most northern blacks were still subjected to the indignities of de facto segregation—corralled, as so many of them were, in the filthy, rat-infested slums of Harlem, Detroit, and Chicago's South Side. Du Bois, therefore, redoubled his search for a usable past.

His *Black Reconstruction in America* (1935) contributed powerfully to that quest. Benefiting from his own earlier research into the subject as well as the work of black scholars like Alrutheus Taylor and progressive southern white historians Francis B. Simpkins and Robert H. Woody, Du Bois fashioned an angry response to the conventional tale of Reconstruction hawked so profitably by Claude Bowers. As well as painting the carpetbag regimes in a positive light, he contended that black workers had contributed decisively to the destruction of the Confederacy by refusing to work for their masters during the Civil War and by fighting for the Union. Du Bois also wrote a scathing chapter titled "The Propaganda of History" in which he indicted the American historical profession for making myths instead of puncturing them.[38] Historians, he wrote, had wittingly participated in "one of the most stupendous efforts the world ever saw to discredit human beings."[39] By divorcing slavery from morality and Reconstruction from the facts, he contended, academics like the Beards and amateurs like Bowers had obscured "the truth" of history. Surely, thought Du Bois, "[n]o serious and unbiased student" could "be deceived by the fairy tale of a beautiful Southern slave civilization."[40] Perhaps so. But one year later, white Americans were lining up to buy a compelling new novel packed with faithful slaves, beautiful belles, and marauding Yankees. While Du Bois's book struck a chord with a handful of progressive white historians, public remembrance of the Civil War in the United States was about to be shaped decisively by a feisty southern writer named Margaret Mitchell.

Gone with the Wind

Margaret Mitchell's 1936 Pulitzer Prize–winning novel, *Gone with the Wind*, and the phenomenally successful movie version that followed three years later generated unprecedented popular interest in the American Civil War. "Peggy" Mitchell was steeped in the mythology of slavery, the Confederacy, and Reconstruction. However, her fictional recreation of a vanished society succeeded beyond her wildest dreams because it combined traditional romance with hard-edged insights into the dilemmas confronting women in contemporary society. Dismissed by modernist critics as just another plantation fable, *Gone with the Wind* was less a nostalgic tribute to the Lost Cause than a highly personal account of the struggle to survive, indeed to thrive, in a society that remade itself after suffering devastating defeat at the hands of the Yankees.

Mitchell's novel bore the imprint of her upbringing in Henry Grady's Atlanta, a city proud of its phoenixlike resurrection to become the primary hub of the bustling New South. Born in November 1900 to parents who owned a Victorian mansion spared by Sherman's army in 1864, Mitchell was reared on family stories of the Civil War and its aftermath, all of them brimming with admiration for the endurance of the embattled Confederates and contempt for the vandal Yankees who had destroyed much of the city and inflicted immeasurable hardships on southern POWs. These tales enabled her to take on a measure of her ancestors' pain—that of her paternal grandfather, for example, who was seriously wounded at the Battle of Antietam.

Physical evidence of the war furnished tangible reminders of Confederate suffering. One day when Mitchell was six years old, her mother, May Belle, a strong-minded supporter of women's suffrage, drove her to nearby Jonesboro to see the ruins of plantation houses as well as some estate homes that were still standing. May Belle used these memory-laden traces of the past to teach her daughter an important contemporary lesson. "[S]he talked," recalled Mitchell thirty years later, "about the world those people had lived in, such a secure world, and how it had exploded beneath them. And she told me that my own world was going to explode under me, some day, and God help me if I didn't have some weapon to meet the new world. She was talking about the necessity of having an education, both classical and practical."[41]

Although Mitchell was not an intellectual, she received a sound education at Westminster Seminary in Atlanta and Smith College in Northampton, Massachusetts. She consumed the racist fiction of Thomas Dixon and even staged a production of one of his Ku Klux Klan novels, *The Traitor*. She endured more than her fair share of personal tragedy too. Her Yankee fiancé died from wounds incurred on the Western Front. Her mother, May Belle, was struck down by the virulent postwar influenza epidemic. And her first husband, a raffish Atlanta bootlegger, proved to be physically abusive. To get by financially she secured a job as a reporter for a local newspaper and began writing fiction. A thoroughly modern woman who liked to drink, smoke, dance, and flirt, Mitchell also yearned for domestic stability. In 1925, she married her second husband John Marsh, a quiet man who encouraged her to embark on a writing career.

The South at this time was still a region on the cusp of modernity. Cities like Atlanta, Houston, and Birmingham benefited from the decade's feverish industrial and commercial growth, but the countryside, populated by sharecroppers and tenant farmers overly dependent on fluctuating world demand for cash crops like cotton, remained impoverished, and the region's extractive industries benefited mainly the wealthy few.

Sectional rivalry in the United States intensified after World War I, partly because of the widening economic gap between North and South. One of its main outlets was the increasingly popular sport of college football, a Yankee invention whose origins lay in the rise of a mechanistic industrial society. White southerners, who regularly sang "Dixie" at games and compared their football heroes to Confederate generals, swelled with pride when the University of Alabama defeated the University of Washington in the 1926 Rose Bowl—the first significant national triumph registered by a team from the old Confederacy. One Atlanta newspaper described the Crimson Tide's dramatic 20-19 win as "the greatest victory for the South since the first battle of Bull Run," without noting that Alabama's achievement belonged more to the New South than the Old.[42] In Nashville, a group of conservative young poets, self-styled "Fugitives" who would become better known as the "Agrarians," were angered by northern condescension toward the South as well as the encroachment of industrial civilization on their storied region. They embraced what one of them, Donald Davidson, called "the cold Civil War," finding inspiration in what they imagined to be the ordered, stable society of the Old South and the noble virtues of Confederate heroes like Stonewall Jackson.[43]

Many southern whites shared the Fugitives' concerns about modernity. However, as automobile traffic from the northeast began to increase after 1918, some were quick to recognize the marketing opportunities presented. Nowhere during the interwar period did Old and New South values combine more publicly than in Charleston, South Carolina, a prime stopping-off point for Yankee snowbirds motoring to and from the Florida coast. The men and women behind the "Charleston Renaissance" readily embraced historical preservation as a means of selling southern culture to tourists eager to visit the city where the Civil War had begun and where the antebellum South's putatively glorious "civilization" had been most securely rooted. By the late 1920s, the city government had installed several authentic cannon on the Battery overlooking the harbor, and a private tour company was taking boatloads of curious visitors out to Fort Sumter. City boosters welcomed not only the building of new downtown hotels like the Francis Marion to accommodate the influx but also efforts to historicize Charleston's physical spaces with monuments to past glories. The Lost Cause flourished amid these changes. In October 1932, North Carolina journalist Gerald W. Johnson addressed a large crowd on the Battery at the unveiling of a new memorial to the city's Confederate defenders. Those men, he said, had fought not for slavery, but "their right to live their lives as they chose to live them."[44]

Proud of her section yet deeply ambivalent about the onset of modernity and women's place within it, Margaret Mitchell hammered away at her Civil

War novel. Although she had completed a draft by the end of the decade, the manuscript remained undiscovered until 1935, when it was picked up by an editor from Macmillan scouting the South for new literary talent. It was a publishing sensation. The book flew off the shelves despite its challenging retail price of $3; by the end of its first month in print, it had sold more than a million copies.[45]

Like *Birth of a Nation, Gone with the Wind* was a defiantly southern creation that transcended its sectional origins. Mitchell later claimed that she had not written "in any spirit of bitterness." Many of her fans, she said, wrote to her saying that it "should help to allay sectional feeling by creating a better understanding of what the South endured in the days of the Civil war and Reconstruction."[46] Whatever the truth of these assertions, strident Lost Cause themes permeated the novel. Mitchell's antebellum South is populated by dashing cavaliers like Ashley Wilkes and loyal slaves like Mammy and Sam; her Confederates fight bravely in a doomed war against destructive Yankees; and her take on Reconstruction is indistinguishable from that of Claude Bowers. What saved Mitchell's book from obscurity and ensured a fan base far beyond Dixie was her unsentimental realization, impressed on her by May Belle during her childhood visit to Jonesboro, that civil war had destroyed the Old South depicted so lovingly by Thomas Nelson Page and that southerners, specifically southern white women, had overcome that long-remembered catastrophe through present-oriented struggle.

Female readers in the midst of America's deepest economic depression were gripped by the book's romantic plot centered on relations between the central character, the strong-willed and scheming Scarlett O'Hara, and her two principal beaux, Ashley Wilkes and Rhett Butler. Crucially, however, they also identified, first, with Scarlett's immense resourcefulness at a time of acute personal and societal crisis and, second, with her deep ambivalence, mirroring that of the author, about patriarchal control. The fact that the heroine's romantic dilemma remained unresolved at the close merely intensified women readers' commitment to the book. But while Mitchell provided no answer to the question of whether Scarlett could ever find happiness with Rhett, the husband who rapes her in her own bed, the trajectory of her own life revealed her conservative conviction that women's destiny was to marry men. This belief helps to explain her own decision to make Melanie Wilkes the most sympathetic character in the book. Only with Melanie's death in childbirth does Scarlett belatedly glimpse the importance of the putative Old South character traits that she herself lacks: generosity of spirit, devotion to duty, and, of course, an unswerving commitment to her husband.

Following the immediate success of her richly textured Civil War tale, Margaret Mitchell sold the film rights to the Hollywood producer David O.

Selznick, son of a Jewish immigrant from Russia, who had made a fortune in California's early movie industry. Securing a distribution deal with Metro Goldwyn Mayer to ensure the casting of MGM-owned star Clark Gable as Rhett Butler, Selznick oversaw production at a prohibitive cost of more than $4 million. The production process was a troubled one. George Cukor, the original director, was fired before the movie was finished, and a battery of writers, among them F. Scott Fitzgerald, had to be employed to knock the screenplay into shape. Selznick, however, cleverly piqued audience interest in the movie ahead of production by staging a well-publicized contest for the part of Scarlett, which eventually went to the accomplished young English actor Vivien Leigh. He also contracted a raft of skilled professionals, including costume designer Walter Plunkett and composer Max Steiner to ensure that *Gone with the Wind*, filmed in Technicolor, was the most visually and aurally stunning movie of its era. Civil War historian and collector Wilbur Kurtz and Margaret Mitchell's friend Susan Myrick worked to ensure both historical authenticity and the closest possible fit with the popular novel.

In December 1939, Selznick flew into Atlanta from Los Angeles with leading cast members to attend the glittering world premiere at the Loew's Grand Theatre. Diminutive Margaret Mitchell was there in person as were a smattering of elderly Confederate veterans. The event attracted extensive newsreel and press coverage, thereby helping to generate huge audiences across the country over the course of the following months. Missing from the cast's expedition to Atlanta were the movie's leading African American actors, including Hattie McDaniel (Mammy), Butterfly McQueen (Prissy), and Oscar Polk (Pork). Selznick had capitulated to pressure from the city's mayor and left them behind in California. Despite his cowardice on this issue, he had taken steps to erase some of the more racist features of the novel. Under pressure from the black press, from the NAACP, from Jewish organizations, and from his own black actors, Selznick excised Mitchell's use of the epithet "nigger," which had been retained in Sidney Howard's original screenplay; her explicit championing of the Klan; and her potentially inflammatory depiction of a freedman's assault on Scarlett, which was dangerously reminiscent of Gus's attempted rape of Ben Cameron's young sister Flora in *The Birth of a Nation*.

The result was certainly not a racially liberal movie. Ben Hecht's opening intertitle went even further than Mitchell's novel in validating the slave South as a "pretty world" where "[g]allantry took its last bow."[47] Yet Selznick's interventions did help to bring the content broadly into line with the racial climate of the 1930s, which was somewhat more enlightened than that of the Progressive era. They may also have contributed to the movie's survival long after its natural shelf life was over.

The tremendous commercial success of *Gone with the Wind*, the novel and the movie, confirmed white Americans' receptivity to many elements of the Lost Cause narrative. The UDC, of course, loved everything about it. One leading Daughter who attended the Atlanta premiere commended the film "for its beauty, its historical accuracy and perfection of detail."[48] But large numbers of non-southerners also embraced the product, happy to identify with the mythic South and Scarlett's negotiation of its greatest crisis. Although African American criticism was more organized than it had been at the time of *Birth of a Nation*, only lone voices criticized the portrayal of the invading Union troops, one of whom, a menacing deserter, is shot dead by Scarlett when she returns home to Tara after the fall of Atlanta. The female Auxiliary to Sons of Union Veterans of the Civil War protested angrily against what it called "this defamatory film," urging movie censors to ban it on the grounds that its "injurious presentation of the Union soldiers as bestial" was "an affront to all who wear our Country's uniform and would create disrespect for our Nation and its defenders and encourage those who advocate the righteousness of National destruction."[49] The storm of praise for Selznick's film drowned out these lingering demonstrations of Unionist memory. Yet what modern devotees of the Old South could not know was that the Lost Cause had reached the peak of its national appeal. One measure of its vulnerability was the shrillness of its tones in the changing political landscape of Franklin D. Roosevelt's America.

Inventing Tradition in New Deal America

In June 1932, Richmond, Virginia, festooned with Confederate battle flags for the occasion, hosted one of the last great reunions of Confederate soldiers. About 1,500 attended, accompanied by a handful of elderly former slaves, including "Uncle" Steve Eberhardt, who cannily styled himself "the biggest chicken-thief in the Confederacy."[50] The old Rebels swapped tales of the war with one another and recorded some of their recollections for NBC radio. They also rode in cars in a grand parade through town. One group drew gales of laughter by holding up a sign calling for repeal of the Eighteenth Amendment, which prohibited sales of alcohol. The veterans blew kisses at adoring women and beamed at children along the way. Douglas Southall Freeman, a local newspaper editor who would soon win international renown as the biographer of Robert E. Lee, captured the pathos underlying the city's joyous celebration of heroic Confederate manhood. "It is the rear guard, engaged with death, that passes now," he wrote: "The deeds that shook a continent belong to history. Farewell; sound taps! And then a generation new must face its battles in its turn, forever heartened by that heritage."[51]

The reunion occurred at the beginning of one of the most portentous presidential campaigns in American history—one that presaged fundamental change to the South and the wider nation. Driving that change was the shuddering collapse of economic activity after the Great Crash, which, many Americans contended, demanded greater federal intervention in society. In November 1932, Franklin D. Roosevelt, the Democratic governor of New York, won a convincing election victory with the backing of the Solid South. In his acceptance speech at the party's national convention, Roosevelt had promised a "new deal" for the American people. In its first hundred days, his administration cranked out relief and recovery programs that would commence the building of "the New Deal order" by a liberalized Democratic Party coalition committed to governmental solutions to the country's enormous social and economic problems.[52]

Southern states benefited greatly from federal spending on agricultural subsidies, major capital projects like the building of the Tennessee River dams, and work relief programs of all kinds. Some of these initiatives altered the appearance of Civil War battlefields and monuments, formal ownership of which was transferred from the War Department to the Department of the Interior in 1933. Day-to-day stewardship of these historic places passed to the National Park Service, which employed men recruited by New Deal agencies like the Civilian Conservation Corps to prepare the properties for a new era of history tourism. Federal workers remade the battlefield landscapes at places like Vicksburg and Gettysburg by constructing roads and interpretive museums and by repairing walls and dilapidated buildings. Abetted by the South's nascent tourist infrastructure, Americans began visiting the battlefields in increasing numbers, their interest in the Civil War stimulated by the drama of *Gone with the Wind*, the homespun lyricism of Sandburg and Benét, and accessible histories like Freeman's best-selling life of Lee that Richmond novelist Ellen Glasgow pronounced the general's "complete and final biography."[53]

Notwithstanding its positive impact on jobs and infrastructural development, the New Deal's enhancement of Washington's powers resulted in growing divisions among the conservative white Democrats who had dominated the region's politics since the late nineteenth century. Most of the federal funds pouring into the region were safely channeled through existing elites at the state and county levels, but many white-supremacist politicians worried that liberal New Deal officials were trying to undermine Jim Crow. Their fears were increased not only by the rising influence of African Americans inside the national Democratic Party (blacks who could vote began to transfer their historic allegiance from the Republicans to the Democrats in the 1934 midterm elections) but also by the attempts of left-wing groups like the Communist

Party of the United States, the Alabama Sharecroppers Union, and the Congress of Industrial Organizations to organize low-paid southern farm and industrial workers on an interracial basis. The result was a new wave of state-supported violence directed against neo-abolitionist "outside agitators" accused of meddling with the South's racially segregated society.

The political ferment of the era induced radicals, moderates, and conservatives to mobilize supporters on the basis of a usable past located in the Civil War era. Communist James S. Allen seized on the writings of Alrutheus Taylor and other scholars to argue that black and white workers in the South should regard the biracial politics of Reconstruction as a model for how to organize in the present. Folk memories of black activism during the late 1860s were revived by civil rights and labor organizers across the region. In Greenville, South Carolina, the NAACP president, James A. Briar, whose father had been an active Republican after the Civil War, inaugurated a voting rights campaign ahead of the 1939 municipal election. The campaign elicited a violent response from local Klansmen, who had their own remembrance of Reconstruction. The state's Grand Dragon issued a press release defending attacks on African Americans and black businesses in the upcountry on the grounds "that almost the same influences which caused the trouble seventy years ago again are at work in our country," and that only the Klan could save South Carolina from "negro rule and northern political domination" as it had done "during Reconstruction days."[54]

The Lost Cause narrative of Reconstruction as a nightmare period for southern whites was so deeply rooted that it would help sustain white resistance to the modern civil rights movement. During the 1930s, powerful conservative politicians relied heavily on this culturally embedded historical memory to defy their liberal opponents. In Congress, they denounced attempts by the NAACP and its allies to secure passage of a federal anti-lynching act by dusting off arguments that Ben Tillman and others had used to disfranchise African Americans. Senator Hugo Black of Alabama described the hated Costigan-Wagner Bill as "a lineal descendant" of the disreputable legislation denounced by his fellow Democrat Claude Bowers in *The Tragic Era*.[55] Senator Ellison D. "Cotton Ed" Smith of South Carolina cited James S. Pike's hoary 1874 exposé, *The Prostrate State*, to help defeat another anti-lynching bill. Ignorant blacks, he said, had been empowered during Reconstruction with disastrous results: "This element, composed of those who but a few short years previously had been imported from the jungles of Africa, with human passion but with undeveloped human reason, was turned loose in a defenseless community."[56] When Smith defeated New Dealer Olin D. Johnston for reelection, this modern-day Tillmanite marked his victory, apparently without irony, at the patrician Wade Hampton monument in Columbia. Proudly sporting a red shirt, he told his supporters that they were the state's bulwark against "the mongrel breed who would take us back to the horrid days of reconstruction." "We conquered in '76," said Smith, "and we conquered in '38."[57]

Southern senators defeated every attempt to pass a federal anti-lynching law during the New Deal. President Roosevelt did not want to alienate white southerners—one of his party's main constituencies—and therefore failed to intervene. However, his patience with conservatives' efforts to block government legislation in other policy areas soon ran out. In early 1937, he embarked on a controversial scheme to pack the US Supreme Court with his own nominees. The following year, he launched what he hoped would be a purge of his opponents within the Democratic Party with a major speech in Barnesville, Georgia. After declaring the South to be the country's chief economic problem, he attacked Georgia's reactionary senator, Walter George, for contributing to this unpalatable state of affairs.

The president's interference ahead of the midterm elections stoked southern sectionalism. Ever since Roosevelt's speech, remarked Margaret Mitchell, "I have heard so many yells of 'states' rights' and 'Northern oppression' and 'sinister centralization of power' and so many bands playing 'Dixie' that I have wondered whether this was 1938 or 1861."[58] Senator George, knowing that fears of outside intervention coursed through the blood of his white constituents, did nothing to discourage these Confederate yells. "Are the people of this state or any other state entitled to choose their own servants?" he asked in a speech at Waycross four days after Roosevelt's appearance in Barnesville. "This is not the first time this has been fought out in Georgia. We settled it once before when honesty walked down through the shadow of bayonets held in carpetbag hands and cast an honest vote for redemption in this state."[59]

Robert E. Lee's biographer Douglas Southall Freeman was a racial paternalist who publicly supported the prosecution of lynchers. However, like most moderate southern Democrats, he feared what he described as "those centralizing influences" that now threatened the United States "with ruin."[60] As well as using his editorial position at the Richmond *Times-Dispatch* to inform Virginians of New Deal excesses, he tried to use his knowledge of "the southern tradition" to alert politicians in Washington to "their duty to support the constitutional division of power between the states and the federal government."[61] Southern senators like Harry S. Byrd of Virginia and Josiah Bailey of North Carolina greatly admired his four-volume study of Lee—a man he saw as the ultimate opponent of centralized tyranny directed against the states. (Bailey thought Freeman's name "would be remembered by posterity in generations to come.")[62] But for Freeman, Lee's importance at this moment in American history lay not only in his model resistance to federal power. What Lee represented above all else, he thought, was character—the kind of character necessary for ordinary Americans to survive the nightmare of the economic depression.

In January 1936, Douglas Freeman delivered an invited address on the anniversary of Lee's birth to the Virginia legislature in Richmond. While the editor described Lee as "our Southern Arthur," he rejoiced that his subject had become a truly national figure. Freeman, like Lee, to whose fame he was yoked, was at the height of his celebrity: the talk was broadcast live by forty-five radio stations across America. For the centerpiece of his speech, he chose the dramatic moment when the great commander steadied his troops at Sayler's Creek on the Confederates' final retreat to Appomattox. Freeman told how Lee "took a battle flag, placed it staff against his stirrup, held it in his left hand and waited—silently waited. In a few minutes, the wounded and the weary, the panting and the panic-stricken had gathered about him, and a line of resistance quickly was formed." Continued Freeman, "The American people, some of them broken, some of them bewildered," were looking to the example provided by practical, clear-sighted men like General Lee to save them from despair at a time when many politicians had fallen prey to "beguiling theories." America would "rally," he concluded optimistically. "The clouds that encompass us are those of dawn, not those of twilight. No surrender lies ahead of the Army that comes up from the Valley. It will go on, and find new leaders and achieve new victories."[63]

Thus, in the depths of the greatest crisis faced by the United States since the Civil War, a renowned southern writer who was himself the son of a Confederate officer proffered the most effective domestic enemy in the history of the republic as an inspiration for the sires of Grant and Sherman as well as those of Davis and Jackson. His oration, devoid of irony, testified to the triumph of sectional reconciliation and the broad appeal of many core elements of the Lost Cause in the 1930s.

If Robert E. Lee seemed to be a plausible role model for ordinary Americans during the Great Depression, Abraham Lincoln proved the more compelling hero for the times. Although Republicans like Herbert Hoover insisted that the industrious Railsplitter possessed all the qualities needed by individuals to survive the slump, liberals and left-wing radicals fashioned an updated version of the Progressive-era Lincoln to bolster their claims that only government action could deliver Americans from grinding poverty. At a moment when some white workers regarded their debased status as a form of slavery, Lincoln found a new "cultural resonance" as the friend of laboring people.[64] The author Carl Sandburg, whose books had cemented Lincoln's reputation as a folk hero, took the lead in establishing his subject's contemporary relevance. In 1934, he compared the Roosevelt administration's attempts to aid industrial workers through its National Recovery legislation with the achievement of abolition in the 1860s. Creative artists, some of them subsidized by New Deal relief programs, disseminated a broad emancipationist memory of the sixteenth president that was far removed from his consensual image of the 1920s. The Mexican communist Diego Rivera painted one of his insurgent murals in New York City. It showed Lincoln brandishing a copy of the Emancipation Proclamation in the company of John Brown and Union soldiers of both races. Robert Sherwood's popular Broadway play, *Abe Lincoln in Illinois* (1938), featured its eponymous subject proclaiming, "Thank God we live under a system by which men have the right to strike."[65] When scores of left-wing Americans opted to fight fascism in the Spanish Civil War, it was no surprise that they enlisted under the banner of "the Abraham Lincoln Brigade."

The politician who benefited most from these progressive reworkings of the Lincoln image was Franklin Roosevelt. The president lacked the kind of autobiographical memory of the Civil War era possessed by his older cousin, Teddy. Nevertheless, he had a shrewd understanding of the way that historical memories of the sectional conflict could be used to advance his domestic and foreign agenda. In July 1938, he spoke at the seventy-fifth anniversary of the Battle of Gettysburg, the last significant gathering of the Blue and the Gray. About 1,900 Civil War veterans were present, including nearly 60 African Americans. Most of the old soldiers were now in their nineties. Along with a vast throng numbering at least a quarter of a million people, they gathered on Oak Hill to see FDR dedicate the new Eternal Light Peace Memorial, conceived by veterans on both sides and financed by donations from northern and southern states.

Although Roosevelt followed Woodrow Wilson's lead by stating that America honored all the veterans, "not asking under which flag they fought then—thankful that they stand together under one flag now," he went even further than his predecessor had gone in hallowing the name of the original Republican hero, Abraham Lincoln.[66] FDR had long been impressed with the power of Lincoln's dual image as statesman and man of the people. In 1929, he told his co-partisan Claude Bowers that it was "time for us Democrats to claim Lincoln as one of our own."[67] Aware that he could promote much-needed change and legitimize his personal authority by drawing parallels between his activist presidency and that of Lincoln, he defended his controversial court-packing scheme by reminding Americans that the savior of the Union had also increased the number of judges on the nation's highest tribunal.[68] At Gettysburg he implicitly attacked his conservative critics by lauding his predecessor's conviction "that when a challenge to constituted government is thrown down, the people must in self-defense take it up" and by insisting that the endless "battle" for democracy had to be fought anew by every generation of Americans.[69] The "fundamental" domestic struggle to "save for our common country opportunity and security for citizens in a free society," he suggested optimistically, was nearly won.[70] Venturing the hope that the United States could learn from Lincoln's Second Inaugural appeal for unity after fracture, Roosevelt knew that the next battle was looming in Europe. So did his listeners, some of whom were doubtless reassured by the presence of troops and military hardware at Gettysburg. The qualities displayed by America's Civil War heroes, Lincoln preeminently, were about to be tested in a global conflict of unprecedented ferocity.

The Greatest Democracy of the Universe

The Civil War provided a usable past for backers of US intervention in the European war that began in September 1939. The film director John Ford, a New Deal supporter, used the arresting image of a violent thunderstorm over the Lincoln Memorial to alert viewers of his 1939 movie *Young Mr Lincoln* to the coming test. President Roosevelt meanwhile compared domestic opponents of US aid for Great Britain to Civil War–era Copperheads, and Carl Sandburg, an interventionist whose four-volume history of Lincoln's active presidency was published to great acclaim in 1939, insisted three months after France and the Low Countries fell to the Nazis that if he was "hysterical" in the words of isolationists like Charles Lindbergh, then so too were Lincoln's Gettysburg Address and Second Inaugural.[71]

The constructed memories of the American Civil War, tapped and molded as they had been by creative artists in the 1920s and 1930s, as well as the ubiquitous parallels between Roosevelt and Lincoln, provided federal officials with an essential cultural resource in the United States's brutal wars against Germany and Japan. These memories functioned in much the same way as they had during World War I and the recent economic collapse. Political leaders and government officials made allusions to well-known Civil War figures and events to explain and legitimize their policies to ordinary people and thereby to inspire popular support for them.

The Gettysburg Address, Lincoln's inducement to his fellow northerners to keep fighting in the midst of mounting slaughter, played a significant role in the US government's efforts to remind Americans that they were fighting for the cause of popular democracy. Shortly after the surprise Japanese attacks on Pearl Harbor finally dragged the United States into the war, Washington's main propaganda arm, the Office of War Information (OWI), issued a striking visual call to arms in the form of a poster. Depicting a tattered Stars and Stripes billowing out against a backdrop of black smoke emanating from the Japanese assault, the poster urged Americans not to forget December 7 and repeated Lincoln's famous utterance that "we here highly resolve that these dead shall not have died in vain."[72]

Foreigners also turned to Civil War memory for succor at this time. British Prime Minister Winston Churchill, whose mother was an American heiress, sought a usable transatlantic past as part of his broader effort to secure US assistance in his country's most desperate hour of need. An enthusiastic historian who had always found war exciting, Churchill empathized with the Lost Cause. In 1929, Douglas Southall Freeman had shown the maverick British politician around the Richmond battlefields while he was staying with Senator Harry Byrd. Churchill subsequently made his own singular contribution to a counterfactual history of the Civil War. In an article for *Scribner's*, he imagined Jeb Stuart's cavalry turning the tide at Gettysburg. The decisive Confederate victory results in Robert E. Lee's triumphal entry into Washington and the Rebel commander's announcement of emancipation for the slaves. These events spark British intervention on the side of the South, a move that forces Lincoln to agree to southern independence. There is no Reconstruction. "Let us only think what would have happened," Churchill wrote ironically, "supposing the liberation of the slaves had been followed by some idiotic assertion of racial equality, and even by attempts to graft white democratic institutions upon the simple, docile, gifted African race belonging to a much earlier chapter in human history."[73] In 1905, the three great Anglo-Saxon powers of Britain, the U.S.A., and the C.S.A. come together and peaceably coerce the militaristic nations of continental Europe to abandon their plans for aggression, thereby preventing the outbreak of World War I.

In the real world of late 1941, Churchill, fearing national collapse at the height of the German bombing offensive against British cities, wisely chose to shift his focus from Lee to Lincoln. Visiting Washington after Pearl Harbor, the arch imperialist assured a joint session of Congress that he had "steered confidently towards the Gettysburg ideal of 'government of the people by the people for the people.' "[74] This avowal from a committed Tory opponent of Indian independence was as implausible as Lee's liberation of the slaves in 1863. But in the struggle to come, the comforting conceit that the Gettysburg Address was a document of Anglo-American history akin to the Magna Carta could only strengthen the Atlantic alliance.

As war raged in Europe and the Pacific, the US government repeatedly used historical memories of Lincoln's wartime leadership to explain the country's military involvement—a task given added urgency by a 1942 Gallup poll finding that nearly a third of Americans lacked a clear understanding of why they were fighting. Seven months after Pearl Harbor the OWI disseminated posters of Lincoln urging his compatriots to "Back the Attack!" and tagged the image with the familiar last line of the Gettysburg Address.[75] Creative artists rallied to the cause. Cartoonists drew pictures of a puny Adolf Hitler beside Lincoln's massive statue in Washington and the Railsplitter destroying a swastika with an ax.[76] Composer Aaron Copland, the son of a Jewish immigrant from Russia, captured the spirit of Carl Sandburg's well-known biography in his patriotic *Lincoln Portrait*, first performed in Cincinnati in May 1942 during the darkest period of World War II. Copland's narrator quotes Lincoln, saying that Americans were "waging the eternal struggle between two principles, right and wrong."[77] While the human costs of this battle were appalling, Lincoln may also have provided the bereaved with a measure of solace. One Cleveland company offered relatives of deceased servicemen a replica of the sixteenth president's 1864 letter to Lydia Bixby, thanking her for laying her fallen sons on the altar of the nation.[78]

While national leaders and artists seized on the Civil War as a usable past to instill patriotic purpose, genuine domestic consensus remained elusive in the early 1940s. Southern white and African American historical memories, invigorated by interracial competition, consistently challenged official efforts to find unity in the nation's turbulent history. Racial tensions dogged the war effort. African Americans, subjected to the daily indignities of segregation at home and abroad, often regarded the federal authorities' self-serving references to "government of the people, by the people, for the people" with understandable cynicism. In April 1939, Secretary of the Interior Harold Ickes permitted Marian Anderson to perform at the Lincoln Memorial after the Daughters of the American Revolution barred the black contralto from using their hall in Washington. But this symbolic act did not alter the government's official policy over Jim Crow. During the riot-torn summer of 1943, the *Chicago Defender*, one of the country's leading black newspapers, featured a letter from a typically disillusioned black serviceman fighting in an army that remained as segregated as it had been during the Civil War. "This country is supposed to be the greatest democracy of the universe," wrote Corporal James Johnson, "and my conception of the word is as Lincoln expressed in his immortal Gettysburg Address, 'All men are created equal.' We are now giving everything to save the same democratic way of life that Lincoln cherished. But I ask myself, why sacrifice everything that we hold dear for something we have never fully shared?"[79]

By contrast, many white southern Democrats in the early 1940s felt that African Americans, pampered by New Deal relief and Roosevelt's limited efforts to outlaw employment discrimination against blacks, were receiving far more government assistance than they deserved. Seething racial tension on military bases and in overcrowded cities fueled widespread fears that segregation was under imminent attack from white radicals and aggressive blacks.

Southern conservatives again framed these fears of racial change in terms of Reconstruction. Serious unrest among members of the all-black 364th Infantry at Camp Van Dorn in southern Mississippi in May 1943 induced a Picayune businessman to assert that whites were "no more ready to tolerate such acts than they were in the carpetbag days."[80] The letter writer's freshman senator, a Democrat named James O. Eastland, who would become a prominent opponent of the escalating black freedom struggle, concurred. "The negro question," asserted Eastland, "must be met and solved by the people of the South after the war, as was done during the Era of Reconstruction."[81] Mississippi's senior senator, Theodore Bilbo, had no doubt that America should settle its racial problem as soon as the fighting ended. Citing Abraham Lincoln's colonization efforts as justification, he urged the deportation of blacks as the solution. "Are our soldiers and sailors fighting to save this Nation," he asked in 1944, "or are they fighting so that we may become a mongrelized people?"[82]

Bilbo's attempt to enlist the protean myth of Abraham Lincoln in the cause of white supremacy, at odds though it was with official discourse during the New Deal and World War II, highlighted the dissonance between federal, black, and southern white narratives of the Civil War as well as the sheer plasticity of historical memory. At the dawn of the modern civil rights movement, competing narratives of the country's greatest catastrophe threatened to undermine the drive for domestic consensus generated by the United States's continuing embroilment in global conflict. The old sectional divide was about to reopen once again over the unfinished business of equal rights for African Americans.

Centennial Blues

Fighting the Cold War

On August 2, 1956, Albert H. Woolson, a drummer boy who had enlisted in the First Minnesota Heavy Artillery in 1864, died at his home in Duluth, Minnesota. Newspapers listed his age as 109. The old man was the last surviving veteran of the Civil War whose military record could be documented reliably. Even though his regiment had never seen active service, Americans paused to recognize the significance of his death in the midst of waging the Cold War against the Soviet Union and its communist allies. Bruce Catton, a well-known chronicler of the North's Army of the Potomac, worried about the disappearance of the veterans' salutary influence on contemporary America. Writing in *Life* magazine, he described the now-defunct Grand Army of the Republic as "the last living link that bound us intimately to the great morning of national youth." As long as that venerable organization survived, he contended, even in the form of one old man, "the great day of tragedy and of decision was still a part of living memory. There was an open door into the past, and what we could see through that opening was magically haunted. . . . But when the final handful of dust drifted down on Albert Woolson's casket, and the last notes of the bugle hung against the sky, the door swung shut. It cannot be reopened."[1]

Writing five years later in anticipation of the centennial commemoration of the Civil War, southern-born author Robert Penn Warren seemed less convinced that Woolson's death had robbed his compatriots of an indispensable connection to their past. Like Catton, who had encountered Union veterans and their patriotic rituals while growing up in Michigan, Warren had personal ties to the Civil War. His grandfather, Gabriel Thomas Penn, had seen action with the Fifteenth Tennessee Cavalry, fighting at Shiloh and participating in a massacre of black prisoners at Fort Pillow. Grandpa Penn's stories of the war furnished useful insights into the swirling mix of fact and fiction that influenced continuing remembrance of the war in the United States. Warren's close relationship with his Rebel forebear also made him aware that the great streams of Civil War memory were still fed by individuals and groups in the present—people born years after the conflict but who glimpsed it at a distance through their interactions with relatives, friends, and neighbors who had belonged to the wartime generation. This was one of the main reasons he could describe the war so confidently as "our only 'felt' history—history lived in the national imagination," even after the death of the last veteran.[2]

Warren had grown intellectually since 1929, when, as a crusading young Fugitive, he had written an unremarkable pro-southern, anti-abolitionist biography of John Brown. Certainly he had learned enough by the late 1950s to recognize that the Lost Cause—what he called the South's "Great Alibi" for the region's failings since 1865—and its northern equivalent, "The Treasury of Virtue," were tales that Americans told one another to consolidate their sense of being.[3] Warren's characteristically thoughtful and penetrating *Legacy of the Civil War* (1961) still betrayed his southern origins. His blanket claim that white northerners were as racially prejudiced as their southern peers spoke to Lost Cause claims of Yankee hypocrisy, but, in view of northern white liberals' rising support for African American civil rights after World War II, it concealed as much as it uncovered. Among Warren's key points, however, was his insistence—following James Randall and other revisionist historians—that the Civil War had been grossly romanticized in American culture. "It was real blood," he asserted, "not tomato catsup."[4] He sensed too that the war remained relevant in the middle of the twentieth century because "it holds in suspension . . . so many of the issues and tragic ironies—somehow essential yet incommensurable—which we yet live."[5] His deep understanding of his native South told him that the most pressing of those issues and ironies was the persistence of racial oppression in a country notionally dedicated to human freedom. By the time *Legacy* was published, the African American civil rights movement had already begun to puncture the era's stifling consensus culture and in the process derail the Civil War centennial that had begun as an exercise in sterile conformism. While the war's memory after 1945 was still felt primarily in the realm of culture, its continuing relevance to the fraught racial politics of the United States was hard to ignore.

The early years of the Cold War had a significant impact on the way several American scholars thought about their civil war. The most important intellectual shift was a renewed awareness among some historians that if the country had no choice but to wage contemporary struggles against vicious regimes like Nazi Germany and the Soviet Union, then perhaps war against the slaveholding Confederacy had been necessary too. This view was expressed most trenchantly by the Harvard academic, Arthur M. Schlesinger Jr., a committed anticommunist who was a founding member of Americans for Democratic Action, a new, left-liberal political pressure group. In 1949, Schlesinger attacked the revisionists for suggesting that the Civil War could have been prevented by better statesmanship. This interpretation, he contended, ignored the fact that slavery was "one of the few issues of whose evil we can be sure."[6] Its extension, wrote Schlesinger, "like the extension of fascism, was an act of aggression which made a moral choice inescapable."[7]

Scholarly reconceptualization of the Civil War era was also triggered by growing domestic support for black civil rights. In 1946, Franklin Roosevelt's successor, Harry Truman, pressed by African American leaders to put the country's house in order while fighting a new crusade for freedom against communism, created the President's Committee on Civil Rights. This body demanded serious federal efforts to curb the impact of racial segregation on black lives, a call that was backed broadly by the Democratic National Convention in 1948.

Washington's gathering assault on Jim Crow stimulated widespread use of the Confederate battle flag and states' rights rhetoric across a Southland that was changing rapidly under the leadership of a new urban and suburban business class. From the early 1940s, students at colleges like the University of Mississippi began to embrace the instantly recognizable saltire as an emblem of sectional pride. A group of student delegates confirmed the battle flag's close connection to contemporary racial struggles in July 1948 when they reverentially carried it into a political convention in Birmingham, Alabama. This meeting of breakaway southern "Dixiecrats" appalled by the national Democratic Party's opposition to segregation drew up a robust states' rights platform and nominated Governor Strom Thurmond of South Carolina for president on a separate ticket. Thurmond won only four states in the election, but southern Democrats' hostility to the federal government intensified after 1954, when the US Supreme Court ruled in *Brown vs. Board of Education* that racially segregated public schools were unlawful.

Federal backing for integration in such a sensitive policy area shocked most southern whites. Schooled in the verities of the Lost Cause, political leaders responded to the court's judgment by mounting a campaign of "massive resistance" to stanch attacks on Jim Crow emanating from Washington and civil rights groups like the NAACP. New Citizens' Councils committed to defending Jim Crow used the battle flag as a symbol of defiance, and in 1956 Georgia legislators incorporated it into their state's official banner. Throughout the late 1950s, white mobs waved it furiously to signal their opposition to integration at flashpoints like the University of Alabama and Central High School in Little Rock, Arkansas.

Other evidence of segregationists' purposeful use of Lost Cause symbolism was not hard to find at this time. Mississippi legislators sang "Dixie" after passing an interposition law to obstruct school integration and a Citizens' Council form letter in the Magnolia state urged southern whites to remember the "dark and bitter days of Reconstruction."[8] Importantly, however, most massive resisters embraced the celebratory Lost Cause, which had always been broadly compatible with American nationalism. Rather than seeking a second secession, they insisted that their fight against centralizing tyranny was in the interests of all their compatriots, North as well as South.

The 1950s also witnessed the development of what historian Edward Linenthal has described as "a distinct Civil War subculture" in the United States.[9] This subculture reflected heightened popular interest in military history—a phenomenon closely linked to the country's emergence as a global superpower during World War II. Interest in the Civil War as the event that had prepared the ground for America's global supremacy was strongest among upper- and middle-class white men whose prosperity was generated by the rapid advance of a formidable consumer economy energized by vast government defense spending in the Cold War.

This interest took several forms. In 1940, a number of Chicago professionals organized the country's first Civil War Round Table, a lecture and discussion group that met every month at the city's prestigious University Club. By 1948, the group boasted 150 members, including local bookseller Ralph G. Newman, Lincoln bard Carl Sandburg, and several prominent historians, among them Douglas Southall Freeman and Avery Craven. Forty Round Tables existed by 1958, most of them in the urban South and Midwest. The preoccupation with military aspects of the Civil War indicated these groups' attachment to ideas of American exceptionalism that had been strengthened by the country's recent victories against Germany and Japan. The New York City Round Table, formed in 1950, declared itself open to "everyone who shares an appreciation of and respect for the singular American qualities of conviction, rugged determination, and loyalty which so marked the majority of Union and Confederate soldiers during the furious tides of a Civil War."[10]

Other manifestations of the subculture included the formation in 1950 of the country's first modern reenactors' organization, the North-South Skirmish

Association; the creation five years later of Ralph Newman's successful Civil War Book Club, whose members soon included Harry Truman and President Dwight D. Eisenhower; and the inauguration in 1956 of *Civil War History*, a new academic journal devoted entirely to the sectional conflict. Popular interest in the Civil War was confirmed by rising visitor numbers to the battlefields administered by the National Park Service. Automobile tourism thrived with the renewed prosperity and enhanced leisure time of the era. Vacation trips to the battlefields proved especially popular with families keen to combine entertainment with patriotic education. More than 800,000 people visited Gettysburg in 1957 compared with just over 650,000 at the start of the decade.[11] Even Shiloh, more remote from major population centers, witnessed a steady increase in visitors during the first half of the 1950s.[12]

Many individuals belonging to the new generation of Civil War enthusiasts (or "buffs" as they were often known) possessed direct ties to the veterans. Some were enthusiastic readers of MacKinlay Kantor's Pulitzer Prize–winning novel, *Andersonville* (1955). Kantor was a midwesterner who belonged to the Sons of Union Veterans. While he claimed to have had eleven relatives in the Union Army, he had no interest in denigrating the Lost Cause.[13] His concern, in the wake of the Nazis' wholesale slaughter of European Jews, was to probe ordinary human beings' capacity to commit evil acts.

The book's uncompromising account of the notorious Confederate prison unlocked powerful autobiographical memories among Kantor's admirers. Many told him about close relatives who had been incarcerated in the deadly Georgia stockade. One Minneapolis woman said that her father weighed only sixty-five pounds after he was liberated, while a New Englander marveled at the "wonderful agreement" between Kantor's description of Andersonville and that of his father, who had spent six months there.[14] Clint Edwards, a Michigan resident, confessed to belonging to "a family that has made the history of the Civil War rather a hobby." Edwards recalled that he had spoken to a Union veteran in 1932, how the old soldier had talked of "the horrible conditions" in the prison as well as being rescued by "a friendly negro."[15] An Illinois man wrote about his father, who had been wounded while participating in Sherman's Atlanta campaign in 1864. "I never remember him without a cane," said C. C. Burford from Urbana, "He bandaged and polticed his leg for 40 years. . . . He was a volunteer and a private soldier. He was never called into high councils and his opinion was never sought. His contribution to the cause of Lincoln and of the Union was humble, but he gave it willingly. I never heard him complain."[16]

Not everyone enjoyed the book. The remorseless detailing of human wretchedness irritated many. So did what some readers felt to be its sectional bias. Kantor, wrote one critic, should write another novel about the ill treatment of Confederate POWs in northern prisons or Sherman's "infamous bloody march to the sea, paralleling the Bataan Death March" of US and Filipino POWs in 1942: "For anyone to write a book so full of venom, vitriol and bitterness against our People—to reopen the wounds of the War Between the States, it takes a mighty unusual person."[17]

The popular historian Bruce Catton played a leading role in expanding the new Civil War subculture in the United States. He did so, first, by tapping the kind of personal memories held by Kantor's readers and, second, by crafting compelling narratives of the war in the middlebrow tradition of Benét and Sandburg. His books made him rich as well as famous. By 1967, Catton had accrued royalties as high as $700,000 with his New York publisher, Doubleday.[18] Although he wrote to make a living, he also wrote with ideological intent. His best-selling accounts of the sectional crisis were deliberate contributions to national defense at the height of the Cold War.[19]

Born in 1899, Catton was reared in the denuded lumber district of northern Michigan. In a memoir written late in life, he remembered marching to the local cemetery behind elderly Union veterans on Memorial Day. He knew some of them by name. One day in 1916, he asked Cassius Judson, one of Sherman's "bummers," what he thought of the battle scenes in *Birth of a Nation*. "Well, it wasn't much like the real thing," reflected the old man.[20] Catton and his boyhood friends refought the war in the fields around town, delivering more beatings to the Rebels. These experiences gave him a permanent fascination for a conflict that always seemed peculiarly immediate to him and whose immediacy he would convey so effectively to modern readers. Too old to fight in 1941, he served the US government in several capacities, notably as director of information at the War Production Board, a post that left him disillusioned by Washington's readiness to prioritize the needs and expertise of big business while claiming to fight a people's war. Capitalist democracy, believed Catton, was superior to fascism and communism, but only if it meant government for "all the people" and not just wealthy elites.[21]

From the late 1940s onward, American political leaders grew increasingly concerned that US leadership of the "free world" was being corroded by a range of debilitating domestic factors. These included postwar affluence, suffocating matriarchy, insidious homosexuality (linked in many minds with communism), and "teenage" disaffection with established authority. They deemed the chief consequences to be complacency, apathy, and an attendant loss of identity and mission. Liberals, no less than conservatives, worried like their predecessors in the late nineteenth century that the American people were going soft at a critical moment in their nation's history.

Bruce Catton's lucid accounts of the Union war effort—*Mr. Lincoln's Army* (1950), *Glory Road* (1952), *A Stillness at Appomattox* (1954), and *This Hallowed Ground* (1956)—earned rave reviews in part because he was an early practitioner of history from the bottom up. These books focused readers' attention on the experiences of ordinary Federal soldiers rather than politicians and generals. If World War II had not been the people's conflict Catton had wanted it to be, he found what he was looking for in the Civil War.

Judging by the popularity of his work as well as the symbiotic growth of the Civil War subculture, many of his compatriots were also seeking affirmation that individual action in pursuit of a grand collective cause could make a difference to their own lives and to the country they loved. They learned by reading Catton's narratives of the soldiers' hardships and courage that Union victory, a prime source of national greatness in the modern age, had been built on the dogged determination of unheralded Americans to see a difficult but necessary task through to the finish. A frustrated novelist as well as former journalist, Catton understood that his readers thirsted for knowledge and understanding in the troubled present. He gave them what they wanted: strong plot lines and vivid human-interest stories couched in accessible, elegiac prose that blended historical explanation, excitement, and sentiment in equal measure.

In common with many like-minded Cold War liberals, Bruce Catton feared ordinary people were so bewildered by the state of the world around them that they were losing their commitment to fundamental values. He tried to keep a foot in the door of American memory in order to persuade his anxious compatriots that they should learn lessons from their divided past. Civil War soldiers, he told students at Duke University in early 1957, "are very close to us. Those of us who are getting on in years can still remember them, gallant old men with white beards, who liked to dress in worn ceremonial uniforms on state occasions and who somehow stood for integrity, for loyalty to an ideal, for plain unvarnished bravery—in a word, for character. They put something beyond price into the mainstream of American life. We are richer for having known them."[22]

One reason for Catton's nationwide popularity in the 1950s was his admiration for southern heroes like Lee and Jackson—an admiration that reflected the power of reconciliatory language and symbols in an era defined by the consensual pressures of the Cold War as much as it did his desire to sell as many books as possible. His positive view of the Confederates also stemmed partly from the fact that he was a prisoner of his generation's racially blinkered historiography. Heavily influenced by the work of revisionists like Craven and Randall, he understated the role of slavery in causing the Civil War and marginalized the part played by slaves and US Colored Troops in the Confederacy's demise. Consequently, most readers below the Mason-Dixon Line found little to concern them in his books. In fact, white southerners responded positively to Catton's attempts to humanize the Yankee foe. Clifford Dowdey, a partisan historian of the Rebel cause, reported that Catton "would be gratified . . . to know of the deep response to your work from devout neo-Confederates who would never before read a line by a non-Southerner."[23]

Catton's empathy for southern whites and inattention to the historical agency of blacks could lead him into dangerous territory. In one 1957 address, he illustrated his point that freedom was challenged periodically in the United States by alluding to the persecution of Brigadier General Charles Stone by the Republican-dominated Joint Committee on the Conduct of the War after the disastrous Union assault at Ball's Bluff in October 1861. Stone's offense, claimed Catton, had been to offend "powerful and suspicious Abolitionists" by returning fugitive slaves to their owners. He presented this episode as evidence "of the way in which fear and hysteria, operating together, can lead even a committee of Congress to narrow the area of American freedom and justice."[24] Although most members of his liberal audience probably appreciated his swipe at right-wing McCarthyism, one listener was puzzled. How, wondered Phineas Indritz, special counsel for a progressive World War II veterans' group, could he attack congressmen for restricting freedom when their objective was the emancipation of the slaves?[25] Catton was hoisted by his own petard. By endorsing the orthodox master narrative that demonized the kind of antislavery "fanatics" who assailed General Stone, he unwittingly uncovered the limits of racial liberalism in the early Cold War era.

Like many liberals, Bruce Catton sent mixed messages on black civil rights to his readers and listeners. In part this reflected his dilemma as a racial moderate. An ardent patriot, he desperately wanted the United States to defeat the Soviet Union—an objective that seemed unattainable if the government angered white southerners by pressing ahead too quickly with its attempts to compel integration. However, by furnishing the Russians with embarrassing propaganda material and exposing the hollowness of State Department rhetoric, violent racial incidents in places like Chicago and Levittown, Pennsylvania, in the North and Montgomery, Alabama; Clinton, Tennessee; and Little Rock, Arkansas, in the South suggested that liberals could not achieve their goals without responding constructively to African American grievances. By late 1960, the year of the first wave of black sit-ins, growing numbers of Americans sensed that Jim Crow was an incubus in the Cold War and that the government must take decisive steps to remove it.

Segregationists' use of Confederate symbols and states' rights rhetoric to defy federal authority challenged the commitment of many liberals to a reconciliatory interpretation of the Civil War. Bruce Catton's initial response to the developing racial crisis was cautious. He told a correspondent in late 1955, "I still think that the Federal side was right, and that a substantial moral issue was involved in the war, but I don't feel any need to let my own blood pressure rise over it at this late date."[26] However, in December 1956, he publicly connected the civil rights struggle to both the Civil War and the Cold War when he spoke at his alma mater. The emancipation of the slaves, he told a group of Oberlin alumni, had finally made Americans "face up to the race problem," but the Civil War was only "a beginning, rather than an end." The modern world, he continued, was a fearful place: "Look afield—to Hungary, perhaps, or even to Clinton, Tennessee—and you see the old forces at work, declaiming that men are not worthy of freedom and that whatever people do must be done within the framework laid down by stone-age folk who have something to lose whenever the shackles that bind men's spirits are broken." The best thing Americans could do, concluded Catton, was to visit a Civil War battlefield in order to derive "from it a new dedication to the unfinished task which falls on all of us."[27]

The conjunction of the upcoming Civil War centennial and the nonviolent civil rights movement posed the greatest test for Catton's slow-burning opposition to racism. It would reveal whether he and other Cold War liberals were capable of meeting the challenge posed by African Americans' demands for equality.

The Civil War Centennial and the Demise of Jim Crow

During the mid-1950s, a range of groups belonging to the country's Civil War subculture called for a comprehensive national commemoration of the one hundredth anniversary of America's greatest conflict. Buffs were especially vocal supporters of such an event. Men like Karl S. Betts, a Kansas-born public relations expert who played a leading role in the Washington, DC, Round Table, envisaged a truly popular pageant that would excite and inspire ordinary Americans in the midst of the Cold War. Professional historians such as Allan Nevins of Columbia and Bell Wiley at Emory, racial moderates who shared Bruce Catton's desire to galvanize his fellow citizens at this dangerous moment in the country's history, had a different vision. They wanted to educate the public about the Civil War in order to promote the growth of an enlightened democratic citizenry. While neither of these interest groups was sufficiently influential on its own to set the centennial in motion, the project received crucial support from agencies and organizations keen to profit from a national commemoration, notably those involved in the country's booming tourist industry.

In the spring of 1957, a congressional subcommittee in Washington gathered testimony on a bill based on the DC Round Table's plans for a federally funded US centennial commission. Although nobody departed from the consensus-oriented script, Colonel H. C. Harrison of the Sons of Confederate Veterans (SCV) indicated that a national commission would guarantee southerners a fair hearing in commemorative exercises. Karl Betts, who had solicited support from patriotic groups like the SCV and the United Daughters of the

Confederacy (UDC), insisted that the proposal would benefit the whole country. There was, he said, "a very wide and growing interest in the history of the Civil War" that would make the centennial a great success, one that would "point up forcefully and dramatically the aspirations, the enthusiasms and the achievements of our forebears in a rededication of our will to achieve a greater American union."[28]

Although the Chicago bookseller Ralph Newman wondered if "some states might resent too active participation by a federal body in their own observation," most congressmen were in thrall to the dominant reconciliatory interpretation of the Civil War as the historic moment when the United States had been reunited and the modern superpower had been born.[29] As Senator Joseph O'Mahoney of Wisconsin put it reassuringly, "The purpose of the observance of this great schism between our people is not to stress that which divides us but rather to reaffirm that which unites us—the basic desire for unity, liberty, freedom, and self-government."[30]

In September 1957, President Eisenhower, a Civil War buff himself, signed legislation creating the US Civil War Centennial Commission (CWCC) as an agency of the National Park Service. Two weeks later, he reluctantly dispatched paratroops to Little Rock to impel the court-ordered integration of Central High School over the opposition of the state's governor. William Tuck, a conservative Virginia Democrat who strongly supported the centennial project, was appalled. Eisenhower's action, he thought, could only rally southern whites in opposition to *Brown* and "the tyranny to which we are now being subjected."[31]

After the appointment of Major General Ulysses S. Grant III, a retired US Army officer and grandson of the famous Union commander, as head of the CWCC, many white southerners feared that the upcoming commemoration would be a noisy celebration of Yankee victory. Grant and his deputy, Karl Betts, however, were right-wing Republicans steeped in the narrative of sectional reconciliation and committed to making their Cold War pageant a positive contribution to the fight against communism. They quickly assured southern white organizers that the latter would have a virtually free hand in staging centennial events. Any lingering anxieties that the federal commission would try to ram civil rights down southern throats were dispelled by Karl Betts in a telling interview for the *Nation* in 1960. When asked how his agency intended to mark the hundredth anniversary of emancipation, Betts responded that the CWCC would not be emphasizing that subject. Besides, he said, black slaves had been loyal to the proslavery Confederacy: "A lot of fine Negro people loved life as it was in the old South."[32]

By 1961, southern state officials had overcome their reservations about the commemoration and were ready to celebrate the Confederacy. One reason for this was their expectation that efficient marketing would bring tourists flocking to the southern battlefields. Contemporary racial politics, however, also influenced local whites' enthusiastic embrace of the centennial. Marking the historic moment when the cotton states had seceded from the Union made perfect sense to the embattled segregationists who dominated the region's state centennial commissions. What better way to mobilize popular opposition to court-ordered public school desegregation and civil rights activism than to remind ordinary whites of their ancestors' uncompromising resistance to assaults on southern institutions?

In February 1961, the white population of Montgomery, Alabama—the first capital of the Confederacy and more recently the scene of a successful bus boycott led by a charismatic black preacher named Martin Luther King Jr.—turned out in force to celebrate the centenary of Jefferson Davis's inauguration as Confederate president. They participated enthusiastically in beard-growing contests, dressed up in period costume, bought tickets for a Confederate belle beauty contest, and flocked to see a weeklong secession pageant that culminated in a colorful fireworks display over the city's Coliseum building. State judge Walter B. Jones, a leading segregationist, marveled at the community's response. The events in Montgomery, he thought, had given his people "a deeper appreciation of the things the Confederacy fought for, and helped them to realize that unrestrained federal power is destroying this nation."[33]

Similar events took place in other southern towns that spring. In Jackson, Mississippi, Governor Ross R. Barnett, an outspoken opponent of black civil rights, led the city's secession-day parade, riding in a horse-drawn carriage while scores of white Mississippians clad in Rebel gray watched him pass. There was so much enthusiasm for the Confederacy in the South at this time that one agitated US serviceman told the new president, John F. Kennedy, that the centennial "could endanger our country so great it might cause the fall of our great nation."[34] White southern moderates also worried about the impact of these theatrics on their region. Ralph McGill, editor of the *Atlanta Constitution*, urged a more temperate and national commemoration of the Civil War. "[W]hat we have now," he wrote, "are increasing numbers of persons wandering about the South wearing sleazy imitations of Confederate uniforms, growing beards, stirring up old hatreds, making ancient wounds bleed again."[35]

The combination of southern whites' attachment to the Lost Cause and the CWCC leadership's lack of empathy for the civil rights struggle soon threatened to undermine the consensual objectives of the centennial. In April 1961, southern organizers launched the one hundredth anniversary commemoration of the American Civil War with a spectacular fireworks "bombardment" of Fort Sumter. The CWCC had scheduled its annual meeting in Charleston to coincide with the events in South Carolina. Having assumed that the centennial would be of interest mainly to whites, Karl Betts was surprised when New

Jersey's state centennial agency demanded that one of its delegates, a black woman named Madaline A. Williams, should be accommodated in the downtown Francis Marion Hotel with the commission's other guests. Charleston was a racially segregated city, and predictably the hotel could find no space for Williams, a Newark Democrat who was married to the president of the local NAACP.

Correctly sensing that the liberal New Jerseyans were trying to derail their Jim Crow commemoration, centennial commission leaders insisted that they had no control over a state's racial customs. The story quickly became front-page news, inducing President Kennedy to scold the agency at a press conference. Wiser heads on the commission eventually prevailed. Following a suggestion from the southern historian Bell Wiley, the delegates reconvened at Charleston's desegregated US Navy base. But the damage had been done. The Civil War centennial was a national embarrassment before it began in earnest. "Just where in the first place the idea of the Civil War Centennial came from we don't know," mused one commentator sardonically, "but we suspect the Russians."[36] Another wearily described the commemoration as "the emptiest and most tedious event ever inflicted upon a free people."[37] It had all gone horribly wrong. An initiative designed to rally Americans for the fight against communism now competed with the civil rights movement to demonstrate the hollowness of America's commitment to democracy.

The coup de grâce was administered by press outrage at a reenactment of the Battle of First Bull Run in July 1961, which took place only weeks after segregationists had attacked black and white "freedom riders" in Alabama. The heavily commercialized event, staged with the full backing of the CWCC and the local Park Service superintendent, attracted tens of thousands of paying tourists. Many visitors were deeply impressed by what they saw. One of them, Millard Crane, drove his family down to Virginia from upstate New York for the occasion. Despite sweltering temperatures, the Cranes' patriotism was strengthened by President Eisenhower's message—contained in their twenty-five cent souvenir program—that "Out of the Civil War came a Nation tempered in liberty destined for leadership in the Free World."[38] They were thrilled by a "Pageant of American Unity" and the crashing recreation of the battle that followed. "Truly," Crane told readers of his hometown newspaper, "our forebears were dedicated men with a cause, no matter which color uniform they wore." The Civil War, he wrote, had preserved the Union and left the nation stronger than ever before: "We have suffered together through four great wars and today present a united front to the foes of our way of life. With God's help, let's be about it."[39]

Other observers were less impressed by the reenactment. The sight of hamburger stalls parked on a field sanctified with the blood of dead Americans sickened many watching journalists already appalled by the ease with which segregationists had co-opted the centennial for their own ends. That summer Karl Betts, the man who had favored a business-friendly centennial to maximize public interest in the event, fell victim to an internal coup. His boss, General Grant, resigned in disgust. Both men were soon replaced by two sober-minded Civil War scholars.

Allan Nevins, the new chairman of the CWCC, was one of the most highly regarded Civil War historians of his day. An indefatigable worker based at the Huntington Library in California, he was a liberal northern Democrat who could be trusted by the Kennedy administration to save the centennial from complete meltdown. After announcing that the reorganized commission would "allow the just pride of no national group to be belittled or besmirched," he worked effectively with his young southern deputy, James A. ("Bud") Robertson, to take the heat out of the whole exercise by prioritizing public education, historic preservation, and academic scholarship over what both men regarded as empty spectacle, and by taking faltering steps to accommodate what they regarded as reasonable African American concerns about the event.[40]

On September 22, 1962, the reorganized commission hosted a gathering at the Lincoln Memorial to commemorate the issuing of the preliminary Emancipation Proclamation. On this occasion, Nevins's liberal anticommunism induced him to connect the famous edict with generic Cold War freedoms rather than the divisive fight for racial justice at home. His failure to invite a single African American to speak at the ceremony drew the ire of Bishop Smallwood E. Williams, a black Baptist minister who headed the District of Columbia affiliate of Martin Luther King's Southern Christian Leadership Conference (SCLC). Williams denounced the planned ceremony as "a mockery" and described Nevins as "prejudiced" and an "apologist for the Confederacy."[41] The negative publicity that ensued forced CWCC officials to limit the damage by allowing the renowned black judge and civil rights advocate, Thurgood Marshall, to make some remarks on the day.

One week after this low-key emancipation ceremony in Washington, President Kennedy and his brother Robert, the US attorney general, were compelled to send federal troops to Oxford, Mississippi, where a howling mob was trying to prevent the admission of a black student, James Meredith, to the University of Mississippi. "Ole Miss" had long been a stronghold of the Lost Cause. Its leafy campus contained a Confederate cemetery as well as the statue of a Confederate soldier and a fine stained-glass window dedicated to the university's Confederate Grays, a unit that had been wiped out during the Civil War. A large battle flag was displayed prominently at local football games, and excited fans of the "Rebels" lustily sang "Dixie" on game days in Jackson and Oxford. On the night of the riot in which two civilians were killed, Edwin A. Walker, a far-right activist and former US major general, tried to rally the demonstrators by clambering onto the Confederate statue on Lyceum Circle. Earlier that day, students hoisted a battle flag in front of the registrar's office where Meredith was seeking admission.

The federal government's use of military force to protect James Meredith angered white Mississippians reared on stories of the Civil War and Reconstruction. Governor Ross Barnett tapped vivid historical memories by exhorting local whites to prove that they would "not surrender to the evil and illegal forces of tyranny!"[42] Many of his supporters denounced President Kennedy as a despot in language reminiscent of the barbs that secessionists had once aimed at Abraham Lincoln. "I am extremely bitter over the invasion of Mississippi by political tyrants," wrote one angry businessman, "About one hundred years ago the southern states were forced at gunpoint to ratify the 14th amendment to the Constitution. Now our state is again invaded by federal troops."[43] "Our forefathers fought and died together," commented a resident of Meridian, "and it seems to me, out of respect to those who spilt their blood on the battlefields together, the least the Southern States could do, would be to stick together."[44] An angry Biloxi man demanded immediate cessation of "[t]his nigger situation" or the country would see "either a civil war or an out and out racial war." A modern-day secession, he thought, might not be a bad idea: "it might make that bastard president stop and think for a minute or two what he is doing."[45]

After the *Brown* decision, southern historian C. Vann Woodward had broached the idea that the South was undergoing a "new" or second Reconstruction.[46] Now some white Mississippians drew strength from the outcome of the first. "During the reconstruction era following the Civil War," said one Greenville resident, "our grandfathers were in a far worse position than we are today. They banded together, ran the carpetbaggers and other damnyankees out of office and Mississippi and demanded that Federal troops be removed. Are we going to let them down?"[47]

Importantly, however, prominent segregationists in the state discounted the idea of violently resisting the authority of the US government even while they drew on constructed memories to bolster their cause. "History is again repeating itself . . . ," commented Citizens' Council leader Tom Brady, "The only difference in us now and our revered grandparents is that we will not secede; we have throughout this country something that is fine and grand, and that is the realization that 'I am an American. And, as an American, I will work my problems out.' "[48] Patriotic statements like this opened up the possibility that once the immediate crisis had subsided, southern conservatives could forge links with their northern peers, for whom federal intervention in local affairs smacked dangerously of socialism.

But for now the momentum lay with moderates, not conservatives. The civil rights movement's attempts to expose the violent heart of Jim Crow not only angered segregationists but also made it increasingly difficult for liberals to ignore what was happening in the South. In a speech at Boston College on May 25, 1963, CWCC member Bruce Catton praised Colonel Robert Gould Shaw, the patrician white officer who had led the black Fifty-Fourth Massachusetts Infantry in its attack on Battery Wagner, for laying down his life for the cause of African American freedom. Catton had previously soft-pedaled racial issues because of his preoccupation with Cold War consensus and his reluctance to alienate southern readers. This time he exhorted his listeners to live up to Shaw's example by making plain their disgust at the violence recently unleashed by police chief Eugene "Bull" Connor on peaceful civil rights demonstrators in Birmingham, Alabama. Modern Americans, he said, might not be called to repeat Shaw's sacrifice but "we are at least obliged to reach into our own hearts and wrench out everything that may stand between us and complete acceptance of the universal dignity and equality of man. . . . We are at least obliged to make clear to everyone which side we stand on—and to make this clear to the authorities in our own state as well as those of a state a thousand miles away."[49]

Segregationist Democrats led the fight against federal efforts to outlaw segregation by statute and enforce black voting rights. In what was becoming an increasingly bitter political battle, several state governors employed Lost Cause rhetoric and symbolism to counter this new round of federal intervention, none more effectively than Governor George C. Wallace of Alabama. In common with many hard-core segregationists, Wallace possessed Confederate connections. His great-grandfather had been wounded at Lookout Mountain, and he treasured boyhood memories of the elderly "graybeards." Alert to the political utility of Lost Cause symbolism in the racially charged present, he delivered his notorious "segregation now, segregation forever" speech on the spot outside the Alabama state capitol where Jefferson Davis was inaugurated Confederate president in February 1861. Watching over him in January 1963 was Frederick Cleveland Hibbard's statue of Davis, built with funds raised by the UDC in the late 1930s. Excited spectators ululated their version of the Rebel yell and a "Confederate" band played patriotic southern airs. Before his stage-managed resistance to court-ordered integration of the state university in June 1963, Wallace ordered the battle flag to be flown over the statehouse as a gesture of defiance aimed at Robert Kennedy, who went to Montgomery in a vain bid to persuade the recalcitrant governor not to impede the legal process.

The following month, the charismatic Wallace sought to make political capital out of the centennial by traveling to Gettysburg to participate in events marking the one hundredth anniversary of the great battle. Although no veterans were alive to attend, their place was filled by reenactors, many of them descendants of Civil War soldiers, who staged "living vignettes" of the battle to the delight of the many thousands of spectators.[50] On July 1, the governor placed a wreath on the UDC's monument to Alabama's fallen soldiers, which had been dedicated on the field in 1933. Aware that many northerners shared his dim views of blacks and big government, he predicted presciently that the "descendants of both sides in the Civil War" would "soon be united in a common fight to end the growing power of a central government." Later that day, Wallace participated in ceremonies at the Eternal Light Peace Memorial. More Rebel yells greeted him as he advanced to lay flowers in tribute to the dead of Gettysburg. "We stand with the descendants of brave men who fought for the North and the South," he told journalists, "and we will stand for defense of the Constitution."[51]

George Wallace's pointedly intersectional remarks anticipated the consolidation of a powerful national conservative response to the racially liberal and statist achievements of the 1960s. However, to a majority of northerners and a minority of southern whites, his rearguard defense of segregation on the centenary of Pickett's Charge appeared profoundly un-American. Several northern governors used the events at Gettysburg to articulate their support for what they saw as the patriotic goals of the civil rights movement. Richard Hughes, a New Jersey Democrat, insisted, "The Civil War was not fought to preserve the Union 'lily-white' or 'Jim Crow'" but "for liberty and justice for all."[52]

Segregationists' opposition to the nonviolent civil rights movement rekindled an often repressed conviction among many northerners that their section had fought a just war in 1861–65. Despite Bishop Williams's criticism of his handling of the CWCC's Emancipation Proclamation ceremony in Washington, Allan Nevins was as worried as any other Cold War liberal by segregationist violence and its disastrous impact on America's standing as leader of the free world. The watershed events in Birmingham led him to insist, against the advice of his deputy Bud Robertson, who wanted to prevent southern centennial commissions from abandoning the official observance, that the anniversary of the Gettysburg Address should be marked with an academic symposium in Washington.

One of the leading contributors was Nevins's fellow liberal Democrat, Senator Paul H. Douglas of Illinois. A former marine with a passionate interest in Abraham Lincoln, Douglas agreed to deliver a paper about the consequences of the North's victory at Gettysburg for the future of racial and sectional relations in the United States. In a revealing assertion of Nevins's personal search for a usable past at this moment, the CWCC chairman told Douglas that his essay would have a "direct pertinence to the problems of our time."[53] The senator produced an unashamedly present-minded paper in which he urged congressional supporters of a comprehensive civil rights bill, stalled in Congress at the time of President Kennedy's assassination in November 1963, "to observe the same energetic steadfastness in the cause of human freedom which the men of the Union displayed on Culp's Hill, Little Round Top, and at the clump of trees in the center of the Union lines where the final agonized gasp of the battle was uttered."[54] This may not have been entirely accurate history, but Nevins set aside his commitment to that objective in order to make the symposium a weapon of civil rights. Six months after Douglas delivered his paper in January 1964, the senator joined his fellow northern Democrats and Republicans in helping to secure passage of the landmark Civil Rights Act that inaugurated the destruction of Jim Crow in the United States.

In demolishing de jure segregation, the new legislation increased southern Democrats' disillusionment with the national party. Florence Sillers Ogden, an outspoken segregationist, urged her fellow Mississippians "to forever break" with an organization that appeared to have been taken over by racial liberals and to vote in the upcoming presidential election for the right-wing Republican candidate, Barry Goldwater. "If our fathers should rise up out of their graves and take a look around," she wrote, "they wouldn't recognize the 'party of their fathers.' . . . I know exactly what my father . . . would do. He would vote for Goldwater. So would my two Confederate grandfathers."[55] Although the Arizona senator proved no match for Lyndon B. Johnson in the fall election, he carried five Deep South states, including Mississippi. This showing prefigured southern whites' rapid shift from the Democratic to the Republican fold in the late 1960s and the 1970s. Conservative intellectuals such as Richard M. Weaver had long mourned the Old South as a victim of big government. Now its progeny were moving into an embryonic right-wing coalition that would render liberalism a dirty word in politics by the end of the century.

When the Civil War centennial drew to a close in the spring of 1965, most Americans had forgotten about it. Even moderate segregationists, worried by the negative impact of white-supremacist violence, had seen enough of an event that had heaped outside scorn on their troubled region. Shortly before the reconciliation-themed closing ceremony at Appomattox, Alabama's *Birmingham News* responded to a widely publicized police attack on peaceful civil rights marchers in Selma by criticizing George Wallace and other political leaders in the state. Several of the paper's readers concurred. "We have listened so often to Gov. Wallace make alibis and proclaim 'segregation forever,'" wrote one of them, "that many of us apparently believe that it can last forever and that it is our inherited right to deny the Negro his right to vote. I have lived in Alabama all my life, and I love the South; but I feel I live in America—not the Confederacy. If it is wrong to discriminate in America, it is wrong in Alabama."[56] Sentiments like these did not necessarily demonstrate that those who uttered them had made their peace with racial integration. While most southern whites accommodated themselves to the demise of Jim Crow, many lost no time moving into new suburbs that were unaffordable to most African Americans.

The Civil War centennial's legacy was not entirely negative. Even though it attracted extensive criticism, Karl Betts's commercial pageant generated enormous popular interest in the Civil War. American children in particular were thrilled by the war's raised media profile, the ubiquity of war-related souvenirs, Bruce Catton's best-selling *Centennial History of the Civil War*, and family visits to the battlefields. Many adults today look back warmly on the centennial. Kenneth Noe, a prominent Civil War historian, "fondly remember[s] a family trip to the Manassas battlefield, where I crawled all over the field pieces, bought my first Civil War books, and marveled at the vista from atop the Stonewall Jackson statue."[57] William Piston, another leading Civil War scholar, recalls that for young boys the commemoration was "a wonderful visual experience. Every newspaper and magazine was flooded with pictures. We traded bubblegum cards. Every restaurant's placemat had a Civil War theme and every packet of Dixie Crystal sugar on the table told a Civil War story on the back."[58] In most respects, the centennial was an object lesson in how not to conjure public memory. But in its ability to create its own community of consumers among young people, it proved remarkably effective.

Unfinished Business

During the first half of the 1960s, leaders of the mainstream civil rights movement made calculated use of the American past to promote their political objectives. In doing so they drew heavily on the emancipationist strain of Civil War memory fostered by Carter G. Woodson, W.E.B. Du Bois, and other African American scholars during the first half of the twentieth century. Although Karl Betts and other centennial organizers made little attempt to include blacks in their segregated Cold War pageant, white supremacists' murderous opposition to liberal reform heightened the significance of the one hundredth anniversary of emancipation in the context of the contemporary struggle for equal rights. But while mainstream activists like Martin Luther King initially saw the black counter-memory of the Civil War as a useful resource in their nonviolent struggle, a growing number of black radicals—angered by the slow pace of change in America—scorned rhetorical strategies anchored by Lincoln's contention at Gettysburg that the Civil War was unfinished business for a nation committed by its founders to the belief that all men were created equal.

Initially, African Americans displayed little interest in the centennial. However, the barrage of adverse national publicity caused by segregationists' attempts to co-opt the event soon attracted the attention of civil rights activists. By the spring of 1961, spokesmen were lining up to denounce the commemoration. Robert F. Williams, a radical black leader who hailed from Monroe, North

Carolina, attacked "the Centennial of Shame" and claimed that "the North is fast becoming a running dog for the southern way of life."[59] Lawrence D. Reddick, one of Martin Luther King's closest allies, warned that the Civil War bonanza was perpetuating historical myths and demanded the burning of Confederate symbols like the battle flag. And in words echoing the late-nineteenth-century warnings of Frederick Douglass and Albion Tourgée, veteran black labor leader A. Philip Randolph described the centennial as "a stupendous brain-washing exercise to make the Civil War leaders of the South on a par with the Civil War leaders of the North, and to strike a blow against men of color and human dignity."[60]

As criticism of the centennial intensified, black historians redoubled their efforts to weaken the influence of the lily-white narratives of the Lost Cause and sectional reconciliation on ordinary African Americans. Members of the financially strapped Association for the Study of Negro Life and History labored hard to disseminate an emancipationist narrative of the 1860s. Using a variety of forums, professional scholars who taught at black colleges, including Charles H. Wesley, Benjamin Quarles, and John Hope Franklin, brought the past to bear on the present by insisting on the centrality of slavery to Civil War causation, the positive role that blacks had played in their own liberation, and—this a critical theme at a time of renewed southern hostility to court-ordered integration—the conflict's ultimate confirmation of federal power.

It was a journalist, Lerone H. Bennett, who reached the widest audience with a series of pathbreaking articles on African American history for *Ebony*, a magazine read by members of the country's growing urban black middle class. The series included an essay on "The Negro in the Civil War," in which Bennett detailed the active combat role of black troops and argued that emancipation was attributable "not to Union humanitarianism but to rebel battlefield brilliance."[61] Readers responded appreciatively to his attempts to stress "the role of the Negro, himself, in the struggle for freedom and equality."[62] Writing from Brooklyn, Marie Josey recalled that she had realized in high school that whites believed "the Negroes were 'docile' slaves." She added honestly, "I must confess that this was my conception of the Negro until I started subscribing to your magazine."[63] Equipped with a raised historical consciousness, African Americans set about wresting control not only of the flagging centennial but also, and more important, of Civil War memory itself.

Martin Luther King, widely regarded by whites as the leader of the civil rights movement, was a skillful manipulator of Civil War themes. Reared by loving parents in a relatively well-to-do black neighborhood in Atlanta, he developed a sound awareness of the emancipationist counter-memory sustained by Woodson and others. In a prize-winning school oration titled "The Negro Constitution" written in 1944, he insisted that the Confederacy's defeat had delivered "freedom for all people" guaranteed by new constitutional amendments. "Black America still wears chains," he wrote, but if they were properly enfranchised, African Americans would "be vigilant and defend even with their arms, the ark of federal liberty from treason and destruction by her enemies." Concluded the young student optimistically, "The spirit of Lincoln still lives."[64]

After *Brown*, King contended that only federal power could achieve equality under the law for African Americans. One of his strategies was to induce President Kennedy to deal with the country's racial crisis as decisively as Lincoln had done during the Civil War. In October 1961, he conferred with Kennedy at the White House and suggested that it was time for the president to issue his own version of the Emancipation Proclamation. Kennedy, as wary as Franklin Roosevelt of alienating southern white voters, bought himself time by saying that he would consider a written proposal for such an edict. On May 17, 1962, an SCLC representative duly submitted King's "Appeal . . . for a National Rededication to the Principles of the Emancipation Proclamation and for an Executive Order Prohibiting Segregation in the United States of America." This document exhibited the close connection that had once existed between the emancipationist and Unionist strains of historical memory. It not only urged Kennedy to reflect seriously on the significance of the Civil War past to the current crisis but also claimed that there was direct continuity between the two events. "The struggle for freedom . . . ," wrote King, "of which the Civil War was but a bloody chapter, continues throughout our land today. The courage and heroism of Negro citizens at Montgomery, Little Rock, New Orleans, Prince Edward County and Jackson, Mississippi is only a further effort to affirm that democratic heritage so painfully won, in part, upon the grassy battlefields of Antietam, Lookout Mountain, and Gettysburg."[65]

On this occasion, King's rhetorical strategy—which foreshadowed that of sympathetic white liberals like Allan Nevins and Paul Douglas—had no immediate impact on President Kennedy, who chose not to mimic Lincoln by issuing his own emancipation edict. The SCLC leader was so frustrated by the administration's gradualist approach to civil rights enforcement that he accepted an invitation from the New York Civil War Centennial Commission to attend a dinner in Manhattan marking the centenary of the preliminary Emancipation Proclamation. The South's continuing resistance to integration, he told a group of distinguished guests including Bruce Catton and the state's liberal Republican governor, Nelson Rockefeller, was making a mockery of America's vaunted commitment to freedom: "Only the undeveloped or primitive nations of the world would tolerate regions which are similar, in which feudal autocrats or military governors hold sway over the federal power. It is a condition unknown to modern industrial democracies except our own." "No president," he added pointedly, "can be great or even fit for office, if he attempts to accommodate injustice to maintain his political balance."[66] Just days later, the Kennedys were forced to dispatch federal troops to quell the rioting at Ole Miss.

Angered by segregationist violence, both for its divisive domestic consequences and its negative impact on America's image abroad, the Kennedy brothers began to inject careful allusions to the Civil War into their own speeches. In February 1963, the embattled president told Congress that the Emancipation Proclamation had been "only a first step" in the struggle for racial equality.[67] Confronted by concerted opposition from southern Democrats, however, the administration's civil rights bill remained stalled in Congress when its supporters converged on the Lincoln Memorial for the March on Washington on August 28.

While the Kennedys hoped this mass demonstration might prod Congress into action, many angry black activists who had suffered beatings in the movement's southern campaigns had lost patience with the White House's constant temporizing on civil rights. In the original draft of his speech that day, John Lewis, the courageous young chairman of the Student Nonviolent Coordinating Committee (SNCC), declared that the civil rights bill was a case of "too little, and too late" and insisted that no one could stop the movement now. "We will march through the South," he promised, "through the Heart of Dixie, the way Sherman did. We shall pursue our own 'scorched earth' policy and burn Jim Crow to the ground—nonviolently."[68] Although white and black leaders at the Lincoln Memorial leaned heavily on Lewis to tone down his remarks, SNCC activists circulated a draft to the crowd as evidence of their deep frustration with the slow pace of change as well as their contempt for the Lost Cause foundations of Jim Crow.

Martin Luther King was just as impatient with the administration as John Lewis and his fellow SNCC workers. He couched his celebrated "I Have a Dream" speech that day in terms less offensive to white southerners weaned on the black legend of General Sherman, but nevertheless drew forcefully on Civil War remembrance to press the case for urgent federal action. King's address was given historical weight by the fact that he spoke in what he called "the symbolic shadow" of French's marble statue of Abraham Lincoln.[69] Even though this classic site of North-South reconciliation paid little heed to the act of black liberation, the memorial had been a sacred space to African Americans since Marian Anderson's concert in 1939.[70] King knew that embracing a memory of Lincoln as the Great Emancipator would invest his call for government action with legitimacy, even if it meant downplaying Lerone Bennett's recent focus on black agency in US history.

King began by merging his own voice with that of the sixteenth president. "Five score years ago," he proclaimed, "a great American . . . signed the Emancipation Proclamation. This momentous decree came as a great beacon light of hope to millions of Negro slaves who had been seared in the flames of withering injustice. It came as a joyous daybreak to end the long night of their captivity."[71] The SCLC leader's purpose, however, was not to praise America but to chastise it for not fulfilling the promise of Lincoln's historic edict. The centenary of emancipation underlined his central, damning point, masterfully repeated, that "one hundred years later, the Negro still is not free; one hundred years later, the life of the Negro is still sadly crippled by the manacles of segregation and the chains of discrimination; one hundred years later, the Negro lives on a lonely island of poverty in the midst of a vast ocean of material prosperity; one hundred years later, the Negro is still languished in the corners of American society and finds himself in exile in his own land."[72]

King did not resort to Civil War themes and images so frequently after his appearance on the Mall, perhaps because he began to lose confidence in the idea that a usable past could effect radical social change in the United States. However, the movement's voting rights campaign in Alabama in the spring of 1965 triggered more segregationist violence—violence that contributed to a passionate speech he delivered before the state capitol in Montgomery at the close of a troubled but ultimately successful protest march from Selma. Speaking this time in the symbolic shadow of Jefferson Davis and blotting out memories of Governor Wallace's rallying call to segregationists, King iterated his belief, rooted in his Christian faith, that "the arc of the moral universe is long, but it bends toward justice." In a rousing peroration, he asked rhetorically how long the fight for equal justice would take. Not long, he answered, because:

> Mine eyes have seen the glory of the coming of the Lord;
> He is trampling out the vintage where the grapes of wrath are stored;
> He has loosed the fateful lightning of his terrible swift sword;
> His truth is marching on.
> He has sounded forth the trumpet that shall never call retreat;
> He is sifting out the hearts of men before His judgment seat.
> O, be swift, my soul, to answer Him! Be jubilant my feet!
> Our God is marching on.
> Glory, hallelujah! Glory, hallelujah!
> Glory, hallelujah! Glory, hallelujah!
> His truth is marching on.[73]

The minister's predominantly black audience shouted their approval at the end of every line of the "Battle Hymn of the Republic" and erupted into applause at the close. King would cite the famous Union anthem again on the night before his murder in Memphis three years later. But by this time, the glacial pace of domestic reform had seriously undermined his faith in America.

Black Power radicals, most of them openly contemptuous of King, integration, and nonviolent protest, had little interest in Civil War memory as a rhetorical tool. At times nationalist leaders reflected on the conflict's significance, but normally they did so in a negative sense: to condemn white liberals and their black allies. The coruscating agitator Malcolm X, for example, debunked the familiar liberal narrative depicting Abraham Lincoln as the president who freed the slaves. Lincoln, he said in October 1963, was "the one who has been dangled in front of our people as a god who brought us out of slavery into the promised land of freedom. Martin Luther King last year was begging President Kennedy to issue another Emancipation Proclamation. If the Emancipation Proclamation of Abraham Lincoln was authentic and produced the results that it was supposed to and if it had been sincere, it would have gotten results. Then Martin Luther King wouldn't have to be begging for another proclamation of emancipation today."[74] Julius Lester, in his polemical text *Look Out Whitey! Black Power's Gon' Get Your Mama!*, adopted the same cynical approach, deriding the self-congratulatory liberal notion, embedded in some school textbooks, that whites had gone to war to free the slaves. "It turned out that way," asserted the combative SNCC activist, "but that ain't the way it started out."[75]

While Black Power activists and intellectuals engaged with Civil War memory, they did not, like civil rights movement leaders, deploy it creatively as part of a patriotic campaign to make whites see the gap between the glittering promise and the often depressing reality of modern American life. This was because they regarded the Civil War as a reactionary site of memory—one that, as they had witnessed during the centennial, was more likely to buttress the cause of segregationists, hypocritical white liberals, or deluded black integrationists than clear-sighted revolutionaries like themselves. Whereas Martin Luther King was a deeply loyal American who sought desperately to make his country live up to its fine ideals, radical black nationalists had no illusions that the United States, as presently constituted, could ever change. In fact, for many of them, America was the enemy they were fighting. "America is truly a disgusting burden upon this planet," asserted the Black Panther leader Eldridge Cleaver. "In order to transform the American social order, we have to destroy the present structure of power in the United States, we have to overthrow the government."[76]

For self-proclaimed black revolutionaries, lauding African American soldiers' efforts to secure equal citizenship by taking up arms in defense of the Union made little tactical sense when they were urging their black compatriots not to go to war against fellow people of color in Vietnam. One gleans a sense of what they may have felt about US Colored Troops in Cleaver's stinging rebuke to black servicemen in Indochina in January 1970: "I know that you niggers have your minds all messed up about Black organizations, or you wouldn't be the flunkies for the white organization—the U.S.A.—for whom you have picked up the gun." Either quit the United States Army, he instructed, or "start destroying it from the inside."[77]

Black Power leaders had a strong sense of the past and frequently used their reading of historians like Lerone Bennett (who damned Lincoln as a white supremacist in a widely read 1968 essay) to legitimize and strengthen their cause. But they focused less on the tainted memory site of the Civil War than on the actions of slave rebels and their free black allies in the antebellum period. Unlike black Union troops or Crispus Attucks, a black American patriot killed in the Boston massacre of 1773, insurrectionary slaves were not compromised by the fact that they had died to help save racist white people.

Black radicals on the socialist wing of the Black Power continuum, however, were willing to celebrate the white abolitionist John Brown. In 1965, Malcolm X described him as "the only good white the country's ever had."[78] Others championed Brown as a role model for America's incipient interracial revolutionary coalition. In an interview with *Playboy* in October 1968, Eldridge Cleaver raised the specter of domestic carnage if the federal government did not accede to the Black Panthers' Ten Point program—"Not just a race war, which in itself would destroy this country, but a guerrilla resistance movement that will amount to a second Civil War, with thousands of John Browns fighting on the side of the blacks, plunging America into the depths of its most desperate nightmare on the way to realizing the American dream."[79]

By the end of the 1960s, America's cities were aflame with racial unrest. The dream of national centennial planners that the country's divisive Civil War could be a platform for domestic consensus in the fight against communism had been shattered. Violent southern segregationists, committed to a racially discriminatory society bolstered by Lost Cause myths, were partly responsible for this development. So was the mainstream civil rights movement, which exposed the inherent flaws in America's claims to be the champion of the free world. Even white liberals like Bruce Catton and Allan Nevins, whose commitment to national victory in the Cold War exceeded their empathy for alienated African Americans, belatedly threw their influence behind the destruction of Jim Crow at the expense of domestic consensus. The era's racial strife, however, shattered more than illusions of national unity. By destabilizing seemingly entrenched grand narratives of the Civil War and legitimizing interest-group politics, it also contributed to a new fragmentation of American memory. In the postmodern, post–civil rights epoch depopulated entirely of people who had lived through the 1860s, the Civil War would remain an object of frequent cultural and political appropriation.

Afterlife

The War That Won't Go Away

On July 1, 1997, visitors to the tourist town of Gettysburg witnessed the latest in a long line of ceremonies linked to the most famous battle of the Civil War. It was staged as carefully as any of its predecessors. Musket-bearing reenactors walked slowly alongside a hearse containing the remains of an unknown soldier uncovered by an archeological dig the previous year. Two elderly women were the stars of the day, riding in a horse-drawn carriage in the procession to the National Cemetery. Ninety-year-old Alberta Martin from Elba, Alabama, widely regarded as the last surviving widow of a Confederate veteran, sat at the front; behind her was ninety-six-year-old Daisy Anderson, an African American resident of a nursing home in Denver, Colorado, who was believed to be one of only two Union widows still alive on the eve of the millennium. At the graveside, the coffin was draped in an American flag, and James M. McPherson of Princeton University, the country's leading Civil War historian, delivered a short speech in which he said the burial of the unknown soldier was "a reminder of a time when the nation's institutions and values hung in the balance of war. His death in the fighting at the Railroad Cut 134 years ago abolished that distinction between enemies . . . [j]ust as the end of the Civil War two years later made all soldiers Americans again, whether they had worn the blue or the gray."[1]

The two widows appeared to share McPherson's belief that the war's primary meaning lay in national reunification. During the day, they shook hands for the photographers. Alberta Martin commented how much she had been looking forward to seeing her black counterpart, the wife of a former slave who had enlisted in the 125th US Colored Infantry. She proffered gifts, including an old locket containing a photograph of herself in front of a Confederate monument back home. Daisy Anderson invited the southerner to visit Denver and remarked on the personal and symbolic importance of their meeting. "I think it shows unity and that's what we need," she said.[2] While this heartwarming ceremony doubtless proved to be a genuinely moving occasion for participants and observers alike, it illustrated three major trends in Americans' efforts to remember the Civil War in the modern era.

First, it demonstrated the way that contemporary concerns and agendas continued to shape the memory of that bitter conflict. The National Park Service, guardian of the battlefields, had stage-managed the funeral of the unknown soldier to illustrate how the war could unite Americans in the divided present. Daisy Anderson, Alberta Martin, and James McPherson each played their allotted parts to perfection.

Second, the ceremony highlighted the versatility of Civil War remembrance. The reconciliatory strain of historical memory that had dominated, though not monopolized, American interpretations of the war since the 1890s had depended on the existence of common ground between northern and southern whites. Consensus was no less the main goal for the country's governing elites in 1997 than it had been in 1897 or 1957. However, the civil rights movement's destruction of Jim Crow and the resulting political and cultural empowerment of African Americans meant that if consensual discourse were to retain the high ground, it must belatedly accommodate black perspectives on the Civil War. What better way to signify the biracial foundations of Civil War memory than to invite two elderly war widows, one African American, the other white and southern, to shake hands before the cameras at Gettysburg?

Third, the carefully orchestrated funeral unwittingly revealed the extent to which time had divorced Americans from what southern historian Shelby Foote memorably called "the cross roads of our being."[3] Park Service officials believed the war widows' presence would highlight the direct connection that still existed between modern-day Americans and the events of 1861–65. In reality, this connection was highly tenuous. Martin and Anderson had been born long after Appomattox. They had married their husbands when the men, both pension holders, were already in their eighties. Both of the old soldiers had died in the early 1930s. Living memories of the sectional conflict could play no role in Civil War commemoration in the late twentieth century. Relatives three or four times removed from the veterans did continue to influence the country's still-flourishing Civil War subculture, most visibly as members of small heritage groups like the Sons of Union Veterans, the United Daughters of the Confederacy (UDC), and the Sons of Confederate Veterans (SCV). However, while it was certainly influenced by evolving collective memories of the Civil War and the grand narratives to which they were connected, this subculture was molded largely by the technologically innovative, fiercely corporate, and socially alienating capitalism of the present.

Racial politics also drove Civil War remembrance and commemoration after 1970. A majority of white southerners reached a grudging accommodation with the social, political, and cultural shifts wrought by the Second Reconstruction, but this did not prevent the majority of them abandoning the increasingly liberal Democratic Party in favor of the more conservative Republicans. Although most southern whites spent less time obsessing about the Civil War than many northerners supposed, several neo-Confederate groups sprang up in the late twentieth century, their support for displays of the Rebel battle flag conditioned by a combination of race hatred, patriarchal decline, hostility to big government, and, in some cases, a deep distrust of global capitalism's impact on the United States.

African Americans were more interested in the history of the civil rights movement than the Civil War, but it was a black politician, Barack Obama, who reenergized the memory of Abraham Lincoln at the start of his presidential campaign in early 2007. Obama's remarkable success demonstrated that nearly 150 years after the attack on Fort Sumter the Civil War still provided American politicians with a usable past. The significance of the Civil War sesquicentennial that began in 2011 was less clear. On the one hand, its low-key tenor, certainly compared with that of the ill-fated centennial, appeared to suggest that the war's influence on the United States was beginning to recede. On the other, its inclusive and educational goals indicated that more Americans than ever were beginning to realize that serious study of the Civil War offered their compatriots a deeper understanding of the republic's turbulent past and present. No event better illustrated the urgent need for such awareness than the tragic murders in Charleston in June 2015.

The Fall and Rise of Civil War Remembrance in the Modern Age

Popular interest in the American Civil War sagged after the centennial. Many children who had been excited by Civil War–themed TV programs, commercial paraphernalia, and family trips to the battlefields moved into adult life with scarcely a backward glance. Their successors in the 1970s were brought up in a country sobered by racial strife, military defeat in Vietnam, and President Richard Nixon's disgracing of the executive office in the Watergate scandal. At the height of the Cold War, American families had visited the battlefield shrines to stoke their civic pride. By the late 1970s, the urge to make patriotic pilgrimages had abated. The number of visitors at most major Civil War sites dipped at some point during this fractious decade, most precipitously at Gettysburg. The latter registered just under one million recreational visitors in 1979 compared with nearly seven million in 1970.[4] Baby-boomers born in the decade and a half after 1945 sought personal fulfillment in many ways, but normally an interest in Civil War history was not one of them. Even white southerners, certainly moderates appalled by the violence of battle-flag waving segregationists, seemed to have had enough of Robert E. Lee, Stonewall Jackson, and other Lost Cause heroes. For concerned patriots thirsting for proof of consensus in the nation's past, the Bicentenary of the American Revolution offered greater sustenance. Surely in 1776 Americans had been united in their opposition to a common enemy and their commitment to human liberty?

Professional historians also seemed to lose interest in the Civil War at this time. The centennial's overriding focus on the conflict's military events left many scholars bored with the whole affair. Academic books on the subject nearly dried up. Heavily influenced by the racial conflicts of the era, as well as a growing trend in favor of writing "history from below," historians turned their gaze from the war itself to reassess what they regarded as more compelling topics like slavery and Reconstruction. The result was an outpouring of books and essays that debunked stale interpretations of docile slaves, fanatical abolitionists, vindictive Radicals, and venal carpetbaggers. Influential works, including John Blassingame's *The Slave Community* (1972) and Eugene Genovese's *Roll, Jordan, Roll* (1974) emphasized the capacity of slaves to influence the world around them—their ability to fashion a distinctive African American culture and even to affect the actions of their white masters.[5] Although scholars in the post–civil rights era were aware of the racially blinkered attitudes of white abolitionists and Radical Republicans, books such as Eric Foner's *Free Soil, Free Labor, Free Men* (1971) and *Reconstruction: America's Unfinished Revolution, 1863–1877* (1988) demonstrated that there had been an ideological basis for the struggles against slavery and white supremacy and that many supporters of those campaigns had pursued idealistic goals within an intellectual framework bounded by economic liberalism and a preference for constitutional restraint.[6]

These fresh assessments kicked away the intellectual props of the reconciliatory and Lost Cause narratives of the Civil War era, those overlapping strains of historical memory that retained their hold on the American public even in the wake of the civil rights movement. By the late 1970s, they were being incorporated into museum exhibits by a new generation of professionally trained specialists who took account not only of the new scholarship but also of African Americans' determination to secure public recognition of their emancipationist counter-memory. The impact of these efforts, however, was limited. Not until the end of the century would revisionist interpretations exert a determining influence on the dominant national narrative of the Civil War.

One of the most striking signs of Americans' waning interest in the watershed event of their history was the rapid decline in Abraham Lincoln's popularity. For the first six decades of the twentieth century, Lincoln had been a usable symbol for governing elites and ordinary people alike. The Black Power movement sparked his eclipse in the 1960s. Few African American radicals had anything good to say about a president who had confessed his preference for his own race and avowed his support for colonization. In fact, as Americans of every hue entered a cynical, "post-heroic era," they seemed to lose not only their faith in towering figures like Abraham Lincoln but also their psychological need for them.[7]

The Great Emancipator's standing was further eroded by the Republican Party's steady abandonment of him. As the party moved to the right to accommodate its new southern white constituency, its leaders had little cause to remind voters of a president who signified black liberation and federal power. The dwindling band of liberal Republicans were loath to give him up, but conservatives in the party, contemptuous of Vietnam-era defeatism and countercultural excess, discovered a new hero in Ronald Reagan during the 1980s. When conservative Republicans made positive references to the country's past, they lodged them in America's celebratory World War II narrative and nostalgia for the prosperous 1950s. Washington's triumphal World War II Memorial, dedicated officially on the Mall by President George W. Bush in May 2004, obscured the sightlines between the Lincoln Memorial, Arlington Cemetery, and the Civil War monuments at the base of Capitol Hill. Its location seemed symbolically to announce the trumping of a distant and divisive war by the historical memory of a victorious national struggle against evil—"the good war" as one best-selling title labeled it—in which all Americans could take pride.[8]

Yet by this date, grassroots interest in the Civil War had undergone something of a popular revival. Three factors spurred the conflict's return to rude health in its afterlife: consolidation of the post-1945 Civil War subculture as a result of major social and economic change; a widespread realization that the old battlefields were threatened with destruction by commercial development; and the war's dramatic return to the television and silver screens.

In his critically acclaimed novel *The March*, written in the midst of the chaotic aftermath of the US invasion of Iraq in 2003, E. L. Doctorow crafted a profoundly modern account of General William T. Sherman's devastating campaign through Georgia and the Carolinas in late 1864 and early 1865. This event, still infamous in southern lore, became in Doctorow's imagination a powerful metaphor for the rampantly capitalist United States—what one commentator described as "a loosely directed, omnivorously consuming, amoeba-like nation that grows with no plan beyond the slaking of its own hungers."[9]

Doctorow illustrates America's transformative capacity by describing how Sherman's campaign inexorably draws in human beings, black as well as white, and then chews them up, leaving them either altered or just plain dead. The march itself takes on the form of a monstrous worm. "Imagine," says the science-obsessed Union doctor Wrede Sartorius, "a great segmented body moving in contractions and dilations at a rate of twelve or fifteen miles a day, a creature of a hundred thousand feet. It is tubular in its being and tentacled to the roads and bridges over which it travels. . . . It consumes everything in its path."[10] Although Doctorow concedes a modicum of moral purpose to some of his creations, the relentless advance of American modernity appears wholly amoral. At the close, Sherman believes that his battle-weary troops have bestowed meaning to the ground they have trod, something even "of moral consequence." But "as the march dissolves," he thinks, "so does the meaning, the army strewing itself into the isolated intentions of diffuse private life, and the terrain thereby left blank and also diffuse, and ineffable, a thing once again . . . completely insensible and without any purpose of its own."[11]

Cast adrift from their moorings by rapid socioeconomic changes associated with the triumph of global capitalism and "neoliberal" ideology, Americans yearned for meaning and identity in the late twentieth century. Growing numbers of them found succor not in academic history but in heritage—history packaged and sold as entertainment by businesses attuned to the demands of specialized groups of consumers forged by the evolving market. The Civil War subculture that had taken shape after 1945 provided such businesses with ample opportunities to turn a profit. Reenactors, for example, mostly middle-aged white men eager to engage in a purposeful male-bonding exercise, were willing to spend thousands of dollars on replica weapons, uniforms, and other military paraphernalia to feed their hobby. Along with Civil War book collectors, board-game players, genealogists, Round Table members, and relic hunters, they belonged to what historian Jim Weeks refers to as "image tribes"—self-selecting consumer groups with their own specialist magazines, networks, and suppliers.[12]

Most of these group members and, indeed, many Americans who did not belong to the evolving Civil War subculture hankered after authenticity in their encounters with the past, largely because of the dispiriting anomie and rootlessness of modern life. During the 1970s and early 1980s, the National Park Service, operating as the tourist arm of the US government, began to take advantage of this demand by introducing "living history" elements into its programs, including those at major Civil War sites. Park rangers guided visitors on walks across portions of the old battlefields, retracing the steps of individual regiments at critical moments in those engagements. Volunteer reenactors, alert to the joys of the "period rush," often participated in Park Service events.[13] By demonstrating how to fire rifled muskets and reenacting Civil War skirmishes and battles, they contributed to the visitors' sense that they were being transported back into history. "Hard-core" reenactors were especially dismissive of "farbs," people who supposed they could represent the past without striving to live it in a manner as close as possible to the way their forebears had lived it. Hence their need to spend a small fortune on the best reproduction clothing and weaponry they could lay their hands on.[14]

The commercial ambitions of profit-oriented heritage purveyors clashed with the rising grassroots demand for authenticity in November 1993 when the Walt Disney Corporation announced plans to install a three thousand–acre theme park called "Disney's America" near the Manassas National Battlefield Park. The ensuing controversy over this grandiose scheme (which included a purpose-built Civil War village and fort) not only energized an emerging battlefield preservation coalition but also helped to revive popular interest in the Civil War.

Concerns about the damaging impact of economic growth on the nation's Civil War sites were long-standing. However, they had increased considerably in 1974 after construction of an imposing viewing tower on the edge of the park at Gettysburg and were intensified further by the destruction of the Chantilly battlefield in Fairfax County, Virginia, in the mid-1980s as well as by proposals to build a large mall adjacent to the Manassas park. Disney's plan to capitalize on the 19 million annual tourist visits to Washington sparked a feeling of real crisis among preservationists, historians, and many other Americans who deplored the impact of suburban sprawl on hallowed Civil War sites. Although two well-known scholars, Eric Foner and James O. Horton, acted as consultants for the $650 million heritage project in the hope that it might assist the popular dissemination of historical knowledge, others, including James McPherson, Shelby Foote, John Hope Franklin, and David McCulloch, organized a new campaign group, Protect Historic America, to fight it. Speaking at a press conference in May 1994, McCulloch bemoaned the fact that Americans "have so little left that's authentic and real." He added, "To replace what we have with plastic, contrived history, mechanical history is almost sacrilege."[15] Combining with other interested parties, including wealthy residents of northern Virginia's horse country, Protect Historic America generated a rash of negative press coverage for the scheme (one iconoclastic newspaper cartoon depicted Abraham Lincoln with Mickey Mouse ears). Disney's ensuing decision to abandon its plans did not end the pressure of ancillary development on Civil War parks. However, it provided a major fillip to savvy battlefield preservation groups like the Association for the Preservation of Civil War Sites, the

Friends of Gettysburg, and the Civil War Trust, which would soon be using the latest Internet technology to launch membership drives and augment campaign coffers.

The pace of modernity also led some Park Service officials to redouble their efforts to render the battlefield landscapes as "real" as possible. Although some policymakers regarded the clutter of monuments and expanse of twentieth-century infrastructure as insurmountable barriers to the attainment of authenticity, popular pressure to restore the sites to something resembling their Civil War appearance proved too intense to resist. By the beginning of the twenty-first century, John Latschar, park superintendent at Gettysburg, was overseeing an ambitious program of tree planting and felling, deer culling, and building reconstruction to restore the battlefield to what it might have looked like in 1863.

Visitor numbers to most Civil War sites were robust in the last two decades of the twentieth century.[16] This was partly because of the war's revitalized status in American popular culture as evidenced by the popularity of the movies *Glory* (1989) and *Gettysburg* (1993) and Ken Burns's landmark television series *The Civil War*, which aired for twelve consecutive nights on the Public Broadcasting Service in 1990. While it is difficult to explain this phenomenon with any degree of precision, it seems probable that the patriotic renewal of the Reagan years combined with the delayed cultural impact of the civil rights movement and the durability of the Civil War subculture to make the conflict a more attractive topic for filmmakers than it had been during the national malaise of the 1970s. Each of these productions left audiences with a patriotic afterglow and revealed the extent to which the stories that Americans told themselves about the 1860s had altered since the centennial commemorations.

In terms of its depiction of racial politics, Edward Zwick's *Glory* was the most significant of the three films. Before its appearance, no Hollywood movie had made black Civil War troops the central focus of attention. Zwick's narrative dramatizes the experiences of the black Fifty-Fourth Massachusetts Regiment that assaulted Battery Wagner in July 1863 and whose bravery had been commemorated in the unique Saint-Gaudens monument on Boston Common. Although the regiment's white commanding officer, Robert Gould Shaw (Matthew Broderick), is a major figure in the movie, his presence is counterbalanced by three fictionalized black soldiers: the rebellious Trip (Denzel Washington), the pragmatic Rawlins (Morgan Freeman), and the bookish Searles (Andre Braugher). During the action, Shaw molds his disparate charges into effective fighting men with a combination of well-intentioned discipline and paternal encouragement. In many respects the film is "a Civil War platoon drama that follows certain predictable formulas," one in which different character types learn to work with one another and embrace the cause for which they are fighting before they go into battle as American comrades.[17] During the dramatic, stylized finale, in which Shaw leads his men along the beach toward the fort, Trip carries the regimental flag to indicate his belated sense of patriotic purpose. In the last scene, after the attack has failed, viewers witness the bodies of Trip and Shaw lying together in a burial trench. Zwick's willingness, reminiscent of William James's speech at the dedication of the Shaw monument on Boston Common, to sanction the use of force in the service of a moral cause like black emancipation is plainly evident, as is his personal commitment to racial integration.

Although *Glory* was only a modest success at the box office, its stirring account of a black Union regiment garnered significant attention from African Americans, many of whom knew nothing of blacks fighting for the United States in the Civil War. In November 1998, a poll carried out by the glossy magazine *Ebony* rated it fifteenth in a list of "the top black films" of all time.[18] The movie provided an additional stimulus to African Americans' growing interest in genealogy, which had received a major boost after the TV series of Alex Haley's *Roots* (1977) and led to the formation of the country's first black Civil War reenactment groups. It also prompted Frank Smith Jr., a former SNCC activist who served as a city councilor in Washington, DC, to initiate efforts to create a national memorial to black Civil War troops. His campaign, supported by prominent African American politicians, culminated in 1992, when Congress appropriated $2.5 million to fund the project.[19] Sculptor Ed Hamilton's statue *The Spirit of Freedom* was dedicated in the capital's Shaw neighborhood in the summer of 1998, where it was soon joined by the country's first museum devoted to the history of US Colored Troops.

Ken Burns's *Civil War* generated enormous interest across the United States in 1990, when more than 23 million people watched the first two episodes of the series, and 14 million viewers stayed the course to watch all twelve episodes transmitted in the first week of the fall season.[20] Whereas Edward Zwick drew heavily on the revitalized emancipationist strain of Civil War memory to inject visual power and moral purpose into *Glory*, Burns—like Zwick a patriotic white liberal—crafted an updated version of the established reconciliatory narrative. His documentary series depicted the Civil War as America's Iliad, a national Cattonesque epic waged by courageous and suffering Americans on both sides. Passing rapidly in the season finale over Reconstruction and the horrors and indignities of Jim Crow, he glimpsed redemption in the abolition of slavery and the rapid restoration of sectional amity.

Although Burns used a number of professionals, including the black historian Barbara Jeanne Fields, to provide expert commentary, the film's power was generated primarily by the director's clever use of sentiment, the main weapon of conciliators in the late nineteenth century, to stir viewers' emotions.

A skillful combination of sources made *The Civil War* a compelling television feast: black-and-white photographs (including images of the battlefield dead taken by contemporary photographers such as Mathew Brady and Alexander Gardner), haunting background music (notably Jay Ungar's "Ashokan Farewell"), and carefully selected extracts from original letters written by protagonists like Sullivan Ballou, a Union officer whose moving words to his wife Sarah before his death at First Bull Run featured prominently at the close of part 1. Viewers' senses were further aroused by the compelling word pictures painted by Shelby Foote, the most memorable of Burns's talking heads. Although Foote, a white Mississippian, had already won plaudits for his three-volume history of the Civil War published between 1958 and 1974, his lilting descriptions of southern successes and failures made him a national celebrity and sent sales of his books into the stratosphere. "Ken," he told Burns, "you've made me a millionaire."[21]

Ron Maxwell's film *Gettysburg* was an intellectually slighter work than the creations of Zwick and Burns, yet it did as much as its two predecessors to stimulate popular interest in the Civil War at the close of the twentieth century. Distributed effectively in the United States by the Atlanta-based media mogul and self-confessed buff, Ted Turner, it was defiantly traditional in its interpretation of the Civil War and located solidly within the familiar reconciliatory framework.

Based on *The Killer Angels* (1975), a best-selling novel by US Army veteran Michael Shaara that attempted to counter the era's prevailing cynicism about war, Maxwell's epic film follows the Union and Confederate armies as they pound one another over three days at Gettysburg. While his respect for the courage displayed by the soldiers on both sides is apparent throughout the action, his attention to the respective causes is limited to sporadic comments from some of the main characters. Union officer Joshua Lawrence Chamberlain, a hero of the movie along with Confederate general James Longstreet, insists, "We are an army out to set other men free," but viewers gain little awareness that most northerners risking their lives in the defense of Cemetery Ridge and Little Round Top were actually fighting to save the United States.[22] Similarly, the Rebels claim vaguely to be waging war for their rights or for their states as opposed to crusading for a new proslavery southern nation. African Americans are a marginal presence in the film, even though many were present in the town of Gettysburg in July 1863. Seen through Maxwell's eyes, the toned-down battle scenes are evidence of *white* American nobility and courage, demonstrated on day two by Chamberlain's stubborn efforts to defend the exposed left flank of the Union line at Little Round Top and on day three by Lee's doomed attack on the Union center. Like Burns, who has a cameo role in the action, Maxwell makes liberal use of sentiment to press his central point that the Civil War was a tragic brothers' war. One of the main leitmotifs of the film is the close relationship between the Confederate brigade commander Lewis Armistead and his old West Point friend Winfield Scott Hancock, who leads the repulse of Pickett's Charge. Although war has interrupted the friendship, Armistead repeatedly expresses his desire to see his comrade again. His dying wish at the conclusion of Pickett's assault is that Hancock should have his Bible by which to remember him.

Perhaps because *Gettysburg* lacked the cynicism of other contemporary Civil War–related films such as Ang Lee's *Ride with the Devil* (1999), Martin Scorsese's *Gangs of New York* (2002), and Anthony Minghella's *Cold Mountain* (2003), it joined Ken Burns's TV series and *Glory* in expanding the consumer-driven Civil War subculture of the modern era. One immediate result was a significant increase in visitors to Gettysburg National Military Park in 1994.[23] Tellingly, however, many of the war's latest recruits expected to see "authentic" evidence of the film when they visited the battlefield. The Park Service, which had cooperated fully with the Turner project by allowing Maxwell to film on its property, obligingly responded to the new demand. It developed a new exhibit highlighting Joshua Chamberlain's role in the battle and built a new parking lot to accommodate tourists wanting to see the place where Chamberlain's Twentieth Maine had apparently saved the Union Army singlehandedly.[24] Federal authorities also gave permission for the construction of a modern equestrian statue to Longstreet, belatedly vindicated by Shaara's book and Maxwell's film, which was dedicated in 1998.[25] At the end of the twentieth century, memories continued to influence the way many Americans related to the Civil War, but these memories were predominantly artificial, fashioned by the skill of filmmakers and other purveyors of modern popular culture. In this respect, Edward Zwick, Ken Burns, and Ron Maxwell can be seen as the legitimate heirs of D. W. Griffith, Margaret Mitchell, and Carl Sandburg.

Culture Wars and the Development of Neo-Confederacy

In January 1995, the Smithsonian Institution's Air and Space Museum in Washington, DC, canceled an exhibition scheduled to coincide with the fiftieth anniversary of the devastating US atomic attacks on Japan in World War II. The decision followed months of wrangling. Veterans groups, including the American Legion and the Air Force Association, had voiced serious objections to the historical narrative fashioned by the Smithsonian to accompany its display of the *Enola Gay*, the giant Boeing B-29 Superfortress that had launched the first strike on Hiroshima. Believing, like their Civil War predecessors, that they were the optimal guardians of their own military past, members of these influential groups denounced the exhibition as revisionist and unbalanced, even after it had been substantially revised to incorporate their objections.

They were angered especially by what they saw as the curators' excessive focus on Japanese civilian casualties as well as suggestions that the United States had harbored other reasons for using nuclear weapons besides wanting to end World War II. Although leading scholars joined the Smithsonian in fighting a strong rearguard action, the exhibition's defenders were ultimately outflanked by proven patriots cloaked in the robust national memory of that conflict as the "good war."

The resulting controversy, which involved the fierce questioning of expert witnesses in hearings held by the Senate Committee on Rules and Administration, highlighted the tension between veterans' memories and historical interpretation undertaken by professional scholars. It was also an important event in the escalating "culture wars" that bedeviled the United States at the end of the twentieth century. These conflicts tended to pit conservatives, mostly Republicans, against liberals who typically identified themselves as Democrats. The former not only possessed hostile attitudes to abortion, gay rights, and what they saw as secular assaults on Christianity but also abhorred what they regarded as attempts by unpatriotic liberals to question America, past as well as present. In this respect, most conservatives saw the planned *Enola Gay* exhibit as an egregious attempt by out-of-touch elites to change the established facts of history. What liberals saw as healthy interpretive debate, their opponents called revisionism—and disloyalty.

The constructed memory of the Civil War emerged as an important point of contention in the culture wars as African American politicians redoubled their efforts to ensure official recognition of the emancipationist countermemory and as Park Service employees moved to make their interpretive narratives more inclusive and thus more attractive to a wider range of visitors. Black political influence was a major factor in the agency's decision to abandon its exclusive focus on military aspects of the Civil War—a focus that had been induced largely by federal officials' long-standing reluctance to antagonize southern whites. Chicago congressman Jesse L. Jackson Jr. raised the battlefield interpretation issue in the US House of Representatives after he had visited several sites and found little reference to the role that slavery and African Americans had played in the Civil War.

Jackson's campaign to induce federal officials to incorporate racial topics into their interpretive narratives coincided with a concerted move by leading park superintendents, aware of the latest trends in academic scholarship, to improve their agency's outdated presentation of the Civil War. In August 1998, they staged a groundbreaking conference in Nashville at which they acknowledged existing failures of interpretation and concluded that battlefield narratives should delineate a "site's particular place in the continuum of war, illuminate the social, economic, and cultural issues that caused or were affected by the war, illustrate the breadth of human experience during the period, and establish the relevance of the war to people today."[26] The Park Service then held a public conference titled "Rally on the High Ground" in Washington, DC, to broaden the discussion by reaching out to academics and the general public. The agency invited several professional historians to join Congressman Jackson as invited speakers at this event. Among them was James McPherson, who had already participated in an Organization of American Historians site review at Gettysburg. This exercise had resulted in a call for the park's hoary interpretive narrative—still fixated on the battle as the high watermark of the Confederacy—to be completely revised and retitled "A New Birth of Freedom."[27]

In 2000, Congress enshrined the didactic mission of black politicians, academics, and Park Service officials into law by directing the secretary of the interior to "encourage" Civil War sites to show visitors "the unique role that the institution of slavery played in causing the Civil War and its role, if any, at the individual battle sites."[28] In the opening decade of the new century, leading parks, including Gettysburg, Harpers Ferry, and Petersburg, incorporated the racial dimension of the war into their interpretive programs. At Gettysburg, galleries at the new $103 million visitor center opened in April 2008 introduced visitors to slavery's part in secession and Abraham Lincoln's focus on equality in his November 1863 address.[29] At Harpers Ferry, visitors could at last see an exhibit that placed John Brown's raid in its proper historical context and highlighted the town's postwar importance to African Americans. And at Petersburg, rangers finally began teaching tourists about the motivations of US Colored Troops involved in the trench warfare of 1864–65.[30]

Not everyone was happy with the federal government's dissemination of a historical narrative that belatedly recognized the once marginalized emancipationist strain of Civil War memory. Conservative white southerners, unhappy with even the limited social and political changes wrought by the civil rights movement, led the criticism. The Sons of Confederate Veterans spearheaded efforts to thwart installation of the new storyline at Gettysburg by bombarding Secretary of the Interior Bruce Babbitt with preprinted cards stating, "To attempt to change the way that a battlefield is interpreted to include social issues of the day does a great disservice to the military strategists and to the soldiers who sacrificed their all at these important battlefields."[31]

By the time it launched this unsuccessful campaign, the SCV belonged to an aggressive coalition of right-wing groups in the South committed to defending the embattled Lost Cause against liberal attacks. Neo-Confederate organizations like the Council of Conservative Citizens (CCC), the openly secessionist League of the South, and the SCV (which was infiltrated by hardliners at the turn of the century) rallied behind the South's orthodox narrative of the Civil War.[32] As well as denouncing the tide of alleged political correctness sweeping across the battlefields and the attendant erosion of "the facts" of history, they extolled the states' rights and small government origins of the Confederacy, the heroism of southern soldiers, and the supposed loyalty of blacks to the Rebel cause. Also important, they adhered to the white South's "truth" about the horrors of Reconstruction.

Neo-Confederates disseminated these views in several ways. Journals such as *Southern Patriot, Southern Partisan*, and *Southern Mercury* carried a range of articles designed to bolster readers' commitment to the endangered myths of the white South. In 2003, Georgian Frank Conner described Reconstruction as the moment when victorious Yankees "deliberately held the devastated South on the knife-edge of mass starvation" and "sought to crush the Southerners' Christian-based independence of spirit and belief in decentralized government."[33] Similarly one-sided accounts of the region's past, suffused with Lost Cause orthodoxy, appeared in books written by Conner, Thomas E. Woods Jr., and the brothers Walter and James Kennedy, and on websites hosted by neo-Confederate groups like the CCC. The League of the South tried to evade the impact of what it regarded as the encroachment of antisouthern history into the public schools by promoting home schooling—a goal that it encouraged by creating its own Institute for the Study of Southern Culture and History in 1996.[34]

The membership of neo-Confederate organizations transcended that of heritage groups like the UDC and the SCV, which demanded proof of linear or collateral descent from a Rebel ancestor. Its devotees' interest in the southern past was often generated less by respect for the Confederates of the 1860s than by their desire to promote white supremacy in the present. While neo-Confederates usually denied being racists, the movement to which they belonged can be seen as a continuation of massive resistance to racial integration. This was evident in a number of respects. Several leading figures in the CCC, for example, belonged to the old Citizens' Councils that had waged war against the NAACP after *Brown*. In addition, neo-Confederate spokesmen and writers openly declared their opposition to government-backed civil rights initiatives like busing and affirmative action. For the most part, they were white southerners unable to come to terms with the results of the Second Reconstruction.

Neo-Confederates explained what they saw as the region's plight in words that could have been understood by any unrepentant Rebel in the late nineteenth century. As Frank Conner put it in his 2003 piece for the SCV's *Southern Mercury,* twentieth-century liberals had used black civil rights "as their main moral weapon against the white South, just as their predecessors had done prior to the War of Northern Aggression." The civil rights movement, he claimed, had destroyed the culture of the Old South but failed to elevate blacks to the level of whites. Now liberals were promoting "Reconstruction II," ongoing since the 1950s, to spread secularism and socialism. "The only way we can prevent them (and their black-activist catspaws) from finishing the job of destroying us as a people and destroying our belief system and our way of life," Conner insisted, "is by counterattacking the liberals successfully and discrediting them in the eyes of the public."[35]

Neo-Confederates' awareness that a fundamental shift had occurred in American historical memory was sharpened by the US government's growing willingness to recognize the achievements of the nonviolent civil rights movement. In 1983, President Ronald Reagan grudgingly signed a bill designating Martin Luther King's birthday a national holiday. In 2011, the federal government dedicated an official memorial to the slain civil rights leader on the Mall in Washington. These initiatives, intended to incorporate memories of the civil rights movement into a more inclusive yet classically linear narrative of national progress, were consistent with efforts to render the federally sanctioned narrative of the Civil War acceptable to black citizens grown more assertive since the Jim Crow era. But to neo-Confederates, who regarded King with disgust, they were just further evidence of liberals' determination to rewrite the facts of history. After all, they contended, King was a lawbreaker who had reenslaved his people by leading them "into a perpetual dependence on the welfare state, a terrible bondage of body and soul."[36] Now he was deemed worthy of public reverence, just like black Union troops and their commander Ulysses S. Grant, the drunken Yankee butcher whose Manhattan tomb was renovated and reopened to the public in 1997 as a gleaming National Memorial long after it had fallen into a chronic state of disrepair.[37]

Angry neo-Confederates directed much of their ire against black and white liberal opposition to public displays of the Confederate battle flag. The Rebel banner emerged as a key battleground in the culture wars afflicting the South after 1980 less because of its role in the Civil War than as a result of its prominence as a symbol of massive resistance to racial integration and the civil rights movement. The fuse for flag controversies in the modern era was lit by a concerted campaign launched by the NAACP in March 1987 to stop the states of Alabama, Georgia, Mississippi, and South Carolina from using Confederate symbols.[38]

Alabama was the initial site of conflict. A battle flag was still flying over the state capitol in Montgomery since it had been placed there at George Wallace's behest in 1963. When a black state legislator, Thomas L. Reed, tried to tear down the flag in February 1988, a menacing crowd gathered to watch him arrested for criminal trespass along with a number of NAACP representatives and other African American legislators. But five years later, after a local circuit court enjoined the state from flying any emblem other than the national and state flags, Governor James Folsom Jr. announced that he favored displaying the battle flag at the Confederate White House near to the capitol. The state subsequently created a Confederate flag display around the Rebel monument within the statehouse grounds but the battle flag was conspicuous by its absence.[39]

Neo-Confederate groups like the League of the South and the SCV led right-wing efforts to defend the Rebel flag against its detractors. They met with only limited success, partly because of the strength of black opposition and partly because southern whites were not united behind their efforts. They triumphed in Mississippi in 2001 when voters decided, largely on racial lines, to retain the existing state flag that had incorporated the Rebel banner since 1894.[40] Two years later, Georgians delivered a partial victory when they voted three to one to abandon the saltire (adopted at the height of massive resistance in 1956) in favor of a new state flag based on the somewhat less controversial "Stars and Bars," the first national flag of the Confederacy.[41] Neo-Confederate attempts to keep the battle flag (technically the rectangular Confederate naval jack) flying over the South Carolina capitol in Columbia, however, were contested by a dogged NAACP campaign involving calls for an economic boycott of the state.

Significantly, neo-Confederate efforts to defend the battle flag as a marker of the Palmetto State's Christian heritage met with little support from local white women.[42] Although their ancestors had played a formative role in fashioning the Lost Cause, modern South Carolina women seemed more concerned about the flag's close association with racism. Among them was Jamie Renda, a politically conservative suburban housewife descended from a family of proslavery Confederates. After watching a TV documentary on the civil rights movement, one of her young daughters asked why whites were so mean to African Americans. Alarmed, Renda formed an organization named United 2000 to help coordinate opposition to the battle flag. Backed by the NAACP, outside bodies like the National Collegiate Athletic Association, and many local ministers and businesses, the anti-flag coalition attracted support from concerned citizens, at least one of whom invoked Robert E. Lee's "good manners" to justify a change that many hoped would improve community relations.[43] Despite strong resistance from patriarchal neo-Confederates, the majority of whom appeared to be working-class white men anxious about their declining social status, the South Carolina legislature passed the Heritage Act in 2000. The act removed the naval jack from the capitol dome and raised a square battle flag at the site of a monument to Confederate soldiers in the capitol grounds.[44] Even though the saltire remained visible (and therefore still controversial), its shift to the Rebel memorial demonstrated the state government's wish, in the wake of black empowerment, that the battle flag should be tied more closely to the cause of those who had fought, suffered, and died beneath its folds.

This compromise solution to the capitol flag controversy in South Carolina seemed to indicate that at the beginning of the twenty-first century neo-Confederates were a marginal force in the Deep South. It was certainly true that only a relatively small number of southern whites belonged to right-wing groups like the League of the South, the SCV, and the CCC and that even this disaffected constituency was divided over key issues such as the wisdom of present-day secession and opposition to American foreign policy in Iraq and Afghanistan. However, the political significance of these groups was enhanced by the support that many members of the new breed of southern Republicans gave to their efforts to preserve and celebrate Confederate history. This backing took several forms. Georgia's Republican governor, Sonny Perdue, for example, was a vocal supporter of his state's 2003 flag that incorporated the Rebel Stars and Bars. Republican governors and Republican-controlled legislatures in Alabama, Georgia, Mississippi, and Virginia regularly proclaimed their backing for Confederate History Month as part of a broader strategy to attract the votes of as many neo-Confederates as possible—certainly of those who did not belong to the openly secessionist League of the South, which was as hostile to both national political parties as the group's fire-eating predecessors. Dick Armey of Texas, Jesse Helms of North Carolina, and Trent Lott of Mississippi—nationally prominent southern Republicans—furthered this strategy by giving interviews to *Southern Partisan*, a well-known neo-Confederate magazine. Lott, the Senate majority leader between 1996 and 2001, made clear where his sympathies lay by moving Jefferson Davis's desk into his congressional office.

Republican efforts to win votes by cosseting neo-Confederates had the potential to backfire. In the spring of 2010, Virginia's Republican governor, Robert F. McDonnell, issued via his website a proclamation designating April as Confederate History Month. The event, he contended, would enable Virginians "to understand the sacrifices of the Confederate leaders, soldiers and citizens during the period of the Civil War." In suggesting that their involvement in this event would enable people "to reflect upon our Commonwealth's shared history," McDonnell was clearly appealing to his core political constituency.[45] However, the governor's failure to reflect on the role of slavery in Virginia's wartime experience brought down a storm of criticism upon his head from the NAACP, Democrats like former governor Douglas Wilder, and several academics (one of whom told National Public Radio that she wondered why Americans would want to celebrate traitors). Under normal circumstances, McDonnell might have been able to weather assaults from liberal opponents like these. Mississippi's Haley Barbour, only the second Republican governor of his state since

Reconstruction, thought the controversy "doesn't matter for diddly," and the SCV rallied to his defense.[46] In 2010, however, McDonnell also had to reckon with stinging criticism from President Barack Obama, who told ABC television that the governor had made an "unacceptable omission" by not mentioning slavery in his proclamation.[47] McDonnell quickly apologized and announced his submission to what had become the dominant national grand narrative of the Civil War. Slavery, he said, was an "abomination" that had caused that sanguinary conflict and "an evil, vicious and inhumane practice."[48]

The perils attached to southern Republican support for Lost Cause symbols were underlined further by the massacre of black churchgoers at Mother Emanuel in June 2015. Even when South Carolina Governor Nikki Haley and other leading Republicans called on the party to reject the battle flag, liberal commentators were swift to suggest that conservatives intended this knee-jerk response to deflect attention from the critical issue of gun control. Confederate emblems continued to be represented officially in other "red states" such as Mississippi and Georgia and to be sold commercially throughout the region. Neo-Confederates, many of whom were Republican voters, insisted they would not abandon the flag of their fathers in the face of pressure from its allegedly hypocritical detractors. "It's a symbol of family and my ancestors who defended the state from invasion," said one SCV member in the wake of the Charleston killings. "It was about standing up to a central government. . . . The things that our ancestors fought for were not novel and they really are the same issues we have today."[49] Opponents of name changes and the removal of Confederate statues adopted similar arguments. "This is a perfect example of the liberal government using 'political correctness' to erase history," wrote one Texan protesting the renaming of Confederate parks in Memphis.[50]

In the minds of embattled neo-Confederates, few liberal enemies loomed larger than Barack Obama, one of the most skilled practitioners of Civil War memory ever to inhabit the White House.

Abraham Obama

Obama, a liberal Illinois Democrat who had spoken out against the invasion of Iraq in 2003 before his election to the US Senate, launched his presidential campaign on February 10, 2007, from the steps of the Old State House in Springfield. His choice of location was a calculated one. Abraham Lincoln had begun his senatorial race against Stephen Douglas from the same spot in 1858. In case anyone missed the connection, Obama made sure to invoke his illustrious predecessor during the course of his brief announcement. Against the backdrop of the historic capitol and an enormous Stars and Stripes hanging from a nearby building, he told the interracial throng before him that Lincoln had shown Americans "that there is power in hope."

In historical terms, the speech was a muddle. Obama praised "[t]he genius" of the Founders for designing "a system of government that can be changed," yet lauded President Lincoln and other opponents of secession for using force to resolve a crisis that had been a consequence of the Founders' flawed creation. Nobody cared. Obama was a politician, not a historian. His speech was a rhetorical artifice, historically inflected to impart substance to his campaign announcement and crafted to appeal to those Americans yearning for a more united, compassionate, and peaceful country in the midst of bloody post-9/11 wars in the Near East and bitter partisan and cultural strife at home. Lincoln, intoned Obama, "through his will and his words" had "moved a nation and helped free a people." "It is," he insisted, "because of the millions who rallied to his cause that we are no longer divided, North and South, slave and free. It is because men and women of every race . . . continued to march for freedom together after Lincoln was laid to rest that today we have the chance to face the challenges of this millennium together, as one people—as Americans." "Together, starting today," he urged in a concluding invocation of the Gettysburg Address, "let us finish the work that needs to be done, and usher in a new birth of freedom on this Earth."[51]

The speech's power lay in Obama's shrewd understanding of how history could be used to promote progressive consensus as well as his own political ambitions. It was a subtle blend of historical memories—not only of the Union cause and its emancipationist counterpart, but also of the civil rights movement. When they referenced the Civil War in the early 1960s, Martin Luther King and other mainstream black leaders had depicted it as unfinished business because it failed to guarantee equality and security to African Americans. Not unlike his fellow Illinois Democrat Paul Douglas before him, Obama positioned himself at the modern end of a linear temporal narrative that fused the achievements of Lincoln, nineteenth-century Unionists, and modern civil rights activists. This was an astute move. Not only did he mark himself as another actor in America's millennial journey to perfection, but he also shielded himself against critics who regarded his identity as questionable. The son of a Kenyan father and a white American mother, Obama had spent his youth in Indonesia and Hawaii. While this background rendered him a living, breathing example of present-day multiculturalism, it made him a deeply suspect figure in the eyes of conservative whites and some blacks. He had tried to counter African American qualms by organizing poor blacks in Chicago's South Side in the 1980s and by consistently acknowledging his debt to the civil rights movement. By embracing Lincoln's memory, he explained his place in American history to black and white moderates who might have been concerned about elevating such an ambiguous and relatively inexperienced figure to the highest office in the land.

The global financial crisis that began in 2007 assisted Barack Obama's restoration of Abraham Lincoln to "active commemorative status" after three decades in which Americans seemed to have forgotten about their sixteenth president.[52] However, during the 2008 campaign, it was Obama's supporters rather than the candidate himself who did most to point out the supposed similarities between their favorite and Abraham Lincoln. Political commentator Garry Wills observed what he saw as Obama's Lincoln-style defense of his membership at Trinity United Church in Chicago, the domain of Rev. Jeremiah Wright, an African American preacher noted for his outspoken comments on a range of issues. Documentary filmmaker Ken Burns endorsed Obama on the grounds that he, like Lincoln, had set out a compelling vision of the future. Positive images intended by Obama's campaign team to embed the linkage in voters' consciousness were ubiquitous. Ron English's composite portrait, *Abraham Obama*, was a familiar, if frequently parodied, image on the Internet. One popular campaign button even depicted Lincoln sporting an "Obama '08" T-shirt.

The Obama-Lincoln connection was widely noted by news media intrigued, and to a large extent persuaded by, these attempts to orientate the public at a time of national crisis. They were also derided by conservative Republicans and by liberal supporters of New York Senator Hillary Clinton's rival presidential campaign. The progressive commentator Sean Wilentz, for example, attacked what he regarded as the preposterous idea that Clinton's dangerous young opponent had a unique sense of history. He compared Obama unfavorably with John F. Kennedy, who, he contended, had "won a Pulitzer Prize for a work of history"—a comment that ignored the fact that Kennedy's *Profiles in Courage* (1956), a celebratory account of the seven Republicans who had voted against the impeachment of Andrew Johnson, was out of date even before it had been written with the assistance of a "committee" of professional historians.[53] Although Clinton tried to negate Obama's sophisticated use of historical memory by challenging him to a series of Lincoln-Douglas–style debates, her opponent rejected the offer. After the Illinois senator's victory at the Democratic National Convention in Denver, former vice president Al Gore announced that Obama was the man for a crisis, just as Lincoln had been in 1860. A majority of American voters thought so too. In the November general election the Democratic nominee won a crushing victory over the Republican candidate, Senator John McCain.

In spite of withering attacks from his opponents, the president-elect did little to damp down media interest in the Obama/Lincoln comparison. In one interview, in which he referred to an award-winning account of Lincoln's cabinet by historian Doris Kearns Goodwin, he raised the possibility of appointing a "team of rivals" to his cabinet as a means of curbing destructive partisanship.[54]

On January 18, 2009, at a pre-inauguration ceremony, he told a large crowd at the Lincoln Memorial in Washington that he drew strength in the current crisis from the fact that "[d]irectly in front of us is a pool that still reflects the dream of a King, and the glory of a people who marched and bled so that their children might be judged by their character's content. And behind me, watching over the union he saved, sits the man who in so many ways made this day possible."[55] Two days later, he was the first American president since 1861 to swear the oath of office on the same Bible used by Lincoln. Presidential Inaugural Committee executive director Emmett Beliveau said the president-elect was "committed to holding an inauguration that celebrates America's unity, and the use of the historic Bible will provide a powerful connection to our common past and common heritage."[56]

In office, Obama resorted less frequently to the pliable memory of Abraham Lincoln. On the rare occasions when he did so, he appeared keener to promote the elusive goal of national unity than economic justice for the millions of poor Americans hit hard by the banking collapse. He told an audience in Washington on the bicentenary of the martyred president's birth, "What Lincoln never forgot, not even in the midst of civil war, was that despite all that divides us—North and South, black and white—we were, at heart, one nation and one people, sharing a bond as Americans that could bend but would not break."[57] Yet in a speech delivered in Springfield, Illinois, later that day in February 2009, he did invoke Lincoln's commitment to the Union to commend the need for state as well as individual action to solve America's problems. A "knee-jerk disdain for government," he insisted, "cannot rebuild our levees or our roads or our bridges. It can't refurbish our schools or modernize our health care system."[58] This was hardly the socialism that conservative opponents feared, but it was evidence of Obama's willingness, reminiscent of FDR and JFK, to press Civil War memory into the service of positive liberal goals.

While the president was reluctant to abandon the consensual, reconciliatory narrative of the Civil War completely, his efforts to connect himself with Lincoln's wartime achievements, as well as his 2011 intervention in the spat over Confederate History Month in Virginia, confirmed the new visibility in official circles of the emancipationist strain of Civil War memory. Partial evidence of its new vitality in popular culture was provided by Steven Spielberg's 2012 movie, *Lincoln*, which not only garnered wide critical acclaim but also proved to be a major commercial success. Assisted by an Oscar-winning performance by Daniel Day Lewis in the role of the president, Spielberg used his film to educate viewers about the centrality of democratic politics to the abolition of slavery in the United States. While acknowledging Lincoln's importance in national memory as the Great Emancipator, it slighted the Emancipation Proclamation itself in order to highlight the decisive contribution to black liberation made by the president's behind-the-scenes efforts to secure passage of the Thirteenth Amendment. Some professional historians found plenty to complain about, including Spielberg's inattention to the slaves' role in their own liberation and his cavalier treatment of historical facts, notably the significance of Lincoln's peace feelers to Richmond, which he exaggerated for dramatic effect.[59] However, although this flawed film was clearly the work of a white liberal committed to familiar ideas about Americans' moral and material progress—precisely the same ideas to which Obama himself was attached—it did at least make it clear that the Civil War was not just about military events and that passionate debates over the place of blacks in society had electrified the politics of the 1860s.

All Aboard for the Sesquicentennial

Planning for the 150th anniversary of the Civil War was conditioned primarily by two factors: first, an awareness that racial divisions and an overriding emphasis on military history had nearly derailed the centennial of 1961–65; second, a conviction at both the national and state levels that the achievements of the rights revolutions of the 1960s and 1970s demanded a genuinely inclusive commemoration.

The National Park Service's official plan for the sesquicentennial, "Holding the High Ground," insisted on the Civil War's central importance to American history and proclaimed that its issues "remain current and relevant." The overriding tone was confessional. "In the aftermath of national trauma," it stated, "we as a Nation (consciously or unconsciously) have assigned the rights of memory to a few select groups. . . . They, in turn, fostered a swift but incomplete reconciliation—one that pasted over but did not extinguish lingering bitterness, one that was based on selective memory, and forged, in part, at the expense of liberty for free blacks and newly freed slaves." The document also conceded the continuing lack of adequate historical contextualization at most of the Park Service's Civil War sites and the exclusionary effect of the agency's long-standing focus on battles. The conventional view that the war had been "a noble adventure, undertaken by noble men on both sides for noble ends with noble results," it contended, ignored "the undeniable fact that the war was experienced differently by different people—depending on race, gender, geography, socioeconomic status, and cultural background." Visitors, it argued, should be informed "that history is a subject of continual debate, rather than a set of fixed facts.[60]

Attempts in Congress to create a national sesquicentennial commission came to naught, quite possibly because legislators feared a repeat of what Park Service historian Robert Sutton refers to as the centennial "debacle."[61] This left the agency as the sole federal body with responsibility for interpreting and commemorating the Civil War in 2011–15. The Obama administration, preoccupied with the economic crisis, made no attempt to press the issue. The president himself may have been concerned about the danger of centennial-style racial conflicts. He was certainly under no illusions about the lingering power of conflicting memories of the Civil War, for he continued the White House tradition of sending flowers to the UDC's memorial in Arlington National Cemetery on Confederate Memorial Day.[62]

Federal inaction meant that much of the organizing for the sesquicentennial was undertaken at the state and local levels. Several states set up their own commissions, as they had done in the late 1950s. Although southern planners had their eyes on the tourist dollar, most shared the Park Service's commitment to an intelligent, educational, and inclusive commemoration. Bill Pencek, director of heritage tourism in Maryland, announced in 2009 that "sesquicentennial events" would "highlight diverse viewpoints on the war, a departure from centennial observances that mainly honored Confederate veterans."[63] The well-funded Virginia commission organized an annual series of conferences intended to bring leading historians and members of the public together to debate key issues of the war such as causation, slavery, and the reasons for southern defeat. Its North Carolina counterpart planned what it described as a "multi-year program of state-sponsored activities to commemorate, in an appropriate and historically accurate manner, the richness, diversity, and significance of the state's participation in and contributions to the American Civil War."[64] Events organized under this expansive rubric included a conference titled "Lay Down My Burden: Freedom and the Legacies of the Civil War" that was held in Winston-Salem in October 2013.

Programs designed to appeal to blacks and women found no support among neo-Confederates. SCV members took the lead in setting up the privately funded North Carolina War between the States Sesquicentennial Commission as a rival to what they regarded as the politically correct body in Raleigh. This shadow "commission" declared its commitment to "a clear, unbiased history of North Carolina's role during America's War Between the States"; its intention to avoid "a social and class perspective of history"; and its overriding desire to "provide a more telling story of why North Carolinians were 'forced out of the Union.'"[65] The group's professionally designed website provided readers with familiar Lost Cause interpretations of the state's history and included the charge that Abraham Lincoln had committed "treason" by warring against sovereign American states in 1861.[66]

The absence of a federal commission and the existence of the Internet made the sesquicentennial a more fragmented commemoration than its predecessor. However, influential forums such as the *New York Times* Disunion blog (which featured regular contributions from experts on a wide range of Civil War themes and events) instigated spirited and often useful debates among readers. In combination with the educational efforts of the Park Service and relevant state bodies, such discussions appeared to suggest that historian David Blight's early hopes for a mature commemoration—one that would give Americans the chance "to find unity in a shared history of conflict, in a genuine sense of tragedy, and in a conflicted memory stared squarely in the face"—were being fulfilled.[67]

The evidence on this point, however, was ambiguous. The overall tenor of the sesquicentennial was sober, just as the planners, keen to acknowledge the heritage of all stakeholders as legitimate, had intended from the outset. Although the commemoration itself triggered no racial crisis comparable to the Charleston controversy in 1961, the downside of an event focused on legacies and community history was that most Americans, young people certainly, were not as excited and thus drawn to US history as their peers had been by the centennial. The anniversary witnessed increased visitor numbers at some major Park Service sites, such as Antietam and Shiloh in 2012. Yet attendances at most state and community-level events were modest, and annual recreational visits to Gettysburg hovered around the million mark—lower than they had been in the years preceding the financial crisis.[68] Writing in the *Wall Street Journal* in April 2014, Cameron McWhirter pronounced the commemoration "disappointing so far." "Promoters of Civil War memorabilia, tourism and reenactments across the country," he observed, "are fighting a losing battle against apathy for one of the most important periods in US history—a cataclysmic event that shaped the nation and helped define its soul. Limited government funding to stage events and public unease over the divisive racial issues that the war represents are two factors for low turnout, say Civil War buffs." McWhirter quoted the dispirited owner of a toy soldier company in New Jersey: "If it's a celebration, it's a celebration that the public is either not aware of or not interested in."[69]

The most popular sesquicentennial events were battle-related ones. Sixty thousand spectators watched a large-scale reenactment at Gettysburg National Military Park in July 2011.[70] Two years later, Park Service rangers led a crowd of about forty thousand across the ground of Pickett's Charge. A dozen buglers met the walkers on Cemetery Ridge and played Echo Taps.[71] Toward the close of the national commemoration, twenty-five thousand people watched more than three thousand reenactors replay the first afternoon of the Battle of Bentonville, North Carolina, one of the Civil War's last engagements. Most of these observers probably learned little about the political context in which the original engagements had been fought and had even less interest in it. A reporter noted that some spectators at the Bentonville event were "cheering for the home team."[72]

Despite the considerable efforts of Park Service officials, state planners, and museum curators to ensure a truly inclusive commemoration, one group of Americans remained largely detached from mainstream Civil War observances. After many decades of being excluded from, or marginalized by, such commemorations, blacks demonstrated only limited interest in events designed to highlight themes such as slavery, emancipation, and the role of US Colored Troops. One reason for this was the fact that national and state officials had only recently begun to include African Americans in their interpretive narratives. As a result, most Civil War sites remained "uncomfortable territory" for blacks.[73] In 2009, Ta-Nehisi Coates, an African American writer and blogger for the *Atlantic*, took his family on a driving tour of Virginia. After visiting the Petersburg battlefield south of Richmond, he reported that his family "were the only black people in the group" taken around the park by a ranger and that most of the talk was of "tactics and strategic errors." It was, he wrote, "like listening to a doctor discuss with great interest and curiosity, your grandmother's cancerous tumors."[74] Perhaps it was unsurprising, then, that there appeared to be "few black faces" among the crowd watching the 2011 reenactment at Gettysburg.[75] Despite the creation of a new visitor center, one academic commentator pronounced the Pennsylvania battlefield "tepid" on race compared with its counterpart at Harpers Ferry.[76]

A second reason for the paucity of African American interest in the sesquicentennial was the fact that even in the wake of *Glory*, many black schoolchildren remained ignorant of the role played by African Americans in their own liberation. Interviewed in 1998, one of the country's new band of black battle reenactors stated, "Fourth-grade history in Virginia is Virginia history. . . . And for a great portion of that you hear about the Civil War, and you hear about Lee and Jackson and Jeb Stuart, and I grew up just thinking that blacks didn't participate in the war. I just thought that all blacks were slaves during that period."[77] Poor-quality textbooks constituted part of the problem in the southern states. Even though Virginia finally discontinued its Jim Crow–era histories in the 1970s, *Our Virginia: Past and Present*, an approved fourth-grade textbook published in 2010, attracted controversy because it repeated the Lost Cause canard that "[t]housands of Southern blacks fought in the Confederate ranks, including two black battalions under the command of Stonewall Jackson."[78]

African Americans did not lack interest in their past. But, as the National Park Service's decision in 2012 to alter its official title for the sesquicentennial from "Civil War 150" to "Civil War to Civil Rights" seemed to acknowledge, the past in which they were mainly interested was that of the fifty-year-old civil rights movement. By 2015, the latter had its own veterans, as determined to take charge of their histories as any aging Union or Confederate soldier.

During the late twentieth and early twenty-first centuries, these veterans wrote a prodigious number of memoirs, many of them intended to undermine or complicate the classic Montgomery-to-Selma narrative that privileged Martin Luther King and nonviolence at the expense of local protests, the role of black women, and the African American tradition of self-defense.[79] This narrative was widely taught in the public schools and disseminated by the South's new civil rights museums—institutions that, in marked contrast to the battlefields, were visited by large numbers of black schoolchildren. In the minds of many African Americans, therefore, the ongoing struggle over the historical memory of the civil rights movement took precedence over debates about how to remember a distant war whose commemorative rituals had been dominated by whites since its conclusion.

The official, federally sanctioned narrative of both the Civil War and the civil rights movement bent toward consensus and a self-reverential notion of American progress. However, the Charleston slayings impelled an angry Barack Obama to assert publicly that Americans could no longer sit on the fence when it came to assessing the relative morality of what he took to be the two causes involved in their Civil War. On June 26, 2015, he delivered a passionate eulogy for Rev. Clementa Pinckney, one of the massacre's nine victims. Speaking at the College of Charleston, he claimed that the recent killings had enabled his compatriots to see that the Confederate battle flag was "a reminder of systemic oppression and racial subjugation." During the course of his oration, in which he sang lines from the antislavery hymn "Amazing Grace," he threw the weight of his office behind removal of the flag from the grounds of the South Carolina capitol. Getting rid of it, he said, "would not be an act of political correctness; it would not be an insult to the valor of Confederate soldiers. It would simply be an acknowledgment that the cause for which they fought—the cause of slavery—was wrong—the imposition of Jim Crow after the Civil War, the resistance to civil rights for all people was wrong."[80] The president's carefully chosen words were punctuated with applause. But on such a noteworthy day for the history of Civil War memory in the United States, a day when the most powerful politician in the land explicitly invalidated the white South's narrative of the Lost Cause, there was no guarantee whatsoever that everyone outside was listening sympathetically.

Conclusion

The Continuing Civil War

Leroy Moffitt's marriage to Norma Jean is in trouble. Leroy, a white Kentuckian like his wife, has had to give up his job as a long-distance truck driver after an accident on the highway. He is living at home and getting under Norma Jean's feet. His wife is deeply unhappy. Leroy knows something is wrong but doesn't know what to do about it. One day his mother-in-law, Mabel, suggests the couple should drive out to the old Shiloh battlefield across the state line in Tennessee. Mabel is proud of her membership of the United Daughters of the Confederacy. She thinks the trip will do them good.

One Sunday, Norma Jean packs a picnic and motors to Shiloh with Leroy. He tries to make conversation but without success. At the battlefield they drive "aimlessly through the park, past bluffs and trails and steep ravines." Leroy finds it hard to imagine that men ever fought on this ground: "It is not what he expected. He thought it would look like a golf course." The site is cluttered with monuments and dotted with tourists searching for evidence of a war long gone. Although the couple venture into the museum, they skip the interpretive film. Instead, they purchase a souvenir Rebel battle flag for Mabel and take their picnic into the National Cemetery. There Norma Jean finally makes clear her frustrations with the marriage. Leroy works hard to take it all in. "He tries to focus on the fact that thirty-five hundred soldiers died on the grounds around him. He can only think of that war as a board game with plastic soldiers." His failure of imagination on this occasion gives him a measure of belated insight. "History was always just names and dates to him," he realizes, "And the real inner workings of a marriage, like most of history, have escaped him." The revelation may have come too late. "Norma Jean is far away, walking rapidly toward the bluff by the [Tennessee] river." She waves, but he has no idea if she is calling him on.[1]

Leroy and Norma Jean, the central characters in Bobbie Ann Mason's short story, "Shiloh" (1982), feel no connection to the bloody Civil War that nearly destroyed the United States. Norma Jean is bored by the subject. Leroy knows a few dubious facts—that Grant was a drunk—but these are not enough for him to connect with, let alone make sense of, all that killing. He and his lonely wife are quintessentially modern Americans, cast adrift from their country's past by the passing of time, the bewildering impact of late-twentieth-century capitalism, and a poverty of education. Like the tourists whom they encounter searching for bullet holes in a wooden building, Leroy yearns to connect with history. Everyone struggles to do so.

Americans who had lived through the 1860s knew that the Civil War was about the survival of the Union, the fight to create a proslavery southern nation, and ultimately the very meaning of the republic's commitment to liberty and equality. Remembering agents from the wartime generation cooperated with their immediate kin in fashioning the master narratives that framed future modes of Civil War commemoration and interpretation in the United States.

Union veterans dominated the collective remembering process above the Mason-Dixon Line, writing and speaking about their wartime exploits, participating in Memorial Day parades, and raising monuments to the Union cause across the country. Not all former Federals joined in these efforts to embed their narrative of republican service into American history. The experience of war was shattering for many bluecoats, and in countless cases peacetime brought only greater suffering. Yet for large numbers of Union volunteers who survived into the late nineteenth and early twentieth centuries, acts of remembrance and commemoration imparted meaning to their lives. In their eyes and those of their immediate family members, they were the brave men who had saved the nation. They had no intention of letting their compatriots, North or South, forget it.

Carving out a respectable social role for themselves as mourners and as the guardians of family and local lore, southern white women collaborated closely with their menfolk in perpetuating memories of the Confederacy and Reconstruction. The diehard phase of the Lost Cause had its origins in the historical activities of the Rebel officer class and elite Ladies' Memorial Associations, but ultimately the assertive Confederate celebration of the late nineteenth century was the work of ordinary Rebel soldiers belonging to the United Confederate Veterans and middle-class women who joined the UDC. While their achievement acknowledged the reality of southern defeat, it constituted a vital contribution to the construction of a modern Jim Crow society that was a fitting legacy of the slaveholding Confederacy.

Interparty competition assisted consolidation of the Unionist and Lost Cause strains of Civil War memory after 1865. A majority of northern Republicans and southern Democrats, many of them veterans, had a vested interest in sustaining divisive memories of the war. These memories, skillfully packaged, forged partisan identity and marginalized opponents. Ideological commitment and fierce interparty rivalry after 1877 sustained heavily sectionalized interpretations of the Civil War into the 1890s.

This critical decade—an era of widespread agrarian and industrial unrest, the creation of the country's first national battlefield parks, and the Spanish-American War—witnessed the flowering of a romantic reconciliatory strain of historical memory that would quickly predominate over its Unionist and emancipationist competitors in the North and in official circles because of its excellent fit with postwar nationalism. Many prominent former soldiers played a constructive role in promoting sectional reconciliation in the closing decades of the nineteenth century. A majority of ordinary veterans on both sides, however, were wary of reconciliation because their memories of the war remained so vivid. While most southern guerrillas and embittered POWs refused point-blank to engage in sentimental remembrance of the conflict, the majority of veterans bided their time, awaiting signs that their opponents respected their courage and their cause. Although many such indications were evident by the 1890s, it was a new generation of Americans who had not experienced the war that proved to be the strongest bulwark of North-South amity. Eager to read about the Civil War era as a gendered realm of romance and fraternal adventure, younger Americans exhibited relatively little interest in the issues that had caused the conflict and helped sustain its hatreds after Appomattox.

Black equality under the law was among the keenest of those issues, even if national independence and survival had been the immediate causes of war. Emancipationist memories, disseminated passionately by the likes of Frederick Douglass and Albion Tourgée, stimulated limited support among white Federal veterans for equal rights into the late nineteenth century. But they were no match for the tide of reconciliation that, alongside white-supremacist terror, economic coercion, political disfranchisement, and de jure segregation, pushed African Americans to the margins of national memory. Unionist memory, which possessed a secondary antislavery dimension, was largely subsumed in the North by its reconciliatory counterpart after the 1890s because most white northerners prioritized allegiance to the nation-state over equal rights for African Americans. In the Jim Crow era, the paramount strains of reconciliatory and Lost Cause memory proved largely compatible. Even members of the UDC and the SCV, devoted to honoring the Confederacy, regarded themselves as patriotic Americans, sure in the knowledge that most northern whites acquiesced to segregation and acknowledged great southern commanders like Lee and Jackson as authentic national heroes.

As the ranks of the veterans thinned, wartime memories were transmitted in different ways, most importantly (owing to the new power of mass culture) in the films and writings of creative artists, some of whom had family ties to the wartime generation. The cultural productions of D. W. Griffith, Margaret Mitchell, Stephen Vincent Benét, Bruce Catton, and many others generated Civil War consumers with artificial memories of their compatriots' suffering, courage, resourcefulness, and devotion to duty in the 1860s and 1870s. Treasured autobiographical recollections of the veterans, their kin, and their commemorative rituals, however, rendered the war a genuinely "felt" memory for many Americans well into the twentieth century. The business-friendly Civil War centennial, though deeply flawed in conception and execution, created its own legion of fans that helped to extend the conflict's mnemonic reach into the twenty-first century.

White southerners retained a disproportionate interest in the Civil War for several reasons. First, the war had been fought mainly on southern soil and therefore memories of the Lost Cause—molded by death, destruction, and defeat—were imprinted especially deeply on the Rebels' descendants. The novelist William Faulkner, whose great-grandfather had fought for the Confederacy, was not alone in imagining southern boys returning to "the instant when it's still not yet two o'clock on that July afternoon in 1863" and hoping Pickett's Charge might achieve a different result.[2] Second, economic change and population movements had less of an impact on the South than the North, with the result that historical memories in the region tended to be more stable than those above the Mason-Dixon Line. Third, white control of the South's Jim Crow society relied partly on the existence of a coherent group memory of the Civil War and Reconstruction. Enshrined in the mythology of the Lost Cause, this instrumental narrative was embedded in school textbooks for at least three generations. It furnished a highly usable past for conservative southern Democrats whose power depended on the existence of white supremacy. Their determination to maintain that power ensured that historical memories of the Civil War and Reconstruction would exercise a heavy influence on racial politics in the South throughout the middle decades of the twentieth century.

Civil War memory in the modern era was driven not only by individuals, organizations, and the spread of mass culture but also by the federal government. Beginning in 1898, when President McKinley publicly acknowledged Washington's responsibility for the Confederate dead, the United States government consistently encouraged consensual modes of remembering and commemorating the sectional conflict. Washington's problem over the years, however, was that different communities nurtured their own historical memories of the country's bloody fracture. These "vernacular" memories, as John Bodnar has termed them—preeminently the celebratory Lost Cause and the samizdat counter-memory of emancipation fostered mainly by African Americans—were not wholly incompatible with the nation-state's "official" narrative of the Civil War, which was grounded firmly in the achievement of national unity.[3] However, neither were they entirely consistent with it. During the first half of the twentieth century, reconciliatory motifs and rhetoric appeared to serve the country well because American political leaders could use them to promote good feeling between northern and southern whites during a period of global warfare when blacks had minimal political influence. But by helping to reempower African Americans, the civil rights movement exploded the uncritical official narrative of the Civil War as a national epic fought by brave, principled white soldiers on both sides.

A new generation of black politicians, aided by paradigmatic shifts in historical interpretation, demanded government recognition for their understanding of the role that slavery and equal rights had played in the struggles of the Civil War era. At the start of the twenty-first century, federal officials scampered to integrate these calls into an updated birth-of-freedom narrative that acknowledged the once-marginalized emancipationist memory of the Civil War without jettisoning every component of the old reconciliatory discourse. Despite the consensual imperative underpinning these efforts, the mnemonic shift that they occasioned outraged right-wing neo-Confederates who saw their Lost Cause "truths" displaced by landmark political and cultural change. In 2009, the United States had a black president eager to connect himself in a direct line to Martin Luther King and Abraham Lincoln. During the course of the subsequent low-key sesquicentennial, neo-Confederates had to stomach the release not only of Steven Spielberg's filmic account of the passing of the Thirteenth Amendment but also of *12 Years a Slave*, black British director Steve McQueen's uncompromising indictment of North American slavery.

All modern nation-states strive to disseminate coherent versions of their history consistent with internal power relations. These grand narratives highlight selected "facts" about a country's past and leave inconvenient truths forgotten. The results can be insidious. The Chinese Communist Party, for example, has used its control over dissent to erase the bloody Tiananmen Square massacre of 1989 from the domestic historical record.[4] Vladimir Putin's authoritarian regime in Russia fosters rose-tinted memories of a glorious Soviet past to legitimize what many commentators see as its revanchist foreign policy.[5] In 2014, Hungary's right-wing government led by Viktor Orbán installed a controversial monument in Budapest ostensibly dedicated to the victims of Nazism but intended in fact to conceal the reality that many Hungarians had been complicit in the crimes of fascism.[6]

In the United States, historical narratives of freedom and progress have traditionally concealed the oppression of blacks and the wholesale slaughter and displacement of Native Americans. The contested realm of Civil War memory suggests that only concerted action by previously disempowered groups and their allies to recover and disseminate their history can reshape the stories that nations tell themselves and others about their past. National Park Service officials at sites like Harpers Ferry and Gettysburg only tell visitors today about the significance of slavery and African Americans in the Civil War era because of the civil rights and Black Power movements of the 1960s. Assertive efforts on the part of Native Americans, also inspired by the rights revolutions of the mid-twentieth century, have recently contributed to the Park Service's campaign to purchase, mark, and interpret the site of the 1864 Sand Creek massacre in which pro-Union Colorado militiamen murdered scores of Arapaho and Cheyenne Indians.[7]

While it is right to regard these developments in a positive light, we should be wary of complacency. US government efforts, often backed by professional historians, to promote a more inclusive interpretation of the American past are laudable, but they present dangers of their own. What art historian Dell Upton refers to as the "dual heritages" approach to the Civil War—one that respects both southern white and African American memories of the conflict—may foster the growth of unchallenging parallel narratives likely to sustain rather than combat racial oppression.[8] The reinvigorated emancipationist narrative of the Civil War, moreover, can be used to legitimize military action in the nominal pursuit of humanitarian goals. This is undoubtedly one reason why some scholars, influenced by the controversial US incursions into Iraq and Afghanistan, have sought to underline and expand the revisionists' insights into the brutality and squalor of America's bloodiest event.[9] However, as Arthur Schlesinger Jr. pointed out in the late 1940s, preoccupation with the slaughter can lead commentators to ignore the moral dimensions of a conflict that finally put an end to slavery in the United States.

Although our temporal distance from the Civil War limits its impact, the conflict remains relevant today. Its implications for the treatment of minorities and the function of government continue to resonate in a society that is, as the rise of the Black Lives Matter movement attests, still burdened with persistent racial injustice. Memories of the great sectional caesura have been vigorously contested by individuals and groups with a vested interest in reifying their particular historical "truths." The task of citizens in a healthy democracy must be to subject such truths to intellectually rigorous scrutiny, even at the cost of cozy consensus. The work of our predecessors is done. It is for us, the living, to ensure that their words and actions cannot be manipulated easily by politicians, groups, and institutions seeking to promote self-serving narratives of the past in the challenging present.

Introduction

1. Quoted in Charles M. Blow, "In Charleston, a Millennial Race Terrorist," *New York Times*, June 21, 2015, http://www.nytimes.com/2015/06/22/opinion/charles-blow-in-charleston-a-millennial-race-terrorist.html.

2. Quoted in Nick Corasaniti, Richard Pérez-Peña, and Lizette Alvarez, "Church Massacre Suspect Held as Charleston Grieves," *New York Times*, June 18, 2015, http://www.nytimes.com/2015/06/19/us/charleston-church-shooting.html.

3. "Statement by the President on the Shooting in Charleston, South Carolina," June 18, 2015, The White House, https://www.whitehouse.gov/the-press-office/2015/06/18/statement-president-shooting-charleston-south-carolina.

4. Roof was convicted of his crimes in federal court on December 15, 2016, and sentenced to death the following month.

5. Quoted in Elahe Izadi and Abby Phillip, "South Carolina House Votes to Remove Confederate Flag from Statehouse Grounds," *Washington Post*, July 9, 2015, https://www.washingtonpost.com/news/post-nation/wp/2015/07/09/south-carolina-house-votes-to-remove-confederate-flag-from-statehouse-grounds/?utm_term=.43a571549521.

6. Quoted in M. J. Lee, "Walmart, Amazon, Sears, eBay to Stop Selling Confederate Flag Merchandise," CNN Politics, updated June 24, 2015, http://edition.cnn.com/2015/06/22/politics/confederate-flag-walmart-south-carolina.

7. Quoted in ibid.

8. Quoted in Natalie Pompilio, "Tug-of-War over Confederate Monuments Rages On," *Chicago Tribune*, April 17, 2016, http://www.chicagotribune.com/news/nationworld/ct-confederate-monuments-20160417-story.html.

9. Gerald Warner, "Hoist It High and Proud: The Confederate Flag Proclaims a Glorious Heritage," Breitbart, July 1, 2015, http://www.breitbart.com/big-government/2015/07/01/hoist-it-high-and-proud-the-confederate-flag-proclaims-a-glorious-heritage.

10. Quoted in Julie Zauzmer, "Southern Baptist Convention Votes to Condemn Confederate Battle Flag," *Washington Post*, June 15, 2016, https://www.washingtonpost.com/news/acts-of-faith/wp/2016/06/15/southern-baptist-convention-votes-to-condemn-confederate-battle-flag/?utm_term=.7b2b2537dd6b.

11. There are several important overviews of Civil War memory before 1914 but none covering the entire span of the past 150 years. See especially Paul H. Buck, *The Road to Reunion 1865–1900* (Boston: Little, Brown, 1937); David W. Blight, *Race and Reunion:*

The Civil War in American Memory (Cambridge, MA: Belknap Press of Harvard University Press, 2001); and Caroline E. Janney, *Remembering the Civil War: Reunion and the Limits of Reconciliation* (Chapel Hill: University of North Carolina Press, 2013).

12. There is a substantial literature on historical memory. Jeffrey K. Olick, Vered Vinitzky-Seroussi, and Daniel Levy, eds., *The Collective Memory Reader* (New York: Oxford University Press, 2011); and Stefan Berger and Bill Niven, eds., *Writing the History of Memory* (New York: Bloomsbury, 2014) are useful introductions to the topic. Modern scholars differ over whether "memory" is an appropriate term to apply to the way communities or societies reflect on historical events in their recent or far-flung past. The historian Jay Winter, for example, insists helpfully: "States do not remember; individuals do, in association with other people" (*Remembering War: The Great War between Memory and History in the Twentieth Century* [New Haven, CT: Yale University Press, 2006], 4). While acknowledging that only human beings can "remember" in the orthodox sense of the word, I use the term "historical memory" to describe how different groups construct their own narratives—based on selected facts or "truths"—of past events.

13. Maurice Halbwachs, *On Collective Memory*, trans. Lewis A. Coser (Chicago: University of Chicago Press, 1992).

14. Barry Schwartz, "Memory as a Cultural System: Abraham Lincoln in World War II," *American Sociological Review* 61 (October 1996): 910.

15. Ralph D. Abernathy, *And the Walls Came Tumbling Down* (New York: Harper and Row, 1989), 33.

16. These strands are identified by Gary W. Gallagher in *Causes Won, Lost, and Forgotten: How Hollywood and Popular Art Shape What We Know about the Civil War* (Chapel Hill: University of North Carolina Press, 2008), 2. Gallagher refers to them as "traditions."

17. David W. Blight, "W.E.B. Du Bois and the Struggle for American Historical Memory," in *History and Memory in African-American Culture*, ed. Geneviève Fabre and Robert O'Meally (New York: Oxford University Press, 1994), 46.

18. Gaines M. Foster, *Ghosts of the Confederacy: Defeat, the Lost Cause, and the Emergence of the New South, 1865 to 1913* (New York: Oxford University Press, 1987), 104–44.

19. Blight, *Race and Reunion*.

20. *Economist*, April 2, 2011.

21. Robert Penn Warren, *The Legacy of the Civil War: Meditations on the Centennial* (New York: Random House, 1961), 4.

Chapter 1 • A Fractured Country and Its Fractured Memories

1. Bruce Levine, *Half Slave and Half Free: The Roots of Civil War* (New York: Hill and Wang, 1992), 21.

2. Stephen F. Hale to Beriah Magoffin, December 27, 1860, in Charles B. Dew, *Apostles of Disunion: Southern Secession Commissioners and the Causes of the Civil War* (Charlottesville: University of Virginia Press, 2001), 98.

3. Benjamin H. Hill, speech of November 15, 1860, in William W. Freehling and Craig M. Simpson, eds., *Secession Debated: Georgia's Showdown in 1860* (New York: Oxford University Press, 1992), 90.

4. Waitman T. Willey, remarks of April 16, 1861, in William W. Freehling and Craig M. Simpson, eds., *Showdown in Virginia: The 1861 Convention and the Fate of the Union* (Charlottesville: University of Virginia Press, 2010), 184.

5. Thomas R.R. Cobb, speech of November 12, 1860, in Freehling and Simpson, *Secession Debated*, 14.

6. Abraham Lincoln, "First Inaugural Address," March 4, 1861, in *The Collected Works of Abraham Lincoln*, ed. Roy P. Basler, 9 vols. (New Brunswick, NJ: Rutgers University Press, 1953–55), 4:271.

7. Ibid.

8. For a convincing reassessment of the number of Civil War deaths, see J. David Hacker, "A Census-Based Count of the Civil War Dead," *Civil War History* 57 (December 2011): 307–48.

9. William W. Freehling, *The South vs. the South: How Anti-Confederate Southerners Shaped the Course of the Civil War* (New York: Oxford University Press, 2001), xiii.

10. Abraham Lincoln, "Address Delivered at the Dedication of the Cemetery at Gettysburg (Second Draft)," November 19, 1863, in *Collected Works*, ed. Basler, 7:18–19.

11. Quoted in James M. McPherson, *Tried by War: Abraham Lincoln as Commander in Chief* (New York: Penguin Books, 2009), 70–71.

12. Bruce Levine, *Confederate Emancipation: Southern Plans to Free and Arm Slaves during the Civil War* (New York: Oxford University Press, 2006), 129.

13. Lincoln, "Second Inaugural Address," March 4, 1865, *Collected Works*, ed. Basler, 8:333.

14. Ulysses S. Grant, *Personal Memoirs* (1885–86; repr., New York: Penguin, 1999), 605.

15. Quoted in Joan Waugh, *U.S. Grant: American Hero, American Myth* (Chapel Hill: University of North Carolina Press, 2009), 99.

16. Quoted in John McKee Barr, *Loathing Lincoln: An American Tradition from the Civil War to the Present* (Baton Rouge: Louisiana State University Press, 2014), 2.

17. Gary W. Gallagher, *The Confederate War* (Cambridge, MA: Harvard University Press, 1997), 29.

18. James M. McPherson, *Battle Cry of Freedom: The Civil War Era* (New York: Oxford University Press, 1988), 619.

19. Caroline E. Janney, *Burying the Dead but Not the Past: Ladies' Memorial Associations and the Lost Cause* (Chapel Hill: University of North Carolina Press, 2008), 21–22.

20. John R. Thompson, "The Burial of Latané," *Southern Literary Messenger* 34 (July–August 1862): 476.

21. See, for example, Wulf Kansteiner, "Generation and Memory: A Critique of the Ethical and Ideological Implications of Generational Narration," in *Writing the History of Memory*, ed. Stefan Berger and Bill Niven (New York: Bloomsbury, 2014), 118.

22. Quoted in Robert McElroy, *Jefferson Davis: The Unreal and the Real* (New York: Harper and Brothers, 1937), 2:544.

23. Quoted in Jason Phillips, "Rebels in War and Peace: Their Ethos and Its Impact," in *The Great Task Remaining before Us: Reconstruction as America's Continuing Civil War*, ed. Paul A. Cimbala and Randall M. Miller (New York: Fordham University Press, 2010), 165.

24. Salmon P. Chase to Andrew Johnson, May 21, 1865, in *Advice after Appomattox: Letters to Andrew Johnson, 1865–1866*, ed. LeRoy P. Graf and John Muldowny (Knoxville: University of Tennessee Press, 1987), 35.

25. Mitch Kachun, "From Forgotten Founder to Indispensable Icon: Crispus Attucks, Black Citizenship, and Collective Memory, 1770–1865," *Journal of the Early*

Republic 29 (Summer 2009): 249–86; Margot Minardi, *Making Slavery History: Abolitionism and the Politics of Memory in Massachusetts* (New York: Oxford University Press, 2010).

26. Quoted in Catherine A. Stewart, *Long Past Slavery: Representing Race in the Federal Writers' Project* (Chapel Hill: University of North Carolina Press, 2016), 223.

27. By comparison 50,000 defeated Republicans were slaughtered by General Francisco Franco's Nationalists *after* the Spanish Civil War of 1936–39, and as many as 400,000 may have rotted in jails and concentration camps. Paul D. Escott, *Uncommonly Savage: Civil War and Remembrance in Spain and the United States* (Gainesville: University Press of Florida, 2014), 14.

28. John R. Neff, *Honoring the Civil War Dead: Commemoration and the Problem of Reconciliation* (Lawrence: University Press of Kansas, 2005), 119. I discuss these northern histories in chapter 3.

29. Lurton Dunham Ingersoll, *Iowa and the Rebellion: A History of the Troops Furnished by the State of Iowa to the Volunteer Armies of the Union, Which Conquered the Great Southern Rebellion of 1861–5* (Philadelphia: J. B. Lippincott and Co., 1866).

30. A. F. Sperry, *History of the 33d Iowa Volunteer Infantry Regiment 1863–6*, ed. Gregory J. W. Urwin and Cathy Kunzinger Urwin (1866; repr., Fayetteville: University of Arkansas Press, 1999), 192.

31. Quoted in Allen W. Moger, "General Lee's Unwritten 'History of the Army of Northern Virginia,'" *Virginia Magazine of History and Biography* 71 (July 1963): 345.

32. Robert E. Lee to Jubal A. Early, November 22, 1865, vol. 4, Jubal A. Early Papers, Library of Congress.

33. Jedidiah Hotchkiss to Early, December 7, 1865, vol. 4, Early Papers.

34. Jubal A. Early, *A Memoir of the Last Year of the War for Independence, in the Confederate States of America, Containing an Account of the Operations of His Commands in the Years 1864 and 1865* (Toronto: Lovell and Gibson, 1866), unnumbered title page.

35. Lee to Early, October 15, 1866, vol. 4, Early Papers.

36. Timothy B. Smith, *This Great Battlefield of Shiloh: History, Memory, and the Establishment of a Civil War National Military Park* (Knoxville: University of Tennessee Press, 2004), 11.

37. Neff, *Honoring the Civil War Dead*, 128.

38. Ibid., 134.

39. Some northern communities remembered the Union dead in more overtly utilitarian ways. Memorial chimes were installed in the Amherst College chapel, and a handful of colleges funded purpose-built memorial buildings. Harvard's Memorial Hall, for example, was dedicated in 1874. Thomas J. Brown, "The Peaceable War Memorial," in *The Civil War in Art and Memory*, ed. Kirk Savage (Washington, DC: National Gallery of Art, 2016; distributed by Yale University Press, New Haven, CT), 251–54.

40. Quoted in William A. Blair, *Cities of the Dead: Contesting the Memory of the Civil War in the South, 1865–1914* (Chapel Hill: University of North Carolina Press, 2004), 53.

41. Paul H. Buck, *The Road to Reunion 1865–1900* (Boston: Little, Brown and Co., 1937), 39.

42. Blair, *Cities of the Dead*, 81.

43. Ibid., 78.

44. Quoted in Janney, *Burying the Dead*, 42.

45. Quoted in Blair, *Cities of the Dead*, 61.

46. Quoted in Janney, *Burying the Dead*, 67.

47. Quoted in Blair, *Cities of the Dead*, 95.

48. Susanna Michele Lee, *Claiming the Union: Citizenship in the Post–Civil War South* (New York: Cambridge University Press, 2014), 37.

49. Quoted in ibid., 118.

50. Gregory P. Downs, "The Mexicanization of American Politics: The United States' Transnational Path from Civil War to Stabilization," *American Historical Review* 117 (April 2012): 395–96.

51. Quoted in Mark Wahlgren Summers, *A Dangerous Stir: Fear, Paranoia, and the Making of Reconstruction* (Chapel Hill: University of North Carolina Press, 2009), 135.

52. Early to his brother, August 21, 1866, vol. 4, Early Papers.

53. US Congress, *Report of the Joint Committee on Reconstruction at the First Session Thirty-Ninth Congress* (1866; repr., Freeport, NY: Books for Libraries Press, 1971), pt. 2, 157.

54. Ibid., 220.

55. Ibid., "Report," xxii.

56. Ibid., x–xi.

57. J. F. Noble to Manton Marble, February 4, 1868, vol. 17, Manton Marble Papers, Library of Congress.

58. Quoted in Mark Wahlgren Summers, *The Ordeal of the Reunion: A New History of Reconstruction* (Chapel Hill: University of North Carolina Press, 2014), 143. Fort Pillow was an infamous massacre of black Union soldiers by Confederates during the Civil War. At least seven African Americans, gathering for a Republican rally, had been murdered in the so-called Camilla, Georgia, riot of September 19, 1868 (ibid., 255).

59. Quoted in Buck, *Road to Reunion*, 77.

60. Quoted in ibid., 77.

61. Summers, *Ordeal*, 311–12.

62. Quoted in Michael F. Holt, *By One Vote: The Disputed Presidential Election of 1876* (Lawrence: University Press of Kansas, 2008), 45.

63. Quoted in ibid., 68.

64. Quoted in ibid., 88.

65. Quoted in ibid., 124.

66. Quoted in ibid., 130.

67. Bradley T. Johnson to Early, January 8, 1877, vol. 9, Early Papers.

68. William H. Payne to Early, February 5, 1877, vol. 9, Early Papers.

Chapter 2 • The Resurgent South and Its Lost Cause

1. Abram J. Ryan, *Poems: Patriotic, Religious, Miscellaneous* (Baltimore, MD: J. B. Piet, 1880), 185–87.

2. "Died, near the South-Side Rail Road," Union broadside (Philadelphia, 1865), Library of Congress, accessed July 10, 2015, https://www.loc.gov/resource/rbpe.15900200.

3. David W. Blight, *Race and Reunion: The Civil War in American Memory* (Cambridge, MA: Belknap Press of Harvard University Press, 2001), 260.

4. Albert Taylor Bledsoe, *Is Davis a Traitor; or Was Secession a Constitutional Right Previous to the War of 1861?* (Baltimore, MD: Innes and Co., 1866), 5.

5. Alexander H. Stephens, *A Constitutional View of the Late War between the States: Its Causes, Character, Conduct and Results; Presented in a Series of Colloquies at Liberty Hall*, 2 vols. (Philadelphia: National Publishing Co., 1867–70), 1:539–40.

6. Ibid., 2:651–52.

7. Edward A. Pollard, *The Lost Cause: A New Southern History of the War of the Confederates* (New York: E. B. Treat and Co., 1866), 679.

8. Bledsoe, *Is Davis a Traitor?*, v, 5.

9. Stephens, *Constitutional View*, 2:645, 651.

10. Pollard, *Lost Cause*, 752.

11. Quoted in Sarah E. Gardner, *Blood and Irony: Southern White Women's Narratives of the Civil War, 1861–1937* (Chapel Hill: University of North Carolina Press, 2004), 57.

12. Ibid., 58–59.

13. "National Glory," *Land We Love* 3 (May 1867): 26, 29.

14. Quoted in Blight, *Race and Reunion*, 104.

15. William Allan to Jubal A. Early, October 25, 1870, vol. 5, Early Papers, Library of Congress.

16. Quoted in Gardner, *Blood and Irony*, 60.

17. Michael A. Ross, "The Commemoration of Robert E. Lee's Death and the Obstruction of Reconstruction in New Orleans," *Civil War History* 51 (June 2005): 145.

18. *Richmond Daily Dispatch*, August 19, 1873.

19. Quoted in Blight, *Race and Reunion*, 79.

20. Dabney H. Maury, review of Chaplain Van Horne, *History of the Army of the Cumberland*, *Southern Historical Society Papers* 1 (June 1876): 424.

21. Maury to Early, March 29, 1870, vol. 5, Early Papers.

22. Pollard, *Lost Cause*, 406.

23. William Garrett Piston, *Lee's Tarnished Lieutenant: James Longstreet and His Place in Southern History* (Athens: University of Georgia Press, 1987), 135.

24. Quoted in ibid., 122.

25. Robert E. Withers to Early, April 24, 1871, vol. 5, Early Papers.

26. James Kemper to Early, October 11, 1875, vol. 8, Early Papers. The Conservative Party of Virginia was founded in late 1867 to oppose Reconstruction. Most of its members joined the Democrats after its demise.

27. Kemper to Early, October 22, 1875, vol. 8, Early Papers.

28. A. K. Young to William E. Chandler, December 13, 1889, vol. 79, William E. Chandler Papers, Library of Congress.

29. Gaines M. Foster, *Ghosts of the Confederacy: Defeat, the Lost Cause, and the Emergence of the New South, 1865 to 1913* (New York: Oxford University Press, 1987), 104–44.

30. Jane Dailey, *Before Jim Crow: The Politics of Race in Postemancipation Virginia* (Chapel Hill: University of North Carolina Press, 2000), 67.

31. Sam R. Watkins, *"Co. Aytch": A Confederate Memoir of the Civil War* (New York: Simon and Schuster, 2003), 3.

32. Ibid., 146.

33. Ibid., 55.

34. Ibid., 33.

35. Ibid., 51.

36. Jefferson Davis, *The Rise and Fall of the Confederate Government*, 2 vols. (1881; repr., New York: T. Yoseloff, 1958), 2:764.

37. Quoted in Donald E. Collins, *The Death and Resurrection of Jefferson Davis* (Lanham, MD: Rowman and Littlefield, 2005), 34.

38. Quoted in ibid., 38.

39. *New Orleans Times-Democrat*, December 10, 1889.

40. Ibid., December 11, 1889.

41. St. George T. C. Bryan to his brother, December 28, 1889, St. George T. C. Bryan Papers, Eleanor S. Brockenbrough Library, Museum of the Confederacy, Richmond, VA.

42. *New Orleans Times-Democrat*, December 11, 1889.

43. *Chicago Herald*, December 12, 1889.

44. *Atlanta Constitution*, December 12, 1889.

45. Undated newspaper clipping, Walter H. Lee Scrapbooks, vol. 3, Southern Historical Collection, University of North Carolina Library, Chapel Hill, NC.

46. *Atlanta Constitution*, December 12, 1889.

47. Collins, *Death and Resurrection*, 78.

48. *Charleston News and Courier*, December 12, 1889.

49. Charles Reagan Wilson, *Baptized in Blood: The Religion of the Lost Cause, 1865–1920* (Athens: University of Georgia Press, 1980), 1.

50. *Galveston Daily News*, December 12, 1889; *Nation*, December 12, 1889.

51. *Atlanta Constitution*, December 6, 1889.

52. Ibid., December 8, 1889.

53. Ibid.

54. *Richmond Dispatch*, December 8, 1889.

55. Henry W. Grady, speech at the Boston Merchants' Association, December 12, 1889, in Joel Chandler Harris, *Life of Henry W. Grady, Including His Writings and Speeches* (New York: Cassell Publishing Co., 1890), 195, 196.

56. *Charleston News and Courier*, December 10, 1889.

57. William Payne to Early, May 24, 1890, vol. 14, Early Papers.

58. Payne to Early, June 8, 1890, vol. 14, Early Papers.

59. Foster, *Ghosts*, 106.

60. Ibid., 107.

61. Ibid., 133.

62. *Confederate Veteran* 1 (January 1893), 1.

63. Thomas J. Brown, ed., *The Public Art of Civil War Commemoration: A Brief History with Documents* (Boston: Bedford/St. Martin's, 2004), 24.

64. Ibid., 38.

65. The SCV dropped the word "United" from its name in 1908. Members worried that the acronym USCV might be confused with that of US Colored Volunteers. Foster, *Ghosts*, 108.

66. Karen L. Cox, *Dixie's Daughters: The United Daughters of the Confederacy and the Preservation of Confederate Culture* (Gainesville: University Press of Florida, 2003), 29.

67. Martin Williams, letter to *Richmond Dispatch*, in *Confederate Veteran* 2 (July 1894): 206.

68. Quoted in Gardner, *Blood and Irony*, 121.

69. Quoted in Thomas J. Brown, *Civil War Canon: Sites of Confederate Memory in South Carolina* (Chapel Hill: University of North Carolina Press, 2015), 114–15.

70. Susan Dabney Smedes, *Memorials of a Southern Planter* (Baltimore, MD: Cushings and Bailey, 1887), 232, 234.

71. Ibid., 260.

72. Quoted in Cox, *Dixie's Daughters*, 107.

73. Quoted in ibid., 108.

74. Quoted in Robin Bates, "'As Gray as the Century Burned Granite': The Confederate Veteran and the Construction of Confederate Historical Memory" (M. Litt. thesis, University of Newcastle, 2014), 27.

75. Quoted in Fred Arthur Bailey, "The Textbooks of the 'Lost Cause': Censorship and the Creation of Southern State Histories," *Georgia Historical Quarterly* 75 (Fall 1991): 518.

76. Quoted in Stephen Kantrowitz, *Ben Tillman and the Reconstruction of White Supremacy* (Chapel Hill: University of North Carolina Press, 2000), 242.

Chapter 3 · Remembering the Victors' War in the Gilded Age

1. Julia Ward Howe, "The Battle Hymn of the Republic" (1862), in John Stauffer and Benjamin Soskis, *The Battle Hymn of the Republic: A Biography of the Song That Marches On* (New York: Oxford University Press, 2013), 298.

2. Quoted in *Daily Iowa State Register* (Des Moines), October 1, 1875.

3. William T. Sherman to Samuel H. M. Byers, May 1, 1887, Samuel H. M. Byers Papers, State Historical Society of Iowa.

4. Joel T. Headley, *The Great Rebellion: A History of the Civil War in the United States*, 2 vols. (Hartford, CT: American Publishing Co., 1865–66), 1:10, 11.

5. Henry Wilson, *History of the Rise and Fall of the Slave Power in America*. 3 vols. (Boston: Houghton, Mifflin, and Co., 1872), 1:[v].

6. Ibid., 3:4.

7. Horace Greeley, *The American Conflict: A History of the Great Rebellion in the United States of America, 1860–'65*, 2 vols. (Hartford, CT: O. D. Case and Co., 1867), 1:[7].

8. Quoted in Paul H. Buck, *The Road to Reunion, 1865–1900* (Boston: Little, Brown, and Co., 1937), 57.

9. Greeley, *American Conflict*, 1:[7].

10. Headley, *Great Rebellion*, 2:614.

11. Wilson, *History*, 3:380; Headley, *Great Rebellion*, 2:84.

12. Quoted in Brian Matthew Jordan, "'Living Monuments': Union Veteran Amputees and the Embodied Memory of the Civil War," *Civil War History* 57 (June 2011): 137.

13. Quoted in ibid., 132.

14. Quoted in ibid., 139.

15. On this subject, see esp. Eric T. Dean, *Shook over Hell: Post-traumatic Stress, Vietnam, and the Civil War* (Cambridge, MA: Harvard University Press, 1997); and Brian Matthew Jordan, *Marching Home: Union Veterans and Their Unending Civil War* (New York: Liveright Publishing, 2015).

16. Mrs. John A. [Mary] Logan, *Reminiscences of a Soldier's Wife: An Autobiography* (New York: Charles Scribner's Sons, 1913), 214.

17. GAR, "Declaration of Principles" (1866), quoted in ibid., 217.

18. Stuart McConnell, *Glorious Contentment: The Grand Army of the Republic, 1865–1900* (Chapel Hill: University of North Carolina Press, 1992), 54; Theda Skocpol, *Protecting Soldiers and Mothers: The Political Origins of Social Policy in the United States* (Cambridge, MA: Belknap Press of Harvard University Press, 1992), 112.

19. Cecilia Elizabeth O'Leary, *To Die For: The Paradox of American Patriotism* (Princeton, NJ: Princeton University Press, 1999), 100, 103. The WRC, a Union benevolent organization, was granted auxiliary status by the GAR in 1883. Unlike the South's UDC, it did not require members to be relatives of Civil War veterans.

20. *Daily Iowa State Register*, September 1, 1870.

21. Ibid.

22. James Marten, *Sing Not War: The Lives of Union and Confederate Veterans in Gilded Age America* (Chapel Hill: University of North Carolina Press, 2011), 17. Skocpol, *Protecting Soldiers*, 102–51, places government pension provision for veterans in comparative international context.

23. Robert J. Cook, "A War for Principle? Shifting Memories of the Union Cause in Iowa, 1865–1916," *Annals of Iowa* 74 (Summer 2015): 256–57.

24. Quoted in David W. Blight, *Beyond the Battlefield: Race, Memory, and the American Civil War* (Amherst: University of Massachusetts Press, 2002), 128.

25. W. Fitzhugh Brundage, *The Southern Past: A Clash of Race and Memory* (Cambridge, MA: Belknap Press of Harvard University Press, 2005), 55.

26. Blight, *Race and Reunion*, 65–71.

27. Quoted in ibid., 170.

28. Kirk Savage, *Standing Soldiers, Kneeling Slaves: Race, War, and Monument in Nineteenth-Century America* (Princeton, NJ: Princeton University Press, 1997), 90–92, 113–22.

29. Frederick Douglass, "The Freedmen's Monument to Abraham Lincoln," speech of April 14, 1876, in *The Frederick Douglass Papers—Series One: Speeches, Debates, and Interviews*, ed. John W. Blassingame and John R. McKivigan (New Haven, CT: Yale University Press, 1991), 4:431, 432, 440.

30. Douglass, "We Must Not Abandon the Observance of Decoration Day," speech of May 30, 1882, in *Frederick Douglass Papers—Series One: Speeches, Debates, and Interviews*, 5:45.

31. Samuel H. M. Byers, *What I Saw in Dixie; or Sixteen Months in Rebel Prisons* (Dansville, NY: Robbins and Poore, 1868), unnumbered dedication page.

32. Scholars continue to debate the impact of the Civil War on Union soldiers' attitudes toward blacks. Chandra Manning charts what she regards as most white Union troops' acceptance of emancipation and black troops in *What This Cruel War Was Over: Soldiers, Slavery, and the Civil War* (New York: Alfred A. Knopf, 2007). Her conclusion that "astonishing changes took place in many white Union men's ideas about slavery and eventually, if more fragilely, about racial equality" (221) is valid, but it may overstate the war's impact on white soldiers' views of African Americans. Gary W. Gallagher, *The Union War* (Cambridge, MA: Harvard University Press, 2011), 80–81, is more skeptical about the racial attitudes of ordinary white Union soldiers. His interpretation is broadly in line with that of Reid Mitchell, *Civil War Soldiers* (New York: Viking, 1988), 117–31, but for a more upbeat account, see James M. McPherson, *For Cause and Comrades: Why Men Fought in the Civil War* (New York: Oxford University Press, 1997), 117–30.

33. *National Tribune*, May 17, 1883.

34. *Historical Sketch by C. H. Fasnacht, and Oration, by E. K. Martin, Esq., Delivered at Dedication of 99th Pennsylvania Monument, Gettysburg, Pa., July 2, 1886* (Lancaster, PA: Examiner Steam Book and Job Print, 1886), 36.

35. Quoted in M. Keith Harris, *Across the Bloody Chasm: The Culture of Commemoration among Civil War Veterans* (Baton Rouge: Louisiana State University Press, 2014), 101.

36. Quoted in Susan-Mary Grant, *Oliver Wendell Holmes, Jr.: Civil War Soldier, Supreme Court Justice* (New York: Routledge, 2015), 107.

37. William James, "Oration at Dedication of the Shaw Memorial, May 31, 1897," in *The Public Art of Civil War Commemoration: A Brief History with Documents*, ed. Thomas J. Brown (Boston: Bedford/St. Martin's, 2004), 123–25.

38. Quoted in Andre M. Fleche, "'Shoulder to Shoulder as Comrades Tried': Black and White Union Veterans and Civil War Memory," *Civil War History* 51 (June 2005): 187.

39. Quoted in ibid., 190.

40. Quoted in Mark Elliott, *Color-Blind Justice: Albion Tourgée and the Quest for Racial Equality from the Civil War to* Plessy v. Ferguson (New York: Oxford University Press, 2006), 89.

41. Quoted in Deborah Beckel, *Radical Reform: Interracial Politics in Post-emancipation North Carolina* (Charlottesville: University of Virginia Press, 2011), 61.

42. Quoted in Elliott, *Color-Blind Justice*, 125.

43. Quoted in ibid., 200.

44. Albion W. Tourgée, *The Veteran and His Pipe* (Chicago: Belford, Clarke, and Co., 1886), 3.

45. Ibid., 10.

46. Quoted in Fleche, "'Shoulder to Shoulder,'" 183.

47. Ulysses S. Grant, *Personal Memoirs* (1885–86; repr., New York: Penguin, 1999), 601, 603.

48. Ibid., 638.

49. Quoted in Anne Sarah Rubin, *Through the Heart of Dixie: Sherman's March in American Memory* (Chapel Hill: University of North Carolina Press, 2014), 125–26.

50. William T. Sherman, "Old Shady, with a Moral," *North American Review* 147 (October 1888): 368.

51. Ibid., 366

52. Cook, "A War for Principle?," 239–40.

53. Caroline E. Janney, *Remembering the Civil War: Reunion and the Limits of Reconciliation* (Chapel Hill: University of North Carolina Press, 2013), 176.

54. *National Tribune*, December 12, 1889.

55. *Ottawa Republican*, July 6, 1886 (clipping), John A. Logan Scrapbook, February 23–December 5, 1886, box 100, John Alexander Logan Family Papers, Library of Congress.

56. Ibid.

57. Quoted in *Iowa State Register*, September 7, 1878. Kirkwood had served as Iowa's governor during the Civil War. He was elected for a third term in 1876.

58. John A. Logan Scrapbook, June 28–December 31, 1884, box 100, Logan Family Papers.

59. Ibid.

60. J. J. Fitzgerrell to Logan, November 6, 1884, box 4, Logan Family Papers.

61. John Palmer to Logan, November 15, 1884, box 4, Logan Family Papers.

62. Quoted in Buck, *Road to Reunion*, 269.

63. Whitelaw Reid to Logan, November 20, 1884, box 4, Logan Family Papers; Reid to Logan, December 31, 1884, box 4, Logan Family Papers.

64. John A. Logan, *The Great Conspiracy: Its Origin and History* (New York: A. R. Hart and Co., 1886), unnumbered preface.

65. Ibid., 672–74.

66. Republican National Platform, 1888, in *History of American Presidential Elections, 1789–1968*, ed. Arthur M. Schlesinger Jr., 9 vols. (New York: Chelsea House Publishers, 1985), 4:1656.

67. Quoted in Robert E. Morsberger and Katharine M. Morsberger, *Lew Wallace: Militant Romantic* (New York: McGraw-Hill, 1980), 369.

68. Quoted in ibid., 370.

69. *Iowa State Register*, November 8, 1888.

70. Quoted in Elliott, *Color-Blind Justice*, 246.

71. Quoted in J. Morgan Kousser, *The Shaping of Southern Politics: Suffrage Restriction and the Establishment of the One-Party South, 1880–1910* (New Haven, CT: Yale University Press, 1974), 22–23.

72. Quoted in ibid., 21.

73. Quoted in ibid., 23.

74. Quoted in Charles W. Calhoun, *Conceiving a New Republic: The Republican Party and the Southern Question, 1869–1900* (Lawrence: University Press of Kansas, 2006), 259.

75. Alexander Martin to Albion W. Tourgée, October 29, 1891, reel 37, Albion W. Tourgée Papers, Chautauqua County Historical Society.

76. David T. Silver to Tourgée, September 7, 1892, reel 35, Tourgée Papers.

77. J. H. Wimpey to Tourgée, November 20, 1891, reel 37, Tourgée Papers.

78. *Plessy* was decided by a Republican-majority court. The only dissenter was Justice John Marshall Harlan, a Union veteran from Kentucky.

Chapter 4 · The Rocky Road to Sectional Reconciliation

1. Quoted in Edward J. Blum, *Reforging the White Republic: Race, Religion, and American Nationalism, 1865–1898* (Baton Rouge: Louisiana State University Press, 2005), 191.

2. Quoted in ibid., 194.

3. Joan Waugh, *U. S. Grant: American Hero, American Myth* (Chapel Hill: University of North Carolina Press, 2009), 235.

4. Ibid., 216, 252.

5. Dabney H. Maury to Jubal A. Early, July 30, 1885, vol. 13, Jubal A. Early Papers, Library of Congress.

6. Quoted in Waugh, *U. S. Grant*, 250.

7. Quoted in ibid., 250, 252.

8. See, for example, David W. Blight, *Race and Reunion: The Civil War in American Memory* (Cambridge, MA: Belknap Press of Harvard University Press, 2001), 381–97; and Nina Silber, *The Romance of Reunion: Northerners and the South, 1865–1900* (Chapel Hill: University of North Carolina Press, 1993), 4, 156–58.

9. Paul H. Buck, *The Road to Reunion, 1865–1900* (Boston: Little, Brown, and Co., 1937), 307.

10. Quoted in Susanna W. Gold, "'Fighting It Over Again': The Battle of Gettysburg at the 1876 Centennial Exhibition," *Civil War History* 54 (September 2008): 283.

11. Quoted in ibid., 303–4.

12. *Richmond Daily Dispatch*, August 5, 1873.

13. Quoted in Blight, *Race and Reunion*, 164.

14. Richard Taylor, *Destruction and Reconstruction: Personal Experiences of the Late War in the United States* (Edinburgh, UK: William Blackwell and Sons, 1879), 36, 51.

15. Quoted in Blight, *Race and Reunion*, 166–67.

16. Blight, *Race and Reunion*, 175, 178.

17. Stephen Davis, "'A Matter of Sensational Interest': The *Century* 'Battles and Leaders Series,'" *Civil War History* 27 (December 1981): 347.

18. Robert Underwood Johnson, *Remembered Yesterdays* (Boston: Little, Brown, and Co., 1923), 189.

19. According to Johnson, the initial offer was $500 each for four pieces, but *Century*, eager to secure the rights to Grant's memoirs, later doubled the figure "voluntarily." Ibid., 213.

20. Ulysses S. Grant, *Personal Memoirs* (1885–86; repr., New York: Penguin, 1999), 601, 609.

21. Quoted in Sarah E. Gardner, *Blood and Irony: Southern White Women's Narratives of the Civil War, 1861–1937* (Chapel Hill: University of North Carolina Press, 2004), 85.

22. Ambrose Bierce, *Phantoms of a Blood-Stained Period: The Complete Civil War Writings of Ambrose Bierce*, ed. Russell Duncan and David J. Klooster (Amherst: University of Massachusetts Press, 2002), 103.

23. Ibid., 331.

24. Ibid., 316.

25. Quoted in Paul Sorrentino, *Stephen Crane: A Life of Fire* (Cambridge, MA: Belknap Press of Harvard University Press, 2014), 119.

26. Quoted in ibid., 120.

27. Stephen Crane, *The Red Badge of Courage: An Episode of the American Civil War* (1895; repr., Charlottesville: University of Virginia Press, 1975), 54. The novel was serialized in 1894 and published in full the following year.

28. Oliver Wendell Holmes Jr., "The Soldier's Faith," May 30, 1895, in *The Public Art of Civil War Commemoration: A Brief History with Documents*, ed. Thomas J. Brown (Boston: Bedford/St. Martin's, 2004), 46, 48, 49.

29. Quoted in Jim Weeks, *Gettysburg: Memory, Market, and an American Shrine* (Princeton, NJ: Princeton University Press, 2003), 65.

30. Henry V. N. Boynton, *Sherman's Historical Raid: The Memoir in the Light of the Record* (Cincinnati, OH: Wilstach, Baldwin, and Co., 1875), 8.

31. Ibid., 65.

32. Ibid., 66.

33. Quoted in Michael Fellman, *Citizen Sherman: A Life of William Tecumseh Sherman* (Lawrence: University Press of Kansas, 1995), 328.

34. Quoted in Timothy B. Smith, *A Chickamauga Memorial: The Establishment of America's First Civil War National Military Park* (Knoxville: University of Tennessee Press, 2009), 19.

35. Quoted in ibid., 22.

36. Quoted in ibid., 31.

37. Quoted in Caroline E. Janney, "'I Yield to No Man an Iota of My Convictions': Chickamauga and Chattanooga National Military Park and the Limits of Reconciliation," *Journal of the Civil War Era* 2 (September 2012): 410.

38. Quoted in ibid., 404.

39. Quoted in ibid., 405.

40. Quoted in Patrick J. Kelly, "The Election of 1896 and the Restructuring of Civil War Memory," in *The Memory of the Civil War in American Culture*, ed. Alice Fahs and Joan Waugh (Chapel Hill: University of North Carolina Press, 2004), 185.

41. Quoted in R. Hal Williams, *Realigning America: McKinley, Bryan, and the Remarkable Election of 1896* (Lawrence: University Press of Kansas, 2010), 82.

42. Quoted in Kelly, "Election of 1896," 194.

43. Quoted in ibid., 189.

44. *Iowa State Register*, October 11, 1896.

45. Quoted in Williams, *Realigning America*, 144.

46. Quoted in Bradley S. Keefer, *Conflicting Memories on the "River of Death": The Chickamauga Battlefield and the Spanish-American War, 1863–1933* (Kent, OH: Kent State University Press, 2013), 167.

47. Quoted in Cecilia Elizabeth O'Leary, *To Die For: The Paradox of American Patriotism* (Princeton, NJ: Princeton University Press, 1999), 139.

48. *National Tribune*, May 12, 1898.

49. *Confederate Veteran* 6 (April 1898): 146.

50. William McKinley, "Address at the Trans-Mississippi Exposition at Omaha, Nebraska, October 12, 1898," in *Speeches and Addresses of William McKinley from March 1, 1897 to May 30, 1900* (New York: Doubleday and McClure Co., 1900), 104.

51. Quoted in John R. Neff, *Honoring the Civil War Dead: Commemoration and the Problem of Reconciliation* (Lawrence: University Press of Kansas, 2005), 222.

52. *San Francisco Call*, February 7, 1899. McKinley's conciliatory remarks in Atlanta were not the only reason why the Senate narrowly voted for the peace treaty with Spain. McLaurin of South Carolina was softened up "in part by promises of patronage" and McEnery of Louisiana successfully demanded Republican support for his resolution denying US interest in annexing the Philippines. Lewis L. Gould, *The Presidency of William McKinley* (Lawrence: Regents Press of Kansas, 1980), 149–50.

53. Mike Sewell, "Humanitarian Intervention, Democracy, and Imperialism: The American War with Spain, 1898, and After," in *Humanitarian Intervention: A History*, ed. Brendan Simms and D.J.B. Trim (New York: Cambridge University Press, 2013), 318–19.

54. McKinley, "Speech at Sioux Falls, South Dakota, October 14, 1899," in McKinley, *Speeches*, 297.

55. McKinley, "Speech at Antietam Battle-Field, Maryland, May 30, 1900," in ibid., 370. In addition to Antietam and Chickamauga/Chattanooga, the other battlefield parks created in the 1890s were Shiloh, Gettysburg, and Vicksburg.

56. *Irish World and American Industrial Liberator*, July 22, 1899.

57. Micki McElya, *The Politics of Mourning: Death and Honor in Arlington National Cemetery* (Cambridge, MA: Harvard University Press, 2016), 153.

58. Quoted in Buck, *Road to Reunion*, 171.

59. Woodrow Wilson, "An Address at the Gettysburg Battlefield," July 4, 1913, in *The Papers of Woodrow Wilson*, vol. 28: *1913*, ed. Arthur Link (Princeton, NJ: Princeton University Press, 1978), 23.

60. Quoted in Daniel Sutherland, "Memories of a Rooted Sorrow: The Legacy of the Guerrilla War," *Civil War History* 62 (March 2016): 30.

61. Benjamin G. Cloyd, *Haunted by Atrocity: Civil War Prisons in American Memory* (Baton Rouge: Louisiana State University Press, 2010), 1.

62. Ibid., 14.

63. Herbert W. Collingwood, *Andersonville Violets: A Story of Northern and Southern Life* (Boston: Lee and Shepard, 1889), unnumbered preface.

64. Quoted in James Marten, *America's Corporal: James Tanner in War and Peace* (Athens: University of Georgia Press, 2014), 81.

65. Charles Francis Adams Jr., "Shall Cromwell Have a Statue?" (1902), in *Public Art*, ed. Brown, 108.

66. [Dudley McEwan Featherston], "Speech to Honor the Confederate Dead" [1904], folder 14, box 7, Featherston Collection, University of Mississippi Library. Although Dudley Featherston is not named in the original document, I believe the evidence is strong enough to identify him as the author of the speech. I thank Jennifer Ford, head of Special Collections at the University of Mississippi Library, for assisting me in this matter.

67. O'Leary, *To Die For*, 172–93; Stuart McConnell, *Glorious Contentment: The Grand Army of the Republic, 1865–1900* (Chapel Hill: University of North Carolina Press, 1992), 192–93.

68. Barbara A. Gannon, "'They Call Themselves Veterans': Civil War Veterans and Spanish War Veterans and the Complexities of Veteranhood," *Journal of the Civil War Era* 5 (December 2015): 530. Although the Spanish-American War veterans' readiness to accept racial segregation illustrated many young Americans' lack of empathy for blacks, it should be noted that some northern college students enthusiastically supported Albion Tourgée's short-lived National Citizens' Rights Association. See Carolyn L. Karcher, *A Refugee from His Race: Albion W. Tourgée and His Fight against White Supremacy* (Chapel Hill: University of North Carolina Press, 2016), 171–72.

69. Booker T. Washington, "The Standard Printed Version of the Atlanta Exposition Address," September 18, 1895, in *The Booker T. Washington Papers*, vol. 3: *1889–95*, ed. Louis R. Harlan (Urbana: University of Illinois Press, 1974), 585.

70. Ibid., 587.

71. Quoted in Blight, *Race and Reunion*, 362.

72. Silber, *Romance of Reunion*.

73. Quoted in Buck, *Road to Reunion*, 212.

74. Johnson, *Remembered Yesterdays*, 121–22; Buck, *Road to Reunion*, 216.

75. Quoted in Gardner, *Blood and Irony*, 87.

76. Adam Fairclough, "Was the Grant of Black Suffrage a Political Error? Reconsidering the Views of John W. Burgess, William A. Dunning, and Eric Foner on Congressional Reconstruction," *Journal of the Historical Society* 12 (June 2012): 160–65.

77. Bruce Baker, *What Reconstruction Meant: Historical Memory in the American South* (Charlottesville: University of Virginia Press, 2007), 46.

78. Thomas Nelson Page, *Red Rock: A Chronicle of Reconstruction* (New York: Charles Scribner's Sons, 1898), vii, viii.

79. Joel Chandler Harris, *Gabriel Tolliver: A Story of Reconstruction* (New York: McClure, Phillips, and Co., 1902), 176, 179.

80. Quoted from a Union veteran's letter to Dixon in William C. Lowe, "'A Grand and Patriotic Pilgrimage': The Iowa Civil War Monuments Dedication Tour of 1906," *Annals of Iowa* 69 (Winter 2010): 44.

81. William Hayes Ward, address of May 31, 1909, in *Proceedings of the National Negro Conference 1909: New York, May 31 and June 1* (New York: The Conference, 1909), 9.

82. Burt G. Wilder, "The Brain of the American Negro," in ibid., 23.

Chapter 5 • Distant Drums in an Age of Global Warfare

1. Caroline E. Janney, *Remembering the Civil War: Reunion and the Limits of Reconciliation* (Chapel Hill: University of North Carolina Press, 2013), 268.

2. Inez Smith to MacKinlay Kantor, May 14, 1939, folder 9, box 24, MacKinlay Kantor Papers, Library of Congress.

3. Grace L. Hosmer to Kantor, June 3, 1939, folder 9, box 24, Kantor Papers.

4. Ida B. Tarbell, chapter 2 of *Abraham Lincoln, McClure's Magazine* 6 (December 1895): 20.

5. Jane Addams, *Twenty Years at Hull-House with Autobiographical Notes* (New York: Macmillan, 1910), 23.

6. Ibid., 29. For a history of the eagle, see J. O. Barrett, *The Soldier Bird: "Old Abe"; The Live War-Eagle of Wisconsin, That Served a Three Years' Campaign in the Great Rebellion* (Madison, WI: Atwood and Culver, 1876).

7. Addams, *Twenty Years*, 42.

8. Mary Raymond Shipman Andrews, "The Perfect Tribute," *Scribner's Magazine* 40 (July 1906): 23, 24.

9. Jared Peatman, *The Long Shadow of Lincoln's Gettysburg Address* (Carbondale: University of Southern Illinois Press, 2013), 82.

10. Melvyn Stokes, *D. W. Griffith's* The Birth of a Nation*: A History of "The Most Controversial Motion Picture of All Time"* (New York: Oxford University Press, 2007), 79. According to Stokes, Dixon may have earned "anything from one to several million dollars" from the deal (80).

11. Ibid., 125.

12. Quoted in Brian Matthew Jordan, *Marching Home: Union Veterans and Their Unending Civil War* (New York: Liveright Publishing, 2014), 195.

13. Minutes of meeting, March 4, 1916, minute book, box 25, Crocker Post No. 12, Post Records, Iowa Department GAR, State Historical Society of Iowa.

14. Alison Landsberg, *Prosthetic Memory: The Transformation of American Remembrance in the Age of Mass Culture* (New York: Columbia University Press, 2004), 19.

15. Quoted in Stokes, *D. W. Griffith's* The Birth of a Nation, 208.

16. David Stevenson, *With Our Backs to the Wall: Victory and Defeat in 1918* (New York: Allen Lane, 2011), 251. World War I generated more bitter memories—not only among blacks who resented their degrading treatment in the army but also some whites, especially those who deplored the industrial scale of the killing and found their service experience far from glorious. Like the Civil War before it, however, the Great War sired a patriotic national veterans' organization. This time it took the form of the American Legion, whose members replaced their GAR and UCV predecessors as lobbyists and

politicians and as organizers of, and participants in, Memorial Day events. While the Legion replicated some of the GAR's paramilitary style, it followed the United Spanish War Veterans in pursuing a policy of racial segregation.

17. Ibid., 44.

18. Samuel S. Wise, "Lincoln and Wilson," *Free Synagogue Pulpit* 7 (1921–22): 9.

19. Quoted in Barry Schwartz, *Abraham Lincoln and the Forge of National Memory* (Chicago: University of Chicago Press, 2000), 244.

20. Christopher A. Thomas, *The Lincoln Memorial and American Life* (Princeton, NJ: Princeton University Press, 2002), 139.

21. Quoted in Scott A. Sandage, "A Marble House Divided: The Lincoln Memorial, the Civil Rights Movement, and the Politics of Memory, 1939–1963," *Journal of American History* 80 (June 1993): 141. The memorial's only reference to black liberation was a hard-to-spot mural by symbolist painter Jules Guérin. Thomas, *Lincoln Memorial*, 126–27.

22. Quoted in Adam Fairclough, "Civil Rights and the Lincoln Memorial: The Censored Speeches of Robert R. Moton (1922) and John Lewis (1963)," *Journal of Negro History* 82 (Autumn 1997): 410–11.

23. Quoted in ibid., 412.

24. Carl Sandburg, *Abraham Lincoln: The Prairie Years*, 2 vols. (London: Jonathan Cape, 1926), 1:49.

25. Ibid., 2:183.

26. R. Blakeslee Gilpin, *John Brown Still Lives! America's Long Reckoning with Violence, Equality, and Change* (Chapel Hill: University of North Carolina Press, 2011), 106.

27. Stephen Vincent Benét, *John Brown's Body* (1928; repr., Chicago: Ivan R. Dee, 1990), 333, 335.

28. Ibid., 162.

29. Quoted in Peter Novick, *That Noble Dream: The "Objectivity Question" and the American Historical Profession* (New York: Cambridge University Press, 1988), 237.

30. Quoted in ibid.

31. Quoted in ibid.

32. Quoted in ibid., 235.

33. Quoted in ibid., 231n42.

34. Charles Edward Russell, "Civil War History as Taught in Certain Text Books," [draft article, c. 1932], box 37, Charles Edward Russell Papers, Library of Congress.

35. Quoted in Bruce Baker, *What Reconstruction Meant: Historical Memory in the American South* (Charlottesville: University of Virginia Press, 2007), 122.

36. Alessandra Lorini, *Rituals of Race: American Public Culture and the Search for Racial Democracy* (Charlottesville: University of Virginia Press, 1999), 219.

37. Quoted in William H. Wiggins Jr., *O Freedom! Afro-American Emancipation Celebrations* (Knoxville: University of Tennessee Press, 1987), 59.

38. W.E.B. Du Bois, *Black Reconstruction in America: An Essay toward a History of the Part Which Black Folk Played in the Attempt to Reconstruct Democracy in America, 1860–1880* (New York: Russel and Russel, 1935), 711–29.

39. Ibid., 727.

40. Ibid., 715.

41. Richard B. Harwell, ed., *Margaret Mitchell's "Gone With the Wind" Letters, 1936–1949* (New York: Macmillan, 1976), 38.

42. Quoted in Andrew Doyle, "Turning the Tide: College Football and Southern Progressivism," *Southern Cultures* 3, no. 3 (1997): 37.

43. Quoted in ibid., 36.

44. Quoted in Thomas J. Brown, *Civil War Canon: Sites of Confederate Memory in South Carolina* (Chapel Hill: University of North Carolina Press, 2015), 176.

45. Molly Haskell, *Frankly, My Dear:* Gone with the Wind *Revisited* (New Haven, CT: Yale University Press, 2009), 5; Leonard J. Leff, "'Gone with the Wind' and Hollywood's Racial Politics," *Atlantic*, December 1999, http://www.theatlantic.com/magazine/archive/1999/12/gone-with-the-wind-and-hollywoods-racial-politics/377919.

46. Harwell, *"Gone With the Wind" Letters*, 57.

47. Quoted in Haskell, *Frankly, My Dear*, 30.

48. *Bulletin: The United Daughters of the Confederacy* 3 (January 1940): n.p.

49. Quoted in Steve Wilson, *The Making of* Gone with the Wind (Austin: University of Texas Press, 2014), 318.

50. Quoted in Virginius Dabney, *The Last Review: The Confederate Reunion, Richmond, 1932* (Chapel Hill: Algonquin Books, 1984), 39.

51. Douglas Southall Freeman, "The Last Parade," in ibid., 157.

52. On the construction of "the New Deal order," see Steve Fraser and Gary Gerstle, *The Rise and Fall of the New Deal Order, 1930–1980* (Princeton, NJ: Princeton University Press, 1989).

53. Ellen Glasgow to Douglas Southall Freeman, February 3, 1935, box 23, Douglas Southall Freeman Papers, Library of Congress. Glasgow told her fellow Richmonder, "As far back as I can remember Lee has been my only hero."

54. Quoted in Baker, *What Reconstruction Meant*, 104.

55. Quoted in ibid., 99.

56. Quoted in ibid.

57. Quoted in ibid., 102.

58. Harwell, *"Gone With the Wind" Letters*, 221.

59. Quoted in Baker, *What Reconstruction Meant*, 100.

60. Freeman to Harry F. Byrd, July 3, 1935, box 21, Freeman Papers.

61. Freeman to Byrd, July 10, 1935, box 21, Freeman Papers.

62. Byrd to Freeman, citing a conversation with Bailey, June 27, 1935, box 21, Freeman Papers.

63. Freeman, "An Address before a Joint Session of the General Assembly of Virginia, Jany. 20, 1936," box 127, Freeman Papers.

64. Nina Silber, "Abraham Lincoln and the Political Culture of New Deal America," *Journal of the Civil War Era* 5 (September 2015): 348.

65. Quoted in Jim Cullen, *The Civil War in Popular Culture: A Reusable Past* (Washington, DC: Smithsonian Institution Press, 1995), 47.

66. Franklin D. Roosevelt, "Address at the Dedication of the Memorial on the Gettysburg Battlefield, Gettysburg, Pennsylvania: July 3, 1938," *The Public Papers and Addresses of Franklin D. Roosevelt—1938: The Continuing Struggle for Liberalism* (London: Macmillan, 1941), 420.

67. Quoted in Cullen, *Civil War in Popular Culture*, 47.

68. Ibid.

69. Roosevelt, "Address at the Dedication," 420.

70. Ibid., 421.

71. Quoted in Cullen, *Civil War in Popular Culture*, 48–49.

72. Quoted in Peatman, *Long Shadow*, 132.

73. Winston S. Churchill, "If Lee Had Not Won the Battle of Gettysburg," *Scribner's Magazine* 88 (December 1930): 589.

74. Churchill, "The Speech to Congress," December 26, 1941, in *The War Speeches of the Rt Hon Winston S. Churchill*, ed. Charles Eade, 3 vols. (London: Cassell and Co., 1952), 2:145.

75. Quoted in Barry Schwartz, "Memory as a Cultural System: Abraham Lincoln in World War II," *American Sociological Review* 61 (October 1996): 916.

76. Ibid.

77. Quoted in Fred Child, "Copland's 'Lincoln Portrait,'" National Public Radio, accessed July 29, 2015, http://www.npr.org/templates/story/story.php?storyId=4165357.

78. Director Steven Spielberg included the Bixby letter in his 1998 movie, *Saving Private Ryan*. General George Marshall reads it to officers after he learns about the deaths of the three Ryan brothers and of the one surviving brother's involvement in the D-Day landings. Marshall is also heard quoting from the Bixby letter when he writes to Mrs. Ryan at the end of the film.

79. Quoted in Peatman, *Long Shadow*, 146.

80. L. O. Crosby to James O. Eastland, June 2, 1943, folder 9, box 30, James O. Eastland Papers, University of Mississippi Library. Camp Van Dorn was named for General Earl Van Dorn, a prominent Confederate commander in the western theater.

81. Eastland to W. C. Adams, May 13, 1943, folder 9, box 30, Eastland Papers.

82. Theodore G. Bilbo, *The War; Constitutional Government; and the Race Issue—America's Greatest Unsolved Domestic Problem* (Washington, DC: US Government Printing Office, 1945), 12.

Chapter 6 • Centennial Blues

1. Bruce Catton, "Muffled Roll for Grand Army," *Life*, August 20, 1956. Open only to Union veterans of the Civil War, the GAR was dissolved formally after Woolson's death.

2. Robert Penn Warren, *The Legacy of the Civil War: Meditations on the Centennial* (New York: Random House, 1961), 4.

3. Ibid., 53–66.

4. Ibid., 50.

5. Ibid., 108.

6. Arthur M. Schlesinger Jr., "The Causes of the Civil War: A Note on Historical Sentimentalism," *Partisan Review* 16 (October 1949): 979. One caustic commentator called the essay "an obvious exercise in historical rearmament for World War III." Quoted in Peter Novick, *That Noble Dream: The "Objectivity Question" and the American Historical Profession* (New York: Cambridge University Press, 1988), 357.

7. Schlesinger, "Causes of the Civil War," 978.

8. Quoted in Joseph Crespino, *In Search of Another Country: Mississippi and the Conservative Counterrevolution* (Princeton, NJ: Princeton University Press, 2007), 51.

9. Edward Tabor Linenthal, *Sacred Ground: Americans and Their Battlefields* (Urbana: University of Illinois Press, 1991), 97.

10. Quoted in Robert J. Cook, *Troubled Commemoration: The American Civil War Centennial, 1961–65* (Baton Rouge: Louisiana State University Press, 2007), 19.

11. NPS Stats, Gettysburg NMP, National Park Service, accessed April 14, 2015, https://irma.nps.gov/Stats/SSRSReports/Park%20Specific%20Reports/Annual%20Park%20Recreation%20Visitation%20(1904%20-%20Last%20Calendar%20Year)?Park=GETT.

12. NPS Stats, Shiloh NMP, National Park Service, accessed April 14, 2015, https://irma.nps.gov/Stats/SSRSReports/Park%20Specific%20Reports/Annual%20Park%20Recreation%20Visitation%20(1904%20-%20Last%20Calendar%20Year)?Park=SHIL.

13. MacKinlay Kantor to Lucy S. Stewart, February 10, 1936, folder 6, box 24, MacKinlay Kantor Papers, Library of Congress.

14. Ernest D. Jackman to Kantor, January 11, 1956, folder 1, box 27, Kantor Papers.

15. Clint Edwards to Kantor, February 3, 1956, folder 1, box 27, Kantor Papers.

16. C. C. Burford to Kantor, April 11, 1956, folder 2, box 27, Kantor Papers.

17. Walter Masterson to Kantor, August 5, 1957, folder 8, box 27, Kantor Papers.

18. Gerald Dickler to Bruce Catton, October 19, 1967, folder "Corr.—1967—Aug.–Oct.," box 12, Bruce Catton Papers, American Heritage Center.

19. Catton was not the only American of his generation to deploy the Civil War as a usable past in the Cold War. During the sesquicentennial of Abraham Lincoln's birth in 1959, the United States Information Service, the propaganda arm of the State Department, furnished allies and "non-aligned" nations with images of the sixteenth president as a self-made man and quintessential American democrat. Jay Sexton, "Projecting Lincoln, Projecting America," in *The Global Lincoln*, ed. Richard Carwardine and Jay Sexton (New York: Oxford University Press, 2011), 288–302.

20. Quoted in David W. Blight, *American Oracle: The Civil War in the Civil Rights Era* (Cambridge, MA: Belknap Press of Harvard University Press, 2011), 83.

21. Bruce Catton, *The War Lords of Washington* (New York: Harcourt, Brace, and Co., 1948), 309.

22. Catton, speech at Duke University, February 7, 1957, folder "Speeches," box 1, Catton Papers.

23. Clifford Dowdey to Catton, November 21, 1954, folder 1, box 2, Catton Papers.

24. *Congressional Record*, 85th Cong., 2nd sess., 1763.

25. Phineas Indritz to Catton, April 22, 1957, folder 4, box 2, Catton Papers.

26. Catton to Hugh A. McCloskey, October 4, 1955, folder 2, box 2, Catton Papers.

27. Catton, speech at Oberlin College, December 11, 1956, folder "Speeches," box 1, Catton Papers.

28. Transcript, House Judiciary Subcommittee Number 4, Hearing on H.J. Res 233, etc., folder 2, box 350, Committee on the Judiciary, HR85A-D10, 85th Cong., Records of the House of Representatives, National Archives, Washington, DC.

29. Ralph Newman to Emanuel Celler, June 5, 1957, ibid.

30. 85th Cong., 1st sess., Senate Report 1076, "Civil War Centennial Commission," August 21, 1957, folder "Commission Legislation," box 69, subject files 1957–66, Records of the Civil War Centennial Commission, National Archives, College Park, MD (hereafter CWCCR).

31. William M. Tuck to E. L. Forrester, December 25, 1957, folder 5263, William M. Tuck Papers, Earl Gregg Swem Library, College of William and Mary.

32. Dan Wakefield, "Civil War Centennial: Bull Run with Popcorn," *Nation*, January 30, 1960.

33. *Montgomery Advertiser*, February 27, 1961.

34. Bill Wallace to John F. Kennedy, February 7, 1961, box 69, subject files 1957–66, CWCCR.

35. *Atlanta Constitution*, April 8, 1961.

36. Cleveland Amory, "First of the Month," *Saturday Review*, April 1, 1961.

37. *New York Post*, March 30, 1961, clipping encl. in Arthur M. Schlesinger Jr. to Bell I. Wiley, April 3, 1961, folder "General Correspondence 1961, April 1–7, box 62, Bell I. Wiley Papers, Manuscript, Archives, and Rare Book Library, Emory University.

38. *Centennial Commemoration July 22–23, 1961: The First Battle of Manassas (Bull Run)*, official commemorative program, folder "Reenactments—Manassas," box 97, subject files 1957–66, CWCCR.

39. *Fonda Democrat*, August 17, 1961, clipping in box 1, scrapbooks and clippings 1961–62, A0208-78, Records of the New York Civil War Centennial Commission, New York State Archives.

40. CWCC, minutes of the meeting held December 4, 1961, folder "Minutes—Commission Meetings, Agendas, etc.," box 184, Wiley Papers.

41. *Washington Post*, September 17, 1962.

42. Quoted in Charles W. Eagles, *The Price of Defiance: James Meredith and the Integration of Ole Miss* (Chapel Hill: University of North Carolina Press, 2009), 283. Barnett's strident public rhetoric did not always match his private actions. During the Oxford crisis, he participated in covert negotiations with Attorney General Robert Kennedy to secure James Meredith's peaceful admission to Ole Miss.

43. Sterling A. Chandler to James O. Eastland and John A. Stennis, October 10, 1962, folder 1, box 41, James O. Eastland Papers, University of Mississippi Library.

44. F. F. Henson to Eastland, October 4, 1962, ibid.

45. Lewis H. Andrews to Eastland, September 23, 1962, ibid.

46. C. Vann Woodward, *The Strange Career of Jim Crow* (New York: Oxford University Press, 1955), 9.

47. George Johnson Jr. to editor of *Jackson Clarion-Ledger*, October 10, 1962, folder 1, box 41, Eastland Papers.

48. Quoted in Crespino, *In Search of Another Country*, 50.

49. Catton, speech at Boston College, May 25, 1963, folder "National Assembly, 1963," box 184, Wiley Papers.

50. Jim Weeks, *Gettysburg: Memory, Market, and an American Shrine* (Princeton, NJ: Princeton University Press, 2003), 137.

51. *Montgomery Advertiser*, July 2, 1963.

52. Speech of Governor Richard Hughes, New Jersey Civil War Centennial Commission press release, folder "Gettysburg Rededication, July 1, 1963," box 3, Records of the New Jersey Civil War Centennial Commission, New Jersey State Archives.

53. Allan Nevins to Paul H. Douglas, September 4, 1963, box 85, Allan Nevins Papers, Rare Book and Manuscript Library, Columbia University.

54. Paul H. Douglas, "The Significance of Gettysburg," in Allan Nevins, ed., *Lincoln and the Gettysburg Address: Commemorative Papers [by] John Dos Passos, Arthur Lehman Goodhart, Reinhold Niebuhr, Robert Lowell, Paul H. Douglas, David C. Mearns* (Urbana: University of Illinois Press, 1964), 115–16. At the behest of JFK's widow, Jacqueline, Kennedy's lying in state at the White House was modeled closely on that of Abraham Lincoln. Assisting in this task, the CWCC's executive director "Bud" Robertson pored over original illustrations of Lincoln's coffin in the Library of Congress and found the Great Emancipator's catafalque, retrieved from the bowels of the Capitol, waiting for him when he arrived at the White House. Larry J. Sabato, *The Kennedy Half Century: The Presidency, Assassination, and Lasting Legacy of John F. Kennedy* (New York: Bloomsbury, 2013), 21–22.

55. Quoted in Crespino, *In Search of Another Country*, 103.

56. *Birmingham News*, April 6, 1965.

57. Robert J. Cook et al., "Historians' Forum: The American Civil War's Centennial vs. the Sesquicentennial," *Civil War History* 57 (December 2011): 391.

58. William G. Piston to the author, February 6, 2004.

59. *Crusader*, March 4, 1961, Special Collections, Duke University Library. I thank Joe Street for this reference.

60. A. Philip Randolph to Howard N. Meyer, July 13, 1961, reel 2, Bayard Rustin Papers (University Publications of America microfilm, 1988).

61. Lerone Bennett, "The Negro in the Civil War," *Ebony* 17 (May 1962): 134.

62. *Ebony*, 17 (July 1962): 13.

63. Ibid.

64. Martin Luther King Jr., "The Negro and the Constitution" [May 1944], in *The Papers of Martin Luther King, Jr.*, vol. 1, *Called to Serve, January 1929–June 1951*, ed. Clayborne Carson (Berkeley: University of California Press, 1992), 110–11.

65. King, "An Appeal to the Honorable John F. Kennedy[,] President of the United States[,] for a National Rededication to the Principles of the Emancipation Proclamation and for an Executive Order Prohibiting Segregation in the United States of America," May 17, 1962, folder "Emancipation Proclamation Centennial Appeal to President Kennedy re: Civil Rights, May 17, 1962," box 5, US Commission on Civil Rights, 1958–1963, Berl I. Bernhard Papers, John F. Kennedy Presidential Library.

66. King, "Address to the New York Civil War Centennial Commission," September 12, 1962, box 3, series 3, Martin Luther King Jr. Papers, King Center Archives, Atlanta.

67. John F. Kennedy, "Special Message to the Congress on Civil Rights, Feb. 28, 1963," *Public Papers of the Presidents: John F. Kennedy, 1963* (Washington, DC: US Government Printing Office, 1964), 222.

68. John Lewis, "Original Text of Speech to Be Delivered at the Lincoln Memorial," August 28, 1963, in *The Eyes on the Prize Civil Rights Reader: Documents, Speeches, and Firsthand Accounts from the Black Freedom Struggle, 1954–1990*, ed. Clayborne Carson et al. (New York: Penguin, 1991), 165.

69. Martin Luther King Jr., "I Have a Dream," August 28, 1963, in *A Testament of Hope: The Essential Writings and Speeches of Martin Luther King, Jr.*, ed. James M. Washington (San Francisco: HarperSanFrancisco, 1986), 217.

70. On this topic, see especially Scott A. Sandage, "A Marble House Divided: The Lincoln Memorial, the Civil Rights Movement, and the Politics of Memory, 1939–1963," *Journal of American History* 80 (June 1993): 135–67.

71. King, "I Have a Dream," 217.

72. Ibid.

73. King, "Address at the Conclusion of the Selma to Montgomery March," March 25, 1965, Martin Luther King, Jr., and the Global Freedom Struggle, accessed May 14, 2015, http://mlk-kpp01.stanford.edu/index.php/encyclopedia/documentsentry/doc_address_at_the_conclusion_of_selma_march.

74. Malcolm X, response to moderator's question at the University of California, October 11, 1963, in Bruce Perry, ed., *Malcolm X: The Last Speeches* (New York: Pathfinder Press, 1989), 76.

75. Julius Lester, *Look Out, Whitey! Black Power's Gon' Get Your Mama!* (1968; repr., New York: Grove Press, 1969), 58.

76. Robert Scheer, ed., *Eldridge Cleaver: Post-prison Writings and Speeches* (London: Jonathan Cape, 1969), 79; G. Louis Heath, ed., *The Black Panther Leaders Speak: Huey P. Newton, Bobby Seale, Eldridge Cleaver and Company Speak Out through the Black Panther Party's Official Newspaper* (Metuchen, NJ: Scarecrow Press, 1976), 25.

77. Heath, *Black Panther Leaders Speak*, 71–72.

78. Quoted in R. Blakeslee Gilpin, *John Brown Still Lives! America's Long Reckoning with Violence, Equality, and Change* (Chapel Hill: University of North Carolina Press, 2011), 185.

79. Scheer, *Eldridge Cleaver*, 165.

Chapter 7 • Afterlife

1. Quoted in Robert Holt, "Battlefield Burial: Union, Confederate Widows Take Part in Ceremony," *Gettysburg Times*, July 2, 1997, http://www.brotherswar.com/Union_Confederate_Burial_at_Gettysburg_1997.htm.

2. Ibid.

3. Quoted in Gabor S. Boritt, "Lincoln and Gettysburg: The Hero and the Heroic Place," in *Ken Burns's* The Civil War: *Historians Respond*, ed. Robert Brent Toplin (New York: Oxford University Press, 1996), 86.

4. NPS Stats, Gettysburg NMP, National Park Service, accessed July 27, 2015, https://irma.nps.gov/Stats/SSRSReports/Park Specific Reports/Annual Park Recreation Visitation (1904 - Last Calendar Year)?Park=GETT.

5. John W. Blassingame, *The Slave Community: Plantation Life in the American South* (New York: Oxford University Press, 1972); Eugene D. Genovese, *Roll, Jordan, Roll: The World the Slaves Made* (New York: Pantheon Books, 1974).

6. Eric Foner, *Free Soil, Free Labor, Free Men: The Ideology of the Republican Party before the Civil War* (New York: Oxford University Press, 1971); Foner, *Reconstruction: America's Unfinished Revolution, 1863–1877* (New York: Oxford University Press, 1988).

7. Barry Schwartz, *Abraham Lincoln in the Post-heroic Era: History and Memory in Late Twentieth-Century America* (Chicago: University of Chicago Press, 2008).

8. Studs Terkel, *"The Good War": An Oral History of World War Two* (New York: Pantheon Books, 1984).

9. Michael Kreyling, *A Late Encounter with the Civil War* (Athens: University of Georgia Press, 2013), 88.

10. E. L. Doctorow, *The March* (London: Little, Brown, 2006), 62–63.

11. Ibid., 362.

12. Jim Weeks, *Gettysburg: Memory, Market, and an American Shrine* (Princeton, NJ: Princeton University Press, 2003), 209–14.

13. Tony Horwitz, *Confederates in the Attic: Dispatches from the Unfinished Civil War* (1998; New York: Vintage Books, 1999), 7.

14. Ibid., 10–11.

15. Quoted in *New York Times*, May 12, 1994.

16. Official visitor statistics for individual parks can be found at NPS Stats, National Park Service, https://irma.nps.gov/Stats.

17. David W. Blight, "The Meaning or the Fight: Frederick Douglass and the Memory of the Fifty Fourth Massachusetts," *Massachusetts Review* 36 (Spring 1995): 143.

18. *Ebony*, 54 (November 1998): 156.

19. Martin H. Blatt, "Glory: Hollywood History, Popular Culture, and the Fifty-Fourth Massachusetts Regiment," in *Hope and Glory: Essays on the Legacy of the 54th Massachusetts Regiment*, ed. Martin H. Blatt, Thomas J. Brown, and Donald Yacovone (2001; Amherst: University of Massachusetts Press; Boston: Massachusetts Historical Society, 2009), 228–29.

20. David Harlan, "Ken Burns and the Coming Crisis of Academic History," *Rethinking History* 7 (Summer 2003): 169.

21. Quoted in C. Stuart Chapman, *Shelby Foote: A Writer's Life* (Jackson: University of Mississippi Press, 2003), 263; Shelby Foote, *The Civil War: A Narrative*, 3 vols. (New York: Random House, 1958–74).

22. Dialogue quoted in Gary W. Gallagher, *Causes Won, Lost and Forgotten: How Hollywood and Popular Art Shape What We Know about the Civil War* (Chapel Hill: University of North Carolina Press, 2008), 100.

23. A total of 1,674,532 recreational visits were made to Gettysburg National Military Park in 1994 compared with 1,411,453 in 1993. This was the highest figure since 1976, when visitor numbers were inflated by the bicentenary of the Revolution. NPS Stats, Gettysburg NMP, National Park Service, accessed July 22, 2015, https://irma.nps.gov/Stats/SSRSReports/Park%20Specific%20Reports/Annual%20Park%20Recreation%20Visitation%20(1904%20-%20Last%20Calendar%20Year)?Park=GETT.

24. Weeks, *Gettysburg*, 190.

25. Jennifer M. Murray, *On a Great Battlefield: The Making, Management, and Memory of Gettysburg National Military Park, 1933–2013* (Knoxville: University of Tennessee Press, 2014), 150–51.

26. Quoted in ibid., 170.

27. Murray, *On a Great Battlefield*, 171.

28. Quoted in ibid.

29. Murray, *On a Great Battlefield*, 187.

30. Kevin M. Levin, *Remembering the Battle of the Crater* (Lexington: University Press of Kentucky, 2012), 133.

31. Sons of Confederate Veterans, "Postcard Objecting to Mention of Slavery at Civil War Sites," 2000, in *The Confederate and Neo-Confederate Reader: The "Great Truth" about the "Lost Cause,"* ed. James W. Loewen and Edward H. Sebesta (Jackson: University of Mississippi Press, 2010), 375; Murray, *On a Great Battlefield*, 170.

32. Heidi Beirich, "The Struggle for the Sons of Confederate Veterans: A Return to White Supremacy in the Early Twenty-First Century?" in *Neo-Confederacy: A Critical Introduction*, ed. Euan Hague, Heidi Beirich, and Edward H. Sebesta (Austin: University of Texas Press, 2008), 280–308.

33. Frank Conner, "Where We Stand Now: And How We Got Here," *Southern Mercury*, September 2003, in *The Confederate and Neo-Confederate Reader*, ed. Loewen and Sebesta, 385.

34. Euan Hague, "Neo-Confederacy and Education," in *Neo-Confederacy*, ed. Hague et al., 211–17.

35. Conner, "Where We Stand Now," 390–91.

36. Euan Hague and Edward H. Sebesta, "Neo-Confederacy and the Understanding of Race," in *Neo-Confederacy*, ed. Hague et al., 139.

37. Joan Waugh, *U. S. Grant: American Hero, American Myth* (Chapel Hill: University of North Carolina Press, 2009), 307.

38. John M. Coski, *The Confederate Battle Flag: America's Most Embattled Emblem* (Cambridge, MA: Belknap Press of Harvard University Press, 2005), 236.

39. Ibid., 237–44.

40. Ibid., 263–66.

41. Ibid., 263.

42. Thomas J. Brown, "The Confederate Battle Flag and the Desertion of the Lost Cause Tradition," in *Remixing the Civil War: Meditations on the Sesquicentennial*, ed. Brown (Baltimore, MD: Johns Hopkins University Press, 2011), 53–55.

43. Quoted in ibid., 59.

44. Coski, *Confederate Battle Flag*, 249–51.

45. Quoted in Paul Quigley, "Refighting the Civil War, Yet Again: Virginia's Confederate History Month Mêlée," *American Nineteenth Century History* 11, no. 3 (2010): 351.

46. Quoted in ibid., 353.

47. Quoted in ibid. 352.

48. Quoted in ibid.

49. Quoted in Nia-Malika Henderson, "Inside the Battle over the Confederate Flag," CNN, updated June 24, 2015, http://edition.cnn.com/2015/06/21/politics/south-carolina-confederate-flag-debate.

50. "Save the South," ipetitions, accessed August 3, 2016, http://www.ipetitions.com/petition/save-the-south.

51. Barack Obama, "Senator Obama's Announcement," *New York Times*, February 10, 2007, http://www.nytimes.com/2007/02/10/us/politics/110bama-text.html?pagewanted=print&_r=0.

52. C. Wyatt Evans, "The Lincoln-Obama Moment," in *Remixing*, ed. Brown, 18–19.

53. Quoted in ibid., 24; Robert Dallek, *Kennedy: An Unfinished Life, 1917–1963* (London: Penguin, 2004), 199.

54. Evans, "Lincoln-Obama Moment," 27.

55. Barack Obama, "Obama's Speech at the Lincoln Memorial," *New York Times*, January 18, 2009, http://www.nytimes.com/2009/01/18/us/politics/18text-obama.html.

56. Quoted in Gail Fineberg, "44th President Takes Oath on Lincoln Bible," *Library of Congress Information Bulletin*, January–February 2009, http://www.loc.gov/loc/lcib/09012/obama.html.

57. Barack Obama, "Remarks at a Lincoln Bicentennial Celebration," February 12, 2009, *Public Papers of the Presidents: Barack Obama, 2009* (Washington, DC: US Government Printing Office, 2010), 94.

58. Barack Obama, "Remarks at the Abraham Lincoln Association Annual Banquet in Springfield, Illinois," February 12, 2009, in ibid., 100.

59. Jon Wiener, "The Trouble with Steven Spielberg's Lincoln," *Nation*, November 27, 2012, http://www.thenation.com/article/trouble-steven-spielbergs-lincoln; Michael Vorenberg, "Spielberg's *Lincoln*: The Great Emancipator Returns," *Journal of the Civil War Era* 3 (December 2013): 553, 562.

60. National Park Service, "Holding the High Ground: A National Park Service Plan for the Sesquicentennial of the American Civil War," May 2008, 3–4, https://hst409509.files.wordpress.com/2011/01/holding-the-high-ground.pdf.

61. Robert Sutton to the author, e-mail communication, June 25, 2015.

62. *New York Times*, May 26, 2009. Acting on a suggestion by the art historian Kirk Savage, Obama attempted to balance this controversial gesture by becoming the first president to send a wreath to the African American Civil War Memorial in Washington. Micki McElya, *The Politics of Mourning: Death and Honor in Arlington National Cemetery* (Cambridge, MA: Harvard University Press, 2016), 159–60.

63. *New York Times*, August 13, 2009.

64. North Carolina Sesquicentennial Committee, "Overview," Facebook, accessed April 15, 2015, https://www.facebook.com/pages/North-Carolina-Civil-War-Sesquicentennial-Committee/105784479554?sk=info&tab=overview.

65. North Carolina War between the States Sesquicentennial Commission, "Our Commission's Purpose," accessed April 15, 2015, http://www.ncwbts150.com/NorthCarolinaSesquicentennialCommission.php.

66. North Carolina War between the States Sesquicentennial Commission, "Acts of Treason Against North Carolina," accessed April 15, 2015, http://www.ncwbts150.com/ActsofTreasonAgainstNorthCarolina.php.

67. David W. Blight, "The Civil War Sesquicentennial," *Chronicle of Higher Education* 55, no. 38 (June 5, 2009).

68. For an assessment of official attendance statistics at the major Civil War parks, see Nick Sacco, "Analyzing Visitor Attendance to Civil War Sites during the Sesquicentennial," April 28, 2014, Exploring the Past, https://pastexplore.wordpress.com/2014/04/28/analyzing-visitor-attendance-to-civil-war-sites-during-the-sesquicentennial.

69. Quoted in Cameron McWhirter, "For Civil War Buffs, 150-Year Anniversary Has Been Disappointing So Far," *Wall Street Journal*, April 10, 2014, http://www.wsj.com/articles/SB10001424052702303847804579481323991648630.

70. Robert E. Weir, "The Graying of Gettysburg National Military Park: Race, Erasure, Ideology, and Iconography," in *The Civil War in Popular Culture: Memory and Meaning*, ed. Lawrence A. Kreiser Jr. and Randal Allred (Lexington: University Press of Kentucky, 2014), 74.

71. National Park Service, "The Sesquicentennial at Gettysburg: 2013—The Year in Review," http://www.nps.gov/gett/learn/management/upload/GETT-150-A-Year-in-Review-2013-report-final.pdf.

72. *Raleigh News and Observer*, March 21, 2015, http://www.newsobserver.com/news/local/counties/johnston-county/article15743138.html.

73. Jill Ogline Titus, "An Unfinished Struggle: Sesquicentennial Interpretations of Slavery and Emancipation," *Journal of the Civil War Era* 4 (June 2014): 342.

74. Ta-Nehisi Coates, "Virginia," *Atlantic*, August 13, 2009, http://ta-nehisicoates.theatlantic.com/archives/2009/08/virginia.php.

75. Weir, "Graying of Gettysburg National Military Park," 74.

76. Ibid., 75.

77. *Washington City Paper*, July 17, 1998.

78. Quoted in Carol Sheriff, "Virginia's Embattled Textbooks: Lessons (Learned and Not) from the Centennial Era," *Civil War History* 58 (March 2012): 41.

79. Kathryn L. Nasstrom, "Between Memory and History: Autobiographies of the Civil Rights Movement and the Writing of Civil Rights History," *Journal of Southern History* 74 (May 2008): 325–64.

80. Barack Obama, "Remarks by the President in Eulogy for the Honorable Reverend Clementa Pinckney," June 26, 2015, The White House, https://www.whitehouse.gov/the-press-office/2015/06/26/remarks-president-eulogy-honorable-reverend-clementa-pinckney.

Conclusion

1. Bobbie Ann Mason, "Shiloh," in Mason, *Shiloh and Other Stories* (New York: Modern Library, 2001), 15, 17.

2. William Faulkner, *Intruder in the Dust* (New York: Random House, 1948), 194.

3. John Bodnar, *Remaking America: Public Memory, Commemoration, and Patriotism in the Twentieth Century* (Princeton, NJ: Princeton University Press, 1992), 13–14.

4. Louisa Lim, *The People's Republic of Amnesia: Tiananmen Revisited* (New York: Oxford University Press, 2014).

5. Timothy Snyder, "Putin's New Nostalgia," *New York Review of Books*, November 10, 2014, http://www.nybooks.com/blogs/nyrblog/2014/nov/10/putin-nostalgia-stalin-hitler.

6. Nora Berend and Christopher Clark, "Not Just a Phase," *London Review of Books* 36, no. 22 (November 20, 2014): 19–21.

7. Ari Kelman, *A Misplaced Massacre: Struggling over the Memory of Sand Creek* (Cambridge, MA: Harvard University Press, 2013).

8. Dell Upton, "The Long Shadow of the Civil War," in *The Civil War in Art and Memory*, ed. Kirk Savage (Washington, DC: National Gallery of Art, 2016; distributed by Yale University Press, New Haven, CT), 180.

9. On this subject, see especially Yael A. Sternhell, "Revisionism Reinvented? The Antiwar Turn in Civil War Scholarship," *Journal of the Civil War Era* 3 (June 2013): 239–56.

BIBLIOGRAPHY

Primary Sources

MANUSCRIPTS

American Heritage Center, University of Wyoming, Laramie
Bruce Catton Papers
Chautauqua County Historical Society, Westfield, NY
Albion W. Tourgée Papers
Columbia University Rare Book and Manuscript Library
Allan Nevins Papers
Earl Gregg Swem Library, College of William and Mary, Williamsburg, VA
William M. Tuck Papers
Eleanor S. Brockenbrough Library, Museum of the Confederacy, Richmond, VA
St. George T. C. Bryan Papers
Emory University Manuscript, Archives, and Rare Book Library, Atlanta
Bell I. Wiley Papers
John F. Kennedy Presidential Library, Boston
Berl I. Bernhard Papers
King Center Archives, Atlanta
Martin Luther King Jr. Papers
Library of Congress, Washington, DC
William E. Chandler Papers
Jubal A. Early Papers
Douglas Southall Freeman Papers
MacKinlay Kantor Papers
John Alexander Logan Family Papers
Manton Marble Papers
Charles Edward Russell Papers
National Archives, College Park, MD
Civil War Centennial Commission Records
National Archives, Washington, DC
US House of Representatives Records
New Jersey State Archives, Trenton
New Jersey Civil War Centennial Commission Records
New York State Archives, Albany
New York Civil War Centennial Commission Records

Southern Historical Collection, University of North Carolina Library, Chapel Hill
Walter H. Lee Scrapbooks
State Historical Society of Iowa, Des Moines
Samuel H. M. Byers Papers
Post Records, Iowa Department, Grand Army of the Republic
University of Mississippi Special Collections, Oxford, MI
James O. Eastland Papers
Featherston Collection
University Publications of America Microfilm
Bayard Rustin Papers

NEWSPAPERS AND PERIODICALS

Atlanta Constitution
Birmingham News
Bulletin: The United Daughters of the Confederacy
Charleston News and Courier
Chicago Herald
Confederate Veteran
Congressional Record
Ebony
Economist
Free Synagogue Pulpit
Galveston Daily News
Iowa State Register
Irish World and American Industrial Liberator
Land We Love
Life
McClure's Magazine
Montgomery Advertiser
Nation
National Tribune
New Orleans Times-Democrat
New York Times
Richmond Daily Dispatch
San Francisco Call
Saturday Review
Scribner's Magazine
Southern Historical Society Papers
Southern Literary Messenger
Wall Street Journal
Washington City Paper
Washington Post

PRINTED PRIMARY MATERIALS

Abernathy, Ralph D. *And the Walls Came Tumbling Down*. New York: Harper and Row, 1989.

Addams, Jane. *Twenty Years at Hull-House with Autobiographical Notes.* New York: Macmillan, 1910.

Barrett, J. O. *Soldier Bird: "Old Abe"; The Live War-Eagle of Wisconsin, That Served a Three Years' Campaign in the Great Rebellion.* Madison, WI: Atwood and Culver, 1876.

Basler, Roy P., ed., *The Collected Works of Abraham Lincoln.* 9 vols. New Brunswick, NJ: Rutgers University Press, 1953–55.

Bilbo, Theodore G. *The War; Constitutional Government; and the Race Issue—America's Greatest Unsolved Domestic Problem.* Washington, DC: US Government Printing Office, 1945.

Blassingame, John W., and John R. McKivigan, eds. *The Frederick Douglass Papers—Series One: Speeches, Debates, and Interviews.* 5 vols. New Haven, CT: Yale University Press, 1979–92.

Bledsoe, Albert Taylor. *Is Davis a Traitor; or Was Secession a Constitutional Right Previous to the War of 1861?* Baltimore, MD: Innes and Co., 1866.

Boynton, Henry V. N. *Sherman's Historical Raid: The Memoir in the Light of the Record.* Cincinnati, OH: Wilstach, Baldwin, and Co., 1875.

Brown, Thomas J., ed. *The Public Art of Civil War Commemoration: A Brief History with Documents.* Boston: Bedford / St. Martin's, 2004.

Byers, Samuel H. M. *What I Saw in Dixie; or Sixteen Months in Rebel Prisons.* Dansville, NY: Robbins and Poore, 1868.

Carson, Clayborne, ed. *The Papers of Martin Luther King, Jr.* Vol. 1: *Called to Serve, January 1929–June 1951.* Berkeley: University of California Press, 1992.

Carson, Clayborne, et al., eds. *The Eyes on the Prize Civil Rights Reader: Documents, Speeches, and Firsthand Accounts from the Black Freedom Struggle, 1954–1990.* New York: Penguin, 1991.

Dabney, Robert L. *Life and Campaigns of Lieut.-Gen. Thomas J. Jackson (Stonewall Jackson).* New York: Blelock and Co., 1866.

Davis, Jefferson. *The Rise and Fall of the Confederate Government.* 2 vols. 1881. Reprint, New York: T. Yoseloff, 1958.

Eade, Charles, ed. *The War Speeches of the Rt Hon Winston S. Churchill.* 3 vols. London: Cassell and Co., 1952.

Early, Jubal A. *A Memoir of the Last Year of the War for Independence, in the Confederate States of America, Containing an Account of the Operations of His Commands in the Years 1864 and 1865.* Toronto: Lovell and Gibson, 1866.

Freehling, William W., and Craig M. Simpson, eds. *Secession Debated: Georgia's Showdown in 1860.* New York: Oxford University Press, 1992.

———. *Showdown in Virginia: The 1861 Convention and the Fate of the Union.* Charlottesville: University of Virginia Press, 2010.

Graf, LeRoy P., and John Muldowny, eds. *Advice after Appomattox: Letters to Andrew Johnson, 1865–1866.* Knoxville: University of Tennessee Press, 1987.

Grant, Ulysses S. *Personal Memoirs.* 1885–86. Reprint, New York: Penguin, 1999.

Greeley, Horace. *The American Conflict: A History of the Great Rebellion in the United States of America, 1860–'65.* 2 vols. Hartford, CT: O. D. Case and Co., 1867.

Harlan, Louis R., and Raymond W. Smock, eds. *The Booker T. Washington Papers.* 14 vols. Urbana: University of Illinois Press, 1972–89.

Harris, Joel Chandler. *Life of Henry W. Grady, Including His Writings and Speeches.* New York: Cassell Publishing Co., 1890.

Harwell, Richard, ed. *Margaret Mitchell's "Gone with the Wind" Letters, 1936–1949*. New York: Macmillan, 1976.

Headley, Joel T. *The Great Rebellion: A History of the Civil War in the United States*. 2 vols. Hartford, CT: American Publishing Co., 1865–66.

Heath, G. Louis, ed. *The Black Panther Leaders Speak: Huey P. Newton, Bobby Seale, Eldridge Cleaver and Company Speak Out through the Black Panther Party's Official Newspaper*. Metuchen, NJ: Scarecrow Press, 1976.

Historical Sketch by C. H. Fasnacht, and Oration, by E. K. Martin, Esq., Delivered at Dedication of 99th Pennsylvania Monument, Gettysburg, Pa., July 2, 1886. Lancaster, PA: Examiner Steam Book and Job Print, 1886.

Ingersoll, Lurton Dunham. *Iowa and the Rebellion: A History of the Troops Furnished by the State of Iowa to the Volunteer Armies of the Union, Which Conquered the Great Southern Rebellion of 1861–5*. Philadelphia: J. B. Lippincott and Co., 1866.

Johnson, Robert Underwood. *Remembered Yesterdays*. Boston: Little, Brown, and Co., 1923.

Link, Arthur, ed. *The Papers of Woodrow Wilson*. 69 vols. Princeton, NJ: Princeton University Press, 1966–94.

Loewen, James W., and Edward H. Sebesta, eds. *The Confederate and Neo-Confederate Reader: The "Great Truth" about the Lost Cause*. Jackson: University of Mississippi Press, 2010.

Logan, John A. *The Great Conspiracy: Its Origin and History*. New York: A. R. Hart and Co., 1886.

Logan, Mrs. John A. [Mary]. *Reminiscences of a Soldier's Wife: An Autobiography*. New York: Charles Scribner's Sons, 1913.

McKinley, William. *Speeches and Addresses of William McKinley from March 1, 1897 to May 30, 1900*. New York: Doubleday and McClure Co., 1900.

Perry, Bruce, ed. *Malcolm X: The Last Speeches*. New York: Pathfinder Press, 1989.

Pollard, Edward A. *The Lost Cause: A New Southern History of the War of the Confederates; Comprising a Full and Authentic Account of the Rise and Progress of the Late Southern Confederacy—the Campaigns, Battles, Incidents, and Adventures of the Most Gigantic Struggle of the World's History*. New York: E. B. Treat and Co., 1866.

Proceedings of the National Negro Conference 1909: New York, May 31 and June 1. New York: The Conference, 1909.

Public Papers of the Presidents: Barack Obama, 2009. Washington DC: US Government Printing Office, 2010.

Public Papers of the Presidents: John F. Kennedy, 1963. Washington DC: US Government Printing Office, 1964.

The Public Papers and Addresses of Franklin D. Roosevelt—1938: The Continuing Struggle for Liberalism. Macmillan: London, 1941.

Scheer, Robert, ed. *Eldridge Cleaver: Post-prison Writings and Speeches*. London: Jonathan Cape, 1969.

Sherman, William T. "Old Shady, with a Moral." *North American Review* 147 (October 1888).

Smedes, Susan Dabney. *Memorials of a Southern Planter*. Baltimore, MD: Cushings and Bailey, 1887.

Sperry, A. F. *History of the 33d Iowa Volunteer Infantry Regiment 1863–6*. Edited by Gregory J. W. Urwin and Cathy Kunzinger Urwin. 1866. Reprint, Fayetteville: University of Arkansas Press, 1999.

Stephens, Alexander H. *A Constitutional View of the Late War between the States: Its Causes, Character, Conduct and Results; Presented in a Series of Colloquies at Liberty Hall.* 2 vols. Philadelphia: National Publishing Co., 1867–70.

Taylor, Richard. *Destruction and Reconstruction: Personal Experiences of the Late War in the United States.* Edinburgh, UK: William Blackwell and Sons, 1879.

US Congress. *Report of the Joint Committee on Reconstruction at the First Session Thirty-Ninth Congress.* 1866. Reprint, Freeport, NY: Books for Libraries Press, 1971.

Washington, James M., ed. *A Testament of Hope: The Essential Writings and Speeches of Martin Luther King, Jr.* San Francisco: HarperSanFrancisco, 1986.

Watkins, Sam R. *"Co. Aytch": A Confederate Memoir of the Civil War.* New York: Simon and Schuster, 2003.

Wilson, Henry. *History of the Rise and Fall of the Slave Power in America.* 3 vols. Boston: Houghton, Mifflin, and Co., 1872.

Secondary Sources

BOOKS

Baker, Bruce. *What Reconstruction Meant: Historical Memory in the American South.* Charlottesville: University of Virginia Press, 2007.

Barnickel, Linda. *Milliken's Bend: A Civil War Battle in History and Memory.* Baton Rouge: Louisiana State University Press, 2013.

Barr, John McKee. *Loathing Lincoln: An American Tradition from the Civil War to the Present.* Baton Rouge: Louisiana State University Press, 2014.

Beckel, Deborah. *Radical Reform: Interracial Politics in Post-emancipation North Carolina.* Charlottesville: University of Virginia Press, 2010.

Berger, Stefan, and Bill Niven, eds. *Writing the History of Memory.* New York: Bloomsbury, 2014.

Blair, William A. *Cities of the Dead: Contesting the Memory of the Civil War in the South, 1865–1914.* Chapel Hill: University of North Carolina Press, 2004.

Blair, William A., and William A. Pencak, eds. *Making and Remaking Pennsylvania's Civil War.* University Park: Pennsylvania State University Press, 2001.

Blassingame, John W. *The Slave Community: Plantation Life in the American South.* New York: Oxford University Press, 1972.

Blatt, Martin H., Thomas J. Brown, and Donald Yacovone, eds. *Hope and Glory: Essays on the Legacy of the 54th Massachusetts Regiment.* 2001; paperback ed., Amherst: University of Massachusetts Press; Boston: Massachusetts Historical Society, 2009.

Blight, David W. *Frederick Douglass's Civil War: Keeping Faith in Jubilee.* Baton Rouge: Louisiana State University Press, 1989.

———. *Race and Reunion: The Civil War in American Memory.* Cambridge, MA: Belknap Press of Harvard University Press, 2001.

———. *Beyond the Battlefield: Race, Memory, and the American Civil War.* Amherst: University of Massachusetts Press, 2002.

———. *American Oracle: The Civil War in the Civil Rights Era.* Cambridge, MA: Belknap Press of Harvard University Press, 2011.

Blum, Edward J. *Reforging the White Republic: Race, Religion, and American Nationalism, 1865–1898.* Baton Rouge: Louisiana State University Press, 2005.

Bodnar, John. *Remaking America: Public Memory, Commemoration, and Patriotism in the Twentieth Century*. Princeton, NJ: Princeton University Press, 1992.

Brown, Thomas J., ed. *Reconstructions: New Perspectives on the Postbellum United States*. New York: Oxford University Press, 2006.

———, ed. *Remixing the Civil War: Meditations on the Sesquicentennial*. Baltimore, MD: Johns Hopkins University Press, 2011.

———. *Civil War Canon: Sites of Confederate Memory in South Carolina*. Chapel Hill: University of North Carolina Press, 2015.

Brundage, W. Fitzhugh, ed. *Where These Memories Grow: History, Memory, and Southern Identity*. Chapel Hill: University of North Carolina Press, 2000.

———. *The Southern Past: A Clash of Race and Memory*. Cambridge, MA: Belknap Press of Harvard University Press, 2005.

Buck, Paul H. *The Road to Reunion, 1865–1900*. Boston: Little, Brown, and Co., 1937.

Calhoun, Charles W. *Conceiving a New Republic: The Republican Party and the Southern Question, 1869–1900*. Lawrence: University Press of Kansas, 2006.

Carwardine, Richard, and Jay Sexton, eds. *The Global Lincoln*. New York: Oxford University Press, 2011.

Cashin, Joan. *First Lady of the Confederacy: Varina Davis's Civil War*. Cambridge, MA: Belknap Press of Harvard University Press, 2006.

Catton, Bruce. *The War Lords of Washington*. New York: Harcourt, Brace, and Co., 1948.

———. *A Stillness at Appomattox*. Garden City, NY: Doubleday, 1954.

———. *The Centennial History of the Civil War*. 3 vols. Garden City, NY: Doubleday, 1961–65.

Chadwick, Bruce. *The Reel Civil War: Mythmaking in American Film*. New York: Alfred A. Knopf, 2001.

Chapman, C. Stuart. *Shelby Foote: A Writer's Life*. Jackson: University of Mississippi Press, 2003.

Cimbala, Paul A., and Randall M. Miller, eds. *The Great Task Remaining before Us: Reconstruction as America's Continuing Civil War*. New York: Fordham University Press, 2010.

Cimprich, John. *Fort Pillow, a Civil War Massacre, and Public Memory*. Baton Rouge: Louisiana State University Press, 2005.

Cloyd, Benjamin G. *Haunted by Atrocity: Civil War Prisons in American Memory*. Baton Rouge: Louisiana State University Press, 2010.

Collins, Donald E. *The Death and Resurrection of Jefferson Davis*. Lanham, MD: Rowman and Littlefield, 2005.

Cook, Robert J. *Troubled Commemoration: The American Civil War Centennial, 1961–1965*. Baton Rouge: Louisiana State University Press, 2007.

Cook, Robert J., William Barney, and Elizabeth Varon. *Secession Winter: When the Union Fell Apart*. Baltimore, MD: Johns Hopkins University Press, 2013.

Cooper, William J. *Jefferson Davis, American*. New York: Alfred A. Knopf, 2000.

Coski, John M. *The Confederate Battle Flag: America's Most Embattled Emblem*. Cambridge, MA: Belknap Press of Harvard University Press, 2005.

Cox, Karen L. *Dixie's Daughters: The United Daughters of the Confederacy and the Preservation of Confederate Culture*. Gainesville: University Press of Florida, 2003.

Crespino, Joseph. *In Search of Another Country: Mississippi and the Conservative Counterrevolution*. Princeton, NJ: Princeton University Press, 2007.

Cullen, Jim. *The Civil War in Popular Culture: A Reusable Past.* Washington, DC: Smithsonian Institution Press, 1995.

Dabney, Virginius. *The Last Review: The Confederate Reunion, Richmond, 1932.* Chapel Hill, NC: Algonquin Books, 1984.

Dailey, Jane. *Before Jim Crow: The Politics of Race in Postemancipation Virginia.* Chapel Hill: University of North Carolina Press, 2000.

Dallek, Robert. *John F. Kennedy: An Unfinished Life, 1917–1963.* London: Penguin, 2004. First published 2003 by Little Brown as *An Unfinished Life: John F. Kennedy, 1917–1963.*

Dean, Eric T., Jr. *Shook over Hell: Post-traumatic Stress, Vietnam, and the Civil War.* Cambridge, MA: Harvard University Press, 1997.

Dew, Charles B. *Apostles of Disunion: Southern Secession Commissioners and the Causes of the Civil War.* Charlottesville: University of Virginia Press, 2001.

Dorsey, Leroy G. *The Presidency and Rhetorical Leadership.* College Station: Texas A&M University Press, 2002.

Du Bois, W.E.B. *Black Reconstruction in America: An Essay toward a History of the Part Which Black Folk Played in the Attempt to Reconstruct Democracy in America, 1860–1880.* New York: Russel and Russel, 1935.

Eagles, Charles W. *The Price of Defiance: James Meredith and the Integration of Ole Miss.* Chapel Hill: University of North Carolina Press, 2009.

Eckert, Ralph Lowell. *John Brown Gordon: Soldier, Southerner, American.* Baton Rouge: Louisiana State University Press, 1989.

Elliott, Mark. *Color-Blind Justice: Albion Tourgée and the Quest for Racial Equality from the Civil War to* Plessy v. Ferguson. New York: Oxford University Press, 2006.

Escott, Paul D. *Uncommonly Savage: Civil War and Remembrance in Spain and the United States.* Gainesville: University Press of Florida, 2014.

Fabre, Geneviève, and Robert O'Meally, eds. *History and Memory in African-American Culture.* New York: Oxford University Press, 1994.

Fahs, Alice, and Joan Waugh, eds. *The Memory of the Civil War in American Culture.* Chapel Hill: University of North Carolina Press, 2004.

Faust, Drew Gilpin. *This Republic of Suffering: Death and the American Civil War.* New York: Alfred A. Knopf, 2001.

Feldman, Glen. *The Irony of the Solid South: Democrats, Republicans, and Race, 1865–1944.* Tuscaloosa: University of Alabama Press, 2013.

Fellman, Michael. *Citizen Sherman: A Life of William Tecumseh Sherman.* Lawrence: University Press of Kansas, 1995.

Foner, Eric. *Free Soil, Free Labor, Free Men: The Ideology of the Republican Party before the Civil War.* New York: Oxford University Press, 1971.

———. *Reconstruction: America's Unfinished Revolution, 1863–1877.* New York: Oxford University Press, 1988.

Foote, Shelby. *The Civil War: A Narrative.* 3 vols. New York: Random House, 1958–74.

Foster, Gaines M. *Ghosts of the Confederacy: Defeat, the Lost Cause, and the Emergence of the New South, 1865 to 1913.* New York: Oxford University Press, 1987.

Fraser, Steve, and Gary Gerstle. *The Rise and Fall of the New Deal Order.* Princeton, NJ: Princeton University Press, 1989.

Freehling, William W. *The South vs. the South: How Anti-Confederate Southerners Shaped the Course of the Civil War.* New York: Oxford University Press, 2001.

Fried, Richard M. *The Russians Are Coming! The Russians Are Coming! Pageantry and Patriotism in Cold-War America*. New York: Oxford University Press, 1998.
Gallagher, Gary W. *The Confederate War*. Cambridge, MA: Harvard University Press, 1997.
———. *Causes Won, Lost, and Forgotten: How Hollywood and Popular Art Shape What We Know about the Civil War*. Chapel Hill: University of North Carolina Press, 2008.
———. *The Union War*. Cambridge, MA: Harvard University Press, 2011.
Gallagher, Gary W., and Alan T. Nolan, eds. *The Myth of the Lost Cause and Civil War History*. Bloomington: Indiana University Press, 2000.
Gannon, Barbara A. *The Won Cause: Black and White Comradeship in the Grand Army of the Republic*. Chapel Hill: University of North Carolina Press, 2011.
Gardner, Sarah E. *Blood and Irony: Southern White Women's Narratives of the Civil War, 1861–1937*. Chapel Hill: University of North Carolina Press, 2004.
Gaston, Paul M. *The New South Creed: A Study in Southern Mythmaking*. New York: Alfred A. Knopf, 1970.
Genovese, Eugene D. *Roll, Jordan, Roll: The World the Slaves Made*. New York: Pantheon Books, 1974.
Gilpin, R. Blakeslee. *John Brown Still Lives! America's Long Reckoning with Violence, Equality, and Change*. Chapel Hill: University of North Carolina Press, 2011.
Goggin, Jacqueline. *Carter G. Woodson: A Life in Black History*. Baton Rouge: Louisiana State University Press, 1993.
Goldfield, David. *Still Fighting the Civil War: The American South and Southern History*. Baton Rouge: Louisiana State University Press, 2002.
Gordon, Lesley J. *A Broken Regiment: The 16th Connecticut's Civil War*. Baton Rouge: Louisiana State University Press, 2014.
Gould, Lewis L. *The Presidency of William McKinley*. Lawrence: Regents Press of Kansas, 1980.
Graham, Allison. *Framing the South: Hollywood, Television, and Race during the Civil Rights Struggle*. Baltimore, MD: Johns Hopkins University Press, 2001.
Grant, Susan-Mary. *Oliver Wendell Holmes, Jr.: Civil War Soldier, Supreme Court Justice*. New York: Routledge, 2015.
Grant, Susan-Mary, and Peter J. Parish, eds. *Legacy of Disunion: The Enduring Significance of the American Civil War*. Baton Rouge: Louisiana State University Press, 2003.
Hagopian, Patrick. *The Vietnam War in American Memory: Veterans, Memorials, and the Politics of Healing*. Amherst: University of Massachusetts Press, 2009.
Hague, Euan, Heidi Beirich, and Edward H. Sebesta, eds. *Neo-Confederacy: A Critical Introduction*. Austin: University of Texas Press, 2008.
Halbwachs, Maurice. *On Collected Memory*. Translated by Lewis A. Coser. Chicago: University of Chicago Press, 1992.
Harris, M. Keith. *Across the Bloody Chasm: The Culture of Commemoration among Civil War Veterans*. Baton Rouge: Louisiana State University Press, 2014.
Haskell, Molly. *Frankly My Dear:* Gone with the Wind *Revisited*. New Haven, CT: Yale University Press, 2009.
Hettle, Wallace. *Inventing Stonewall Jackson: A Civil War Hero in History and Memory*. Baton Rouge: Louisiana State University Press, 2011.
Hirshson, Stanley P. *Farewell to the Bloody Shirt: Northern Republicans and the Southern Negro, 1877–1893*. Bloomington: Indiana University Press, 1962.

Hobsbawm, Eric, and Terence O. Ranger, eds. *The Invention of Tradition*. New York: Cambridge University Press, 1983.

Hoganson, Kristin L. *Fighting for American Manhood: How Gender Politics Provoked the Spanish-American and Philippine-American Wars*. New Haven, CT: Yale University Press, 1998.

Holt, Michael F. *By One Vote: The Disputed Presidential Election of 1876*. Lawrence: University Press of Kansas, 2008.

Horwitz, Tony. *Confederates in the Attic: Dispatches from the Unfinished Civil War*. New York: Vintage Books, 1999. First published 1998 by Pantheon Books.

Janney, Caroline E. *Burying the Dead but Not the Past: Ladies' Memorial Associations and the Lost Cause*. Chapel Hill: University of North Carolina Press, 2008.

———. *Remembering the Civil War: Reunion and the Limits of Reconciliation*. Chapel Hill: University of North Carolina Press, 2013.

Jensen, Richard. *The Winning of the Midwest: Social and Political Conflict, 1888–1896*. Chicago: University of Chicago Press, 1971.

Jordan, Brian Matthew. *Marching Home: Union Veterans and Their Unending Civil War*. New York: Liveright Publishing, 2014.

Kachun, Mitch. *Festivals of Freedom: Memory and Meaning in African-American Emancipation Celebrations, 1808–1915*. Amherst: University of Massachusetts Press, 2003.

Kammen, Michael. *Mystic Chords of Memory: The Transformation of Tradition in American Culture*. New York: Alfred A. Knopf, 1991.

Kantrowitz, Stephen. *Ben Tillman and the Reconstruction of White Supremacy*. Chapel Hill: University of North Carolina Press, 2000.

Karcher, Carolyn L. *A Refugee from His Race: Albion W. Tourgée and His Fight against White Supremacy*. Chapel Hill: University of North Carolina Press, 2016.

Kaser, James A. *At the Bivouac of Memory: History, Politics, and the Battle of Chickamauga*. New York: Peter Lang, 1996.

Keefer, Bradley S. *Conflicting Memories on the "River of Death": The Chickamauga Battlefield and the Spanish-American War, 1863–1933*. Kent, OH: Kent State University Press, 2013.

Kelly, Patrick J. *Creating a National Home: Building the Veterans' Welfare State, 1860–1900*. Cambridge: Harvard University Press, 1997.

Kelman, Ari. *A Misplaced Massacre: Struggling over the Memory of Sand Creek*. Cambridge, MA: Harvard University Press, 2013.

Kousser, J. Morgan. *The Shaping of Southern Politics: Suffrage Restriction and the Establishment of the One-Party South, 1880–1910*. New Haven, CT: Yale University Press, 1974.

Kreiser, Lawrence A., Jr., and Randal Allred, eds. *The Civil War in Popular Culture: Memory and Meaning*. Lexington: University Press of Kentucky, 2014.

Kreyling, Michael. *A Late Encounter with the Civil War*. Athens: University of Georgia Press, 2013.

Laderman, Gary. *The Sacred Remains: American Attitudes toward Death, 1799–1883*. New Haven, CT: Yale University Press, 1996.

Landsberg, Alison. *Prosthetic Memory: The Transformation of American Remembrance in the Age of Mass Culture*. New York: Columbia University Press, 2004.

Lassiter, Matthew D., and Joseph Crespino, eds. *The Myth of Southern Exceptionalism*. New York: Oxford University Press, 2010.

Lears, Jackson. *Rebirth of a Nation: The Making of Modern America, 1877–1920*. New York: Harper Collins, 2009.

Lee, Susanna Michele. *Claiming the Union: Citizenship in the Post–Civil War South*. New York: Cambridge University Press, 2014.

Lester, Julius. *Look Out Whitey! Black Power's Gon' Get Your Mama!* 1968. Reprint, New York: Grove Press, 1969.

Levin, Kevin M. *Remembering the Battle of the Crater*. Lexington: University Press of Kentucky, 2012.

Levine, Bruce. *Half Slave and Half Free: The Roots of Civil War*. New York: Hill and Wang, 1992.

———. *Confederate Emancipation: Southern Plans to Free and Arm Slaves during the Civil War*. New York: Oxford University Press, 2006.

Lim, Louisa. *The People's Republic of Amnesia: Tiananmen Revisited*. New York: Oxford University Press, 2014.

Linenthal, Edward Tabor. *Sacred Ground: Americans and Their Battlefields*. Urbana: University of Illinois Press, 1991.

Link, William A. *Atlanta, Cradle of the New South: Race and Remembering in the Civil War's Aftermath*. Chapel Hill: University of North Carolina Press, 2013.

Logue, Larry M., and Michael Barton, eds. *The Civil War Veteran: A Historical Reader*. New York: New York University Press, 2007.

Lorini, Alessandra. *Rituals of Race: American Public Culture and the Search for Racial Democracy*. Charlottesville: University of Virginia Press, 1999.

Manning, Chandra. *What This Cruel War Was Over: Soldiers, Slavery, and the Civil War*. New York: Alfred A. Knopf, 2007.

Marshall, Anne E. *Creating a Confederate Kentucky: The Lost Cause and Civil War Memory in a Border State*. Chapel Hill: University of North Carolina Press, 2010.

Marten, James. *Sing Not War: The Lives of Union and Confederate Veterans in Gilded Age America*. Chapel Hill: University of North Carolina Press, 2011.

———. *America's Corporal: James Tanner in War and Peace*. Athens: University of Georgia Press, 2014.

McConnell, Stuart. *Glorious Contentment: The Grand Army of the Republic, 1865–1900*. Chapel Hill: University of North Carolina Press, 1992.

McElroy, Robert. *Jefferson Davis: The Unreal and the Real*. 2 vols. New York: Harper and Brothers, 1937.

McElya, Micki. *The Politics of Memory: Death and Honor in Arlington National Cemetery*. Cambridge, MA: Harvard University Press, 2016.

McPherson, James M. *Battle Cry of Freedom: The Civil War Era*. New York: Oxford University Press, 1988.

———. *For Cause and Comrades: Why Men Fought in the Civil War*. New York: Oxford University Press, 1997.

———. *Tried by War: Abraham Lincoln as Commander in Chief*. New York: Penguin Books, 2009.

McPherson, James M., and William J. Cooper, eds. *Writing the Civil War: The Quest to Understand*. Columbia: University of South Carolina Press, 1998.

Meier, August, and Elliott Rudwick. *Black History and the Historical Profession, 1915–1980*. Urbana: University of Illinois Press, 1986.

Micale, Mark S., and Paul Lerner, eds. *Traumatic Pasts: History, Psychiatry, and Trauma in the Modern Age, 1870–1930*. Cambridge: Cambridge University Press, 2001.

Miller, Brian Craig. *John Bell Hood and the Fight for Civil War Memory*. Knoxville: University of Tennessee Press, 2010.

Mills, Cynthia, and Pamela H. Simpson, eds. *Monuments of the Lost Cause: Women, Art, and the Landscapes of Southern Memory*. Knoxville: University of Tennessee Press, 2003.

Minardi, Margot. *Making Slavery History: Abolitionism and the Politics of Memory in Massachusetts*. New York: Oxford University Press, 2010.

Mitchell, Reid. *Civil War Soldiers*. New York: Viking, 1988.

Moody, Wesley. *Demon of the Lost Cause: Sherman and Civil War History*. Columbia: University of Missouri Press, 2011.

Morgan, Iwan W., and Philip John Davies, eds. *Reconfiguring the Union: Civil War Transformations*. New York: Palgrave Macmillan, 2013.

Morsberger, Robert E., and Katharine M. Morsberger. *Lew Wallace: Militant Romantic*. New York: McGraw-Hill, 1980.

Murray, Jennifer M. *On a Great Battlefield: The Making, Management, and Memory of Gettysburg National Military Park, 1933–2013*. Knoxville: University of Tennessee Press, 2014.

Neff, John R. *Honoring the Civil War Dead: Commemoration and the Problem of Reconciliation*. Lawrence: University Press of Kansas, 2005.

Nevins, Allan, ed. *Lincoln and the Gettysburg Address: Commemorative Papers [by] John Dos Passos, Arthur Lehman Goodhart, Reinhold Niebuhr, Robert Lowell, Paul H. Douglas, David C. Mearns*. Urbana: University of Illinois Press, 1964.

Nolan, Alan T. *Lee Considered: General Robert E. Lee and Civil War History*. Chapel Hill: University of North Carolina Press, 1991.

Novick, Peter. *That Noble Dream: The "Objectivity Question" and the American Historical Profession*. New York: Cambridge University Press, 1988.

O'Leary, Cecilia Elizabeth. *To Die For: The Paradox of American Patriotism*. Princeton, NJ: Princeton University Press, 1999.

Olick, Jeffrey K., Vered Vinitzky-Seroussi, and Daniel Levy, eds. *The Collective Memory Reader*. New York: Oxford University Press, 2011.

Peatman, Jared. *The Long Shadow of Lincoln's Gettysburg Address*. Carbondale: Southern Illinois University Press, 2013.

Peterson, Merrill D. *Lincoln in American Memory*. New York: Oxford University Press, 1994.

Phillips, Christopher. *The Rivers Ran Backward: The Civil War and the Remaking of the American Middle Border*. New York: Oxford University Press, 2016.

Piston, William Garrett. *Lee's Tarnished Lieutenant: James Longstreet and His Place in Southern History*. Athens: University of Georgia Press, 1987.

Poole, W. Scott. *Never Surrender: Confederate Memory and Conservatism in the South Carolina Upcountry*. Athens: University of Georgia Press, 2004.

Pressly, Thomas J. *Americans Interpret Their Civil War*. Princeton, NJ: Princeton University Press, 1954.

Reardon, Carol. *Pickett's Charge in History and Memory*. Chapel Hill: University of North Carolina Press, 1997.

Rubin, Anne Sarah. *Through the Heart of Dixie: Sherman's March and American Memory*. Chapel Hill: University of North Carolina Press, 2014.

Sabato, Larry J. *The Kennedy Half Century: The Presidency, Assassination, and Lasting Legacy of John F. Kennedy*. New York: Bloomsbury USA, 2013.

Sandburg, Carl. *Abraham Lincoln: The Prairie Years*. 2 vols. London: Jonathan Cape, 1926.

Savage, Kirk. *Standing Soldiers, Kneeling Slaves: Race, War, and Monument in Nineteenth-Century America*. Princeton, NJ: Princeton University Press, 1997.

Savage, Kirk, ed. *The Civil War in Art and Memory*. Washington, DC: National Gallery of Art, 2016. Distributed by Yale University Press, New Haven, CT.

Schivelbusch, Wolfgang. *The Culture of Defeat: On National Trauma, Mourning, and Recovery*. London: Granta Books, 2003.

Schlesinger, Arthur M., Jr., ed. *History of American Presidential Elections 1789–1968*. 9 vols. New York: Chelsea House, 1985.

Schwartz, Barry. *Abraham Lincoln and the Forge of National Memory*. Chicago: University of Chicago Press, 2000.

———. *Abraham Lincoln in the Post-heroic Era: History and Memory in Late Twentieth-Century America*. Chicago: University of Chicago Press, 2008.

Shaffer, Donald R. *After the Glory: The Struggle of Black Civil War Veterans*. Lawrence: University Press of Kansas, 2004.

Sherman, Richard B. *The Republican Party and Black America: From McKinley to Hoover, 1896–1933*. Charlottesville: University of Virginia Press, 1973.

Silber, Nina. *The Romance of Reunion: Northerners and the South, 1865–1900*. Chapel Hill: University of North Carolina Press, 1993.

Simms, Brendan, and D.J.B. Trim, eds. *Humanitarian Intervention: A History*. New York: Cambridge University Press, 2011.

Skocpol, Theda. *Protecting Soldiers and Mothers: The Political Origins of Social Policy in the United States*. Cambridge, MA: Belknap Press of Harvard University Press, 1992.

Smith, Timothy B. *This Great Battlefield of Shiloh: History, Memory, and the Establishment of a Civil War National Military Park*. Knoxville: University of Tennessee Press, 2004.

———. *A Chickamauga Memorial: The Establishment of America's First Civil War National Military Park*. Knoxville: University of Tennessee Press, 2009.

Sorrentino, Paul. *Stephen Crane: A Life of Fire*. Cambridge, MA: Belknap Press of Harvard University Press, 2014.

Sproat, John G. *"The Best Men": Liberal Reformers in the Gilded Age*. New York: Oxford University Press, 1968.

Stauffer, John, and Benjamin Soskis. *The Battle Hymn of the Republic: A Biography of the Song That Marches On*. New York: Oxford University Press, 2013.

Stevenson, David. *With Our Backs to the Wall: Victory and Defeat in 1918*. New York: Allen Lane, 2011.

Stewart, Catherine A. *Long Past Slavery: Representing Race in the Federal Writers' Project*. Chapel Hill: University of North Carolina Press, 2016.

Stokes, Melvyn. *D. W. Griffith's* The Birth of a Nation*: A History of "The Most Controversial Motion Picture of All Time."* New York: Oxford University Press, 2007.

Strode, Hudson. *Jefferson Davis: Tragic Hero—The Last Twenty-Five Years, 1864–1889*. New York: Harcourt, Brace, and World, 1964.

Summers, Mark Wahlgren. *A Dangerous Stir: Fear, Paranoia, and the Making of Reconstruction*. Chapel Hill: University of North Carolina Press, 2009.

———. *The Ordeal of the Reunion: A New History of Reconstruction.* Chapel Hill: University of North Carolina Press, 2014.

Terkel, Studs. *"The Good War": An Oral History of World War Two.* New York: Pantheon Books, 1984.

Thelen, David, ed. *Memory and American History.* Bloomington: Indiana University Press, 1990.

Thomas, Christopher A. *The Lincoln Memorial and American Life.* Princeton, NJ: Princeton University Press, 2002.

Toplin, Robert Brent, ed., *Ken Burns's* The Civil War: *The Historians Respond.* New York: Oxford University Press, 1996.

Trout, Steven. *On the Battlefield of Memory: The First World War and American Remembrance, 1919–1941.* Tuscaloosa: University of Alabama Press, 2010.

Waldrep, Christopher. *Vicksburg's Long Shadow: The Civil War Legacy of Race and Remembrance.* Lanham, MD: Rowman and Littlefield, 2005.

Wang, Xi. *The Trial of Democracy: Black Suffrage and Northern Republicans.* Athens: University of Georgia Press, 1997.

Warren, Robert Penn. *The Legacy of the Civil War: Meditations on the Centennial.* New York: Random House, 1961.

Waugh, Joan. *U. S. Grant: American Hero, American Myth.* Chapel Hill: University of North Carolina Press, 2009.

Waugh, Joan, and Gary W. Gallagher, eds. *Wars within a War: Controversy and Conflict over the American Civil War.* Chapel Hill: University of North Carolina Press, 2009.

Weeks, Jim. *Gettysburg: Memory, Market, and an American Shrine.* Princeton, NJ: Princeton University Press, 2003.

Wiggins, William H., Jr. *O Freedom! Afro-American Emancipation Celebrations.* Knoxville: University of Tennessee Press, 1987.

Williams, R. Hal. *Realigning America: McKinley, Bryan, and the Remarkable Election of 1896.* Lawrence: University Press of Kansas, 2010.

Wilson, Charles Reagan. *Baptized in Blood: The Religion of the Lost Cause, 1865–1920.* Athens: University of Georgia Press, 1980.

Wilson, Edmund. *Patriotic Gore: Studies in the Literature of the American Civil War.* New York: Oxford University Press, 1962.

Wilson, Steve. *The Making of* Gone with the Wind. Austin: University of Texas Press, 2014.

Winter, Jay. *Sites of Memory, Sites of Mourning: The Great War in European Cultural History.* Cambridge: Cambridge University Press, 1995.

———. *Remembering War: The Great War between Memory and History in the Twentieth Century.* New Haven, CT: Yale University Press, 2006.

Woodward, C. Vann. *The Strange Career of Jim Crow.* New York: Oxford University Press, 1955.

Zenzen, Joan M. *Battling for Manassas: The Fifty-Year Preservation Struggle at Manassas Battlefield Park.* University Park: Pennsylvania State University Press, 1998.

ARTICLES

Adams, Amanda. "'Painfully Southern': *Gone with the Wind*, the Agrarians, and the Battle for the New South." *Southern Literary Journal* 40 (Fall 2007): 58–75.

Bailey, Fred Arthur. "The Textbooks of the 'Lost Cause': Censorship and the Creation of Southern State Histories." *Georgia Historical Quarterly* 75 (Fall 1991): 507–33.

Berend, Nora, and Christopher Clark. "Not Just a Phase." *London Review of Books* 36, no. 22 (November 20, 2014): 19–21.

Bever, Megan L. "Paths to Reconciliation: Northern Intersectional Romances of the Civil War Era." *Civil War History* 60 (March 2014): 32–57.

Black, Brian. "The Nature of Preservation: The Rise of Authenticity at Gettysburg." *Civil War History* 58 (September 2012): 348–73.

Blight, David W. "The Meaning or the Fight: Frederick Douglass and the Memory of the Fifty Fourth Massachusetts." *Massachusetts Review* 36 (Spring 1995): 141–53.

———. "The Civil War Sesquicentennial." *Chronicle of Higher Education* 55, no. 38 (June 5, 2009).

Broomall, James J. "'The Interpretation Is A-Changin': Memory, Museums, and Public History in Central Virginia." *Journal of the Civil War Era* 3 (March 2013): 114–24.

Brundage, W. Fitzhugh. "Commemoration and Conflict: Forgetting and Remembering the Civil War." *Georgia Historical Quarterly* 82 (Fall 1998): 559–74.

———. "'Contentious and Collected': Memory's Future in Southern History." *Journal of Southern History* 75 (August 2009): 751–66.

Cobb, James C. "Beyond Planters and Industrialists: A New Perspective on the New South." *Journal of Southern History* 54 (February 1988): 45–68.

Cook, Robert J. "A War for Principle? Shifting Memories of the Union Cause in Iowa, 1865–1916." *Annals of Iowa* 74 (Summer 2015): 221–62.

———. "The Quarrel Forgotten: Toward a Clearer Understanding of Sectional Reconciliation." *Journal of the Civil War Era* 6 (September 2016): 413–36.

Cook, Robert J., Kenneth Noe, Dana Shoaf, Jennifer Weber, and Daniel E. Sutherland. "Historians' Forum: The American Civil War's Centennial vs. the Sesquicentennial." *Civil War History* 57 (December 2011): 380–402.

Davis, Stephen. "'A Matter of Sensational Interest': The *Century* 'Battles and Leaders Series.'" *Civil War History* 27 (December 1981): 338–49.

Dickson, Keith. "Douglas Southall Freeman, the Civil War, and the Idea of the South." *Civil War History* 60 (March 2014): 66–77.

Downs, Gregory P. "The Mexicanization of American Politics: The United States' Transnational Path from Civil War to Stabilization." *American Historical Review* 117 (April 2012): 387–409.

Doyle, Andrew. "Turning the Tide: College Football and Southern Progressivism." *Southern Cultures* 3, no. 3 (1997): 28–51.

Fahs, Alice. "The Feminized Civil War: Gender, Northern Popular Literature, and the Memory of the War, 1861–1900." *Journal of American History* 85 (March 1999): 1461–94.

Fairclough, Adam. "Civil Rights and the Lincoln Memorial: The Censored Speeches of Robert R. Moton (1922) and John Lewis (1963)." *Journal of Negro History* 82 (Autumn 1997): 408–16.

———. "Was the Grant of Black Suffrage a Political Error? Reconsidering the Views of John W. Burgess, William A. Dunning, and Eric Foner on Congressional Reconstruction." *Journal of the Historical Society* 12 (June 2012): 155–88.

Faust, Drew Gilpin. "Clutching the Chains That Bind: Margaret Mitchell and *Gone with the Wind*." *Southern Cultures* 5, no. 1 (1999): 5–20.

Fleche, Andre. "'Shoulder to Shoulder as Comrades Tried': Black and White Union Veterans and Civil War Memory." *Civil War History* 51 (June 2005): 175–201.

Fox-Genovese, Elizabeth. "Scarlett O'Hara: The Southern Lady as New Woman." *American Quarterly* 33 (Autumn 1981): 391–411.

Franco, Barbara. "Planned Commemorations, Unexpected Consequences." *Journal of the Civil War Era* 1 (September 2011): 444–49.

Gannon, Barbara A. "'They Call Themselves Veterans': Civil War Veterans and Spanish War Veterans and the Complexities of Veteranhood." *Journal of the Civil War Era* 5 (December 2015): 528–50.

Giesberg, Judith Ann. "'To Forget and Forgive': Reconstructing the Nation in the Post–Civil War Classroom." *Civil War History* 52 (September 2006): 282–302.

Gold, Susanna W. "'Fighting It Over Again': *The Battle of Gettysburg* at the 1876 Centennial Exhibition." *Civil War History* 54 (September 2008): 277–310.

Grant, Susan-Mary. "The Lost Boys: Citizen-Soldiers, Disabled Veterans, and Confederate Nationalism in the Age of People's War." *Journal of the Civil War Era* 2 (June 2012): 233–59.

Griffin, Larry J. "'Generations and Collective Memory' Revisited: Race, Region, and Memory of Civil Rights." *American Sociological Review* 69 (August 2004): 544–57.

Grow, Matthew J. "The Shadow of the Civil War: A Historiography of Civil War Memory." *American Nineteenth Century History* 4, no. 2 (2003): 77–103.

Hacker, J. David. "A Census-Based Count of the Civil War Dead." *Civil War History* 57 (December 2011): 307–48.

Hall, Jacquelyn Dowd. "The Prong of Love." *Southern Cultures* 5, no. 1 (1999): 44–48.

Harlan, David. "Ken Burns and the Coming Crisis of Academic History." *Rethinking History* 7 (Summer 2003): 169–92.

Hillyer, Reiko. "Relics of Reconciliation: The Confederate Museum and Civil War Memory in the New South." *Public Historian* 33 (November 2011): 35–62.

Hurlbert, Matthew C. "Constructing Guerrilla Memory: John Newman Edwards and Missouri's Irregular Lost Cause." *Journal of the Civil War Era* 2 (March 2012): 58–81.

Janney, Caroline E. "Written in Stone: Gender, Race, and the Hayward Shepherd Memorial." *Civil War History* 52 (June 2006): 117–41.

———. "'I Yield to No Man an Iota of My Convictions': Chickamauga and Chattanooga National Military Park and the Limits of Reconciliation." *Journal of the Civil War Era* 2 (September 2012): 394–420.

Jordan, Brian Matthew. "'Living Monuments': Union Veteran Amputees and the Embodied Memory of the Civil War." *Civil War History* 57 (June 2011): 121–52.

Kachun, Mitch. "From Forgotten Founder to Indispensable Icon: Crispus Attucks, Black Citizenship, and Collective Memory, 1770–1865." *Journal of the Early Republic* 29 (Summer 2009): 249–86.

Lowe, William C. "'A Grand and Patriotic Pilgrimage': The Iowa Civil War Monuments Dedication Tour of 1906." *Annals of Iowa* 69 (Winter 2010): 1–50.

Moger, Allen W. "General Lee's Unwritten 'History of the Army of Northern Virginia.'" *Virginia Magazine of History and Biography* 71 (July 1963): 341–63.

Nasstrom, Kathryn L. "Between Memory and History: Autobiographies of the Civil Rights Movement and the Writing of Civil Rights History." *Journal of Southern History* 74 (May 2008): 325–64.

Nora, Pierre. "Between History and Memory: Les lieux de mémoire." *Representations* 26 (Spring 1989): 7–24.
Pettegrew, John. "'The Soldier's Faith:' Turn-of-the-Century Memory of the Civil War and the Emergence of Modern American Nationalism." *Journal of Contemporary History* 31 (January 1996): 49–73.
Quigley, Paul. "Refighting the Civil War, Yet Again: Virginia's Confederate History Month Mêlée," *American Nineteenth Century History* 11, no. 3 (2010): 351–59.
Reardon, Carol. "Writing Battle History: The Challenge of Memory." *Civil War History* 53 (September 2007): 252–63.
Rogin, Michael. "The Sword Became a Flashing Vision: D. W. Griffith's *The Birth of a Nation*." *Representations* 9 (Winter 1985): 150–95.
Ross, Michael A. "The Commemoration of Robert E. Lee's Death and the Obstruction of Reconstruction in New Orleans." *Civil War History* 51 (June 2005): 135–50.
Sandage, Scott A. "A Marble House Divided: The Lincoln Memorial, the Civil Rights Movement, and the Politics of Memory, 1939–1963." *Journal of American History* 80 (June 1993): 135–67.
Schlesinger, Arthur M., Jr. "The Causes of the Civil War: A Note on Historical Sentimentalism." *Partisan Review* 16 (October 1949): 969–81.
Schwartz, Barry. "Memory as a Cultural System: Abraham Lincoln in World War II." *American Sociological Review* 61 (October 1996): 908–27.
Sheriff, Carol. "Virginia's Embattled Textbooks: Lessons (Learned and Not) from the Centennial Era." *Civil War History* 58 (March 2012): 37–74.
Silber, Nina. "Abraham Lincoln and the Political Culture of New Deal America." *Journal of the Civil War Era* 5 (September 2015): 348–71.
Smyth, J. E. "Young Mr. Lincoln: Between Myth and History in 1939." *Rethinking History* 7, no. 2 (2003): 193–214.
Starnes, Richard D. "Forever Faithful: The Southern Historical Society and Confederate Historical Memory." *Southern Cultures* 2 (Winter 1996): 177–94.
Sternhell, Yael A. "Revisionism Reinvented? The Antiwar Turn in Civil War Scholarship." *Journal of the Civil War Era* 3 (June 2013): 239–56.
Stokes, Melvyn. "Abraham Lincoln and the Movies." *American Nineteenth Century History* 12, no. 2 (2011): 203–31.
Sutherland, Daniel. "Memories of a Rooted Sorrow: The Legacy of the Guerrilla War." *Civil War History* 62 (March 2016): 8–35.
Sutton, Robert K. "Holding the High Ground: Interpreting the Civil War in National Parks." *George Wright Forum* 25 (2008): 47–57.
Titus, Jill Ogline. "An Unfinished Struggle: Sesquicentennial Interpretations of Slavery and Emancipation." *Journal of the Civil War Era* 4 (June 2014): 338–47.
Turpie, David C. "A Voluntary War: The Spanish-American War, White Southern Manhood, and the Struggle to Recruit Volunteers in the South." *Journal of Southern History* 80 (November 2014): 859–92.
Vogel, Jeffrey E. "Redefining Reconciliation: Confederate Veterans and the Southern Responses to Federal Civil War Pensions." *Civil War History* 51 (March 2005): 67–93.
Vorenberg, Michael. "Spielberg's *Lincoln*: The Great Emancipator Returns." *Journal of the Civil War Era* 3 (December 2013): 549–72.

Warren, Craig A. "Lincoln's Body: The President in Popular Films of the Sesquicentennial." *Journal of the Civil War Era* 4 (March 2014): 146–54.

Yaeger, Patricia. "Race and the Cloud of Unknowing in *Gone with the Wind*." *Southern Cultures* 5, no. 1 (1999): 21–28.

UNPUBLISHED SOURCES

Bates, Robin. " 'As Gray as the Century Burned Granite': The Confederate Veteran and the Construction of Confederate Historical Memory." M. Litt. thesis, Newcastle University, 2014.

INTERNET SOURCES

Anonymous. "Died, near the South-Side Rail Road." Union broadside. Philadelphia, 1865. Library of Congress, accessed July 10, 2015, https://www.loc.gov/resource/rbpe.15900200.

Blow, Charles M. "In Charleston, a Millennial Race Terrorist." *New York Times*, June 21, 2015, http://www.nytimes.com/2015/06/22/opinion/charles-blow-in-charleston-a-millennial-race-terrorist.html.

Child, Fred. "Copland's 'Lincoln Portrait,' " National Public Radio, accessed July 29, 2015, http://www.npr.org/templates/story/story.php?storyId=4165357.

Coates, Ta-Nehisi. "Virginia." *Atlantic*, August 13, 2009, http://ta-nehisicoates.theatlantic.com/archives/2009/08/virginia.php.

Corasaniti, Nick, Richard Pérez-Peña, and Lizette Alvarez. "Church Massacre Suspect Held as Charleston Grieves." *New York Times*, June 18, 2015, http://www.nytimes.com/2015/06/19/us/charleston-church-shooting.html.

Fineberg, Gail. "44th President Takes Oath on Lincoln Bible," *Library of Congress Information Bulletin*, January–February 2009, http://www.loc.gov/loc/lcib/09012/obama.html.

Henderson, Nia-Malika. "Inside the Battle over the Confederate Flag." CNN.com, updated June 24, 2015, http://edition.cnn.com/2015/06/21/politics/south-carolina-confederate-flag-debate.

Holt, Robert. "Battlefield Burial: Union, Confederate Widows Take Part in Ceremony." *Gettysburg Times*, July 2, 1997, http://www.brotherswar.com/Union_Confederate_Burial_at_Gettysburg_1997.htm.

Izadi, Elahe, and Abby Phillip. "South Carolina House Votes to Remove Confederate Flag from Statehouse Grounds." *Washington Post*, July 9, 2015, http://www.washingtonpost.com/news/post-nation/wp/2015/07/09/south-carolina-house-votes-to-remove-confederate-flag-from-statehouse-grounds.

King, Martin Luther, Jr. "Address at the Conclusion of the Selma to Montgomery March." March 25, 1965, Martin Luther King, Jr. Research and Education Institute, http://mlk-kpp01.stanford.edu/index.php/encyclopedia/documentsentry/doc_address_at_the_conclusion_of_selma_march.

Lee, M. J. "Walmart, Amazon, Sears, eBay to Stop Selling Confederate Flag Merchandise." CNN.com, updated June 24, 2015, http://edition.cnn.com/2015/06/22/politics/confederate-flag-walmart-south-carolina.

Leff, Leonard J. " 'Gone with the Wind' and Hollywood's Racial Politics," *Atlantic*, December 1999, http://www.theatlantic.com/magazine/archive/1999/12/gone-with-the-wind-and-hollywoods-racial-politics/377919.

National Park Service. "Civil War to Civil Rights Commemoration: Summary Report." November 2016. https://www.nps.gov/civilwar/upload/CIVIL-WAR-TO-CIVIL-RIGHTS-SUMMARY-REPORT-1-v2.pdf.

———. "Holding the High Ground: A National Park Service Plan for the Sesquicentennial of the American Civil War." May 2008, https://hst409509.files.wordpress.com/2011/01/holding-the-high-ground.pdf.

———. "NPS Stats: National Park Service Visitor Use Statistics." National Park Service, https://irma.nps.gov/Stats.

———. "The Sesquicentennial at Gettysburg: 2013—The Year in Review." http://www.nps.gov/gett/learn/management/upload/GETT-150-A-Year-in-Review-2013-report-final.pdf.

North Carolina Sesquicentennial Committee. "Overview." Facebook.com, accessed April 15, 2015, https://www.facebook.com/pages/North-Carolina-Civil-War-Sesquicentennial-Committee/105784479554?sk=info&tab=overview.

North Carolina War between the States Sesquicentennial Commission. "Our Commission's Purpose," accessed April 15, 2015, http://www.ncwbts150.com/NorthCarolinaSesquicentennialCommission.php.

———. "Acts of Treason against North Carolina," accessed April 15, 2015, http://www.ncwbts150.com/ActsofTreasonAgainstNorthCarolina.php.

Obama, Barack. "Senator Obama's Announcement." February 10, 2007, http://www.nytimes.com/2007/02/10/us/politics/110bama-text.html?pagewanted=print&_r=0.

———. "Obama's Speech at the Lincoln Memorial." *New York Times*, January 18, 2009, http://www.nytimes.com/2009/01/18/us/politics/18text-obama.html.

———. "Statement by the President on the Shooting in Charleston, South Carolina, June 18, 2015." White House, https://www.whitehouse.gov/the-press-office/2015/06/18/statement-president-shooting-charleston-south-carolina.

———. "Remarks by the President in Eulogy for the Honorable Reverend Clementa Pinckney." White House, June 26, 2015, https://www.whitehouse.gov/the-press-office/2015/06/26/remarks-president-eulogy-honorable-reverend-clementa-pinckney.

Pompilio, Natalie. "Tug-of-War over Confederate Monuments Rages On." *Chicago Tribune*, April 17, 2016, http://www.chicagotribune.com/news/nationworld/ct-confederate-monuments-20160417-story.html.

Sacco, Nick. "Analyzing Visitor Attendance to Civil War Sites during the Sesquicentennial." Exploring the Past, April 28, 2014, https://pastexplore.wordpress.com/2014/04/28/analyzing-visitor-attendance-to-civil-war-sites-during-the-sesquicentennial.

Snyder, Timothy. "Putin's New Nostalgia." *New York Review of Books*, November 10, 2014, http://www.nybooks.com/blogs/nyrblog/2014/nov/10/putin-nostalgia-stalin-hitler.

Warner, Gerald. "Hoist It High and Proud: The Confederate Flag Proclaims a Glorious Heritage." Breitbart, July 1, 2015, http://www.breitbart.com/big-government/2015/07/01/hoist-it-high-and-proud-the-confederate-flag-proclaims-a-glorious-heritage.

Wiener, Jon. "The Trouble with Steven Spielberg's Lincoln." *Nation*, November 27, 2012, http://www.thenation.com/article/trouble-steven-spielbergs-lincoln.

Zauzmer, Julie. "Southern Baptist Convention Votes to Condemn Confederate Battle Flag." *Washington Post*, June 15, 2016, https://www.washingtonpost.com/news/acts-of-faith/wp/2016/06/15/southern-baptist-convention-votes-to-condemn-confederate-battle-flag.

FICTION

Benét, Steven Vincent. *John Brown's Body*. 1928. Reprint, Chicago: Ivan R. Dee, 1990.

Bierce, Ambrose. *Phantoms of a Blood-Stained Period: The Complete Civil War Writings of Ambrose Bierce*. Edited by Russell Duncan and David J. Klooster. Amherst: University of Massachusetts Press, 2002.

Collingwood, Herbert W. *Andersonville Violets: A Story of Northern and Southern Life*. Boston: Lee and Shepard, 1889.

Crane, Stephen. *The Red Badge of Courage: An Episode of the American Civil War*. 1895. Reprint, Charlottesville: University of Virginia Press, 1975.

Doctorow, E. L. *The March*. London: Little, Brown, 2006.

Faulkner, William. *Intruder in the Dust*. New York: Random House, 1948.

Harris, Joel Chandler. *Gabriel Tolliver: A Story of Reconstruction*. New York: McClure, Phillips, and Co., 1902.

Mason, Bobbie Ann. *Shiloh and Other Stories*. New York: Modern Library, 2001.

Page, Thomas Nelson. *Meh Lady: A Story of the War*. 1887. New York: Charles Scribner's Sons, 1893.

———. *Red Rock: A Chronicle of Reconstruction*. New York: Charles Scribner's Sons, 1898.

Ryan, Abram J. *Poems: Patriotic, Religious, Miscellaneous*. Baltimore, MD: J. B. Piet, 1880.

Tourgée, Albion W. *The Veteran and His Pipe*. Chicago: Belford, Clarke, and Co., 1886.